Beijing

Beijing

FROM IMPERIAL CAPITAL TO OLYMPIC CITY

Lillian M. Li
Alison J. Dray-Novey
Haili Kong

Excerpts from the following sources appear in the text and have been reprinted with kind permission:

Three quotes in English from *Camel Xiangzi,* translated by Shi Xiaojing, Hong Kong: Chinese University Press, 2005. Permission fom Foreign Language Press, Beijing

Quote from *Teahouse,* translated by John Howard Gibbon, Hong Kong: Chinese University Press, 2004. Permission fom Foreign Language Press, Beijing

China's New Voices: Popular Music, Ethnicity, Gender, and Politics, 1978–1997, University of California Press, 2003.

BEIJING

First published in 2007 by
PALGRAVE MACMILLAN™
175 Fifth Avenue, New York, N.Y. 10010 and
Houndmills, Basingstoke, Hampshire, England RG21 6XS.
Companies and representatives throughout the world.

PALGRAVE MACMILLAN is the global academic imprint of the Palgrave Macmillan division of St. Martin's Press, LLC and of Palgrave Macmillan Ltd. Macmillan® is a registered trademark in the United States, United Kingdom and other countries. Palgrave is a registered trademark in the European Union and other countries.

ISBN-13: 978-0-230-60527-5 paperback
ISBN-10: 0-230-60527-3 paperback

Library of Congress Cataloging-in-Publication Data is available from the Library of Congress.

A catalogue record of the book is available from the British Library.

Design by Letra Libre, Inc.

First PALGRAVE MACMILLAN paperback edition: May 2008

10 9 8 7 6 5 4 3 2 1

Printed in the United States of America.

To

Stephen Dale, Michael Novey, and Xiaodong Zhang

Contents

Color Plates appear between pages 82–83
Black and White Figures appear between pages 178–79

Maps

Acknowledgments

THE WRITING OF THIS BOOK HAS DEPENDED ON THE GENEROSITY OF friends and colleagues in China, the United States, and Europe.

We are especially indebted to Susan Naquin, of Princeton University, for her encouragement and advice on many aspects of this project. Her book *Peking: Temples and City Life, 1400–1900* is the authoritative and classic work on Beijing's history.

Many scholars and friends in Beijing shared their knowledge and experience with us. In particular, we are grateful to Li Xiaocong, of Beijing University, for his guidance and knowledge of Beijing's past and present. Many others gave their time and insights. We warmly thank: Alexander Beels, Bi Qiong, Bi Xidong, Sabina Brady, Marianne Brujard, Joe Carter, Chen Bali, Chen Huaihuai, Cheng Yinong, Michael Crook, Dai Jianzhong, Du Yan, Guo Junxi, Han Guanghui, He Shuzhong, Anthony Kuhn, Li Li, Li Xiaobin, Li Zehou, Lin Shu, Liu Jinshu, Freda Murck, Su Lin, Brian Wallace, Wang Hansheng, Wang Jun, Wang Xuemei, Wu Jianyong, Wu Menglin, Xiao Jiabao, Xu Qing Qing, Steven Xu, Kippy Ye, Yin Junke, Yue Shengyang, Zhang Yiwu, Zhao Yonglai, and Zhu Saihong.

We are grateful to friends and scholars outside Beijing for sharing unpublished materials and insights: Lisha Chen, Robert DuPlessis, Luca Gabbiani, Jiawan Huang, Sophia Lee, Xiang Li, Eva Lim, Liu Jianmei, Liu Xinru, Susan Milmoe, Regine Thiriez, Yamin Xu, and Zheng Lianjie.

For support in research and publication, we thank Swarthmore College and the College of Notre Dame of Maryland. Lillian also acknowledges the support of the Fulbright Hays Faculty Research Abroad Program for her work in Beijing.

Family members provided not only encouragement but direct assistance in various ways. Stephen Dale was instrumental in the development of the project and contributed to each later stage. Kong Rui, Li Yunzhu, Shi Yuanchun, Shi Qiong, and Yan Lichun shared their knowledge of Beijing. Michael Novey, Joelle Novey, Elizabeth Novey, and Zhang Xiaodong provided editorial and technical support. Philip Dray gave professional advice.

Chronology and
Note on Chinese Words

Chronology

Qin	221–206 BCE
Han	202 BCE–220 CE
Tang	618–907
Northern Song	960–1127
Southern Song	1127–1279
Liao	916–1125
Jin	1115–1234
Yuan	1279–1368
Genghis [Chinggis] Khan	lived ca. 1162–1227
Khubilai Khan	reigned 1260–1294
Ming	1368–1644
Hongwu	r. 1368–1398
Yongle	r. 1403–1424
Zhengtong	r. 1436–1449
Qing	1644–1912
Shunzhi	r. 1644–1661
Kangxi	r. 1662–1722
Yongzheng	r. 1723–1735
Qianlong	r. 1736–1795
Jiaqing	r. 1796–1820
Daoguang	r. 1821–1850

Xianfeng	r. 1851–1861
Tongzhi	r. 1862–1874
Guangxu	r. 1875–1908
Xuantong	r. 1909–1911

Republican period	1912–1949
May Fourth incident	May 4, 1919
War against Japan	1937–1945
Civil War	1946–1949
People's Republic of China established	October 1, 1949
Great Leap Forward	1958–1960
Cultural Revolution	1966–1976
Death of Mao Zedong	September 1976
Tiananmen Crisis	April–June 1989
China hosts Summer Olympic Games	2008

Reign name dates listed here are traditional ones based on the Chinese lunar calendar. Actual years of a reign may differ slightly. For example, the Qianlong emperor ascended the throne on October 18, 1735 and abdicated on February 9, 1796.

Note on Chinese Words

We employ the standard Pinyin system of romanization for Chinese words and names. In the case of terms that are widely known in another romanized form, the Pinyin is added in parentheses after the first use.

In general, we use the word "gate" to translate Chinese *men* after the names of gates, but for the two best-known surviving gates of Beijing we use their more common forms, Qianmen and Tiananmen. A number of Chinese words (*miao, guan, si,* and a few others) can be translated as "temple." We use the names of temples both with "temple" and without—Dongyue Temple and Dongyuemiao, Baiyun Temple and Baiyunguan, Baita Temple and Baitasi.

It will help the reader in pronunciation of Chinese words to note that "x" in the Pinyin system replaces "hs" in an earlier one, "q" replaces "ch," and "c" replaces "ts." For example, *xi* (west) sounds like "she," Qing (the name of the last dynasty) like "ching," and *cun* (village) like "tsun."

Introduction

BEIJING IS ONE OF THE WORLD'S MEGACITIES. CONSTANTLY IN THE international news, it commands attention and often inspires controversy. Beijing is the political voice of China, as London, Washington, and Tokyo are the voices of their nations. But far beyond this, to most of the outside world, Beijing *is* China. News events concerning China are overwhelmingly situated in Beijing, the capital and political center of the nation. In the 1950s and after, whenever Mao Zedong and other Communist leaders stood on the balcony at Tiananmen to review parades in the square below, they were symbolically reviewing all of the Chinese people. Major political upheavals since that time—such as the Cultural Revolution (1966–1976) and the pro-democracy movement (1989)—have played out on Tiananmen Square, the world's largest stage. Although there are dozens of huge Chinese cities—Shanghai, Guangzhou, Wuhan, Tianjin, Chongqing, to name just a few—the international media report the social, cultural, and economic news of Beijing as that of all China. It often seems to be the only city that matters.

Beijing was the last and most enduring of China's imperial capitals. Chang'an (modern Xi'an) in the Western Han (202 BCE–9 CE) and Tang (618–907) dynasties and Kaifeng and Hangzhou in the Song (960–1279) were each in their time major world cities. In the tenth and twelfth centuries the city that we know as Beijing was twice chosen as one of several capitals for regional Inner Asian empires. It became capital of all China for the first time under the Mongols in the thirteenth century. They called it Dadu (Great Metropolis) in Chinese and Khanbalikh (the khan's city) in Mongolian; for more than a hundred years, their world empire spread the city's reputation for wealth and grandeur. In the fifteenth century, under Chinese Ming dynasty rulers, the population of Beijing reached close to 1 million, probably the largest in the world at that time. Beijing continued as capital throughout the subsequent Manchu Qing dynasty and afterward until 1928. During the interval from 1928 to 1949, the Nationalist Party established its base at Nanjing, but when the Communists came to power in 1949, they returned the capital to Beijing, where it remains today.

What attracted dynastic rulers to Beijing's border location was certainly not its natural environment or economic potential. The capital is unusual, perhaps unique, among great world cities in not being located on a coast or major river. In past centuries, the area was considered well watered by rivers and lakes and swept by fresh breezes from the hills to the west. But for Chinese literati from the Yangzi valley or from semitropical Guangzhou in the south, Beijing hardly could compare with their home regions in scenery, climate, or agricultural productivity. The beautiful gardens and fertile fields of the lower Yangzi area were admired by all Chinese, including northern rulers themselves.

The great advantage of Beijing's location was its proximity to Inner Asia, to Mongolia and Manchuria, where premodern contenders for power in China often arose. These steppe and forest lands produced the four non-Chinese dynasties that ruled from the site of Beijing—the Khitan Liao (916–1125), Jurchen Jin (1115–1234), Mongol Yuan (1279–1368), and Manchu Qing (1644–1912). Indeed, Beijing was attractive to the Chinese Ming rulers (1368–1644) for closely related reasons. Soon after they established their first capital at Nanjing on the Yangzi River in the fourteenth century, Ming leaders realized that they were too far from borders that they needed to defend and from mountain passes controlling access to the north China plain. They not only moved their capital to Beijing, but also rebuilt both the Grand Canal that supplied southern grain to the city and the Great Wall that marked China's northern border.

The capital had its own boundaries, both external and internal. The massive city walls protected the populace from outside invaders, but that was not their only function. They also enclosed walls of the Imperial and Forbidden Cities, walls of houses and temples, and smaller but extremely numerous barriers, such as street gates that could be closed at night. The whole complex of walls and gates facilitated a compartmentalization of space that made it easier to control the city population itself. In imperial times, today's vast and open Tiananmen Square contained offices and other structures; there were no places where masses could gather. Police watched even sizable crowds at temples and fairs. Dynasties sought the acquiescence of the people, not their active support. Emperors neither reviewed parades nor countenanced demonstrations for or against the state. It is no accident that one of the world's oldest cities of great population is also famous for its walls and gates.

At the center of imperial Beijing, the Forbidden City usually was closed, its palace life hidden. Ceremonies there, enacted at dawn, deliberately created a sense of awe in participants. Chinese officials and visitors privileged to approach the emperor showed their humility by performing the ritual kowtow, prostrating themselves and knocking their foreheads on the paving stones. Reports of these rituals fed the fantasies of outsiders both in China and beyond, because what was forbidden and closed was also seductive.

Throughout its history Beijing has attracted people of many kinds: officials, examination candidates, scholars, merchants, ambassadors, missionaries, laborers, and—even centuries ago—sightseers. Western readers long have been fascinated by accounts of visits to Beijing by merchants like Marco Polo, missionaries like Matteo Ricci, and diplomats like Lord Macartney. For long periods in its history the city was relatively open to newcomers. With each change of dynasty, conquerors replaced the vanquished; new ruling elites and their military supporters displaced the former ones. With new rulers came shifts in the city population. In the mid-twentieth century, a similar process occurred when Mao Zedong and the Communists took over Beijing. Party leaders and their followers, supported by the People's Liberation Army, occupied the former centers of imperial power. From all over China, new bureaucrats arrived to run the central government, and highly educated specialists came to staff universities and other supporting institutions.

As the twenty-first century begins, Beijing—as capital, center of Chinese finance, and international metropolis—is more open to outside influence than ever before. No longer restrained by household registration laws, people from all over China come to Beijing to seek their fortunes. Expatriate communities of Koreans, Taiwanese, and Europeans have established residential areas in the city. Artists and filmmakers find Beijing a stimulating center of creativity. Globalization, popular culture, and the Internet have broken age-old constraints. Yet the political core of Beijing is still closed; most top leaders live and work in an exclusive compound just to the west of the Forbidden City called Zhongnanhai. So symbolic and powerful is Zhongnanhai that ordinary citizens have only to sit silently in front of its entrance, as did adherents of the Falun Gong religious sect in 1999, to be regarded as dangerous lawbreakers rather than peaceful petitioners.

Indeed, Beijing has been so closely identified with central political authority that the city's history is difficult to separate from that of the empire or nation. Unlike early modern European city-states that were independent political entities, all Chinese cities developed in the context of a centralized administrative system. As an imperial capital, Beijing came under direct dynastic rule and its governance often bypassed normal hierarchies of imperial administration. In local functions such as police, multiple and overlapping jurisdictions ensured the security of the capital and safeguarded the power of the rulers. They also prevented the slightest whiff of urban autonomy.

Thus because of shifting populations and close state control, Beijing did not have an historical tradition of local elites—either hereditary aristocracy or local gentry. Nor did merchants there amass great wealth and influence, as they did in Constantinople and other Islamic cities. No social group resembled the bourgeoisie of post-revolutionary Paris. Top officials and other important people in Beijing often were sojourners from elsewhere. In a cosmopolis such as New York, many inhabitants historically have been immigrants or their children who planned to stay indefinitely; in Beijing, high-level outsiders often intended to return to their native places. Local elite leadership and participation in governance—strong Chinese traditions in general—were weak in Beijing.

Only in the early twentieth century, after the fall of the last imperial dynasty in 1912, did Beijing come close to having an independent urban identity. In that era the city developed some forms of self-government. Local leaders, many from other places, took the initiative in social welfare efforts. A new sense of localism and nostalgia prompted the writing of histories and memoirs. The concept of the "Beijingren" (Beijing person) drew attention: Who was a Beijingren? What were his or her attributes? In this era, some considered the so-called bannermen, the main military servitors of the last dynasty, the true Beijingren. Over time, however, the designation became more a cultural identity than a genealogical assertion. Beijing was a place to which people came for various reasons and to which they or their descendants later might claim an affiliation. This remains true today. Suppose we ask a local acquaintance, "Are you a Beijingren?" If he or she replies in the affirmative, it may mean only that his or her parents or grandparents came to Beijing in the 1950s.

Beijing, a city embodying the imperial past, evolved an even stronger identity or image in contrast to Shanghai, a Westernized and rapidly modernizing treaty port. In the 1920s and 1930s, intellectuals drew a cultural distinction between "Jingpai" and "Haipai"—the Beijing school and Shanghai school among literati circles. The former leaned toward political gradualism and scholarship while the latter included writers and leftist radicals who preferred direct social action and quick solutions. In a general sense, Jingpai referred to a certain cultural refinement, conservative elitism, and disdain for money, while Haipai was often interpreted as the Westernized, money-grubbing, and somewhat vulgar Shanghairen. Even today old Beijing residents and most northern Chinese maintain similar prejudices: Shanghai people are shrewd with money and calculate transactions down to the last dime; Beijing people are above caring about the small change. The people of Beijing are straightforward and honest; the people of Shanghai are cunning and practice flattery, and the girls are coy. Southerners, however, long have regarded northerners as rather blunt and arrogant. Today the characterization of "true" Beijingren—those whose roots go back more than a generation or two—by other locals who are more recent arrivals can also be unflattering. Here social class enters the picture. Beijingren in this context are lower class, while the people voicing these opinions are highly educated, sometimes entrepreneurs. They consider Beijingren to be lazy, rude, and arrogant—people who would rather be poor than do the hard jobs as construction workers and nannies that migrants from the countryside happily undertake.

With all its swirling undercurrents of prejudice and opinion, Beijing urban society today stands at a crossroads. The 2008 Olympics will confirm the city as an international metropolis and enhance national pride. Beijing will be placed in the spotlight by international media and will represent—and in a sense, *be*— China to the rest of the world. At the same time, since about 1990, the old residential areas of the city largely have been destroyed to make way for extensive real estate development. The disappearance of the old *hutong* (narrow streets) with their courtyard houses (*siheyuan*) has aroused protests from all directions. Beijing seems to have lost its quintessential architectural plan and city design, and to many this represents the loss of its historic identity. To address this problem, local, national, and international authorities have engaged in preservation or restoration of ancient structures, temples, and old residences. They are protecting fragments of the past while others are destroying it. Thus in addition to being a national showcase and a monument to rampant economic growth—complete with traffic jams, pollution, and social problems—Beijing has become a museum. Now, more than ever, it is important to tell the story of its glorious but also tortuous path from imperial capital to Olympic city.

Chapter 1

The Emergence of Beijing as an Imperial Capital

HISTORIES OF BEIJING OFTEN BEGIN WITH PEKING MAN, AN IMPORtant specimen of *Homo erectus,* whose remains were discovered at Zhoukoudian, southwest of the city, in the 1920s. The history of Beijing as a settlement of course begins much later, and its history as a capital later still.

Towns have existed on or near the site of Beijing since antiquity. A city called Ji was at the center of the state of Yan in the war-torn era that preceded China's first imperial unification in 221 BCE. Soon afterward the First Emperor linked the northern wall of Yan with those of other states to create the Great Wall of China. Later the locale of Ji under the names Youzhou and Yanjing (Yan capital) served as a distant northeastern outpost for the early imperial dynasties of Han (202 BCE–220 CE) and Tang (618–907), as well as during the centuries of disunity between them. Thus today the names Ji, Yan, Yanjing, and Youzhou evoke the origins of Beijing. In the mid-tenth century rulers from north of the Great Wall took what was then an obscure border town and set it on a new course as a capital city. That career has lasted more than a thousand years and continues today.[1]

The name "Beijing" itself is old, but its use for the current city is relatively recent. The first of four non-Chinese dynasties to make the city a capital, the Liao (916–1125), called it Nanjing (Southern Capital) because most of their empire was to the north; thus we may refer to it as Liao Nanjing. The following dynasty, the Jin (1115–1234), called the city Zhongdu (Central Capital), so it was Jin Zhongdu; and the third, the Yuan (1279–1368), called it Dadu (Great Capital), hence Yuan Dadu. The name "Beijing" (Northern Capital) was applied to the city for the first time in the fifteenth century under the Ming, a Chinese dynasty

(1368–1644). But during the Ming and the succeeding Manchu Qing dynasty (1644–1912), another name, Jingshi (Capital City), predominated in daily usage. Only in the twentieth century did Beijing (Northern Capital) become the name most often written and spoken, and even then there was a period of two decades (1928–1949) when the name "Beiping" (Northern Peace) supplanted it because the Republic of China had moved its capital to the south. Since 1949 Beijing has been the capital of the People's Republic of China. ("Peking" is "Beijing" in an earlier romanization.)

By either world or Chinese standards, Beijing is not an ancient city. Today most of its older structures date from no earlier than the Ming and Qing dynasties. The underlying plan, however, can be traced back to the beginnings of Chinese civilization. Elements of the city's distinctive symmetrical layout had appeared in earlier imperial capitals at Chang'an (modern Xi'an), Loyang, and Bianjing (modern Kaifeng). Successive builders of Beijing drew on common precedents that reflected ancient beliefs and institutions, especially those that proclaimed the unique authority of the emperor. The long continuity in city planning and architecture in China's capitals sprang from the close association of those traditions with the political legitimacy of successive dynasties.[2]

Liao Nanjing and Jin Zhongdu, 916 to 1234

When the future Beijing was first chosen as a capital in the tenth century, Chinese civilization was politically divided after the end of the almost three-hundred-year-long Tang dynasty. In northern border areas, non-Chinese peoples lived by animal herding, agriculture, hunting, and fishing. Although their economic base was quite different from that of the Chinese, these groups on the perimeter were familiar with China's agrarian society and bureaucratic government. Far from being primitive outsiders, they lived within the Chinese universe and participated in its politics. They even could aspire to rule inside the Great Wall; they had done so earlier in the north, though not yet in south China. In this context Khitan (Qidan) warriors, who came from the Liao River valley of southern Manchuria, created a dynasty called Liao whose empire included both neighboring tribal peoples and Chinese farmers. Semi-nomadic in origin, the Khitan rulers still thought in terms of their own seasonal migration and therefore had not one capital but five.[3] Among them was Yanjing, from which they administered, with the necessary Chinese help, agricultural regions that they had recently acquired.

The Khitan called the city Southern Capital (Nanjing), which should not be confused with the better-known Nanjing in central China. Liao Nanjing was the main city of the Khitan southern circuit but not their most important base. Its relative significance increased as the Liao rulers gave up efforts to conquer more of China and consolidated their economy and defense at Liao Nanjing.[4] Modern archeologists have found the exact locations of the city's wall corners in the southwestern part of contemporary Beijing. (See Map 1.) The official history of the Liao dynasty reveals that the imperial palace enclave was in the southwest corner of the Southern Capital and that "buildings, shops, markets, offices, hostels, and Buddhist and Daoist monasteries were [so] numerous [that they were] impossible to describe."[5]

The Liao rulers at their Southern Capital mastered some Chinese ways but were careful to avoid assimilation in a region where they were greatly outnumbered. (Of 4 million people in their entire border empire, only about 750,000 were Khitan.) For governmental purposes, the elite adopted much of Confucian ancestor reverence and values, Chinese written language, and bureaucracy; in other ways, however, they preserved Khitan culture. Retaining their tribal organization, dress, and cuisine, they continued to speak their own language and for the first time began to write it as well in Chinese-like characters arranged vertically.

The leaders of the transplanted Liao embraced a tradition that, like them, had come to China from the outside: Buddhism. They patronized temples, generously providing land and funds. More than thirty-six major temples and countless smaller ones were founded in and near Liao Nanjing, and a single temple could house as many as a hundred monks. Stone pillars carved with protective religious texts stood amid the temples' pine and gingko trees. In later ages, such pillars surrounded by evocative, ancient trees often convinced people that a particular temple dated from the Liao era.[6]

The vibrant economic and cultural life of Liao Nanjing reflected both general Chinese technology of the time and Song dynasty artistic skills. The Liao ruled only the northeast region, while the Chinese Song dynasty ruled most of the rest of the country. (During the Northern Song dynasty [960–1127], the capital was in the north at Kaifeng; during the Southern Song dynasty [1127–1279], the capital was in the south at Hangzhou.) Workers in *shuyuan* (embroidery courtyards) mastered advanced textile arts in order to make beautiful women's clothing patterned with delicate flowers. At government kilns, skilled artisans crafted ceramic vessels, including the many yellow, green, and white equestrian water bottles that later would be unearthed by archeologists in the Beijing area.

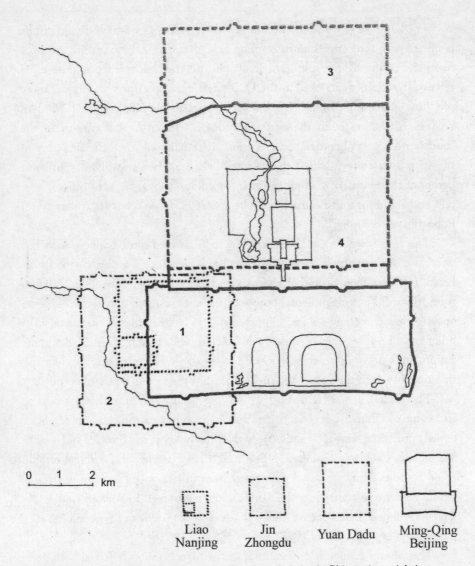

Map 1. From Liao to Qing. Source: *Nancy Shatzman Steinhardt*, Chinese imperial city planning. *Honolulu: University of Hawai'i Press, 1990. Drawn by Huang Yunsheng. Reprinted by permission of University of Hawai'i Press.*

Workers manufactured paper and printed books by a woodblock method. To create a single multicolored image of the Buddha, they would hand-carve several blocks, one for each color. Large markets drew merchants from great distances and particularly from the Northern Song capital at Kaifeng. Shoppers crowded together so densely that merchants in charge of each market watched and controlled commerce from a tower (*kanlou*). Many inns in Nanjing and its suburbs housed visitors; musical and acrobatic performances entertained them along with local audiences. Sanmiao lu, modern Beijing's oldest street, probably dates from the Liao era.[7]

Because peoples north of the Great Wall continually competed with each other over access to the relative wealth of agricultural areas, the embattled Liao empire survived only a little more than a century. Its rulers, who were related to the people later called Mongols, were defeated in 1122 by the Tungusic Jurchen tribes of Manchuria, ancestors of the people later called Manchus. The Jurchen included both plains and forest dwellers; they were more acquainted with agriculture and less with nomadic pastoralism than either their Liao predecessors or their Mongol successors. The former Liao Southern Capital now became the Southern and in 1153 the Central Capital (Zhongdu) of the Jurchen dynasty, which was called Jin. The Jin rulers pushed the Liao city walls outward on three sides, leaving the northern wall in place, and erected a large central palace. After they forced the Chinese Song dynasty rulers to retreat to Hangzhou in the south in 1126, they recycled building material left behind at the former Northern Song capital, Kaifeng.[8] A workforce of 800,000 men and 400,000 troops used these architectural fragments (especially screens, doors, and walls) to create the Jin palace at Zhongdu in the mid-twelfth century. Significantly, the Jin appropriated not only Kaifeng's palace debris but also its technical diagrams and human resources, particularly skilled artisans. Construction of Jin Zhongdu improved on Liao Nanjing achievements by drawing upon ongoing advances in Chinese technology, especially in hydraulic engineering.[9]

The Jin moved large numbers of their Jurchen tribesmen to Zhongdu, and there was a great influx of soldiers and their families. Under the Jin, the urban population was more Jurchen and less Chinese than before, with relatively few Chinese commoners. Chinese who had lived in Zhongdu earlier were expelled to the suburbs or rural areas. The city contained mainly officials, soldiers, artisans, entertainers, and slaves. (Members of the last group came from among the conquered peoples.) The overriding Jin concern was to control the surrounding villages and repress potential uprisings against the dynasty's heavy taxes.

Jin adaptation to life in Zhongdu required major adjustments, some of which would prove important for the future of the city. Although as under Liao just one of five capitals, and not the most populous one, Jin Zhongdu and the surrounding area still contained over 225,000 households. To feed so large a population in a region that was relatively unfavorable for agriculture, officials improved routes for grain transport from the more productive lower Yangzi area, especially along canals and rivers.[10] The Jin rulers also faced another problem: Zhongdu's climate was uncomfortably warm during the summer months, especially for people accustomed to living north of the Great Wall. Seeking relief from the crowded city and access to more water resources, they frequented rural retreats to the immediate northwest, and in 1179 they added a large summer residence with landscaped gardens and lakes northeast of Zhongdu. About a century later the Great Khan Khubilai would turn the ruins of this resort into the palace city of a new Mongol dynasty. The Jin summer structures thus became the oldest element of the future Imperial and Forbidden Cities. Most places in Beijing later associated with the Jin were located either in this summer palace or in the western suburbs, at the former imperial retreats of Deer Park (Luyuan), Fishing Terrace (Diaoyutai), Fragrant Hill (Xiangshan), and Jade Spring Hill (Yuquanshan).[11]

Compared to the Liao dynasty, the Jin ruled much more territory and many more people. Their dominion extended as far south as the Huai River (between the Yellow and Yangzi rivers), and the total population under their sway in 1207 numbered 53 million, of whom only 4 million were Jurchen. They followed the Khitan pattern of combining Chinese-style bureaucratic administration with preservation of much of their own culture, including clothing and language. In the initial period of their rule they even asked the Chinese to adopt Jurchen dress and hairstyles, an idea that did not last but did prefigure the later Manchu demand that Chinese officials wear Manchu clothing and Chinese men wear the queue (pigtail). To write their own language, they used the scripts invented by the Liao and created two others, also arranged vertically in characters resembling, but different from, those of Chinese. Like the Liao they were attracted to Buddhism, and seventeen Beijing-area temples of Jin provenance survived into later times.[12]

More than the Liao, the Jin rulers employed Han officials and learned Chinese quickly. (The Chinese call themselves *hanren* [people of Han] from the name of a long and formative early dynasty.) The Jin admired Chinese civilization and created an atmosphere conducive to art and scholarship. After publishing new editions of Chinese classics, such as ancient books of Confucian philosophy, they then assigned thousands of Jurchen to study them and prepare for special examinations leading to civil office. To their Manchu descendants who founded the Qing dynasty more than five hundred years later, the Jin rulers sometimes even appeared to have gone too far in acculturation. With Jurchen and Chinese frequently marrying each other, the rulers legalized intermarriage in 1191; as time went by, Jurchen often dropped their ancestral language and many completely assimilated. By contrast, the Khitan Liao, even under the Jin dynasty, retained their distinctiveness more easily because a greater reservoir of Khitan tradition endured in tribal areas in their homeland.[13]

It was not only transportation of grain from the south and construction of a summer retreat on the site of the future Forbidden City that marked the emergence of characteristic aspects of later Beijing in Jin Zhongdu. Following the lead of the Song dynasty rulers then at Hangzhou, the Jin began in 1157 to issue paper money.[14] Using this currency, people more easily undertook long-distance trade and contact, including ties with the wealthy Song area itself. They sent goods mostly by water, while government officials dispatched documents overland by mounted courier in a regular postal service. Merchants operated in huge markets in the southeast area of Zhongdu; conscripted artisans on fixed wages in official workshops produced textiles, printed books, and ceramic items.

The Jin continued traditional artistic styles in painting, poetry, and calligraphy that had been typical of the Tang and Northern Song dynasties. At the popular level, however, they were more innovative. The Jurchen were a musical people who, at the time of their victory over the Liao, already enjoyed theater arts, such as acrobatics and pantomime. An important kind of musical performance of the time was called *zaju* (variety show). Male and female entertainers performed hundreds of *yuanben* (playhouse scripts), comical sketches that later would be incorporated in Yuan drama. Just as Shakespeare's plays drew on older plots and stock characters from the popular Italian stage (*commedia dell'arte*), Yuan dynasty opera had roots in the Jin theater. Figures of *yuanben* theatrical characters on north China tomb tiles, as well as terra-cotta tomb sculptures of model stages and actors, show that Jin people hoped to continue attending performances in the spirit world.[15] The Jin and their Han Chinese subjects shared common religious and cultural interests that drew them together at temples and plays.

Yuan Dadu, 1260 to 1368

Like nomadic life itself, steppe politics entailed constant jockeying for position. The rise of the Mongols resembled that of their Liao and Jin predecessors in many ways: it sprang from tribal warfare and drew on familiarity with key elements of Chinese civilization, including writing, record keeping, and law. The Mongol founding leader, Genghis (Chinggis) Khan (1162–1227), was a kind of genius of the steppe who happened to appear at a time when all the surrounding

sedentary states were weak. The Mongol empire was the "perfect storm" of nomadic history. As the largest empire of its kind that the world had ever seen, it
brought widely separated major cultures into contact for the first time.

As before, a relatively small but mobile population used toughness and military skill to threaten a much larger sedentary one. At a time when the total number of people under Jin control was about 53 million, there were only about 1
million Mongols. Yet as the Jin had ousted the Liao, the Mongols eventually defeated the Jin in 1234.[16] The Mongol conquest of north China, however, caused
much more death and loss of property than had occurred in the earlier Liao and
Jin victories. Subsequent conquest of the south was less destructive because the
Mongols had learned to value the Chinese agricultural economy and wanted to
keep it intact as a basis for taxation. Yelu Qucai (1189–1243), a sinicized descendant of the Liao founder whose pragmatic arguments had a mellowing influence
on Mongol rule, is still honored today at his tomb and shrine, now within the
grounds of the Summer Palace northwest of Beijing.[17]

In 1279 the Mongols extinguished the Song at Hangzhou and proceeded to
found a dynasty called Yuan (Origin). The choice of the name Yuan, from the
classic *Yi Jing* (Book of changes), showed their wish for Chinese legitimacy.
Such recognition mattered greatly to the new rulers because China was the richest, most populous, and most advanced state in their extensive Eurasian territo-
ries. Moreover, where the Liao had controlled only the northeastern corner of
China and the Jin only the territory north of the Huai River, the Mongols ruled
the entire country—more than 100 million people—as part of a world empire.
The pattern of hybrid Sino-nomadic rule was not only successful but expanding
in scale.[18]

In 1215 the Mongols, on their way to domination of all China, had destroyed the Jin Central Capital, Zhongdu. The capital of their world empire in its
early decades was at Khara Khorum in Mongolia. In 1260, however, Khubilai, the
grandson of Genghis, became Great Khan; soon afterward he happened to camp
near the Zhongdu ruins. Apparently influenced by Chinese advisers, he decided
to move his main imperial headquarters there from Mongolia and proceeded to
rebuild the former Jin capital. In 1272 he renamed the city Dadu (Great Capital
or Metropolis); henceforth Dadu also would be known in Mongolian and Turkic
as Khanbalikh, the khans' city.[19] (See Color Plate 1.)

Khubilai's decision to rebuild the Jin Zhongdu site as Dadu would have
enormous consequences for the city in the long term. In the short term, he faced
many critical questions. Never before had the Mongols, who customarily lived in

movable yurts, built a capital inside a settled agricultural society. They had no tradition of permanent architecture or city planning.[20] Political motives guided Khubilai's design decisions. In the 1260s, decades after the death of his grandfather in 1227, he was struggling to cope with centrifugal tendencies in the far-flung Mongol empire. He hit upon a strategy of great promise, new to him but clearly reflecting earlier Liao and Jin patterns of rule. From youth he had been deeply impressed by Chinese civilization, and now he concluded that he could base his political power partly on the strength of the Chinese. He needed to do this, however, from a border location where he also could keep control over Mongolia and beyond. His imperial capital had to be first of all a place from which he could monitor the ever-shifting politics of his native land. At the same time, by placing that capital inside the Great Wall and by following Chinese architectural and city planning traditions, the khan signaled to his Chinese subjects that he intended to identify more closely with them. By welcoming the help of craftsmen and architects from many quarters, he also addressed the wider world of the Mongol empire. Khubilai thus skillfully appealed to his Mongol, Chinese, and universal audiences in the creation of Yuan Dadu.[21] For the Mongol rulers, cosmopolitanism was both the natural outlook of a nomadic people and a strategy of empire.

Beginning in the 1260s, Dadu rose quickly as a triple-walled city immediately northeast of the old Liao and Jin capitals.[22] While the ruins of the Jin summer retreat remained on the site, the fundamentals of the *city* as a large architectural ensemble—with its striking grace, balance, and beauty—first came into existence at this time. Advanced engineering and hydraulic capacities underlay the overall plan, which incorporated channels for water supply that had been built by the Jin.[23] Dadu's symmetrical design along a north-south axis running through the palace expressed both the pivotal role of the emperor in politics and the centrality of politics in culture. As in earlier Chinese capitals, the entire city, not just the palace complex, was a unified work of art displaying imperial power. Modern archeologists have found a marker placed, apparently during construction, at a point intended to be central with respect to the outermost, rammed earth walls.[24] (Earthen mounds marking part of the Yuan northern wall and a gate of the western wall are still visible today.) Of only eleven gates, two were on the northern side and three on each of the others. Leading from the gates were broad avenues that intersected narrower lanes at right angles, creating fifty-four wards as territorial units for local government. The second walled enclosure was an imperial city mainly used by the emperor's family and officials;

the third contained a palace city with audience halls near the front and living areas at the back that opened onto courtyards and gardens. The imperial and palace cities were off-limits to the ordinary populace except for servants and workmen.

By channeling three rivers running through the city, the Yuan builders created a chain of picturesque lakes west of the palace enclosure. Today restored gardens, pavilions, and temples dating from the Yuan era in Beihai Park preserve these thirteenth-century achievements. Excavated earth became the artificial hill north of the palace city now called Jingshan (Prospect Hill). An Ancestral Temple (Taimiao) to the east of the imperial city, and Altars of Land and Grain (Shejitan) to the west, provided settings for Chinese rituals. Similarly, a Confucian Temple in the northeastern part of the city honored the ancient founder of China's most important philosophical tradition. (See Figure 1.) Khubilai held court in Dadu for the first time in 1274.[25]

Because the Mongols, building on Jin ruins, created much that would become characteristic of Beijing for centuries, it is worth exploring the sources of the Dadu city plan. One influence may have been the placement of tents in a typical Mongol military camp, with the leader at the center systematically surrounded by his most trusted protectors and their men. The enclosure of undeveloped land within the northern city wall may have reflected a pastoral people's wish to stay close to their flocks.[26] In the service of Khubilai's political goals, however, the layout of the city drew mainly on Chinese tradition. Art historian Nancy Steinhardt traces numerous influences of earlier Chinese capitals on Yuan Dadu. She suggests that Liao Nanjing (with dual walls) and Jin Zhongdu (probably with dual walls and a third enclosure for the palace) as well as the former Northern Song capital at Kaifeng were key models. Kaifeng is the earliest example of a Chinese city with triple walls nested one inside the other. Both the Kaifeng and Jin Zhongdu city plans show the T-shaped formation of an imperial way or road starting at the southern outer wall and passing through a gate of the imperial city to the south gate of the palace city, where it joins a rectangular "palace place" in front of the structure itself.[27] Other models for Yuan Dadu appear in the even older city plans of early capitals Chang'an and Loyang: rectangular outer walls, broad avenues leading from a relatively small number of gates, lanes crossing the great avenues to create wards, and similar placement in the city of the Ancestral Temple and the Altars of Land and Grain.[28]

Another important source of the Dadu plan was the ancient Chinese classical text *Zhou Li* (rites of Zhou) that described an ideal city.[29] This city was square, with three gates on each side, nine north-south and nine east-west avenues, the Ancestral Temple on the east, the Altars of Land and Grain on the west, and royal structures at the exact center. The same plan probably had been used earlier (in 1256) in the construction, two hundred miles to the north in Mongolia, of Shangdu, Khubilai's original summer retreat. (This fabled city, used as a Mongol hunting resort after the building of Dadu, was the "Xanadu" of Samuel Taylor Coleridge's 1797 poem beginning "In Xanadu did Kubla Khan/A stately pleasure dome decree.") In Khubilai's capital, however, the *Zhou Li's* ideal city was realized more completely than ever before; the literary vision became fully manifest in the orderly layout of Dadu.

Without Chinese help, the Yuan rulers never could have developed Dadu as they did. Liu Bingzhong (1216–1274), a Chinese adviser to Khubilai, strongly influenced the design of both Shangdu and Dadu. He shrewdly advised the Khan that the metropolis at Dadu inside the Great Wall was more likely to be the capital of a long-lived empire than the much smaller town outside it at Shangdu. Khubilai especially valued the judgment of Liu Bingzhong; they were about the same age, had met in their twenties, and enjoyed great personal rapport. A statesman, painter, and poet, Liu also knew mathematics; once a Zen Buddhist monk, he also was conversant with Daoist and Confucian philosophy. He was the source of many of Khubilai's ideas, especially those about ruling China. As one of the khan's four wives commented to Liu, "When you speak, he listens."[30]

The eclectic Khubilai listened to many people, and not to Chinese alone. As rulers of a world empire, the Mongols brought together the skills of diverse civilizations to an extent rare at the time and long afterward. Although the main models for Dadu and most of its myriad builders were Chinese, people and ideas of many origins also contributed to the new capital. Learned Persians and Arabs versed in mathematics and engineering cooperated with Chinese scholars. A later funerary inscription even identifies Yeheidie'er, a Muslim of a family of Central or West Asian origin, as the architect of Dadu. Lists of workers on the various construction projects include Muslim, Persian, Khitan, and Jurchen names. Many of these "artisans" may have been conscripted laborers, and Yeheidie'er may have been carrying out the plans of mostly Han Chinese superiors.[31] That said, however, the architectural brilliance of Dadu clearly resulted at least in part from an extraordinary intercultural collaboration. It was not the last time in Chinese history that a dynasty of Inner Asian origin would tap the skills of people from many lands to enhance its image and power. This pattern would recur under the last dynasty, the Qing, when eighteenth-century Jesuit architects would contribute to imperial court capabilities and especially to the design of part of a summer palace. Throughout its existence as a capital, Beijing has been molded by both Chinese and non-Chinese influences.

Urban Society under the Mongols, 1279 to 1368

Not surprisingly, in the new but traditionally designed Dadu, the Mongols carried on urban practices of earlier rulers of large Chinese capitals. They divided day and night into watch-periods and marked their passage with routine noises. In particular, the Bell and Drum towers north of the palace city along the north-south axis informed the populace of the successive watches of the night, facilitating patrols and enforcement of a curfew. Continuing a Jin effort, Persian astronomers tracked the calendar at an observatory near the eastern outer wall.[32] For hundreds of years, and on through the first decades of the twentieth century, noises heard in every street and lane from the Bell and Drum towers marked the daily flow of time, while the antique astronomical instruments became a well-known historical feature of the city. (See Figure 2.) Again like the Jin rulers before him, Khubilai speeded grain transport to the capital from the south. Simultaneously maintaining transport by sea, the Mongols eventually extended the Grand Canal, which had helped to supply earlier northern capitals, from the Yellow River to Dadu. The Grand Canal route from Hangzhou would support the city's economic and political stability for centuries. Without grain from the south, Yuan Dadu could not have sustained its population, estimated to have been as high as 500,000 or more.[33]

The multiethnic planners and builders of Dadu created a city well suited to diverse inhabitants. Its walled courtyards and multiple enclosures helped to order the groups of which urban society was composed. As imperial rulers whose attention focused only partly on China, the Mongols never completely assimilated Chinese culture or habits. They neither adopted Chinese governmental ways as much as the Liao nor mandated study of Chinese classics as much as the Jin.[34] In central Dadu, numerous buildings included Mongol décor alongside traditional Chinese art motifs. The khan displayed animal skins on curtains and screens in the palace. His sons, as well as his concubines about to give birth, slept in yurts in imperial parks. There was precedent for these practices: a rare illustrated map from the fourteenth century shows that the Jin rulers had resided in conical-topped tent structures within the city of Zhongdu.[35] Khubilai ordered grass and soil from Mongolia placed in royal courtyards, both to remind the Mongols of their origins and to provide a setting for shamanistic religious rites. Although the khan "observed" Chinese rites at the appropriate temples in other parts of the city, he usually did so by proxy, sending Chinese court officials to carry out the ceremonies on his behalf. Indeed, separate ethnic spaces within Dadu itself were not sufficient for the rulers. Enduring cultural differences between Mongols and Chinese—not just Dadu's hot summers—may account for Khubilai's decision to spend as much as half of each year at Shangdu in Mongolia. Typically, the Yuan rulers left Dadu in the fourth lunar month and returned in the eighth. At Shangdu, ten days by horse from Dadu, they enjoyed hunting and a general respite from governmental responsibility.[36]

The Mongols brought western Asians with them into Yuan Dadu; they called these Persians, Arabs, Uighurs, and others "people of varied categories" (*semuren*). Many were Muslim merchants who had long cooperated with the Mongols and provided them with valuable knowledge of agricultural societies. Eclectic in religion, the Yuan rulers readily accepted allies of diverse traditions. For their part, the merchants saw the Mongol empire as good for commerce because it secured long-distance trade routes and made new markets accessible. Yuan princes and Islamic merchants pooled investment in lucrative merchant associations called *ortagh*. West Asians also worked for the Mongols in government. Yuan rulers ranked the four main population groups in China in a fixed order: first, Mongols; second, *semuren* (West Asians); third, *hanren* (north Chinese, the Jin population conquered in 1234); and fourth, *nanren* (south Chinese, the Song population conquered in 1279). The southerners understandably were more restive; the Yuan was the first dynasty of Inner Asian origin that they had ever known, although it would not be the last.

The category of *semuren* included people from distant, relatively backward corners of Eurasia. The most exotic participants in Mongol rule were a handful of western Europeans, of whom the Italian merchant Marco Polo is the best known. His account of Yuan Dadu is so famous that Lugou Bridge, originally built in Jin times (in 1189) southwest of Beijing, is also known as Marco Polo Bridge simply because he mentioned it. There is, however, considerable doubt whether Polo reached China either in 1275, as he claimed, or at all. When he described "Cambaluc" (i.e., Khanbalikh or Dadu) in his *Travels*, he may have been retelling stories heard in the Near East, perhaps at Constantinople, from Persian or Arab merchants who actually had ventured much farther in Asia. Scholars still debate many points of Marco Polo's narrative. For example, Polo said that he assisted in a certain Mongol siege during the conquest of the south, but the episode in question occurred in 1273, two years before his arrival. Moreover, although Polo asserted that he, along with other West Asians, worked for Khubilai, there is no mention of him in Yuan records. His failure to touch even briefly on aspects of Chinese life that a medieval European surely would have found noteworthy, such as the Great Wall and women's bound feet, may be yet another indication that his account was not based on firsthand experience.[37]

Whether based on direct observation or on hearsay derived from vivid descriptions by others, Marco Polo's is a uniquely valuable record. His treatment of north and south China as distinct countries tells a great deal about the era. Not until the later sixteenth century would Europeans know for certain that the southeast coast that they by then had reached by sea and Polo's "Cathay" (a name for north China derived from Khitan) were in fact different parts of a single ancient and continuous polity. The *Travels* reported that a huge population filled both Dadu and the dense suburbs outside the eleven major gates. Inns for traveling merchants extended a mile or two beyond the gates on every side, much as motels cluster on the outskirts of modern cities. So crowded was the city that burial of the dead could not be allowed within the walls. Booths and shops lined the main streets, especially near the Drum and Bell towers; merchants were attracted to the rich markets of the capital from north and south and from the huge Mongol empire, which included Central Asia, Persia, Russia, and northern India. Large quantities of costly goods for the khan, his entourage, and others constantly entered the city. Polo noted with amazement that this busy commerce was financed in part by paper money, an idea that was entirely new to him. Like the *Travels,* contemporary accounts by scholar-officials from southern China reported the luxurious way of life of Dadu's rulers and elite.[38]

Marco Polo, or those who were his sources, saw Yuan Dadu when it was newly built. Thus they were among the first to notice an enduring feature of the city plan: by restricting free movement, the nested walls and gates not only protected the large population, they controlled it. Massive walls announced the "presence of government" and the attitude of rulers who valued "security over convenience."[39] Substantial military forces guarded the eleven city gates both day and night. After the Bell Tower signaled curfew in the evening, residents might walk in the streets only in emergencies, and even then only if carrying lights. Groups of mounted guards regularly rode about at night, enforcing the curfew.

Many characteristics of Dadu emphasized in Polo's account were signs of the city's unusually large size. With half a million or more people, Dadu's scale was on an order of magnitude rare in the thirteenth century, when the population of even the largest cities in Europe was counted in the tens, not hundreds, of thousands. Still, the *Travels* presented the capital as not only populous but well organized. Walls and gates, curfew and night patrols, regular sounding of drums and bells—all were aspects of that organization. Whether Polo saw the city with his own eyes or through those of others, and even allowing for travelers' exaggerations, the *Travels* were right that "Cambaluc" was exceptional among world cities of its era.[40]

Yuan rule united north and south China and absorbed the Chinese world into the Mongol empire that dominated Asia and reached as far west as Russia. For almost a century after 1260, these contacts and interactions continued to stimulate Chinese and world cultural developments. Forty-three temples of later Beijing can be firmly dated as originating in Yuan Dadu, and fifteen more make that claim. The former include the Dongyue (God of the Eastern Peak) Temple (Dongyuemiao) built just east of the city in the 1320s and recently restored. To the west, the Daoist Baiyun (White Cloud) Temple (Baiyunguan) flourished in Yuan times based on twelfth-century beginnings; it too still exists.[41] The Yuan rulers patronized artists and craftsmen, both Chinese and *semuren*. They wrote Mongolian with the Uighur script, which they read vertically, and they experimented with a universal alphabet called the Phags-pa script after its creator, a Tibetan lama who was a Buddhist dignitary at the court and high adviser to Khubilai.

Yuan interest in the Chinese vernacular ("everyday") language—as opposed to the ancient, terse classical language—contributed to the development of theater and popular literature in Dadu and in many Chinese cities. Of six to seven hundred Yuan dramas, at least 160 have survived, although the accompanying music has been lost. These poetic and musical pieces, usually in four acts, combined song, dance, acrobatics, pantomime, and lavish costumes. Audiences thrilled to the exploits of generals, the travails of seekers of salvation, the battle of wits between judges and bandits, and the passion of lovers weighing the competing claims of romance and family duty. Even the illiterate were conversant with the many plots drawn from history. Almost all plays contained at least a little humor and a happy ending. Some authors were scholars with extra time to fill because the Yuan discontinuance of state examinations had deprived them of official employment; others were professional playwrights patronized by the court. Both kinds of writers produced masterpieces during the reign of Khubilai (1260–94). Yuan emphasis on colloquial language also favored the evolution of storytelling into the Chinese novel. Employing everyday speech made it easier for writers to tell stories about ordinary folk and easier for a popular audience to read them. As in Song times, the number of books printed by the woodblock method continued to increase, part of a long-term trend toward growth of publishing and literacy.[42] Although Mongol rule had originated in conquest and destruction, it had many constructive outcomes in the cultural realm.

Reconstruction as Ming Beijing, 1402 to 1421

By the middle of the fourteenth century, the Yuan dynasty was disintegrating. Hunger, famine, and disease accompanied an economic crisis in the 1350s and 1360s, but Yuan Dadu saw no major battle and sustained only minor damage in the dynastic transition that followed. The ruling Mongol elite retreated to Mongolia, leaving behind the Yuan imperial capital. Many ordinary Mongol and Chinese residents remained in the city, and some who had left during the midcentury troubles returned.[43]

The founding emperor of the Ming dynasty in 1368 was a Han Chinese commoner from the south, Zhu Yuanzhang, by reign title the Hongwu emperor. Under his leadership, north China came under Chinese rule for the first time since the Song emperor had left Kaifeng for Hangzhou in the early twelfth century. Even from north of the Great Wall, however, the Mongols could pose a serious threat, and that is why Zhu's initial choice of the ancient southern city of Nanjing as capital did not last. (This city on the Yangzi River should not be confused with Liao Nanjing.) Nanjing's many economic advantages were outweighed by its one great disadvantage: it was too far from the Inner Asian frontier. The new rulers needed to control the Mongols and to be able to mount an expansive policy in the steppe quickly if necessary. They also feared the difficulty of managing their own generals and border defense forces from a too-distant capital. The outflow of power to regional commanders had been a major cause of the fall of the Tang dynasty (618–907), a lesson not lost on later rulers.

The return to Dadu by the third Ming emperor was just as crucial to the city's history as its selection by the Great Khan Khubilai had been 140 years earlier. Following the Ming founder's death in 1398, his son Zhu Di rebelled and seized the throne from his own nephew, becoming the Yongle emperor. (See Color Plate 2.) He already had been based in Dadu for two decades as the Prince of Yan. Although he opened his reign in Nanjing, he apparently intended from the start to make Dadu his primary headquarters and Nanjing secondary. The former Dadu had been known since the early Ming as Beiping (Northern Peace); it was now officially named Beijing (Northern Capital); the surrounding prefecture henceforth would be called Shuntian (Obedient to Heaven). After a mere fifteen years of construction, the emperor presided in 1421 over inaugural rites for the restored city. The Ming dynasty now ruled from a border metropolis chosen, after four centuries of growing nomadic power, because it was well situated to stabilize both north China and the steppe.[44] While the Liao and Jin each had established five capitals, the Yuan had used two (Dadu and Shangdu), and the early fifteenth-century Ming two (Beijing and Nanjing). After the 1440s Beijing was the dominant capital in every way, although Nanjing continued in a nominally secondary role until the end of the dynasty.

The reconstruction of the old Dadu as Ming capital drew on the great strength of Chinese civilization in large-scale human organization. This capacity had been demonstrated earlier not only in the building of Dadu itself, but also in such enormous projects as the Great Wall and the First Emperor's capital and tomb (including the now-famous terra-cotta army) near modern Xi'an (all in the third century BCE), and the Grand Canal (beginning in the sixth century CE). As in those undertakings, the emperor did not hesitate to transfer populations in the rebuilding of Dadu. In 1404 he moved ten thousand households—headed by able-bodied men, often of landless families—from Shanxi Province in the northwest to the capital, in order to boost its diminished numbers. Around the same time, at government order, three thousand wealthy southern families settled in the city to increase its cultured population and to remove potentially independent leaders from their home areas. Organizers of the massive capital-building project drew manpower even from among criminals, placing those with the least serious offenses closest to the site. The military population of the city rose steeply: about 250,000 men, many with their families, moved to the area in connection with early Ming reorganization.[45] Streets in narrow alleys near the Xuanwu Gate on the southwest were named for places—Shanxi, Sichuan—from which soldiers and their families had come.[46]

During his reign (1368–1398), the Ming founder had prepared systematically for the rebuilding of the city by ordering survey and repair of walls and moats. The northern wall had been rebuilt south of its Yuan location, probably to make it more easily defensible. (See Map 1.) The names of the two northernmost gates had been changed to Anding (Pacification) and Desheng (Virtuous

Victory) to honor Ming achievements. (The Desheng Gate still stands amid a sea of traffic along the Second Ring Road.) In 1406 the Yongle emperor summoned hundreds of thousands of workers to begin large-scale construction. They started with the palace city in that year and worked outward, reaching the imperial city in 1417 (as the emperor moved north for good) and the main city wall in 1420. Conscripted laborers and convicts endured conditions so difficult that some tried to escape. Thousands of artisans were captives from Annam (North Vietnam), which fell under Ming rule for a brief period beginning in 1407. By 1417 to 1420, a million convicts and conscript laborers, including about 100,000 specialized craftsmen, were at work in Beijing. Wishing to rid themselves of Mongol *fengshui*—of any geomantic link to Yuan décor, such as animal skins on the walls and yurts in the courtyards—the builders destroyed much of what remained of the Yuan palace before constructing the new compound, which they called the Purple Forbidden City (Zijincheng).[47]

Like any army, the battalions of builders needed an extensive supply line to maintain their progress. Officials fanned out to distant provincial forests to supervise cutting of logs—fir, elm, oak, camphor, catalpa—and to dispatch them down rivers for use in Beijing. Other imperial representatives were busy in north China setting up the manufacture of custom-designed bricks and tiles. So great was the intensity of their demands that in 1408 the emperor had to warn his minions—both supervisors and those collecting building material elsewhere—to stop abusing the populace.[48] By 1415 the improved Grand Canal had eased supply problems and expedited construction. By 1420 the city featured a restored Bell Tower as well as new and renovated moats, walls, bridges, palace buildings, and suburban altars for sacred imperial rituals. The 35-foot (10.7-meter)–high city walls consisted of layers of mud, gravel, and lime.

The Yongle emperor rewarded the builders of his northern capital, including officials and all levels of construction workers. But any mood of celebration was short-lived. In 1421 fire destroyed three of the new audience halls. So ominous an event obliged him to invite criticism, because ancient beliefs held that natural disasters might be caused by the ruler's misconduct. Some officials took the opportunity to note abuses connected with rebuilding the Northern Capital; the emperor, they suggested, had aroused the anger of Heaven by asking too much of the people. Such complaints were incautious, to say the least. Having ignored the same criticism when the project began twenty years before, and having exerted himself to control official excess afterward, the emperor refused to listen to those who now said "I told you so." Execution of his most vocal critic silenced all the others.[49]

The cause of the protestors was hopeless in any case, because rebuilding of the city no more depended on the opinions of high officials than on those of captive artisans or relocated farmers. The manner of conflict resolution during construction of the city was one sign that the dynasty was moving toward autocracy, toward concentrating all power in the emperor. In 1380 the Ming founder even had gone so far as to eliminate the office of the prime minister. Power relationships had evolved to favor the emperor alone; by the time of the Ming founding, only imperial decisions really mattered. One modern historian compares the Yongle emperor to Augustus Caesar (63 BCE–14 CE), who said that he found Rome a city of brick and left it a city of marble. The Yongle emperor too found Beijing in relative decay and left it at a completely new level of magnificence.[50] But differences between the two rulers also are instructive. Augustus had seen his adoptive father, Julius Caesar, assassinated for seeking to become a dictator; therefore, he carefully maintained a pretext of republican institutions and titles to mask his power. By contrast, at least in this important instance, the Yongle emperor seems to have felt no need to appear to share decision-making power with anyone, let alone actually to share it.

A second round of building at Beijing under the Zhengtong emperor (1436–1449) employed a labor force of 66,000.[51] The effort added new palaces and pavilions, gate and corner watchtowers, and crescent-shaped outer walls (enceintes) at each gate. (See Figure 4.) Workers also deepened moats and glazed their sides, removed wooden bridges and built stone ones in their place, and thickly faced the city walls with gray brick. In general, they replaced earth, reeds, and wood used in Yuan and early Ming with more enduring brick and stone.[52] A century later, in 1553, a Mongol threat to the city prompted enclosure of the commercial and semiagricultural southern suburbs by a wall. This area, called Nancheng (Southern City), incorporated large parts of the old Liao and Jin capitals on its western side. The mid-sixteenth-century Ming rulers spent far less treasure on the Southern City than their fifteenth-century ancestors had on the northern one: the seven gates of the Southern City were comparatively low and roughly built, and the turrets at the four corners of the Southern City wall were two storeys in height as opposed to four in the Northern City wall.[53] Still, the Southern City wall was a significant addition. Without the strengthening and extension of many structures in the 1430s–40s and 1550s, the architectural complex at Beijing might not have survived into the twentieth century.

As early as 1450, the Ming reconstruction of Beijing had produced a capital much grander, though slightly smaller, than Dadu had been. The northern wall was now about 2.7 kilometers (1.7 miles) south of its former location, and the southern wall also had been moved to the south, but not as far as the northern wall had been drawn in. The Ming east and west walls were rebuilt on Yuan foundations but, because they were shorter, each had lost one gate; in this way, the number of city gates fell from eleven to nine. (In later ages, the words "nine gates" [*jiumen*] alone would serve as literary synecdoche for the entire city.) The section of Ming Beijing with the most direct continuity was its core, which had been central Yuan Dadu. The imperial and palace cities, although reshaped by the Ming builders, retained something of the Yuan past.[54] The Ancestral Temple and Altars of Land and Grain, however, were rebuilt on east and west inside the Imperial City rather than outside it as in Dadu. Unlike the Mongols, the Ming rulers—Chinese themselves—had no reason to distance themselves from Chinese rites.[55]

In the same years when the Ming government was rebuilding Beijing, it also was sponsoring a series of maritime expeditions that reached as far as India, the Persian Gulf, and the coast of East Africa. Motives both political and commercial appear to have been in play: the legacy of the Mongol empire included a taste for tributary states and for lucrative long-distance commerce. Seven large-scale expeditions were remarkable achievements in seamanship: one voyage to India between 1405 and 1407 involved sixty-two vessels and 28,000 men. The necessary technology had accumulated over centuries and included the maritime compass, a much earlier Chinese invention. The court thus commanded a new level of mastery of the seas well before Columbus discovered America (1492) or Vasco DaGama rounded the Cape of Good Hope and reached India (1498).

Ming rulers might well have moved on toward global expansion of their power, as Europeans soon would do, but they chose to end the expeditions in 1433. Why did they face toward Inner Asia instead and turn away from the seas when they might have dominated them? The most important reason was that they wanted to be sure the Mongol conquest would not recur. They focused their resources on projects closely related to that goal: restoration of the Grand Canal, reforestation of north China, revival of agriculture, rebuilding of the Great Wall, and reconstruction of Beijing. Continued fighting with the Mongols during this era kept their reasons for forsaking the seas fresh in their minds. With the benefit of hindsight, however, we can observe that the stakes were far greater than anyone could have foreseen in the fifteenth century. By shifting their attention from the seas to Inner Asia, the Ming rulers chose the conservatism of northwest

China over the modernity and enlightenment that might have been available to them through oceanic commerce. They left the seas to the Portuguese, the Spanish, the Dutch, and the English.

In the long run, moving the Ming capital from the south to Beijing had both major advantages and significant costs. On one hand, the border location of the city not only served crucial strategic purposes but also fostered cultural creativity. Like Yuan Dadu, Ming (and later, to an even greater extent, Qing) Beijing became a place that brought a wide variety of peoples from China and beyond into contact. On the other hand, maintaining so populous a capital hundreds of miles from a main source of its food supply was a drain on revenues and a cause of vulnerability.[56] This indeed was the paradox of Beijing. Emperors selected its peripheral location to consolidate their dominion, but having moved large populations into place in a border city, they were dependent on the steady and uninterrupted flow of grain from the south. As long as the empire lasted, rulers in Beijing recognized that the capital's great size, along with its geographical location, made its tranquility a matter that required their constant attention.

Ming Beijing, 1421 to 1644

After 1421 Beijing more than ever became a magnet for people, goods, and services. Population increased during the Ming era, reaching near 1 million at its highest point in the mid-fifteenth century. Grain and manufactured goods such as ceramics and textiles poured into the city in quantities far larger than the rulers themselves could use. The surplus entered the market. Growing commercialization fostered greater social mobility and a less tightly controlled population. Yuan state-sponsored households of hereditary craftsmen, like the earlier Jin official workshops of conscripted artisans, became outdated. Although trade was limited in the early Ming years, the government deliberately set out to encourage it by building several thousand *langfang* (dwelling compounds with porches) near the main gates and the Bell and Drum towers and by insisting that merchants rent them and undertake commercial activities there. Growing prosperity in Beijing reflected the wealth of the country, especially the southern provinces, and the capacity for efficient transport on the restored Grand Canal. Transplanted southern merchants kept up ties with their places of origin, contributing to the emergence of national business networks. A center of consumption, Ming Beijing further developed publishing and handicraft industries based on capabilities that had first flourished in the city in Liao-Jin times.[57]

A thriving street life reflected the growing size and heterogeneity of the capital. In a pattern going back to Yuan Dadu and earlier cities, Beijing's broadest avenues ran north and south, crossed by many smaller lanes in a chessboard pattern. (A few streets, such as the large Gulou xi dajie [West Drum Tower Avenue] leading diagonally to the northwest from the front of the Drum Tower, were slanted in relation to others because the terrain of the city is not perfectly flat. It inclines from the northwest to the southeast, with streams flowing through the Northern City toward lower-lying land to the south.[58]) The Mongolian word *hutong* began to be used for the city's narrower streets in the Yuan dynasty (1279–1368). By Ming times residents traveled by way of almost 1,200 streets, of which 459 were *hutong*. In the sixteenth century they began to take an interest in street names and to record them in published descriptions of the capital.[59] From that time on street names were passed down by such printed descriptions as well as orally; actual street signs appeared only in the early twentieth century, when there were over 3,000 *hutong*, and elimination of duplicate names became an issue. People named streets based on major markets nearby (Caishikou hutong, Vegetable Market Intersection); merchandise sold there, especially necessities of daily life (Dachaye hutong, Great Tealeaf Alley); the names of eminent persons or craftsmen who once lived there (Shi jia hutong, Shi Family Alley); notable buildings (Jiu gulou dajie, Old Drum Tower Avenue; Xunbuting hutong, Lane of the Constable Headquarters); and scenery or terrain (Dazhalan, Great Street-gate).

Even when a street lost the activity from which its name had come, the name often stuck. Long after it became a book, art, and curio market, Liulichang in the Southern City was still called Glazed Tile Factory in recollection of a government enterprise that had stood there beginning in the Yuan era.[60] Some names were so humble that residents of later ages changed them. A donkey market, *lüshi*, gave its name to Lüshi hutong (Donkey Market Lane); today the same street is called Lishi hutong (Gentleman Lane). The Ming-era Zhushi hutong (Pig Market Lane) in the Southern City is (by substitution of a different character also pronounced *zhu*) today's Pearl Market Lane. Such changes would take, however, only if people accepted them over time. Puns, to which the Chinese language readily lends itself, also appeared in street names; thus the Ming Northern City's Dong jiangmi xiang (East Lane of the Riverine Rice Merchants) later became the Qing-era Dong jiaomin xiang (East Lane of the Exchange of Peoples, also known as Legation Street). The distinctive "*erh*" of the Beijing accent gave many street names a colloquial sound, as in Yu'erh hutong (Rain Lane) or Mao'erh hutong (Hat Lane) or the shopping area Dashalar (Dazhalan).[61]

In Ming Beijing, shops and residences, government offices and temples, homes of rich and poor residents usually were found close together in the same area, in an endlessly mixed arrangement that most modern city dwellers would find disorienting. As we have suggested, however, there already were some exceptions to this pattern in Yuan Dadu, such as the tendency to separate Mongols and Han Chinese. In the Ming capital, the nucleus of official activities was located in the central Northern City. Residences of the rich (along with luxury-level markets and inns) tended to be located in that area as well, especially along the east side of the Northern City near the Imperial City. The poor were more likely to reside at the capital's periphery, especially outside the western wall of the Northern City. They entered the walled area daily as laborers and returned home at night. In addition, the city contained many small "cellular" areas that were ethnic or occupational colonies. Muslims who butchered cattle lived in the western part of the Southern City just outside the Xuanwu Gate, in the vicinity of Niu jie (Ox Street).[62] Today a mosque near the same street faces Mecca and bears the name Niujie libaisi (Ox Street Mosque). In the Ming era, shops in the same or related trades often were grouped together. People who wished to buy pears, for example, knew that they needed to try Guozishi dajie, Fruit Market Avenue, in the Northern City near the Drum Tower. Those in need of bargains in secondhand clothing went to Guyi hutong, Old Clothes [Dealers] Lane, south of Chang'an dajie near the southwestern wall of the Imperial City. In the same immediate neighborhood they would find apparel, textile, and other businesses on Straw Hat Lane, Hemp Rope Lane, Stone Stele Lane, Horsepost Lane, Millers Lane, Curtain Lane, and Felt Cloth Lane.[63]

In a city without street signs where most people got around on foot, mistakes in finding a destination were easy to make and very time-consuming. Moving about in two-wheeled carriages and sedan chairs on main streets crowded with pedestrians cannot have been much faster than walking. The advantage of clustering of shops, often along a street with a name that identified the category of their wares, was that when buyers had arrived in the right place, they could choose among a number of stores relevant to their needs. The Southern City had an especially wide variety of trades available to consumers on Reed Mat Lane, Beancurd Alley, Gold Foil Lane, Hairpin Lane, Tea Delicacies Lane, the Wood Market, Wu's Rug Street, and other streets devoted to special products.[64] Rural wholesale suppliers needed to go to only a few areas to sell their produce to city buyers. Merchants in the same or related trades, for their part, benefited from the acquaintance and mutual help that proximity facilitated. Not coincidentally, the

Chinese word for trade guild, *hang*, is written with a character showing two sides of a street.

For the merchant, a single structure commonly housed living quarters, a workshop at the back, and a store at the front. Inside, a well-established family business could make and sell products in a practical way that allowed for just-in-time delivery and convenient repair. Many lanes were named for a family that had been the first, largest, or most skillful in the neighborhood at developing a particular trade or manufacture: grinding grain, dyeing textiles, working copper, making wine, weaving cloth, fashioning metal or bamboo items, or creating medicine. Tang dao'erh hutong was Tang [Family] Knife Lane; along Shen bizi hutong, the Shen family manufactured bamboo items (*bizi*); on Shih nan hutong, the Shih family dyed garments.[65]

Of course, businesses that did not have streets named for them still could be well known, and specialization helped them to succeed. Officials seeking the large Ming-style formal hats with two perpendicular "fins" at the back knew that they should visit the Li family shop near the southern wall of the Northern City and adjacent grain transport canals. If they needed shoes, they would not forget the Song family shop in the Southern City or the Tang family in the East Yangzi Rice Market. Need incense for religious ceremonies? Try the Li shop outside Qianmen. A sore throat would remind the sufferer of the lane where soothing pills were produced according to a secret formula. Some products were seasonal; southwest of the You'an Gate of the Southern City, gardeners raised flowers in accordance with the weather and the holiday calendar.[66]

The street scene was colorful and exciting, though often crowded and demanding. Ming merchants painted and decorated the fronts of their shops; tall signs outside Qianmen in the Southern City rose high above street level. On busy commercial thoroughfares, inscriptions and symbols of trade told passersby, even illiterate ones, what product or service was offered. Wine cups identified a wine shop, just as apothecary jars marked drugstores and striped poles barber shops in the early modern West. Carved commemorative arches (*pailou*), a borrowing from Indian architecture, decorated streets in both the Northern and Southern cities.[67] Appealing though these avenues may have been to the eye, they were often hard to negotiate. Shoppers and sightseers contended with mud in winter and with dust, flies and heat in summer; a longtime sojourner remarked that it was hard to say which of the two seasons was worse for walking. Some who traveled the streets of Ming Beijing wore black veils to protect themselves from the dust storms that blew in from Mongolia. One advantage of the veil was that wearers could allow themselves to be recognized only when they so wished, avoiding elaborate rituals of public greeting of acquaintances. Moreover, early Christian missionaries found that they could use veils to move about the city without drawing unwanted attention.[68]

Customers and merchants bought and sold extensively in both the Ming Northern and Southern Cities and in suburbs beyond the walls. Some markets in the Southern City may have acted as wholesalers for retail operations in the Northern City. Still, the largest markets, and the main rice market, were in the Northern City just south of the Forbidden City (in the area of today's Tiananmen Square), where traders from many places crowded and jostled daily from well before dawn. Other major markets operated in the densely populated area of the Southern City outside the Qian and Chongwen gates; in the Northern City on the east side near palaces, state granaries, and connections to the Grand Canal; along the north-central Drum Tower Avenue; in the west near the temple to the City God; and just outside the Desheng Gate on the northwest.[69] Because of the advantages of its location near transport routes, the east side of the Northern City became more commercialized than the western side. Everything from necessities to luxury items, even foreign goods, could be found for sale in Ming Beijing, though middlemen and transport costs often resulted in high prices.[70]

Ming Beijing had daily, periodic, and temple markets. Periodic markets were held at street or temple locales on fixed days of every month. Temple markets had grown up around religious festivals, such as the birthday of the Buddha, to take advantage of large crowds that would gather for the day's ceremonies. Many markets specialized in customers of a particular kind. A paupers' market in the Southern City near Qianmen opened at dusk and operated into the early morning hours, with darkness concealing seller, buyer, and the possibly shady origins of the goods. It was a place where no questions were asked. At the other end of the social scale, the "inner market" inside the Imperial City sold luxury products to eunuchs, imperial relatives, palace women, collectors, and other wealthy customers. An even higher-level periodic market was held in the northwestern part of the Forbidden City itself on the dates ending in "four" in each month, all days when the gates were opened so that refuse could be removed. Wishing to promote commerce and protect popular welfare, Ming rulers increased regulation of all Beijing markets. The state announced opening and closing hours, determined permissible locations, and set uniform standards of measurement.[71]

The Ming was an era of achievement in traditional forms of high culture and of growing literacy and knowledge on the popular level. The capital's book trade expanded. A well-known painting shows books for sale at a market, displayed on the ground on a *baitan* (spread) of cloth or a mat.[72] Booksellers would show their wares in front of examination grounds, at temple markets, and at the annual Lantern Festival. By the later Ming period, however, the temporary, movable *baitan* had become a permanent bookstore (*shushi*). Bookstores were found in all parts of the city; some not only sold books but also produced them in a print shop (*shufang*), with the most ambitious proprietors specializing in woodblock publishing and in wholesale rather than retail trade.[73] Works of the time included poetry, history, and philosophy in the classical language as well as stories, novels, and plays based on traditional oral material in the vernacular. Literature that sought mainly to entertain, in everyday language, represented a relatively new "semi-learned, semi-popular" culture that first flourished in large cities.[74] Even readers who knew only a limited number of characters could enjoy vernacular literature, especially since much of its content was already familiar. For their part, the well educated were not only conversant with this material but often its anonymous authors. They usually did not wish to be identified openly with such creations because, in the Confucian view, only literature that contributed to moral understanding could be considered art. Wu Cheng'en, the author of the comic novel *Xiyouji* (Journey to the West, translated by Arthur Waley as *Monkey*) was a sixteenth-century scholar-official whose identity was uncovered only after intensive modern detective work.

Ming scholarship was far-ranging. At the Imperial College (Guozijian), built in the Yuan era, literary tradition reigned. Where Mongol rulers once had sent representatives to intellectual discourses, now emperors themselves discussed the Confucian classics for an audience of students and scholars. Later, in the eighteenth century, stone tablets containing the full text of the classics would be placed in the college, where they remain today. Preparation for the regular civil service examinations was extremely demanding; those who passed at the highest level were honored by having their names engraved on stelae that still stand in the Confucian Temple, down the street from the Imperial College. (See Figure 1.) Ming compilers produced massive surveys of the inherited texts of the Chinese world, among which the *Yongle dadian* (Great encyclopedia of the Yongle era, 1407) in 11,095 volumes and *Bencao gangmu* (Materia medica, 1593) are the best known. Educated readers also were interested in the world beyond China. Among writings that attracted their attention were missionary-sponsored works, produced with the help of Chinese scholars, on astronomy, mathematics, geography, medicine, ethics, and linguistics.

In the thirteenth century, Marco Polo's amazement at the wealth and scale of Dadu had reflected the imbalance between China and late medieval Europe, which lagged behind China in many ways. Three hundred years later, Matteo Ricci (1552–1610) exemplified a different balance between China and the West. An Italian Jesuit of rare ability and powerful memory, Ricci lived in China for almost three decades, taking the Chinese name Li Madou; he learned to speak the Chinese language and read its classical literature. He then used this fluency to teach not only Christianity but also science, mathematics, and cartography. In Polo's time, European stimulation at the discovery of advanced societies in Asia had contributed to the Renaissance; in Ricci's, Renaissance achievements came back to China, where some in the imperial court and bureaucratic elite appreciated them. Operating at the pinnacle of Chinese society, Ricci and other Jesuits practiced astronomy (although they still employed the Ptolemaic rather than the new Copernican, sun-centered system, which had been published in 1543). They added European instruments to the older ones used in Beijing by Persian and Chinese astronomers since the Jin-Yuan era. They demonstrated mechanical clocks and introduced up-to-date world maps. Ricci, who never returned to Europe, attained his goal of residence in the capital in 1601 and remained there until his death in 1610, when he was buried in a plot provided by the emperor as a mark of special respect. His pioneering work initiated decades of missionary activity at the Chinese court. Jesuits built the first Roman Catholic church in Beijing, completed in 1652 just north of the Xuanwu Gate of the Northern City, the locale where Ricci had lived and established a chapel in 1605. A successor to this church, later called the Nantang (Southern Cathedral), stands on the same site today.

A calendar of seasonal festivals added customary pleasures and commercial opportunities to the life of the city. Four were especially well known: the Lunar New Year during the first fifteen days of the new year, when residents visited friends and family and paid their respects at temples; Qingming (Clear and Bright) in the early spring, when families visited ancestral graves; the Dragon Boat festival in the fifth month, which people in Beijing marked by picnics, horse riding, and archery competitions rather than boat races; and the mid-autumn festival after the harvest, on the fifteenth day of the eighth month, when families made offerings to the full moon and gathered to enjoy moon cakes.[75] A fifth, the locally important and picturesque Lantern Festival (Dengshi), continued from the eighth through the eighteenth of the first month along both sides of a broad avenue on the east side of the Northern City. Merchants set up temporary booths and curtains; the rich rented small houses nearby to enjoy the colorful lanterns, the night moon, the music of drums, flutes, and cymbals, and the remarkable wares for sale. The crowd was so large that carriages could not turn around and it was dangerous for their drivers even to look back for a moment.[76]

Fairs and even everyday streets offered extensive popular entertainment. Cricket-fighting, fortune-telling, and card games were common pastimes. Some decks of cards bore the faces of fictional heroes of the Robin Hood type from popular novels such as *Shuihu zhuan* (Water margin, translated by Pearl Buck as *All Men Are Brothers*). A place called Gaoliang Bridge, not far west of the capital outside the Xizhi Gate of the Northern City, was lined with wine shops and places of entertainment. Fairgoers rich and poor entered large tents to watch astounding acrobatic and magic performances.[77] The Qingming fair at Gaoliang Bridge, which could attract thousands of people on a single spring day, was only one of many interesting annual excursions around Ming Beijing.[78] But a person also could be well entertained without leaving the city. Storytelling and ballads (often accompanied by the *pipa*, a four-stringed instrument) enlivened Beijing teahouses and streets. A blind man, having learned to play the *pipa* at one of several stores that offered lessons, could make a living by storytelling. Young female singers became skillful at stirring emotions. Performers proficient in many Chinese dialects—all of which could be heard in the capital because of the travel of officials, merchants, and sightseers—developed elaborate oral tales and routines.

Ballads sometimes criticized the rich and powerful, especially corrupt court eunuchs. Already in the Ming era some felt that the direct, straightforward character considered natural to Beijing local residents was being undermined by a love of profit and luxury. Steady, honest, and experienced people sometimes seemed to do less well than the young, the sharp, and even the unscrupulous. Merchants cheated by manipulating measurements. Emperors and high officials modeled conspicuous overindulgence in partying and gambling. Wealthy families kept female slaves as maids or concubines. Critics saw in Beijing a kind of gilded squalor and "artificial splendor—the great wealth of the south displayed at the edge of the steppe."[79] More than ever before, rural people from around the Beijing region were drawn to the capital, where they worked as laborers, sedan-chair carriers, maids, and printers' helpers. But they did not always find the work that they sought. With all its prosperity, the city was also the scene of great suffering; thousands of beggars struggled to survive on its streets, especially in the winter months.[80]

The Ming–Qing Transition, 1640s

The fall of the Ming dynasty was caused by repeated northward military expeditions, inflationary pressures created by an overspent imperial treasury, epidemics, and natural disasters. Amid court and bureaucratic corruption, in the reign of the last of a series of weak emperors, a peasant rebellion led by Li Zicheng exploded into Beijing on April 25, 1644. Meanwhile the Manchus, a new Inner Asian claimant for power, waited outside the Great Wall. After the capital had been occupied by Li, the emperor hanged himself at a spot still marked today just north of the Forbidden City. A leading Ming general, Wu Sangui, then defected to the Manchus, and together they ejected the peasant rebels from the city. Extended fighting between Manchus and Ming loyalists lay ahead both in Beijing and elsewhere. Ming forces held out for years in south China, and more than a generation would pass before the Manchus were completely victorious in 1683. (The Manchus later renamed the hill where the last Ming emperor committed suicide Jingshan [Prospect Hill] because the previous name, which referred to imperial long life [Wansuishan] was inappropriate.)

The Manchus presented themselves as preservers of Chinese legitimacy, as the new holders of the ancient Mandate given by Heaven to rulers of human society, as "more Chinese than the Chinese."[81] They chose the name "Manchu," probably from a Buddhist term for "great good fortune," in 1636.[82] As descendants of the Jurchen Jin who, five hundred years earlier, had ruled China as far south as the Huai River, the Manchus drew on centuries of familiarity with Chinese political ideas. They did not stake their position only on their military superiority over China, which was not as great as that wielded by their predecessors from north of the Great Wall. Even more than those rulers, therefore, the newly founded Qing dynasty needed assistance, not just acquiescence, from its Chinese subjects. A Chinese official, Hong Chengchou (1593–1665), wrote the regent Dorgon's major early proclamations on behalf of the Shunzhi emperor, still a young boy at the time of the conquest. Hong, who had been both a provincial governor and a military commander, concluded that Ming frontier policy was ineffective after he was captured by the Manchus in 1642. He surrendered and agreed to help his captors by joining one of the military units that they had created for Chinese adherents. In 1644 he advised the regent to fight Chinese bandits and soldiers but not to harm ordinary people or take their property. "If it is done in this way," he predicted, "far and near the word will spread, and on hearing it people will submit."[83]

As Chinese advisers to Mongol khans had done in the thirteenth century, Hong helped to modify the rule of a conquest dynasty to make it more acceptable in China. Like his contemporary Wu Sangui, he judged that a Manchu dynasty assisted by educated Chinese would be preferable to one founded by the commoner rebel Li Zicheng. Such a conclusion was expedient in a premodern context; Inner Asian groups often had played a role in Chinese politics. Moreover, unlike Li and his peasant followers, the Manchus had been preparing for decades to offer themselves as an alternative to the decaying Ming regime.

In Beijing, however, the Manchus soon disregarded Hong's advice to avoid seizing Chinese property. In 1648 they announced that henceforth the Northern City would become the preserve of the Qing military forces ("banners") and their families and that its current Chinese residents would be relocated in the Southern City but compensated financially. The new rulers claimed that conflicts between Manchu and Chinese were responsible for this decision, but they may have intended all along to segregate the two groups and simply waited to consolidate their victory before doing so. Another motive may have been to protect Manchus and Mongols from exposure to smallpox, a disease to which they had not acquired immunity. Only later, in the last decades of the seventeenth century, would the practice of variolation reduce this particular anxiety.[84] Manchu actions in moving soldiers and their families into the city en masse and displacing many Chinese residents resembled Jin behavior when they had first taken over the city that became Zhongdu in the twelfth century.[85]

The "bannermen" (qiren) for whom Chinese Northern City residents now had to make way were products of a distinctive social and military institution. The Eight Banners (baqi) were hereditary military units that had supported the Manchu rise to power. In origin the banner system may have been related to the Ming government's own border military colonies (wei). Beginning in the later sixteenth century, Manchu military men and their families were organized under eight hereditary banners (flags)—plain yellow, white, red, and blue and bordered banners of the same four colors. Among all the Manchus—men, women, and children—only the emperor was not enrolled in a banner. As the Manchus extended their power in Inner Asia prior to the conquest of China, eight Mongol and eight Chinese (hanjun) banners of the same colors and bordered colors were added. For example, the captured commander who gave crucial help to the Manchus, Hong Chengchou, joined the Chinese bordered yellow banner.

Having founded the Qing dynasty, the Manchus now secured themselves in the Forbidden City by stationing the banner forces and their families around it in the Northern City. The territorial arrangement of the banners there probably was *not* derived from the correspondence of their colors with the cardinal compass points, as a common myth has it. It is more likely that the origin of this arrangement lay in the nomadic tradition of protecting the leader's yurt by stationing his closest followers all around it. In Yuan Dadu the Mongols had followed a similar pattern. The Qing rulers carefully placed the Manchu units and their families closest to the Forbidden and Imperial Cities and the Mongol and Chinese units farther away.[86] (See Map 5 in Chapter 3.) In the mid-seventeenth century transition, 300,000 Han Chinese (60,000 to 80,000 households) were displaced from the Northern City and about the same number of people affiliated with the banners were moved into their vacated houses. The number is smaller than might be expected because the population of the Northern City, estimated to have been as high as 600,000 in 1621, had fallen sharply in connection with Li's peasant rebellion and the subsequent fighting. Still, for those forced to move from the Northern to the Southern City, the experience was wrenching and painful. With an Inner Asian dynasty's characteristic respect for religious institutions, however, the new rulers made an exception for Buddhist and Daoist temples and their resident priests and monks. Allowed to stay where they were, these temples, numbering in the hundreds, became "islands of stability" and sites of potential reconciliation between bannermen and the Chinese whom they had evicted.[87]

New names for the two main parts of the city reflected the major changes that were under way. After the enclosure of the Southern City by a wall in the 1550s, it was referred to as the Outer City, while the Northern City was more often called the Inner City.[88] Qing usage continued this practice. In the Qing era, Western visitors often referred to the two areas as the "Tartar" (Inner) and "Chinese" (Outer) Cities. "Tartar," originally a term for the Mongols, in this case referred both to the Manchus and to Mongols closely associated with Manchu rule. It is significant that, compared to the original Ming terms ("Northern" and "Southern"), both "Inner" and "Tartar" emphasized dynastic control and "Tartar" and "Chinese" focused on growing ethnic separation.

The new dynastic rulers, again following Jin precedent, appropriated for themselves and the banners the best land surrounding the city. They exploited farm properties as absentee landlords, with the former owners becoming their tenants.[89] Despite the invaders' many privileges, however, actually living in Beijing and its environs did not come easily to them. They were vulnerable to smallpox;

they had not yet learned the Chinese language; and, like northern peoples before them, they found the summer climate oppressive. They were unaccustomed even to living in a large city; in 1648–1649 the regent Dorgon silenced all the peddlers in the capital because their noise disturbed him.[90] For all these reasons, the rulers soon established a court residence at Rehe (Chengde), beyond the Great Wall in Manchuria. Later they would build other retreats closer to Beijing, especially on the northwest side. Their impulse to leave the city in the summer followed the consistent practice of earlier Inner Asian dynasties. The Qing dynasty, however, would prove more politically adroit and enduring than any of them.

Like the Liao, Jin, Yuan, and Ming choices of the city as a capital at critical earlier junctures, initial Qing dynasty changes had far-reaching consequences. Much more than before, commerce was concentrated in the Southern (now Outer) City as Chinese merchants relocated their shops and workshops there. Some earlier ethnic enclaves continued to exist, but the trend was toward larger-scale ethnic separation in a "newly compartmentalized" landscape.[91] A Qing rule against inns in the Inner City caused the few hostels for visitors from the same province or area (native-place lodges) to join the majority already in the Outer City.[92] The new Inner City mainly contained Manchus, Mongols, and Chinese bannermen and their families; the Outer City and the extramural suburbs were for all other Chinese. The Qing rulers were quick to see that this arrangement achieved more than protecting the dynasty. Their placing most commerce, entertainment, inns, and hostels in the Outer City made the Inner City easier to control by reducing daily traffic. The Qing gendarmerie would press this advantage even further by limiting numbers and kinds of shops both in the Inner City itself and along routes used by imperial processions in the Outer City.[93]

Although, for premodern urban authorities, Qing officials paid an unusual amount of attention to regulating the use of space, they did not forget to regulate appearances as well for dynastic and social purposes. Styles of dress, details of housing, and modes of transportation depended on a person's rank, as had long been the case. But now there was more: in Beijing as elsewhere in China, the new regime required from 1645 on that almost all adult males, except for priests and monks, adopt the Manchu hairstyle (a long queue down the back, with shaved head). Serious resistance followed. Han Chinese resented these orders coming from the Manchus, whom they regarded as their cultural inferiors. That some minority peoples—Mongols, Tibetans, Uighurs—were exempt from the new rules (and others, such as Turks or the Miao, could limit the new-style haircuts to their leaders) only further inflamed feelings on the Chinese side. Tensions over hairstyle crystallized anger aroused by the forced turnover of housing in the Northern City and the expropriation of desirable land in the capital region. For some time, Beijing became "more like occupied territory than the lively capital it had been."[94] The traumatic passage from Ming to Qing was so sensitive a subject that it was almost never discussed openly during the Qing era, and infrequent references employed euphemisms. People often referred to the year corresponding to 1644 as *jiashen*, a name derived from a traditional cyclic system; by using this term, the speaker artfully avoided identifying the year as either the last of the Ming or the first of the Qing.[95]

When the Shunzhi emperor died of smallpox at the age of only twenty-four in 1661 (the regent Dorgon having died a decade earlier), his successor was a seven-year-old son who already had survived the disease. He became the Kangxi emperor, and his long and successful reign lasted until 1722. The transition to yet another dynasty of Inner Asian origin had aroused significant hostility between rulers and subjects. The Manchus had redefined and reallocated familiar spaces; people belonging to diverse groups or engaged in different kinds of activities were now more separated than they had been under the Ming. New fault lines created a need for fresh social integration and opportunities for institutions that could foster it. During the Kangxi reign and after, the resilient society of Beijing gradually revived after a long period of troubles and began to develop and thrive in a new Qing dynasty world.

Chapter 2

The Forbidden City
and the Qing Emperors

THE REIGNS OF THE KANGXI, YONGZHENG, AND QIANLONG EMPERORS
stand out as a high point of imperial and dynastic power in all of Chinese history.
In a remarkable era from 1662 to 1796 that has been called China's long eighteenth century, the three rulers saw themselves as heads of a great, multiethnic
empire. They also aspired to inherit ancient traditions of universal rule by the
Chinese Son of Heaven and by the Buddhist wheel-turning *cakravartin* king.[1]

After consolidating their power, the Manchus achieved a vast territorial expansion. The empire would come to include Manchuria and Mongolia to the
north, Xinjiang to the west, Tibet to the southwest, and the island of Taiwan. At
the same time, emperors worked with the bureaucracy to promote peace and
prosperity. The wealth of the empire seemed unbounded, and the treasuries and
granaries were amply filled. Much of this wealth benefited the people, not just the
rulers, and population may have doubled in size to about 300 million.[2] The
Kangxi and Yongzheng emperors often made a point of frugality, but the Qianlong emperor spared no expense in supporting architectural projects and patron-
izing the arts, religion, and scholarship. The Qing court both enhanced and
turned to maximum effect the distinguished architecture of the capital and of the
Forbidden City. (See Color Plate 3 and Map 2.)

In recent years the Chinese authorities have promoted public admiration for
the accomplishments of this "high Qing" period and for the vigor and skills of the
three emperors. Many books, films, and television programs have made them familiar and popular figures.

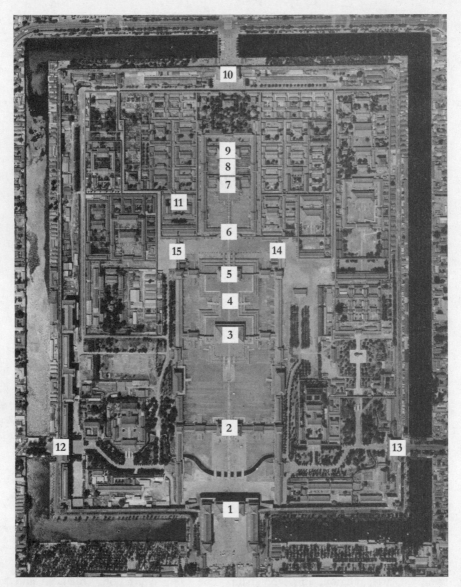

THE FORBIDDEN CITY:

1. Meridian Gate - Wumen
2. Gate of Supreme Harmony - Taihemen
3. Hall of Supreme Harmony - Taihedian
4. Hall of Central Harmony - Zhonghedian
5. Hall of Preserving Harmony - Baohedian
6. Gate of Heavenly Purity - Qianqingmen
7. Palace of Heavenly Purity - Qianqinggong
8. Hall of Union - Jiaotaidian
9. Palace of Earthly Tranquility - Kunninggong
10. Gate of Spiritual Valor - Shenwumen
11. Hall of Mental Cultivation - Yangxindian
12. West Flowery Gate - Xihuamen
13. East Flowery Gate - Donghuamen
14. Gate of Great Fortune - Jingyunmen
15. Gate of Eminent Ancestors - Longzongmen

Map 2. The Forbidden City. *Source: Palace Museum, Beijing*

The Forbidden City:
The Ceremonial and Official View

The Forbidden City was both the private residence of the emperor and his family and the place where he conducted the business of state. The names by which we call the main halls of the Forbidden City today were given them by the Manchus starting in 1645, but the term "Purple Forbidden City" (*Zijincheng*) had been used in Beijing from about the 1420s. It alludes to an ancient conception of rulership: *zi* refers to purple, a color associated with martial bravery, and to the "purple bright" constellation of the *ziwei* star, the pole star to which others do homage. Similarly, the emperor occupied a unique status as the representative of all humanity to Heaven in annual ceremonies at the Temple of Heaven. The word *jin* means off-limits, and *cheng* a walled space, a city. The Forbidden City normally was closed to the people. A recent study of Beijing architecture suggests that this closure served the political interests of autocracy by creating a great disparity in the power to observe. The emperor, aided by his officials, could see out to the Imperial City, the Inner City, the Outer City, and beyond, but the populace, with occasional exceptions, could not look back into his stronghold.[3]

The Forbidden City was and is a rectangle bounded on four sides by an external wall and moat. (See Map 4 in Chapter 3.) Originally each side had one gate. The area measures 961 meters (1051 yards) north to south and 753 meters (823 yards) east to west, covering in all about 723,600 square meters (179 acres). The structures within are laid out along a north-south axis that forms part of a longer Beijing axis beginning at the Yongding Gate of the Outer City and ending at the Bell Tower in the Inner City. The Ming rulers had used the southern part of the Forbidden City for ceremonies and formal audiences and the northern part for the private, residential space of the imperial family and its many servitors. The Manchu emperors took over this pattern and developed it further, performing impressive rituals amid the beautiful structures and extensive spaces of the Outer Court. Ceremonies at dawn in the vast, quiet courtyards imbued ambassadors, officials, and other attendees with deep respect for the rulers.

A tributary envoy arriving for an audience would enter at the southern end of the complex, where the Daqing (Great Qing) and Tianan (Heavenly Peace) gates of the Imperial City led on to the Forbidden City's Wu (Meridian) Gate. (See Map 2.) There he was obliged to dismount. This was the important gate where candidates awaited the results of the court-level examinations for office and where, on rare occasions, vanquished enemies led by silken cords around their necks were presented to the throne before execution. If he wished, the emperor could look down on these events from the top of a wall twelve meters (forty feet) above the courtyard where his subjects knelt.

Proceeding on foot through the Meridian Gate, the tributary representative would arrive at the vast courtyard of the Taihedian (Hall of Supreme Harmony), the largest and tallest building in the Forbidden City. (See Color Plate 9.) The emperor would come to the same building from the north and take his seat on the throne to receive his guest, who, like Chinese officials, would show deference by performing the kowtow (*ketou*), kneeling three times, prostrating himself, and knocking his head on the courtyard stones three times for each kneeling. (See Figure 3.) The hall and courtyard where the two met in formal audience were the most symbolic spaces in the Forbidden City. The bronze turtle in front symbolized longevity and stability; on special occasions, incense lit inside would cause smoke to billow from its mouth. In the Taihedian, the emperor received large groups of guests at the new year, at the end of winter, and at other times. At the new year, princes, officials, and tributary envoys performed the kowtow amid spoken commands—"Kneel!" "Knock!" "Rise!"—and the music of bells and drums.

Beyond the Taihedian to the north were two other major structures, the Zhonghedian (Hall of Central Harmony) and the Baohedian (Hall of Preserved Harmony). In the Zhonghedian, emperors inspected agricultural tools before symbolic annual plowing rites and prepared themselves before ceremonies in the Taihedian; in the Baohedian, they received ambassadors and presided over palace examinations. Emperors also used the three great halls—Taihedian, Zhonghedian, Baohedian—for marriages, funerals, enthronements, and celebrations.[4]

Court artists carefully recorded the reception of guests in the Forbidden City and at imperial retreats. Their works emphasized the strength of the dynasty and the unification of diverse peoples in the Qing empire. Extravagant visual representation of diplomatic scenes had many historical precedents. On one occasion in the Tang dynasty (618–907), at the then capital of Chang'an, a widowed empress had a nearly life-size stone sculpture made of every ambassador in a large group at her husband's funeral.[5] In the high Qing era, cosmopolitanism and new pictorial techniques contributed further to the projection of a broad imperial vision in art.[6]

The three great halls, and the Hall of Supreme Harmony (Taihedian) alone, are major points rather than the climax of the Forbidden City or of the entire capital architectural ensemble. There is no single climax. The power of the arrangement comes from its impact on the visitor as a long series of related structures in a perfect state of balance with each other. Chinese civilization has a genius—in literature, in art, and in architecture—for episodic forms that link many elements not by logic but by association, like beads on a string, in such a way that they make up a whole greater than the sum of its parts.[7] A historian of architecture suggests that the realization of this concept in the Forbidden City, compared to monumental buildings in the capitals of other countries, is a more subtle, "less obvious, perhaps less pretentious" way of showing power and prestige.[8] The "Palace Museum" (Gugong bowuyuan) strikingly differs from other such collections—the Louvre, Versailles, or the Hermitage in St. Petersburg, for example—because the palace is an extensive ensemble rather than a single structure of great size.

Beyond the three great audience halls lay a transitional gate, the Qianqing (Heavenly Purity) Gate, a pivotal divider between the outer court (*waichao*) and the inner palace (*neiting*), the two great worlds of the Forbidden City. It is characteristic of Beijing that the inner palace was an inner part of a Forbidden City that was itself an inner area within an Inner City. To the north were three residential palaces, the Qianqinggong (Palace of Heavenly Purity), the Jiaotaidian (Hall of Union), and the Kunninggong (Palace of Earthly Tranquility). The Kangxi emperor had moved his residence from the Baohedian to the Qianqinggong in 1669, reinforcing the distinction between the inner and outer zones of the Forbidden City. Another compound to the west in the inner palace zone, the Yangxindian (Hall of Mental Cultivation), was the actual residence of Qing rulers beginning in the 1720s. Earlier it had been, among other things, the place where the Kangxi emperor studied mathematics with the Jesuit Jean-François Gerbillon.[9] The rulers kept imperial seals in the Jiaotaidian; they maintained a bridal chamber and altars for shamanistic rites in the Kunninggong, where Ming emperors once had lived. Imperial princes, consorts, and concubines lived in palaces and residences to the east and west of the central axis in the northern part of the Forbidden City, amid gardens and courtyards. The adjacent Western Park (Xiyuan), including three artificial lakes, extended the imperial private area. (Today part of this park is Zhongnanhai, where high Communist Party leaders live and work.) The architecture of the inner palace was on a more human scale than that of the majestic outer court to the south. Residential rooms faced south into courtyards and had a far more intimate feeling than the large, high-ceilinged living spaces of Versailles or other European palaces.[10]

In the Qing era the path of a civilian official coming to see the emperor on business, rather than on a ceremonial occasion, lay not through the Meridian Gate and along the north-south axis but rather along a diagonal route from the east, entering at the Donghua (Eastern Flowery) Gate of the Forbidden City and progressing to the transitional area between the outer court and inner palace, marked by the Qianqing Gate, and from there sometimes to the emperor's residence itself. A military official, however, would enter at the Xihua (Western Flowery) Gate. An important place for officials was the gate building at the entrance to the Qianqinggong. A throne set up behind a table covered in yellow silk had carpet in front of it; here officials offering documents for imperial consideration would prostrate themselves to show their veneration of the ruler.[11] Even a high official far from the capital would bow to his memorial (a kind of official document) before sending it off by fast horse post to the emperor; how much more intense the sensations of reverence and/or apprehension must have been within the Forbidden City.

An important development of Forbidden City institutions, as well as of their associated buildings and pathways, had followed the Ming founder's abolition of the prime minister's office in 1380. In the 1420s the Yongle emperor had created the Grand Secretariat (Neige) to help handle official correspondence. This office was located in the outer court area of the Forbidden City, along its southern wall near the Donghua Gate. In 1729, however, the Yongzheng emperor set up a new agency that became the Grand Council in the inner palace area of the Forbidden City, adjacent to the private so-called great within (*danei*) and close to the emperor's residence. The location of the Grand Council—much closer to the emperor than the Secretariat was—reflected its dominance over the older institution. Because these two institutions successively became the only channel of regular governmental access to the ruler, they both were connected with limits on officials' power vis-à-vis the emperor.

The influence of the bureaucracy, although limited in the Forbidden City, was pervasive in Beijing as a whole. The Six Boards—ministries of Personnel, Revenue, Rites, War, Punishments, and Works—as well as the Censorate that watched the performance of all of them, were among the major offices in the Inner City. High-level civil service examinations occurred twice in every three years in the southeast Inner City and also in the Forbidden City; they attracted candidates from the whole empire. By one estimate there were about five thousand metropolitan officials in 1800, served by an equal number of secretaries, clerks, and copyists.[12] The state was highly centralized, and, except for routine matters, emperors dealt with provincial officials directly rather than through the

ministries. At the apex of the judicial system, capital cases (those involving offenses punishable by death) had to be reviewed by the emperor himself. Management of populous Beijing was just one of the dynasty's many difficult problems,
and the head of the city gendarmerie was among those allowed to memorialize—
to send the communications known as memorials to—the throne. The narrow-
ness of the institutional channels—such as the Secretariat and the Grand
Council—through which bureaucratic matters entered the Forbidden City gave
the emperor some control over his home territory. They did not, however, reduce
his workload. With many important matters constantly flowing upward toward
imperial decision, the challenge of being Son of Heaven was great indeed.

The Three Emperors

In light of the many demands on the emperor, it was fortunate for Qing rule that
from 1662 until the end of the eighteenth century, the dynasty saw only three
reigns, two of exceptional length, and all by men of unusual energy and ability.
Xuanye, the Kangxi emperor, ruled from 1662 to 1722; Yinzhen, the Yongzheng
emperor, from 1723 to 1735; and Hongli, the Qianlong emperor, from 1736 to
1795. (For simplicity the Qing emperors' better-known reign names sometimes
appear in place of their personal names in this book; although it is more correct to
say "the Kangxi emperor" to show that this is a reign name rather than a personal
name, we also use "Kangxi.") All three high Qing emperors had long life spans,
reaching the ages of sixty-eight, fifty-six, and eighty-seven, respectively. They had
quite different personalities but shared patterns of activity that contrasted with
those of the Ming emperors. More mobile than their predecessors, they traveled
often in the Beijing area. They hunted in Manchuria and visited summer retreats,
dynastic tombs, water control projects, and historic sites. Kangxi and Qianlong
also embarked on longer expeditions for political and military purposes; each of
them toured south China six times, and Qianlong more than once took his
mother along. All were hardworking emperors who on normal days awoke early,
limited the time spent at meals, conferred extensively with advisers, and read and
commented personally on many documents.

The Qing emperors keenly understood the importance of ceremony in the
affirmation and display of power. Interested in religion and aware of the pain that
the conquest had inflicted on local people, they patronized city temples and diligently carried out their ritual responsibilities. Ming rulers often had sent substi-
tutes to perform annual winter-solstice observances or prayers for rain at the

Temple of Heaven. Kangxi, Yongzheng, and Qianlong almost always went in person, even when they were old and ill.[13] Religion also enabled them to conciliate various social groups. In addition to establishing many new temples, especially those devoted to Tibetan Lamaist Buddhism and to Confucianism, they also donated funds to religious institutions supporting Daoist priests, Buddhist monks and lamas, and even Muslims and Roman Catholics. Once a temple had been added to the imperial payroll, it tended to stay there, and its long-term advantage in wealth made it more likely to survive.[14]

Conscious of the ancient Chinese roots of imperial institutions, the early Qing emperors at the same time realized, to a greater extent than had the Ming rulers, that they could benefit from the ideas and technology of other peoples. Even at times when they were trying to curtail the spread of Christianity, they consulted missionaries in Beijing both out of curiosity and because they wished to use the Europeans' knowledge for Qing purposes. Employment of people of varied backgrounds by a dynasty of Inner Asian origin was a long-established pattern. That tradition took new forms in the Qing era, however, because of changes in the outer world. Reformation and Counter-Reformation Europe had produced a small but dynamic Catholic missionary effort. We saw in the last chapter how the pioneer Matteo Ricci had reached Beijing by 1601, after spending almost two decades in other parts of China, and how the Jesuits led by Ricci used secular learning to attract the interest of the Chinese elite. After the Ming fell, the Jesuits served the Manchus. Noting that the Europeans' predictions were more often correct than those of his Muslim experts, Kangxi placed the missionaries in charge of the Imperial Board of Astronomy. The Jesuits in Beijing also contributed to the expertise available to the Qing court in painting, cartography, and architecture—all fields reflecting the improved understanding of space, geometry, and optics in Renaissance science.

The personal rule of the Kangxi emperor, born in the Forbidden City in 1654, began in his early teens. Having lost both his young parents to illness, the boy emperor apparently was sustained emotionally in part by his Mongolian paternal grandmother. She encouraged his love of reading and stressed the importance of compassion as well as knowledge. He could converse easily in Chinese, and he dedicated himself early to the study of Chinese classics. In later years Kangxi credited his grandmother, who lived until he was thirty-four years old, with helping him to develop the mental and physical discipline necessary to be emperor.[15] In crucial ways, Kangxi stabilized the new dynasty and created a political order favorable to the resurgence of the capital. In the 1670s and 1680s he completed the Qing conquest by suppressing lingering revolt in the south and establishing control of Taiwan. Turning to the north, he fought Russians who had clashed with the Manchus along the Amur River in the Manchurian border area. Jesuits served as translators when Kangxi and the Russians negotiated a treaty at Nerchinsk in 1689, using Chinese, Manchu, Mongolian, Russian, and Latin as working languages. With all rebellions quelled by 1696, Qing territory was significantly larger than the Ming empire had been and would grow further. Attention to fundamentals such as water control and grain transport also helped the frugal Kangxi to build up the economic reserves needed for architectural projects in Beijing. (See Color Plate 4.)

Kangxi possessed the priceless virtue of intellectual curiosity. His patronage of scholarship followed the precedent of his Jin dynasty ancestors and set a standard for his successors. He sponsored work on the official history of the Ming dynasty that was published decades later under his grandson Qianlong. The *Kangxi zidian,* named for his own reign, was an authoritative dictionary containing almost fifty thousand Chinese characters. The *Qinding gujin tushu jicheng* (Synthesis of illustrations and books past and present) was a huge encyclopedia that appeared under his son Yongzheng in 1728. This monumental work synthesized Chinese knowledge of the time with elements of Western learning. The emperor's interests embraced both humanistic subjects and natural science.

When Kangxi died in 1722, Yongzheng, born in 1678, came to the throne; the circumstances surrounding his ascension at age forty-five remain controversial. Amid intense competition among twenty eligible sons, Kangxi by 1712 had rejected his previously chosen heir, accused him of planning patricide, and refused to name a replacement prior to his own death. Yongzheng may have won out against his remaining brothers because he either changed his father's will secretly after his death or, in the absence of a will, took power by force with the help of the head of the Beijing gendarmerie. Some historians have depicted Yongzheng as suspicious, ruthless, and a far lesser man than Kangxi, his father, or Qianlong, the son who succeeded him; others, however, stress his conscientious rulership and complex personality. He was a serious student of art and of Zen Buddhism.[16]

Although his reign lasted only thirteen years, Yongzheng introduced important governmental reforms. He streamlined tax and fiscal practices, thus increasing revenue; he systematized the administration of the Eight Banners at Beijing and beyond, checking the power of individual princes. Battling corruption, he invented an extra stipend given to officials to "cultivate incorruptibility." Following the lead of his father, who had initiated a confidential system of palace memorials, he created modes of communication that helped emperors to cut through bureaucratic tangles in relations between the capital and the provinces. The Junjichu (literally "office of military affairs") that Yongzheng introduced in the 1720s became in the 1730s the Grand Council, a significant innovation. This group of five or six Manchus and Chinese, served by a secretarial staff of about 250, became the means by which Yongzheng centralized power and made the empire even more autocratic, but also more efficient. Its members talked with the emperor frequently, sometimes daily, at a location near his residence in the Forbidden City or at a branch office near the imperial summer villas. More than twenty thousand surviving documents contain Yongzheng's lengthy comments, in which he used Beijing colloquialisms that he apparently picked up from soldiers and workmen. Some of his comments were longer than the original memorial.

Although his historical legacy was primarily political, Yongzheng wished to create a public image of himself as closely involved with cultural matters. He liked to be painted in different roles. Color Plate 5 shows the emperor in an intimate palace setting in an informal, languid posture, reading a book amid carefully chosen art objects and antiques. A particularly intriguing portrait album shows him trying on more exotic identities: he appears in thirteen roles, including those of Tibetan monk, Daoist immortal, Mongol nobleman, and European hunter. Art historians debate what was in the emperor's mind when he commissioned this album intended for private viewing: "Was the album created as a calculated political strategy to reinforce Manchu subjugation of other ethnic groups; was it creative recreation, with the ruler engaging in fantasy, perhaps inspired by knowledge of European masquerade; or was it a sincere reflection of the ruler's belief that as the supreme monarch he truly embraced the entire spectrum of humanity within his own person?" Such speculative questions about the consciousness of Yongzheng are difficult to answer, but they do suggest the depth of his mind. Secure in his identity as Qing emperor despite questions about his accession, deeply interested in Zen Buddhism with its love of multiple truths and rapidly shifting frames of reference, Yongzheng felt comfortable experimenting with alternative personae in art.[17]

Yongzheng's successor Qianlong reigned for most of the eighteenth century and presided over the greatest era of Qing prosperity and imperial expansion. Sometimes described as a child prodigy, he was Kangxi's favorite grandson. He was born in 1711 in Yongzheng's princely palace in the northeastern Inner City. (In 1723, after Kangxi died and Yongzheng took the throne, this residence became the Yonghe Palace [Yonghegong]; later, under Qianlong, it was converted into a lamasery for monks from Mongolia and Tibet. The "Lama Temple" benefited from imperial patronage and survives today as a religious institution and tourist site.) Qianlong defeated a new challenge from the western Mongols between 1755 and 1757, and he proceeded to integrate Xinjiang, the "new dominion," into the empire. He settled Tibetan troubles by establishing a Qing protectorate in Lhasa. His reign saw the completion of a comprehensive collection of books in four traditional categories (classics, history, philosophy, and belles-lettres) in the *Siku quanshu* (Complete Books of the Four Treasuries) in 36,000 paperbound volumes, containing about 3,450 complete works. (Unfortunately, the twenty-year-long project that produced this collection also destroyed works deemed seditious, punished people who even appeared to criticize the Manchus, and frightened writers away from controversial subjects.) Qianlong was so avid an art collector that he inscribed some of his favorite paintings not just once but twice, or in some cases many times. He even took paintings along on his travels so that he could view them in different circumstances; many of his inscriptions document his lifelong aesthetic experience. He collected ancient bronze ritual vessels, jade objects, and porcelain. Always his purpose was not merely to possess but to know, to discriminate, to comment critically. His judgments have influenced the world's understanding of Chinese art down to the present day.[18]

The Three Qing Emperors as Builders of Beijing

Often starting from fifteenth-century Ming foundations, the three high Qing emperors built or restored palaces, princely mansions, gardens, and temples.[19] Happening to pass a temple and admire its scenery, an emperor might later renovate it and then continue to provide funds periodically on special occasions. These efforts dated from the very outset of the dynasty. In 1657, when Kangxi was a small boy and Shunzhi was on the throne, the new Qing rulers rebuilt the Confucian Temple in the northeast Inner City, thus conciliating Chinese literati. After the military and diplomatic successes of the 1680s, Kangxi increasingly turned his attention to construction. In the first decade of the eighteenth century, he ordered the Board of Revenue to build new Outer City houses and stores and to renovate many structures there. In 1703 he created the summer retreat at Rehe (Chengde) beyond the Great Wall; his Rehe replica of the Tibetan Potala Palace in Lhasa showed the importance of Tibetan Buddhism to the rulers. Earlier (in

1690) Kangxi had restored the garden of a Ming nobleman to establish the summer retreat Changchunyuan on a site northwest of the city that had been used by the Jin and Yuan rulers for the same purpose. Flowing lakes and streams in the area in Jin, Yuan, Ming, and Qing times, not found there more recently, appealed to dynasties of north Asian origin and were related to its name, Haidian (marsh). (Waterways have dried up because of agricultural and industrial encroachment on the land.) The use of the Mongolian word *hutong* (literally "water well") for narrow streets was another sign of the importance of water in the early attraction of people to the city. In the Ming era, the soil of the Haidian area was considered especially moist and fertile.[20] Kangxi enjoyed spending several months of each year at this retreat.

A half mile north of the Garden of Joyful Springtime, Kangxi in 1709 began work on a palace for his son Yinzhen, the future Yongzheng emperor. This garden would become the larger and more famous summer palace known as Yuanmingyuan (literally round bright garden, "Garden of Perfect Brightness"). Later both Yongzheng and Qianlong expanded it. The name had been chosen by Kangxi, who also founded nearby banner villages to house the labor force that the imperial presence required for security and other purposes. Like his father, Yongzheng spent so much time in these northwestern garden villas that the Grand Council and other state agencies had to establish branch offices in the vicinity. These imperial retreats were more informal, closer to nature, and probably more comfortable for daily living than any part of the Forbidden City. Because emperors were so often in residence, population in the northwest suburbs grew and those areas became more closely tied to the walled cities. Centuries earlier the Forbidden City itself had first come into existence as a summer retreat northeast of the Jin capital, Zhongdu, partly because of its better access to water; now the Qing summer palace zone on the northwest was repeating the same process relative to the Forbidden City.[21]

During his reign from 1723 to 1735, Yongzheng built houses to rent to examination candidates in the Outer City and undertook general renovation there.[22] In 1726 he constructed a temple to the City God in the northwest corner of the Forbidden City. He repaired great damage at both Yuanmingyuan and Beijing from a severe earthquake in the fall of 1730 that caused the deaths of hundreds. When the disaster first struck, Yongzheng was riding for pleasure on a canal barge at Yuanmingyuan. While onboard he issued an edict assuming personal responsibility for Heaven's dissatisfaction. Soon afterward the emperor sent for the Jesuits, questioned them about the nature of earthquakes, and donated funds to repair their churches.[23]

Ascending the throne while still in his twenties, Qianlong had a personal impact on Beijing greater than that of any of his Qing ancestors and comparable in importance only to that of the Mongol ruler Khubilai in the thirteenth century and the Yongle emperor of the Ming in the early fifteenth century. Inheriting the sound economy of his grandfather and the streamlined administrative system of his father, Qianlong presided over a relatively wealthy government and society. The Imperial Household Department (Neiwufu), the Inner City's biggest landlord and its largest employer of workers and artisans, multiplied its revenue by loans to merchants at high rates of interest. Better tax collection increased state income; imperial monopolies on essentials such as salt were highly lucrative.

Given favorable economic and political conditions, and motivated by his own love of art, Qianlong for six decades enhanced the architecture of Beijing. He constructed five pavilions at the top of Jingshan, just north of the Forbidden City; and he renovated a building erected by Yongzheng on its north side, the Shouhuangdian (Hall of the Sovereign of Longevity), where deceased rulers lay in state and ancestral portraits were displayed. Qianlong began the custom of making sacrifices in this hall at the new year. The Ziguangge (Pavilion of Purple Brightness), one of many buildings he constructed in the chain of lakes west of the Forbidden City, became a place used to celebrate military victories and entertain representatives of tributary states. Military examinees competed there in archery and riding contests; the emperor also liked to visit in winter to watch bannermen ice-skating. Eight groups of seven or eight skaters, each with flags attached to their backs, represented the eight banners. After the annexation of Xinjiang in the 1750s, the Ziguangge became a memorial hall for military men, with poems, portraits, and paintings of battles.[24]

Within the Forbidden City, Qianlong in 1771 enlarged the Ningshougong (Palace of Tranquil Longevity), first built by his grandfather in 1689, and he constructed the Leshoutang (Hall of Pleasurable Old Age) in 1774–1775. The Wenyuange (Pavilion of Literary Profundity) was erected between 1774 and 1776 to house just one copy of the 36,000 volumes of the great collection *Siku quanshu*.[25] Another Forbidden City structure, created by Qianlong in 1740 for his mother, was the Jianfugong (Palace of Established Happiness), which is being rebuilt in the twenty-first century, eighty years after its destruction by fire in 1923.[26] This complex, landscaped with perfect rocks from Suzhou in the south, was a favorite of the emperor, as it would be later for the last Qing ruler and court ladies. (See Figure 12.) Even amid all these additions to the Forbidden City, however,

Qianlong did not forget the Outer City; in 1765 and again in 1785 he ordered the construction of clusters of new houses and shops there. When, in 1767, Xu Yang illustrated a poem by the emperor about the capital, he depicted Beijing under snow and placed the lively Outer City in the foreground. (See Color Plate 3.)

When Qianlong was a boy, his grandfather had taken him on many trips to the Changchunyuan and to Rehe; during the reign of his father, he had lived alternately at Changchunyuan and Yuanmingyuan. Having known these places from childhood, he was emotionally attached to them. As an adult, Qianlong transformed Yuanmingyuan into a scenic garden containing many palaces, and he published art and poetry that spread its fame. In the later 1740s, he chose the Jesuit lay brother Giuseppe Castiglione to design a group of buildings in the Italian style for a northeastern corner of the garden.[27] Yuanmingyuan was Qianlong's preferred residence, and he spent more of each year there as his reign progressed.

Ironically the Jesuits, whose letters had introduced Chinese ideas of informal gardening to Europe, became at Yuanmingyuan the builders of European palaces and formal gardens in a late baroque and rococo style then becoming outdated in Europe itself.[28] In 1743 a description of Yuanmingyuan in a letter by Jean-Denis Attiret had attracted wide attention and influenced English gardening toward natural curves rather than French geometric lines and patterns.[29] In the letter Attiret had observed that at Yuanmingyuan "there reigns almost everywhere a graceful disorder, an anti-symmetry. . . . It is a natural, rustic countryside they wish represented. . . ."[30] A 1782 Jesuit letter explained: "Everything that is ruled and symmetrical is alien to free Nature. There one never finds trees growing in lines to form avenues, flowers brought together in beds, water enclosed in ponds or in regular canals."[31] In the landscape-design universe of eighteenth-century Europe, the Chinese garden was better suited to the coming age of romanticism than was the formal garden typified by those of the French royal capital at Versailles. New construction in the small European section of Yuanmingyuan, however, reverted to Western styles of much earlier decades. Time had passed since the Jesuits had left their homelands, in many cases never to return; in the eighteenth century it was difficult for them to keep pace with cultural changes from afar. In the long run, however, not everyone agreed that Chinese gardens had influenced those of Europe. George Lord Macartney, head of the British mission to Beijing in 1793, wrote: "Whether our style of gardening was really copied from the Chinese, or originated with ourselves, I leave for vanity to assert, and idleness to discuss. A discovery which is the result of good sense and reflection may equally occur to the most distant nations, without either borrowing from the other."[32]

Qianlong's fancy initially had turned to the construction of a European-style fountain like one that he had seen painted by Castiglione in 1747. This challenge fell to the Jesuit Michel Benoit because of his skills in hydraulics, mechanics, and mathematics. The emperor was so pleased with the resulting design that he asked Castiglione to plan a palace to accompany it. The fountain became a nucleus for European-style buildings, and many more fountains and palaces followed. These structures contained "numerous false windows and doors, excessive ornamentation in carved stone, glazed tiles in startling color combinations, imitation shells and rock-work, meaningless pyramids, scrolls and foliage, and conspicuous outside staircases."[33] Their internal furnishings included gifts from European kings, such as tapestries, glassware, mechanical toys, and pendulum clocks.[34] Nearby gardens were landscaped in a strictly symmetrical manner that, being alien to Chinese gardening practice, perhaps appeared intriguing and exotic to Qianlong and the Qing court. The fountains' mechanical devices were not always repaired when they wore out, and a Jesuit letter of 1786 revealed that when the emperor announced a visit to the European buildings, "they employ sufficient labor for a couple of days to fill the enormous pond, so that all the fountains can play along the route that the emperor will follow." Even with its distinctive aspects, however, the European architecture corner, like the rest of Yuanmingyuan, had its own attractiveness and natural beauty. Qianlong wrote that he was merely following the path of his ancestors:

> Although, in conformity with the frugal principles of my Imperial Grandfather, my Imperial Father did not richly ornament the [Yuanmingyuan] palace, the buildings were spacious and open, and hills and dales were secluded and quiet, the configuration of the land, and the plants and trees were well arranged and beautiful. . . . Protected by Heaven and blessed by Earth, it is a place of recreation worthy of the emperor. . . . Later generations will certainly not desert this place to build other gardens and thus twice consume the wealth of the people, but in this respect they will sincerely follow my attempt to conform to the examples of diligence and frugality set by my Imperial Father and myself.[35]

Despite these filial words, however, Qianlong was markedly less frugal than his father and grandfather, and he did *not* refrain from building other gardens near Yuanmingyuan called Jingyiyuan (Villa of Peace and Harmony), Changchunyuan (Garden of Long Spring),[36] Qiqunyuan (Garden of Variegated Spring), and Qingyiyuan (Villa of Clear Ripples). The last of these would provide the foundation for a new summer palace, built in the late nineteenth century, which today is known simply as the Summer Palace (Yiheyuan, Villa of Smiling Harmony) in contrast to the Old Summer Palace (Yuanmingyuan), now in ruins.[37]

Life in the Palace

Kangxi, Yongzheng, and Qianlong might spend long months in their summer villas, but then as now the Forbidden City was unquestionably the center of gravity in Beijing. The Qing Forbidden City was home to several thousand people. High-status residents included the emperor, the empress (his highest consort), his mother (the empress dowager), his grandmother (the grand empress dowager), and imperial princes and princesses and their families. When a new emperor ascended the throne, his brothers who were married—and therefore counted as adults—moved out of the Forbidden City, which thus housed only one adult male of the senior generation. For the sake of dynastic prestige, the residents of the Forbidden City had to live in a luxurious style; given premodern technology, only a huge supporting cast could make this possible.

The emperors' personal lives took a peculiar turn because of the dynastic requirement of an heir—preferably a strong and capable one, or more than one—in a time when even royal children often did not survive to adulthood. Imperial existence was supposed to include great bodily comfort and pleasure, and the residential areas of the Forbidden City and the summer palaces were similar to the homes of wealthy commoners. The emperor, however, conducted his family life on a scale different from that of any commoner. It was not unusual for wealthy elite men to have concubines, but Kangxi, who died at sixty-nine in 1722, had twenty-five empresses and consorts and twenty-nine concubines. He was the father of thirty-four sons, of whom slightly more than half survived long enough to marry, and twenty daughters, of whom only eight survived that long. As we have seen, twenty of these sons contended for the succession in the first quarter of the eighteenth century, with Yongzheng the winner. Yongzheng, who died at fifty-six in 1735, had ten sons and four daughters, of whom only four sons and one daughter lived to marry. Qianlong, who died at eighty-nine in 1799, had twenty-four higher consorts and fifteen concubines. He fathered sixteen sons, of whom slightly more than half lived to marry, and ten daughters, of whom five married.[38] The effects of so unusual a family life are hard to glimpse in the biographies of the Qing emperors, but we can observe that they also had other kinds of personal relationships. For example, Kangxi was deeply attached to his grandmother and, with his intellectual bent, enjoyed teaching his children himself. Although he came into serious conflict with some of his sons, he found satisfaction in the tie to his grandson Qianlong. For his part, Qianlong saw himself as a family man, as the idealized portrait by Castiglione shows. (See Color Plate 6.) He was devoted to his first wife, Xiaoxian, whom he married in 1727, and he was famously filial and considerate toward his mother.[39]

At its outset the Manchu dynasty had reduced the number of eunuchs, but in the early Qing era there were still more than thirteen hundred in the Forbidden City and another seven hundred in imperial retreats near Beijing. Some had been Ming palace eunuchs. One way the Qing rulers avoided excesses of eunuch corruption until the last decades of the dynasty, however, was by giving oversight of eunuch-related matters to the Imperial Household Department. This key institution, located in the southwestern part of the Forbidden City, was run by bondservants attached to the banners and was independent of the regular bureaucracy. The Imperial Household Department supervised more people and activities than did comparable institutions in European royal courts. Moreover, under the Qing, eunuchs were not permitted to work in fields other than the care of the imperial family and the palace, a great change from the preceding dynasty. The days of eunuch admirals and architects were over.[40]

The bondservants (Manchu *booi*, Chinese *baoyi*) who ran the Imperial Household Department embodied an ironic combination: low in original status, they could find themselves in high positions.[41] Descended from Chinese and other captives of the mid-seventeenth-century conquest era, they had been enrolled in lower-level banner companies whose members were barred from intermarriage with other banner families. In the 1630s the three upper banners (plain and bordered yellow, plain white) were distinguished as superior banners run directly by the emperor. The emperor then took over the *booi* in those banners as imperial household servants. It was closeness to emperors, combined with complete dependence on them, that made the *booi* ideal servitors and could result in upward mobility. Cao Xueqin, author of the eighteenth-century novel *Honglou meng* (Dream of the red chamber), came from a family that traced itself to a bondservant of the Kangxi reign.

Kangxi had been determined to keep eunuchs under control: "For eunuchs are basically *yin* in nature. They are quite different from ordinary people; when weak with age they babble like babies. In my court I never let them get involved with government. . . . I only have about four hundred, as opposed to the immense numbers there were in the Ming, and I keep them working at menial jobs, ignore their frowns and smiles and make sure that they stay poor."[42] Imperial control of eunuchs was relative, however, and eventually they were "everywhere" in the Qing

Forbidden City, though concentrated in the inner palace area on the north. Their total numbers, including those at retreats outside the city, increased to over 3,000 by 1750 and just over 2,500 in 1797.[43] They carried out countless daily tasks at the court: cleaning, guarding, receiving and dispensing imperial revenue, caring for clothing, cooking, performing in court theatricals and in staged tableaux of urban life at Yuanmingyuan, serving as personal aides to imperial family members, and supervising workshops and storehouses.[44] The Imperial Household Department managed eunuchs specifically through an Attendants' Office in the northeastern, inner-palace part of the Forbidden City. The eunuch world was large and stratified; the chief eunuch reported to the Imperial Household Department and the emperor.

Most eunuchs originated in poor families in the capital region, and their visits home were one channel through which news of the Forbidden City reached the outside world. Their numbers decreased in the nineteenth century, but there were still 1,137 eunuchs in 1922, eleven years after the fall of the dynasty and two before militarists evicted the last emperor from the Forbidden City. Interviews with eunuchs surviving after 1949 point to motives such as poverty, lack of other alternatives, and the religious conviction (born of childhood illness or injury) that a boy's life was destined to be saved by departing from conventional paths.[45] It need hardly be added that a premodern age did not have the contemporary world's idea of self-determination, or that as late as the nineteenth century, European boys with beautiful voices sometimes became *castrati* to enhance choirs.

The persistence of large numbers of eunuchs at the Qing court despite explicit imperial mistrust of them suggests the indispensability of their role. Eunuchs were the discreet observers who kept a record of the emperor's encounters with palace ladies. Such a role hardly could be trusted to men with family and sexual interests of their own. When a child was born, eunuchs had to be prepared to document his or her parentage correctly and without question. Given the presence in the palace of many imperial consorts and their differing ranks, precise data were essential. Record keeping became more difficult with time because imperial family numbers increased geometrically with each generation. Kangxi had 34 sons but 123 grandsons and, of course, many daughters and granddaughters. By the end of the Qing era in 1912, the dynasty had more than 80,000 official members.[46] Recent work by a team of Chinese and English geneticists suggests that at least 1.6 million men alive today carry a Manchu Y-chromosome that marks them as descendants of the Qing rulers. The researchers hypothesize that the lineage has spread so far because of the Qing emperors' and nobles' practice of keeping many concubines.[47]

Young maidservants were another large group of Forbidden City staff. Each member of the imperial family was allotted a certain number of maids according to rank. In 1734 there were more than five hundred in all. Maids came from an annual draft by the Imperial Household Department among daughters of men in bondservant companies. After passing inspection, thirteen-year-old girls came to the Forbidden City for a term of five or ten years. If they caught the emperor's eye, they might become imperial concubines and never return to their former lives. Yongzheng's mother had been a maidservant in the palace; a year after his birth she was elevated to be an imperial consort of the fourth rank. Most maidservants were released when of marriageable age. When the emperor traveled between the summer villas and the Forbidden City, these young women were allowed to visit and exchange presents with their relatives and friends along the roadside. On these hurried occasions and in long lives following their service, they even more than the eunuchs became a source of information and gossip that spread all over China. The populace did not entirely lack knowledge of the Forbidden City. The memoir of a Russian envoy to Beijing in 1849–1850 suggests that gossip about the emperor, his relatives, and those around him was pervasive in the capital area. Although Egor Kovalevsky had at best limited knowledge of the Chinese and Manchu languages, and lived in the Russian hostel near the Forbidden City for less than a year, he was extremely well versed in contemporary rumors and anecdotes about court life.[48] People naturally were curious about a large, centrally located, and highly populated place that was closed and forbidden.

Another kind of female servant in the Forbidden City was the wet nurse. Each of the emperor's children had two or three wet nurses selected from among the wives of bannermen, including bondservants. The selection was rigorous and competitive; candidates had to be attractive, healthy, and mother of at least three children, including both sons and daughters. Forty women would be picked at one time, with forty as alternates. The winner, who was considered highly honored, wore a special costume.[49] Her own child would be fed by another nurse. As a result of wet nurses' intimate relation with imperial children, they and their husbands often were rewarded with silver, residences, or rank, especially if the child became an emperor.[50] Bernardo Bertolucci's film *The Last Emperor* (1987), made in Beijing, dramatized the close relationship of the last Qing emperor with his wet nurse and with court eunuchs who were his servants and playmates.

Imperial ladies were organized in an elaborate hierarchy in the Forbidden City. A multi-step pyramid had one empress, one imperial consort, two high consorts, three or four consorts, five or six imperial concubines, and unlimited lesser concubines. The ladies lived in six eastern and six western palaces located east and west of the central axis in the inner palace area. Qing rulers feared that eunuchs would use imperial ladies to ensnare the emperor in sensual excess and corruption.[51] Kangxi advised his many sons "to avoid too much sex when you are young and too much fighting when you are strong. I keep only three hundred women around the palace, and those who have not served me personally I release when they are thirty years old and send them home to be married. . . . Don't waste money on cosmetics for the women."[52] The court insisted on status-appropriate behavior between eunuchs and imperial women, and it was a serious offense for a eunuch to joke or chat with the ladies. Documents of the Imperial Household Department reveal significant tensions in the relations between the Qing rulers and their eunuchs and other servants. As Kangxi wrote in exasperation: "Eunuchs are the lowest status, persons like ants: how dare they not stand up when they see an official or guard? To bow slightly while squatting is extremely ill-behaved. Henceforth let them stand up respectfully."[53] The emperor and his officials knew or suspected that eunuchs and other servitors had not only interests but an entire backstage world of their own. They were unlikely to see themselves as "persons like ants," and they were not necessarily as respectful of imperial authority as their superiors thought appropriate.[54]

Workmen and artisans who entered the Forbidden City from outside wore belt tallies issued by the Imperial Household Department. Their every entry into the Forbidden City was recorded by guards, with summary reports sent to the emperor. In 1773, for example, the department issued 3,668 belt tallies, each valid for three years. More numerous, however, were laborers called *sula* (Manchu "idle, unemployed"), bannermen attached to the bondservant companies. The Imperial Household Department hired them by the day for many kinds of jobs—carrying loads, moving furniture, sweeping floors, pulling weeds, and removing snow. The Forbidden and Imperial Cities and Qing retreats at other locations included thirty-eight workshops, where skilled local craftsmen produced textiles, clothing, furniture, glass, enamel, porcelain, books, and paintings for the court. The Wuying dian (Hall of Military Eminence), on the western axis of the Forbidden City, contained a printing and editorial office for palace books.[55] In addition, thousands worked to fill imperial orders in southern silk factories at Suzhou and Hangzhou. The Qing court also routinely commissioned the work of non-Chinese artists and craftsmen, including Tibetans, Uighurs, and Jesuit missionaries.

⊷⟹   ⟸⊷

According to the memoirs of the last Qing emperor, food was the costliest category in the palace budget.[56] Meals for the imperial family and the large number of maidservants, eunuchs, and other staff were prepared by the Yuchashanfang (Imperial Pantry), subordinate to the Imperial Household Department. A separate institution, the Guanglusi (Banqueting Department) under the Board of Rites, created state banquets that enlivened many occasions—especially the new year, visits of tributary envoys, and imperial family birthdays. Painters often recorded these celebratory meals in the Forbidden City and at imperial retreats. By the later eighteenth century there were about four hundred chefs, and court cuisine had branched out from Manchu tastes. Palace menus included culinary influences from all over the empire and drew on supplies from many directions. There were seventy-two wells in the Forbidden City, but Qianlong decided that emperors would use the superior spring water from Yuquanshan in the western suburbs. Every evening a cart flying the yellow imperial flag carried water via the Xizhi Gate of the Inner City to the Shenwu (Spiritual Valor, the northern) Gate of the Forbidden City.[57] Imperial estates supplied a great deal of the food consumed in the Forbidden City, including the highest-quality rice raised especially for the emperor and his family as well as many varieties of vegetables and fruit. Items such as butter, milk cakes, and *koumiss* (fermented mare's or camel's milk)—eschewed by the Chinese but enjoyed by the Manchus—came from flocks raised at Nanyuan, an imperial hunting area south of Beijing, or from beyond the Great Wall. Coastal areas supplied the emperor with seafood. At the new year, servants in the Forbidden City prepared large amounts of special congee (rice cooked with red dates, chestnuts, and beans) for ancestral rites, gifts to servants and officials, and charity distribution in the city.[58]

Surviving menus and records give some idea of the style of imperial meals. The emperor usually ate only two meals a day, an early one between 6 and 8 A.M. and a second between noon and 2 P.M. Eunuchs served the meals whenever and wherever he asked for them, and the same was true of drinks and snacks. The Imperial Pantry proposed the daily menu for approval by the Imperial Household Department. More than twenty eunuchs set up several different-size tables for various kinds of food, while servants brought the cooked dishes themselves. The emperor ate alone and his meals invariably contained much more food of many varieties than he could consume. One menu shows breakfast served to the retired Qianlong on a winter day in 1799 in the Yangxindian residence. Forty dishes included "bird's nest soup, duck, chicken, venison and pork dishes, and small steamed buns, New Year cake (made of glutinous rice flour) and other cakes." The midday meal was similar in content. The attending eunuchs received what must have been substantial leftovers.

The food habits of the palace ranged from the commonplace to the unique. Emperors ate popular seasonal foods of the capital such as dumplings (*jiaozi*) at the new year and sweet dumplings made from glutinous rice flower (*fuyuanzi*) at the winter Lantern Festival. A strip of silver in every dish guarded against poisoning, which would be revealed by a change in color of the strip; as an additional precaution, a eunuch tasted every dish before it was served.[59] Favorite imperial foods became less exclusive just a year after the last emperor left the Forbidden City. In 1925 a restaurant in Beihai Park, which Qianlong had done so much to create, began imitating imperial dishes and sauces so that wealthier members of the public could enjoy palace cuisine.

The Forbidden City was closed to the people most days, but not every day. In the Ming era there even had been a periodic market in its northwest corner.[60] Under the Qing about six hundred banner guards preserved the tranquil atmosphere of the Forbidden City. Former maids were not welcome to return for a visit, and even families of imperial consorts needed special permission to enter or to send gifts to their grandchildren.[61] The latter rule was easier to enforce because, given Qing caution to avoid interference by imperial in-laws, emperors married women of less elite families than had been the case in the Ming era. In Qing times too, however, there were many occasions when outsiders entered the Forbidden City, and access increased over the course of the dynasty, particularly after 1800. The inner palace, where imperial women resided, was the most likely Forbidden City area to be off-limits to outsiders. Still, eighteenth-century banquets, receptions, audiences, and theatrical performances involving large numbers of guests occurred in both the outer court and inner palace as well as in the adjacent Western Park. In April 1713 Kangxi invited many men his age or older to his sixtieth birthday banquet in the Qianqing hall in the inner palace area, and in 1783 Qianlong entertained more than thirteen hundred members of the imperial lineage there. Five thousand people helped the aged Qianlong mark his formal abdication inside the Forbidden City. Officials and imperial family members came to pay their respects annually at the lunar new year. Like the visits of envoys and officials, the coming and going of eunuchs and maidservants, and the daily entrance and exit of workmen, such occasions were moments when the emperor's figurative gaze out over the populace could be returned literally by at least some favored commoners.[62]

The emperor and all the residents of the Forbidden City were carefully protected even though their space itself was occasionally open to selected visitors. Guarding of the Forbidden City employed large numbers of banner soldiers chosen with close attention to status and ethnic categories. Most of those assigned were Manchus and Mongols of the three superior banners, and some were bondservants. High officers of the Flank Division of the Banners (Hujun ying) were part of the daily guard at the key Taihe and Qingyun internal gates of the Forbidden City. Men of these units acted as sergeants-at-arms at receptions, state banquets, and imperial sacrifices. At night, they closed all the gates of the Forbidden City and controlled the keys. They performed regular rounds of patrol starting west from the Qingyun Gate and returning there by way of twelve intermediate posts. Guards on this beat passed a wooden token from hand to hand in the "patrol of the thirteen tokens." Two other banner divisions manned eight firefighting stations within the Forbidden City. Detailed plans for firefighting included specification of who might enter, by which gates, and carrying what equipment.[63] Huge bronze cauldrons of water outside palace buildings were ever-ready for use in case of fire. In winter, cotton-padded coverings and heating from beneath by fire on the cauldrons' stone platforms kept the water inside from freezing.[64]

By day, anyone approaching one of the four external gates of the Forbidden City would encounter two seated guards holding a red bar across the entrance. Their job was to admit only authorized persons, and they were supplied with bows and arrows, quivers, and spears. At night, a wooden-tally system allowed imperial messengers to leave the Forbidden City without delay. Keepers of several internal and external Forbidden City gates held the concave (*yin*) side of the incised tally. A messenger dispatched by the emperor carried the convex (*yang*) side. If the two parts matched, the officer opened the gate and reported to his superior. A similar system was employed at the Qian and Xizhi gates of the Inner City; the former was the main exit from the capital toward the south, and the latter toward the northwest.[65]

Emperors in Motion:
The Birthday Processions of 1713 and 1790

Several hundred gendarmes usually protected an imperial procession. For most such occasions, police and their servants cleared the streets of people, curtained off the side streets with blue-cloth hangings, and strewed the entire route with yellow sand (yellow being the imperial color). Visitors to the city from other countries normally were notified that they should stay indoors at the hour appointed for the procession.[66]

It would not be correct, however, to conclude that emperors hardly saw the capital or its people and rarely mingled with commoners. Rumors occasionally circulated that an emperor had visited the Outer City incognito so as to be free of his customary guards and other encumbrances. Moreover, the emperors actually did learn something of their subjects' daily lives through their many excursions to temples and other places. They and their courtiers enjoyed these fleeting glimpses of reality so much that they created mock city streets at Yuanmingyuan just for fun. Merchants, beggars, and peddlers, all convincingly played by eunuchs, offered real goods provided by Beijing stores for sale. Some of these pretend streets were modeled not on Beijing but on Suzhou and other cities of the south that the emperors had visited. A letter by Attiret described how the producers of the make-believe urban scene even went so far as to assign some of the best eunuch actors to take the parts of thieves, play-acting but risking and even experiencing theatrical capture and appropriate punishment. He also noted that the emperor "always buys a good deal on these occasions, and you may be sure that nothing is sold cheaply to him. But the ladies and eunuchs themselves also make purchases. This commerce would not offer such a piquant interest and provoke so much noisy fun if it had no foundation in reality." The same summer retreat also maintained agricultural areas for the sole purpose of giving the emperor and court a glimpse of the realities of farming. This experience was not necessarily softened for them, as might be expected. One painting of Prince Yinzhen, the future Yongzheng emperor, pictured him as a farmer ladling manure onto rice paddies, yet another experimental persona.[67]

Imperial portraits sometimes seem to depict actual events but do not. It is not safe to assume that Yongzheng actually tried his hand at farming. A painting of Kangxi working on a piece of calligraphy may be less a snapshot of reality than a way of projecting a scholarly image.[68] There is, however, a category of Jesuit-influenced Qing paintings that unquestionably documents historical occurrences.

Both Kangxi's 1689 and Qianlong's 1751 tours of the prosperous and cultured region south of the Yangzi were depicted in many scrolls. These records of imperial activity far from the capital inspired similar treatment of events in Beijing itself. Large, collaborative projects by court artists employed the emerging Sino-Western style (*zhong xi he bi*) influenced especially by Castiglione, whose long career (1715–1766) spanned the reigns of all three high Qing emperors. The European techniques involved—the mathematics of perspective, the arrangement of effects of light and shade (chiaroscuro)—enabled artists to capture a picture in three dimensions and with striking verisimilitude.

The ability of European artists to observe a complex and highly peopled scene in life and then produce a remarkably accurate version of it appealed greatly to the Chinese court. The emperors' recognition of the political usefulness of these skills and of the relation between record keeping and power drew them to artists like Attiret, Castiglione, Gerbillon, Giovanni Gherardini, and Matteo Ripa. As an art historian observes, the rulers were fascinated by "optical realism as a seemingly objective lens to document their place in history."[69] Use of these capabilities both demonstrated Qing power and augmented it. They enabled the state to save certain data and to project the chosen self-images of emperors. The Manchus explicitly sought legitimacy in the eyes of the Chinese scholar class, and the portrayal of Kangxi, Yongzheng, and Qianlong reflected this underlying motive. The Qing court saw the new artistic skills as means of strengthening their hold on their own world, and partly for this reason the volume and quality of imperial painting increased throughout the eighteenth century.[70]

Kangxi's sixtieth birthday procession was an extraordinary day that left behind an extraordinary record, an idealized portrait of a rare Qing dynasty Beijing public celebration. It was held the day before Kangxi's sixtieth birthday, the eighteenth day of the third lunar month of the fifty-second year of the Kangxi reign, corresponding to April 11, 1713. The procession was unusual because city and suburban people remained in the streets to watch its progress over fifteen kilometers (9 miles) from the northwestern imperial retreat at the Changchunyuan (the Garden of Joyful Springtime) through the Xizhi Gate facing west at the northwest corner of the Inner City wall, to the Imperial and Forbidden cities. Contrary to the usual procedure, the front curtains of the emperor's palanquin remained open. The artist Wang Yuanqi and his assistants painted scenes from the procession on a silk scroll of great length; woodcuts later were copied from the scroll. The numerous and highly detailed scenes depict the entire route as it would have appeared at one moment. There are some points where the emperor's palanquin has already passed, some where it is now passing, others where the crowds excitedly await the procession. The effect is reminiscent of modern newsreel treatment of a parade, and the artists appear to have wished to preserve, as a record, pictures as close to what today would be called photographic detail as possible.[71] Music of drums, flutes, gongs, and horns accompanied the emperor's passage through the streets. Imperial elephants and colorful flags and inscriptions displayed along the way further enlivened the scene. (See Color Plates 7 and 8 and Figure 4.)

The Kangxi birthday scroll and later copies of it depict the palanquin open at the front but do not actually show the emperor, though scholars commonly assume that on this occasion Kangxi could see the spectators and be seen by them. The court artist Ripa, an eyewitness, paints a slightly different picture:

> Upon this celebration of the sixtieth anniversary of the Emperor's birth, the [lane] openings were not stopped nor the doors shut, nor were the people driven away [as usual]. The streets and roads were now crowded with countless multitudes desirous of beholding their sovereign. He rode on horseback, wearing a robe covered with dragons, magnificently embroidered in gold. . . . He was preceded by about two thousand horse-soldiers . . . and immediately followed by the princes of the blood, who were succeeded by a great number of mandarins. After these came a large body of soldiers. . . . We Europeans were disposed in a rank near a bridge at no great distance from the palace, where we awaited the arrival of his Majesty upon our knees. On passing by, he paid particular attention to each of us, and smilingly inquired which were those employed in drawing the map.
>
> A vast number of aged but healthy men had been sent to [Beijing] from all the provinces. They were in companies, bearing the banner of their respective provinces. They also carried various other symbols and trophies, and being symmetrically drawn up along the streets through which the Emperor was to pass, they presented a very beautiful and uncommon appearance. Every one of these old men brought a present of some kind to the Emperor, which generally consisted of vases and other articles in bronze. His Majesty gave to each of them twelve silver [taels], a coin worth about five shillings, together with a gown of yellow silk, which is the imperial color.[72]

The failure to depict the emperor in his palanquin does not necessarily mean that he was not in it. Only the front curtain was open. But Ripa's description of the scene does suggest that, perhaps fatigued after traveling most of the distance from Changchunyuan in a palanquin, the experienced rider Kangxi may have mounted a horse when inside the city wall and approaching the Forbidden City.

The 1713 birthday procession included a degree of popular participation that the Qing emperors rarely tolerated. The city lacked public squares where large crowds could gather, and this characteristic was not coincidental. (During the Qing era, today's Tiananmen Square was not yet an open space; many buildings stood there.) On this unique occasion, however, not only did crowds line the streets, but hardly any social category was overlooked. Men, women, and children; imperial relatives, eunuchs, and bondservants; officials high and low; representatives of all the provinces and of other lands; people who had attained the age of sixty-five and over; salt merchants; Muslims; descendants of the ancient philosopher Confucius and of his favorite disciple Yan Hui; descendants of the later Confucian philosopher Mencius—all took part in the events of the day. Residents of the Outer City enjoyed a separate, contemporaneous celebration. As Ripa confirmed, Kangxi paid close personal attention to the elderly, who numbered about four thousand, including individuals ninety to one hundred years old. He ordered that they receive meals, medical care, and gifts of food and cloth; he even stopped to talk with them. With masses of people on all sides, gendarmes and police servants also were numerous. The crowds knelt when the emperor's palanquin passed by, but before and after they had many other diversions, including outdoor theater on open stages, temple observances, and vendors selling snacks and toys.[73]

Seen in the context of earlier history, the 1713 procession and associated events appear to reflect an ancient Chinese view of the universe as an organic whole, with a place for every person and every constructive human activity normally pursued in an organized group. It was a vision that harked back to an idealized, pre-Confucian Golden Age of social harmony represented in the ancient poetry of the *Shijing* (Book of Songs).[74] Seen in another way, however, the procession also eerily foreshadows a Chinese Communist celebratory parade in the 1950s or early 1960s, with numerous slogans and portraits displayed, and with party members, workers, farmers, women, students, and youth all exalting a lone and aging moral leader at the top, in the later case not the emperor of a dynasty but the chairman of a political party. The two views, looking backward and forward in time, are quite compatible.

Impressed by the scroll of Kangxi's birthday procession and by the woodcut edition of the same pictures published in 1718, Qianlong for his own eightieth birthday observance in 1790 deliberately copied his grandfather's celebration of seventy-seven years earlier. The date was the thirteenth day of the eighth lunar month of the fifty-fifth year of his reign, corresponding to September 21, 1790. He too is said to have opened the front palanquin curtain while remaining partly shielded from view, although once again the emperor is not depicted. He allowed kneeling crowds to line the streets along almost the same route[75] and arranged for the presence of a wide variety of his subjects, including wealthy merchants, Taiwanese, and Mongols. A pictorial scroll and a book of congratulatory songs (*Baxun wanshou shengdian,* Magnificent record of the emperor's eightieth birthday, 1792) document this celebration. (See Color Plate 10.)

Both the Kangxi and Qianlong birthday scrolls reveal a great deal about the paths of the processions as seen and interpreted by eighteenth-century artists, but the Kangxi scroll tells more. In the Qianlong procession, temporary pavilions and stages take up most of the route, obscuring the everyday streets behind them. In the Kangxi scroll ordinary shops, many with legible names, and even dwellings and adjacent *hutong* are visible. Both scrolls show piles of gifts and offerings guarded by the gendarmerie, commemorative arches, temples open as the procession passes, and auspicious sayings and birthday greetings posted along the way. The routes and appearance of the crowds suggest that many of the thousands of individuals depicted are banner people.

Routes of the 1713 and 1790 processions can be traced on a comprehensive map of the capital produced with Jesuit assistance around 1750. This map, which still survives in Beijing, appears to show every house and larger structure as well as every avenue, lane, and bridge in the Inner and Outer cities. (There is, of course, no way to be sure that it actually does so.) The map labels streets and buildings, including hundreds of temples. The inclusion of symbols for streetgates (*zhalan*) at lane entrances suggests that the map, having been produced for the throne, may have met some of the practical needs of the gendarmerie.[76] (See Map 3.) Even earlier, the government under Kangxi had collaborated with the Jesuits in a nine-year geographic survey that produced a map of the entire empire in 1718.[77] The emperor asked the kneeling European artists about their work on this map during his birthday procession in April 1713, according to Ripa's account.

The close of Qianlong's reign in the mid-1790s marked both a Qing apogee that would not be seen again and the first failures of the dynasty to maintain so high a level. The end of the emperor's rule was overshadowed by rebellions and by the demoralizing behavior of his fabulously corrupt favorite, the Manchu Heshen. In 1793 the aged Qianlong refused with great condescension the invitation

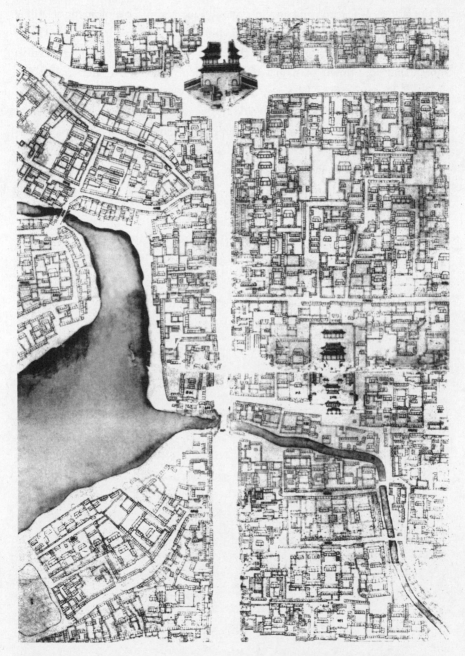

Map 3. The Drum Tower and its neighborhood in the "Qianlong map" of 1750. *Source:*
Qing neiwufu cang jingcheng quantu *(Complete map of the capital kept in the Qing Imperial
Household Department). Beiping, 1940*

of the British Macartney mission to expand trade and place diplomatic relations on a new footing. Recent Chinese scholarship has implied that in doing so, Qianlong allowed an opportunity to pass that, had it been seized, might have led to more rapid adjustment of China to the modern world than later in fact occurred.[78] Moreover, the Macartney mission itself was a sign that a day was coming when Sino-European contact would not be left to missionaries alone. Before facing the post-Qianlong world, however, let us follow the imperial processions out of the summer villas and the Forbidden City and discover the everyday Beijing of the high Qing era.

Chapter 3

Daily Life in the
Inner and Outer Cities

BEIJING IN THE YEAR 1800, WITH ABOUT ONE MILLION INHABITANTS, was not only one of the world's most populous and prosperous cities but also one of its best organized. At a time when outbreaks of mob violence threatened London and night watchmen were so ineffective that the wealthy hired their own guards, Beijing had a large police force that patrolled day and night, conducted a regular census, fought fires, and provided cool drinking water at the gates on hot summer days. In an era when socially incendiary conflicts over the price of grain helped to ignite ten years of revolution in Paris, large granaries and state economic policies safeguarded Beijing's food security. In Europe and even the United States cities were seen as dangerous, unhealthy and conducive to immoral behavior. Beijing, however, offered both a higher level of culture and a more secure life than were available in the countryside. The only other world city close to Beijing in population was the shogunal capital of Edo (later Tokyo) in Japan, but its insular character, intensified by the strict seclusion policy of the Tokugawa rulers, minimized cosmopolitan influences. At this time Beijing had few if any world peers in size, diversity, and administrative control.

The division of the capital into distinct sections facilitated the maintenance of order and social stability. Different kinds of activities (such as government and commerce) and different groups (such as Manchus and Han Chinese, or scholar-officials and merchants) tended to be separated in space much though not all of the time. In Beijing this segmentation took a characteristic form—city walls, walls of houses and temples, city gates, street gates—that human institutions, especially the gendarmerie, reinforced. (See Map 4.) As historian Susan Naquin

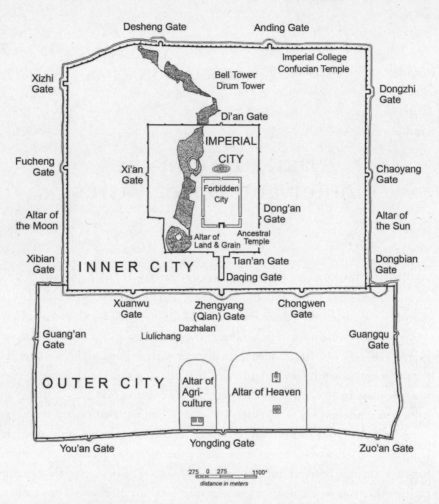

Map 4. Beijing in the Qing era, 1644–1912. *Credit: Elizabeth Novey*

writes, "Walls within, walls without, enclosure nested inside enclosure, cities within cities—compartmentalization was fundamental to [Beijing's] history and identity before the twentieth century."[1]

The Imperial City with its beautiful gardens and many imperial workshops was a sparsely inhabited buffer area between the Forbidden and Inner cities.[2] Its residents included high officials, bondservants, and eunuchs. The Inner City was the principal home of the bannermen, the main military support of the dynasty; it also was the site of government offices and academies, civil service examination grounds, and state granaries. Qing authorities paid close attention to the Inner City, both because of its own great political significance and because of its proximity to the Forbidden City.

The Outer City was a commercial settlement most densely built up outside the three gates that it shared with the Inner City. After the Qing rulers required the Han Chinese population of the Inner City to move there in the 1640s, the Outer City developed rapidly. Even so, much of its territory toward the south was semiagricultural and less densely populated than the Inner City. The Outer City contained the state Temples of Heaven and Agriculture, but its most crucial role during the Qing era was to relieve cultural pressure on the Inner City. The latter was a place of prohibitions, things that residents, at least on paper, could *not* do— build new theaters, hoard rice, practice bribery or usury, gather to plan religious pilgrimages, gamble, set off firecrackers (except at festivals), present plays or sing songs in questionable taste, and so on. In the Outer City, however, Inner City restrictions gave way to permissions both open and tacit, to a general understanding of many things that people *could* do. Because the Outer City was still part of the capital, the throne maintained an underlying dominance there, but it usually did not involve itself directly in local matters.[3]

A system of governance that was intentionally layered and overlapping contributed to the complex spatial and social division of the city. The Imperial Household Department and high banner divisions played the greatest role in the Forbidden and Imperial cities. The gendarmerie policed the Inner and Outer cities. The Censorate monitored the performance of all officials but focused on the nonbanner population and therefore on the Outer City and the suburbs. With Beijing's territory divided yet another way, the Inner and Outer cities formed part of the two counties (*xian*) of Daxing and Wanping in Shuntian Prefecture of Zhili Province. Although the prefecture connected Beijing to the empire's civil administrative hierarchy, matters relating to the capital were not included in provincial or prefectural reports. The dynasty treated the city as unique, as sui generis. The different agencies—Imperial Household Department, banners, gendarmerie, Censorate, counties, prefecture—watched not only the same territory but also each other, and the competition among them served the purposes of the rulers.

The Manchus and Banner Society

Beijing under the Qing resembled in some ways the expansive, multilingual capital that it had been under the Mongols in the thirteenth and fourteenth centuries.[4] The Manchu language constantly was heard in the streets, and the bannerman's greeting of social superiors was noticeably different from that of the Chinese: a Manchu dropped his right knee to the ground and let his arms hang down, while a Chinese clasped both hands in front of his chest and bowed. The Mandarin Chinese speech of the city absorbed Manchu influences that included not only loan words but also patterns of formation of words and sentences. The capital became a center of publishing in Manchu, Mongolian, and Tibetan as well as in Chinese.[5] Some cultural elements spread from the Manchus to the Chinese (men's dress and hairstyle); some spread the other way (Chinese cuisine). Entertainment diffused in both directions: Inner Asian amusements such as kite-flying and acrobatics had long appealed to the Han Chinese, and the city's traditional theatrical forms strongly attracted the Manchus. Indeed, the two peoples already were well acquainted at the theater; ancestors of the Manchus had joined their Chinese subjects in watching *yuanben,* comical sketches that were forerunners of Yuan drama, in Jin Zhongdu in the twelfth century. Five hundred years later, a distinctive Qing-era Beijing identity—a fresh synthesis of cultural elements both Manchu and Han—was beginning to evolve.

We have seen how, within a few years of the conquest in 1644, the Qing rulers took over what had been the Ming Northern City as a place for bannermen and their families to live. (See Map 5.) The three superior banners—the two yellow plus the plain white—were larger than the others, and their northern neighborhoods were considered the most desirable. Bannermen guarded the city gates in their own and other areas through the regular posting of some of their members to the gendarmerie; Manchus and Mongols guarded the Inner City gates and Chinese bannermen (*hanjun*) the Outer City gates. Within the Inner City, Manchus lived closest to the Forbidden City, followed by Mongols and *hanjun.*[6] Banner affiliation thus determined *where* in the Inner City a family's house was located, but rank dictated its size and style. The Imperial Household Department collected rents and provided repair and maintenance.[7]

Other small groups joined the banners in the early to mid-Qing era. In the 1680s the Manchus captured Russians after they clashed with Qing troops at Albazin on the Amur River. Brought to Beijing, the captives became bondservants, working as bowmakers and guards, in the bordered yellow banner in the northeast corner of the Inner City. They married local women and founded a Russian Orthodox colony known to the Russian government as Albazinians. Similarly, Tibetan artisans whom the Qing state brought to the capital in the eighteenth

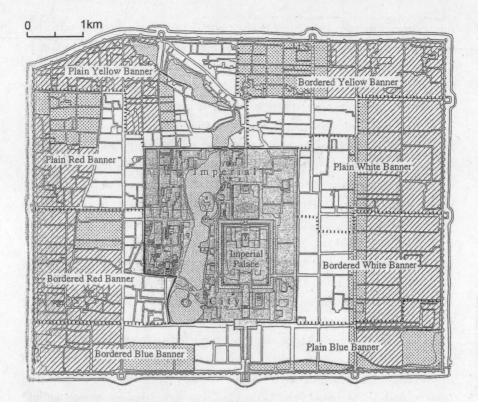

Map 5. Eight Banner Neighborhoods in the Qing-era Inner City.
Unshaded areas: Manchu banners
Shaded areas: Mongol banners
Diagonally barred areas: Chinese banners
(Data from Baqi tongzhi chuji)

Source: *Mark C. Elliott,* The Manchu Way: the Eight Banners and Ethnic Identity in Late Imperial China. *Stanford: Stanford University Press, 2001. Reprinted by permission of Stanford University Press.*

century became bondservants in the plain white banner. After the conquest of Xinjiang in Central Asia in the 1750s, the Qianlong emperor enrolled eight hundred members of elite Muslim families in a Mongol banner. He even ordered new residences and a mosque built for them in the southwest corner of the Imperial City. Moving hundreds of families or artisans with desired skills to enhance a capital city had many precedents; in Beijing history, the Yongle emperor already had done so on a large scale in the early fifteenth century.[8]

The banners were divided into two wings according to their pattern of residence in the Inner City. "Left" and "right" referred to the Inner City on the two sides of the Forbidden City when facing south. The left wing, on the east, contained two of the three superior banners and inhabited the more favored space. In a pattern already noticeable before the Qing era, the two sides of the Inner City had developed differently. The east side, closer to the link to the Grand Canal, contained more significant institutions and more large markets than did the west. The Imperial College (Guozijian), which attracted students from tributary states as well as the empire, was located on the east side, as were two hostels of the Russian Ecclesiastical Mission that St. Petersburg maintained after 1727 to minister to the Albazinians. The walls of the Imperial City and the city's chain of lakes slowed traffic on the main east-west streets compared to the north-south ones; on the latter avenues, it was possible to see from one end of the Inner City to the other, especially on the east side. Less frequent travel and contact east to west than north to south, year in and year out, contributed to the distinctiveness of the east and west sides. The terms "east city" (*dongcheng*) and "west city" (*xicheng*) were in use by the end of the seventeenth century, and by the later Qing era they denoted significant cultural differences, even in accent, storytelling styles, and peddlers' cries. Major monthly temple fairs associated with the east at the Longfu and Dongyue temples (Longfusi and Dongyuemiao) (see Figure 45) or with the west at Huguo Temple (Huguosi) also helped to give the two sides of the city separate identities. The "west city" was considered more isolated and home to a more purely banner population.[9]

Inner City society, like society in the eighteen smaller banner-garrisoned cities in the empire, was closely related to the organization of the banner system. Legal categories separated "banner" (*qi*) and "civilian" (*min*) populations. Unlike everyone else in the empire, banner people did not belong to a county. Wherever they lived, Beijing was their native place and the banner into which they had been born their most important identity; intermarriage of bannermen and civilians was forbidden. In each banner, a lieutenant-general (*fudutong*) held both civil and military authority over bannermen and their families. The company captain (*zuoling*) early in the dynasty led about three hundred men, later about half that number. He was to bannermen what the county magistrate was to civilians, except that the captain could not try legal cases and had to send them to his superiors.[10]

The company and the captain, even more than the family, controlled the lives of banner people. The company kept track of births, deaths, marriages, and houses; the captain allotted funds for weddings and funerals. The company and the banner bureaucracy helped the Board of Revenue to dispense monthly banner stipends in silver and grain. A major source for these payments was rental income from land around the capital that had been appropriated by the dynasty at the time of the conquest. Until 1763 bannermen were forbidden to take up any non-military occupation, and even afterward they needed permission from their captain to do so. Some who were literate found employment handling stipends, census registration, and other paperwork.[11]

Any institutional framework is vulnerable to social and economic changes that occur after the system is fixed in place. In Japan in the Qing era, the Tokugawa rulers (1603–1868) faced urban and mercantile growth that creators of their well-organized feudal social system had never envisioned. In China, the banner system too faced challenges as its population increased over time, doubling through natural increase as early as the 1720s. With banner armies mobilized only occasionally in the eighteenth century, bannermen became less effective as a military force. They gradually valued less the martial skills of the "old Manchu way." Military posts were not available for all, and alternatives such as civil office became increasingly important. Some banner people moved out of the Inner City, and some Han Chinese moved into it; by the late eighteenth century, the throne had given up trying to prevent these moves in either direction. The rulers even offered land to encourage superfluous soldiers to leave the banners and settle as farmers outside the city.[12] But it was not easy to persuade bannermen to leave Beijing once they had learned to enjoy the urban life of theaters, teahouses, and pawnshops; in addition, they often were tied down by debt. After they could speak Chinese and felt at home in Chinese culture—a process well under way by 1700—the throne faced the problem of how to preserve their ability to speak Manchu and their traditional customs. In short, the Qing rulers had to cope with challenges posed by change throughout the life of the banner system.[13] As the Kangxi emperor recalled his advice to his sons: "I told them not to lose their Manchu traditions even in such things as dress, food, utensils, not to get too dyed in Chinese ways like the later rulers of [Jin] and Yuan. I told them to get their pleasures from living in wide spaces, not to close themselves in with screens and connecting rooms the way the Chinese consider clever."[14]

Housing and Dress

Residential architecture of the Inner and Outer cities was similar, but Inner City neighborhoods were more clearly defined geographically by the city gates and by barricades around each banner quarter. By Qing times, the number of *hutong* had increased to over two thousand. The walled "courtyard house" (*siheyuan*) carried out on a smaller scale the architectural concept of a symmetrical ensemble of structures that also was typical of temples, the Forbidden City, and the capital layout as a whole. In the courtyard house as in the other cases, nature played a prominent role: rather than gardens and courtyards being the setting for the house, the house was the setting for them. Just as the balance of many structures (rather than a single monumental palace) in the Forbidden City was a relatively modest way of showing political power, the architectural approach to construction of ordinary dwellings reflected an underlying philosophical view of the modest human place in the world.[15]

Most residences had only one storey. Away from the main avenues, all was quiet, with only occasional exceptions, such as peddlers' cries or noises made by night patrolmen. Houses were constructed of gray brick, with gray roof tiles in two layers and windows made of thick translucent paper. When the windows were rolled up in spring, wide eaves protected rooms from rain and the hot sun. A home consisted of several buildings; the largest and most important structure faced south in order to receive maximum sunlight. In front of the main building was a courtyard with smaller buildings along its east and west sides. Larger houses and mansions would have one or more courtyards, each with lesser buildings on east and west. The northernmost building might contain the living and reception rooms, parents' bedrooms, a young child's bedroom, and a study. Older children lived in side suites; a married son might occupy one side suite; yet another would be for guests. In a wealthy home, a suite on the south would be for male servants; female servants would sleep in the rooms of the women and girls whom they served.[16]

Beijing lies in the latitude of Philadelphia, Madrid, and Naples. Its residents are accustomed to occasional snow and dust storms, to cold winters and hot summers. In relative terms, however, the climate cannot be called especially severe, and its dryness and sunniness have positive aspects for health. In a Qing-era courtyard house, portable charcoal braziers and a heated sleeping platform provided warmth when needed. When residents shivered in the late fall, they put on fur-lined or quilted gowns and thick felt-soled shoes. Despite these comforts, it is fair to say that the courtyard house was at its best in the warmer seasons.[17]

Most houses were not large, but the city map of 1750 included thirty-seven mansions with at least three large courtyards, side gardens, and wide front gates. (See detail from 1750 map in Map 3.) During the Qianlong reign, *The Dream of the Red Chamber* described life in the multicourtyard compound of a wealthy family in a fictional city based on both Beijing and the southern city of Nanjing. Because all Inner City houses ultimately belonged to the dynasty, and because Qing princely titles lost a step in rank when they passed between generations, few mansions remained in the same family for long.[18]

The courtyard-house way of life was already old when the banner people arrived, and many of its details reflected established custom. Rooms were measured by *jian*, the area conventionally allowed by builders between two parallel roof beams. For example, sumptuary rules might state that a bannerman of a certain rank was allowed a living room of three *jian*. A southern wall contained an arched gateway painted with bright color on the doors and eaves leading out into the lane. A "spirit wall" at the entrance was intended to deflect evil influences and preserve privacy. The front gate had large wooden crossbars, though no locks, and usually would be guarded by servants; houses rarely were left completely unoccupied. Ladies of the house or servants might venture out at the front entrance to talk with neighbors or to buy items from peddlers.

The kitchen of a courtyard house was likely to be in a small outbuilding or on a veranda. Bathing and washing took place in living quarters, with water brought to private rooms by servants. The privy, housed in a small corner shed, would be emptied at night by door-to-door collection. Carts run by private enterprise delivered waste to farms around the city, where it was composted and used for fertilizer.

A courtyard often had at least one blossoming shade tree and could be a peaceful place despite its location inside a huge and busy city. People commonly decorated these spaces with crabapple, date, and fig trees; pomegranate, oleander, and other plants in pots; and pools stocked with goldfish. The trees' brief blossoming was a reminder of Buddhist themes of impermanence but also of natural sources of spiritual comfort. In a mostly one-storey city, residents could see the entire sky from their courtyards, along with the tops of trees and, for some, the sun touching the yellow roof tiles of the Forbidden City. Before industrialization, motorized traffic, and air pollution, the sky over the city was known for its bright clarity and azure color. Residents of the *siheyuan* found pleasure in nature and in subtle changes of atmosphere in their courtyards at different times of day, before and after rain, and in diverse seasons. The changing pattern of light and shade; the buzzing of insects in the linden trees in early summer; the touch of autumn amid chrysanthemums; conversation and tea; painting and calligraphy; the sheltered play of small children under the eye of a grandparent or *amah* (nanny)—these were among many quiet sources of happiness in the Beijing courtyard. Daoism taught that the greatness of the Dao (the way of nature) could be sensed even, and sometimes especially, in its small-scale manifestations.

During warmer weather much of family life, including meals and entertainment of guests, took place outdoors in courtyards. Larger houses had an outer courtyard used for acquaintances and parties and an inner one for relatives and close friends—exactly the arrangement found on a grand scale in the Forbidden City.[19] When a theater troupe entertained at a private party, the stage would be set up in the outer courtyard. In a city of a million or more people, there was perhaps a certain joy, at least for a man, in voluntarily secluding himself from time to time, or in being included in a small and intimate group enclosed in a garden setting.

⟿   ⟿

When people emerged from their houses, no matter where they were in the capital, they joined a street crowd that was predominantly male. Among the Chinese, only poor women appeared on the streets. Most women spent a great deal of their time at home, and the Qing state favored this custom as conducive to moral behavior. The gendarmerie regarded with suspicion the public mixing of the sexes that was likely to occur at a market or temple festival or on a religious pilgrimage. Probably because women's housebound way of life gave them only limited opportunities to observe and borrow each other's styles, the dress of females of different ethnic groups remained distinct throughout the Qing era. There were, however, occasional links between men's and women's attire. When the Board of Rites signaled that it was time for officials to change to summer hats, the ladies of the officials' families changed their hair ornaments from gold to jade.[20]

Dress was not the only way in which Manchu women stood out from Han women. With their active Inner Asian background, they not only never had bound their feet but were robust walkers and experienced horsewomen. They were so often seen in the streets, both on foot and astride, that early twentieth-century Western visitors described Manchu women as Beijing's "American girls." They wore platform shoes and a one-piece gown, as opposed to the Han female costume of a loose three-quarter-length garment over trousers. Chinese women combed their hair back and coiled it in a bun at the back or in two at the sides of the head; Manchu women built up their hair on top of their heads, sometimes adding decorations. Only in the twentieth century under the republic, when all women appeared much more than before on the streets and when ethnicity was less emphasized, did Chinese women wear the high-collared one-piece *qipao* (banner gown). At that point, somewhat paradoxically, the *qipao* began to be recognized internationally as Chinese "national" female dress.[21]

Male dress, however, already had converged during the Qing era. Initially, in the mid-seventeenth century, Manchu equestrian-style dress had been required of all bannermen and Chinese officials. The long-sleeved tunic was narrow and tight above the waist, loose below, and slit front and back and along the sides to allow for riding; men often wore the tunic under a three-quarter or half-length riding or "horse" jacket (*magua*). Completion of this outfit required shoes with rigid soles as well as summer bamboo and winter fur-rimmed hats. Glass or jewel balls on top of the hats revealed the wearers' ranks by their color; long necklaces also showed officials' high rank. In addition, almost all males were obliged to wear the queue. This hairstyle became so nearly universal for men that mid-nineteenth-century Russian diplomats attached false queues under their hats so that they would not attract undue attention in the streets. Over time too, most Han Chinese men, not only bannermen and officials, voluntarily adopted the conquerors' long gown and riding jacket. Ming-style robes, hats, and shoes were consigned to history.[22] .

Children wore bright colors and old people soft and muted ones. Neighbors might give a baby a brilliant quilted coat assembled from many pieces of silk from their own homes, thus confusing any nearby malicious spirits as to the child's identity. Meanwhile the dark blue, deep purple, gray, and mauve of the elderly conveyed their dignity in approaching the time when they would become honored ancestors who could send blessings to their descendants.[23]

Food and Food Security

In Qing-era Beijing a varied and delightful cuisine, one of the notable achievements of Chinese civilization, coexisted with tastes introduced by the Manchus and other Inner Asian peoples. Restaurants and teahouses, especially numerous in the Outer City, catered not only to capital residents but also to visitors from the provinces and the steppe. Throughout the year, street vendors sold seasonal selections of cooked and uncooked foods—including dumplings, rice-stuffed lotus roots, baked yams, roasted chestnuts, sweet potatoes, iced sweets, and dried fruits. Frequent temple and secular fairs provided markets and food stalls; banner people at a fair liked to enjoy a refreshing drink of soy bean milk, as well as buckwheat buns, sausages, and sweetened fruit. According to a Qing-era report, the white cold-weather treat made from cooked sheep milk and sugar (*shuiwuta*) had the texture of crunching snow.[24]

Itinerant merchants hawked food items throughout all the streets and lanes of the city, employing distinctive cries and musical tunes to announce their approach. They earned a precarious living by following a predictable routine reminiscent of summer ice-cream vendors in an American city, but sold foods of many kinds and in all seasons. Nonfood items such as cloth and services such as hair-cutting (the queue hairstyle required frequent attention from barbers), tooth-pulling, knife-sharpening, fortune-telling, and letter-writing also were peddled through the city. Widespread mobile commerce enabled women, the elderly, and others to shop without long excursions on the major streets. Peddlers' cries were not easy on the ear and were conventionalized to the point that, although neighborhood residents easily recognized them, they often could not say what the words literally meant. In hot weather poor boys would make the rounds selling ice with the cry "*Bing hu-erh!*" *Bing* is "ice," but a "*hu-erh*" is a seed. "*Bing hu-erh!*" meant "Small lumps of ice!"—roughly comparable to a cry of "Ice cubes!" Peddlers generally specialized in a particular area where they knew the customers; at dusk they carried lanterns to light the road and to enable them to spot counterfeit coins.[25]

Residents purchased everyday food both from peddlers and markets. Ordinary people ate mainly coarse grains, such as millet or sorghum, with vegetables. Fine grains—rice and wheat—were not part of their daily fare and, like meat and even fish, tended to be consumed only on special occasions. Their customary diet included millet gruel, cornbread, buckwheat noodles, and bean products such as bean curd (*doufu*, i.e., tofu). The most common winter vegetables were turnips and cabbage, often stored in cold weather on the tile roofs of houses, with beans and eggplant in summer. On holidays or special occasions, people celebrated with steamed bread, deep-fried crepes (*youbing*), or Mongolian "hot-pot," thin slices of mutton cooked in a chafing dish (*shuan yangrou*). Mutton or pork-filled fried dumplings (*guotie*) were treats at the new year. *Huntun* (meat dumplings) helped to celebrate the winter solstice and noodles, the summer one.[26]

Emperors and officials enjoyed local cuisine and also understood that food security was a key problem of statecraft. To compensate for the region's limited rainfall and relative lack of natural resources, the capital relied on immense grain shipments from central China, especially from the agriculturally rich lower Yangzi region. Grain shipments along the Grand Canal consisted mostly of rice, which was not widely grown or eaten in the north. (Millet, sorghum, and wheat

Color Plate 1. Khubilai Khan (Yuan).
*Credit: National Palace Museum,
Taiwan, Republic of China*

Color Plate 2.
The Yongle
emperor (Ming)
in court dress.
*Credit: National
Palace Museum,
Taiwan, Republic
of China*

Color Plate 3. Snow Scene of Forbidden City, painting by Xu Yang, 1767. A scene described in the Qianlong Emperor's poem "Bird's-Eye View of the Capital." *Credit: The Palace Museum, Beijing*

Color Plate 4. The Kangxi emperor in court dress. *Credit: The Palace Museum, Beijing*

Color Plate 5. The Yongzheng emperor at leisure. *Credit: The Palace Museum, Beijing*

Color Plate 6. The Qianlong emperor and royal children on the New Year's Eve. Painting attributed to Giuseppe Castiglione (Lang Shining). 1736–37. *Credit: The Palace Museum, Beijing*

Color Plate 7. Royal palanquin and carriage in the Kangxi emperor's sixtieth birthday procession, 1713. Scene from a late eighteenth or early nineteenth century copy of the 1718 *Wanshou shengdian* (Magnificent record of the Emperor's birthday). *Credit: The Palace Museum, Beijing*

Color Plate 8. The Kangxi emperor's sixtieth birthday procession, passing by crowds and street entertainment, 1713. Scene from *Wanshou shengdian,* as above. *Credit: The Palace Museum, Beijing*

Color Plate 9. Tributary envoys approaching the Hall of Supreme Harmony (Taihedian). Anonymous court artists, second half of eighteenth century. Calligraphy by the Qianlong emperor. *Credit: The Palace Museum, Beijing*

Color Plate 10. The Qianlong emperor's eightieth birthday procession in 1790, showing Beijing scenery, including the Baita Temple (Baitasi), the white stupa at the upper left. *Credit: The Palace Museum, Beijing*

Color Plate 11. "The Liberation of Beiping," poster by Ye Qianyu depicting the grand entrance ceremony, February 3, 1949. The Temple of Heaven is depicted at the upper left, and the Qianmen at the top center. *Credit: Courtesy of University of Westminster Chinese Poster Collection*

Color Plate 12. Tiananmen Square during the student hunger strike, May 1989. The Monument to the People's Heroes is at the center. The Great Hall of the People is in the back. *Credit: Collection of the authors.*

Color Plate 13. Palace of Established Happiness (Jianfugong) construction in Forbidden City, 2001. *Credit: China Heritage Fund*

were the main grain crops of north China.) Running about sixteen hundred kilometers (a thousand miles) from Hangzhou to Tongzhou, the canal brought grain
that either could be stored at Tongzhou or transported by canal or mule cart over
the last nineteen kilometers (twelve miles) to Beijing. At the capital it was placed
in large granaries, most located near the east wall of the Inner City. These granaries, some of which still stand, were supervised by the banners and the Board of
Revenue and guarded by the gendarmerie. They were large structures about
ninety meters (three hundred feet) long and nine to twelve meters (thirty to forty
feet) high. Their visibility was itself an important message to the populace; it as-
sured them of the rulers' political will to protect the city's food supply and its relatively low grain prices.

The impact of tribute grain on the capital was far from a simple one of
southern supply and northern consumption. A person's relation to tribute grain
had everything to do with social status. The imperial family and its high
courtiers never touched tribute rice and ate instead the exquisitely flavored variety grown on imperial estates near the capital. Tribute grain provided a monthly
food stipend for princes, imperial clansmen, bannermen, and officials. The highest Manchu princes received, in addition to payment in silver, several thousand
shi of milled rice per year. Each *shi* weighed about 79–88 kilograms (175–195
pounds). A low-ranking bannerman, however, received one *shi* per month. The
large difference reflected the assumption that the simple bannerman was supporting a nuclear family of about four, while princes and high officials had large
households including multiple consorts, extended family, and servants. By the
time tribute grain reached Beijing, though, it was usually stale and moldy; much
of it was known candidly as *laomi,* "old rice." Although *laomi* doubtless could
have saved lives in a famine, Inner City residents avoided eating it if they could.
Wealthy stipend recipients typically sold all or part of their grain and used the
proceeds to buy regionally grown wheat or millet. Poor recipients also sold their
stipendiary grain but then bought less costly, inferior grains, such as sorghum. In
this way, large amounts of tribute grain reached the market, reducing prices in
the city and the region.

Food security for the capital was so important that the government could
not even consider failing to keep prices low. Officials employed numerous time-
honored policies—sequentially or simultaneously—to be sure that they achieved
this goal. In addition to the effect on the market of the grain stipends themselves, there were numerous other tactics for reducing and stabilizing prices.
Grain might be brought into the city from the surrounding area for sale, but in

times of scarcity the authorities did not allow grain to be removed from the city for the same purpose. Before spring and fall harvests or when local prices rose because of flood or drought, officials sold off granary contents to the city populace at below-market prices, an ancient practice. They often enlisted private merchants to help carry out these reduced-price sales. Officials could control their distaste for "mean merchants" when they needed them, much as emperors somehow found that they could tolerate eunuchs when convenient. The gendarmerie checked to prevent grain shops from keeping large inventories ("hoarding") and insisted that grain businesses remain relatively small in scale so that none of them could dominate the market. Yet another measure was state operation of winter "soup kitchens" where the poor could obtain one free meal a day, usually millet and rice gruel. Location of many of these soup kitchens in temples just outside the city gates encouraged refugees from natural disasters in the wider region to return home without ever entering the Inner or Outer cities.

Although the state was the largest wholesaler of grain, it never tried to substitute itself for the market. Instead, officials made sophisticated use of market mechanisms and had a long record of success in doing so. Beijing and its region certainly knew times of flood and famine. Nonetheless, the capital benefited from a protected food supply and, unlike Paris under Louis XVI, was never troubled by political conflicts over the price of grain and grain products.[27]

Public Order

Like residents of Chinese capitals for at least a millennium, Beijing residents of the Qing era were familiar with policemen on the beat, regular census-taking, and night-time curfews. The banners' large Gendarmerie Division, along with Five Battalions of the Chinese Army of the Green Standard, carried out systematic policing. With about 23,000 policemen under the banners, and another 10,000 under the Five Battalions, Beijing had an extremely high ratio of police to population, roughly one gendarme for thirty persons. In 1793 a British diplomatic visitor, George L. Staunton, was so struck by the Inner City's orderliness that he likened the place to a military camp: "Great order is preserved among such multitudes; and the commission of crimes is rare. . . . The police is observed with particular strictness within the walls. The city partakes of the regularity and interior safety of a camp; but is subject also to its constraints."[28] The segmented Beijing layout functioned as a protective architectural ensemble as well as an aesthetic one. The multitude of barriers impeded free movement and reflected the priorities of rulers who did not mind adding time to intra-capital trips for the sake of increased security.

The gendarmerie used a network of structures as landmarks of patrol. Street gates (*zhalan*), numbering more than a thousand in the Inner City, were movable railings or doors made of upright posts placed between the walls of houses on either side of a lane. The street gates were manned at night to shut lanes to everyone but their residents. Over seven hundred sentry boxes for police convenience were found in the Inner City, often located next to street gates. In the Outer City, the Five Battalions also maintained fixed routines of patrol on designated beats. The gendarmerie monitored comings and goings at all sixteen city gates, which usually closed soon after sundown with a ceremony that allowed time for stragglers to pass through. Night patrol was supposed to be so pervasive that wrongdoers would "hear the wind blowing and stay at home."[29] There were, indeed, few incentives to nocturnal activity; with light only from oil lamps and candles, Inner City residents went to bed at sunset. Like their emperor, they rose early, when in the words of the British Macartney mission's John Barrow, "from the moment the day begins to dawn, the buzz and the bustle of the populace is like that of a swarm of bees."[30]

At night, policemen on the beat made a distinctive noise by striking together two pieces of hollow bamboo or shaking a wooden rattle. Like peddlers, they used familiar sounds to make their presence known. The policeman's sounds were intended to reassure the householder, intimidate the petty criminal, and synchronize patrol across many streets and lanes. The night from sunset to sunrise was divided into five watches that varied in length with the time of the year. A series of strokes designating the number of the watch was sounded from the Bell and Drum towers in the northern Inner City. In response, all stations drummed the same number out to their patrolmen, who continuously repeated the current number with their rattles or bamboo rods. In 1793 this "dull hollow sound" kept Lord Macartney himself awake for several nights until he "became used to the noise and grew to mind it as little as the ringing of a church bell."[31]

Once darkness fell, a person of any rank needed a good excuse to be out on the street. Night curfews were suspended, however, to allow celebration of the first fifteen days of the first lunar month (the new year holiday) and the spring festival season.[32] At other times, legitimate reasons for passing street gates at night were limited to urgent tasks, such as running errands for the emperor or seeking a midwife or other help in an emergency. Residents who needed permission to be out after curfew could recognize policemen by their distinctive dress and trappings, which could include bamboo rattles and rods, swords, daggers in the belt, whips, and a long hooked pole used to catch thieves around the neck. Lists of gate equipment included light guns, but the evidence does not show how many actually were stored there. Just as the populace knew that the city walls and granaries represented the government, everyone recognized the police and understood their implied coercive powers. As Susan Naquin suggests, the "lack of large-scale violence in Beijing was primarily the combined result of state willingness to keep the locals happy and the ever-present threat of overwhelming force."[33] Low grain prices kept the locals happy, and the large gendarmerie, backed up by banner and other forces in the city and region, conveyed the threat of overwhelming force. Given widespread understanding of this threat, the gendarmerie usually could keep order merely by being in a place or by peaceful mediation. The presence of government that they embodied was marked by a "watchman style" rather than one calling for frequent or overt assertions of authority.[34] As a French missionary astutely observed in the eighteenth century: "Princes and mandarins, citizens and foreigners, soldiers and courtiers, bonzes and lamas, are all subject to their rule, and they keep everyone on the path of order and duty without arrests, and without harsh actions, [seeming] hardly to touch them."[35]

Temples and Fairs

As soon as the banner population had settled in the Inner City, bannermen and their families began to participate in local Chinese society. At the elite level, they took up the literati culture that centered on gardens, poetry, and gatherings of friends in scenic surroundings. In all strata of banner society, they showed a strong interest in the religious life of Beijing, elements of which had been known to them long before they entered China; some of their ancestors had patronized Buddhism in Jin Zhongdu.

Different terms that were used to designate temple buildings tell something about the god(s) enshrined there, the resident priests or monks, or the buildings that housed them. Often there was more than one god in a temple to whom people made offerings and prayers. The term *guan* or *gong* usually designated temples with deities of Daoist origin; *si* or *yuan* suggested Buddhist ones, but *si* also could be used for a mosque. *Miao* designated temples for popular gods not closely tied to either Buddhism or Daoism. Popular religion freely mixed Daoist and Buddhist deities with nature spirits and historical persons. The word *tang* denoted a room where rituals could be performed, and it was this word that Christian missionaries adopted for their churches.

Temples still standing today in and near the former Qing Inner City include Baitasi (White Dagoba Temple—see Color Plate 10), Guangjisi (Universal Rescue Temple), Dazhongsi (Great Bell Temple), and Fayuansi (Source of Law Temple)—all Buddhist establishments. The Yonghegong ("Lama Temple") and Huangsi (Yellow Temple) practice the Tibetan form of Buddhism. The name "Yonghegong" literally refers to the Yonghe Palace, an imperial residence that became a lamasery in the 1740s. (The word *gong* can mean either "temple" or "palace," depending on context.)

Still standing too are the Baiyunguan (White Cloud Temple), a Daoist center for all north China; the Dongyuemiao (Temple of the God of the Eastern Peak), dedicated to a popular north China mountain deity loosely associated with Daoism; Dongsi Qingzhen si and Niujie Libaisi (Dongsi Mosque and Niujie [Ox Street] Mosque); and Nantang and Beitang (North and South cathedrals), Roman Catholic churches. The number of temples grew steadily from early Ming times onward; more than twenty-five hundred temples can be documented in the entire city, including its suburbs, at some time between 1400 and 1900, and this figure is a conservative estimate.[36]

Integration of banner people with the older Beijing population in religious activities helped to mend the social fabric that had been torn by the conquest. An early example is Hong Chengchou, the Ming general who had joined the Qing side and the Chinese bordered yellow banner in 1642. He continued in high office after the conquest and marshaled resources for the campaign against the Ming in the south. In 1651 he was the highest-ranking of more than six hundred people, all or nearly all Chinese bannermen, who contributed to restoration of a Ming temple, the Guandimiao, located along the north wall of the Inner City. The temple's main deity was Guandi, a historical figure of ancient times associated with martial valor and protection against disaster; a new side-hall added at this time honored the Medicine-king, a popular god to whom people prayed for protection against smallpox. Chinese bannermen led the way in this kind of community involvement, and other banner people quickly followed.[37]

Imperial, banner, and nonbanner patronage flowed to hundreds of temples (mostly Buddhist, but some of Daoist and other origins) in the Inner City and to not a few in the Outer City as well. As we have seen, temples and their resident monks and priests had *not* been obliged to leave the Inner City with the Han Chinese population in the 1640s. Supported by believers high and low, temples provided sites for many constructive social purposes. They were places where many came for spiritual refreshment and some planned religious pilgrimages to sacred mountains in the Beijing region. Judging by the number of temples, the three most popular Beijing gods were Guandi, Guanyin (the Buddhist goddess of mercy and compassion), and Bixia Yuanjun (daughter of Dongyue, the God of the Eastern Peak). The father and daughter were both regional north China deities with a cult centered in Shandong. Dongyue was a powerful male judge with authority over life and death, Bixia a ruler with female attendants, gracious and benevolent.[38]

Outer City temples received much less patronage from the throne than did Inner City ones, but officials, bannermen, and temporary residents took up the slack. In addition to giving expression to their religious commitment, acts of generosity helped donors to establish themselves socially. By the nineteenth century, 213 or more temples were found throughout the Outer City. (At about the same time, an 1851 census showed 866 temples in the Inner City.) In the Outer City as in the Inner City, the full range of popular deities was represented, especially Guandi, Guanyin, Bixia Yuanjun, Dongyue, the Medicine-king, the Fire God, and the Stove God. The first five already have been discussed. The Fire God (huoshen) protected against fires and the Stove God (caojun) of each family was believed to make a report to Heaven at the new year. Sweet foods were given to him so that he would say sweet things, or perhaps so that his mouth would be sticky and he would be unable to speak.[39] Interestingly, people conceived the Stove-god as a bureaucrat who had to submit annual reports but who was not so inflexible or humorless as to reject a small, good-natured bribe or to resent a playful trick.

As in the Ming era, the generosity of donors from the emperor down to the ordinary believer helped to sustain temples that otherwise might have disappeared. Imperial patronage of temples was another way, in addition to low grain prices, of "keeping the locals happy." Although Qing-era women played a somewhat smaller role in philanthropy than they had in the Ming, there was much to interest women in the city's varied religious observances. Two of the three most popular gods (Guanyin and Bixia) were female; merciful and compassionate, they were believed to assist in conception and childbirth. The lesser role of eunuchs as temple patrons in the Qing compared to the Ming era reflected their more limited scope under the new dynasty. But as in all periods eunuchs in the Qing had the complex fate of seeking spiritual peace in a society whose oldest and deepest religious concern was ancestral rites. Knowing that they would have no descendants, eunuchs were strongly interested in Buddhist ideas that spoke to every mortal regardless of family status. These ideas included compassion for all living things and the accumulation of moral merit through good deeds, leading at death to endless rebirths in a Pure Land. Similarly, Daoism's view of life as emerging from and ultimately returning to the Dao, the Way of Nature, transcended the family context.

Temples typically were open daily to all for devotion, and each temple also had a calendar of fairs. During the Qing, however, commercial activities in both Inner and Outer cities increasingly occurred at secular as well as temple markets.[40] For example, by 1713 the Tudimiao (Earth God Shrine) outside the Xuanwu Gate in the western Outer City held a fair on the "threes" (dates ending in three) of each month. On the eastern side of the Outer City, there was a similarly regular secular market at Huashikou (Flower Market Intersection). Constantly repeated, calendar patterns for temple and secular fairs were easily remembered. People enjoyed the opportunity to socialize, to attend theater performances, and to buy appealing foods from vendors. Many customary observances provided occasions for regular temple happenings that attracted men and women, adults and children. The Birthday of the Queen Mother of the West at the Daoist Pantaogong, in the northeast corner of the Outer City, was the occasion of a major festival and fair lasting three days at the beginning of the third lunar month.

The rulers tried to reduce the number of events capable of drawing large crowds in the Inner City by moving some of them to the Outer City. During the Qing era, the Lantern Festival, formerly held in the Inner City to the east of the Forbidden City, relocated to several commercial intersections in the Outer City. A thrice-monthly fair formerly at the Inner City temple of the City God moved to the Baoguo Temple (Baoguosi) in the western Outer City. Similarly motivated efforts to move whole categories of institutions to the Outer City affected inns, native-place lodges, theaters, and even teahouses.

An annual, secular new year fair at Liulichang (on the site of an earlier Glazed Tile Factory) in the Outer City reached its peak in the last quarter of the eighteenth century. Readers, collectors, and lovers of music and art gathered from the first to the sixteenth of the lunar new year on streets crowded with cultural goods. They purchased jade and ivory carvings, books, paintings, and antiques of all kinds. When a Qing-era official who lived in the Xuannan area south of the Xuanwu Gate attained high status, his old friends remarked that they only could catch a glimpse of him at the annual fair at Liulichang. The fair's reputation attracted elite persons from all over the city as well as members of tribute missions from distant countries that paid their respects to the court at the new year and stayed afterward to trade.[41] (See Figure 23.)

At the largest fairs, crowds would spill out from temple courtyards to the space in front of the temple and onto adjoining streets, while vendors went from the streets into the temples. The gendarmerie took particular note of such occasions because of the great size of the gatherings. For the same reason, new year fairs in and near the Inner City at the Yonghegong—devoted to exorcism by means of ritual drama—and at the Daoist Baiyunguan regularly drew police attention.[42] The spillover of crowds from temples to streets and the watchfulness of the gendarmerie suggest the key role of temples in the life of the entire city, providing not only spiritual teaching but also countless occasions conducive to the integration and flourishing of urban society. It was perhaps at temples more than anywhere else that the Han Chinese population recovered from the trauma of the conquest, and the bannermen, over nine generations and 267 years, became "Beijingren," natives of Beijing.

Native-Place Lodges, Craft Enterprises, and Theaters

Some institutions of high Qing Beijing could be found at various times in both Inner and Outer cities, but they were especially characteristic of the Outer City and particularly numerous there. In many cases, their location was the result of state policy.

The native-place lodge (*huiguan*) appears to have been invented in the Ming era. According to one account, an early fifteenth-century official, on leaving the capital for the last time, turned over his house for use as a lodge.[43] The *huiguan* was an inn and social club where male natives of the same province or area—metropolitan and provincial officials, degree-holders awaiting appointment, civil service examination candidates, successful merchants—stayed while visiting the capital. Other Chinese cities also had *huiguan*, but the institution had appeared first in Beijing and beginning in the Ming many more lodges were found there than anywhere else. The larger number in Beijing resulted from its status as the capital; the *huiguan* was a place that facilitated the activity of officials and merchants at the political center of the empire. Of seventy *huiguan* in Ming times, only thirteen had been in the Northern City, with the rest in the Southern. Qing regulation soon placed all of them in the Outer City. By the end of the eighteenth century there were almost two hundred lodges; by the later nineteenth century, twice that number.[44] The Chinese empire was comparable in size to all of Europe; a single province, such as Sichuan, was as large as Germany, and a major dialect such as Cantonese (as different from Mandarin as Spanish is from Italian) had millions of native speakers. The cosmopolitanism of the capital resulted in part from the strong attraction that it exerted on the scholars, officials, and merchants of China's own diverse regions. They traveled to Beijing for both business and pleasure, and the *huiguan* met their needs during their stay.

Often connected with a temple, a *huiguan* commonly included both a lodge and a place for religious rituals. Many also had banquet halls, opera stages, gardens, libraries, and study rooms for examination candidates. The *huiguan* offered a common space to those from the same area, but in the Qing era more than in the Ming, lodges distinguished between officials and merchants; most focused on one group or the other, with more catering to officials. For its patrons, the *huiguan* was a "home away from home." Its dialect and perhaps some of its food were familiar. Networking could be beneficial, whether conversation focused on politics, money, or examinations. The *zhangban*, a kind of *huiguan* servant, specialized in familiarizing men from the provinces with current intrigues in the official world, giving advice, and delivering confidential messages in high places. Some of those who frequented the *huiguan* were not visitors at all, but long-term Beijing residents with roots in the region concerned; they were well placed to give valuable advice to new arrivals. Thus the *huiguan* provided all its members with a practical base of operations in a crowded and heterogeneous city.[45] The *huiguan* also was useful to the state: in the native-place lodge as in the temple, travelers obtained a suitable place to stay, and the authorities acquired an institutional lever that they could use to find a visitor should that be necessary.

Also characteristic of the Outer City was a kind of proto-industrial production that needed more space to spread out than was usually available in the Inner City. Qing-era Beijing contained many enterprises larger than a family business that were dedicated to craft manufacture or to cultivation and enhancement of natural products. The Russian envoy Kovalevsky provided glimpses of several of them in describing his stay in the city in 1849 and 1850. For example, Kovalevsky visited a district outside the Chongwen Gate in the Outer City where most of the residents, including women and children, made colorful paper flowers that Manchu and some Chinese women liked to wear in their hair. Near the Dongbian Gate of the Outer City, more than six hundred shops produced different parts of these flowers—some specialized in petals, leaves, or stems, and some in particular blossoms. Young workers learned the art from master craftsmen, who often came from the imperial court. The flowers produced in this district not only supplied palace and capital ladies but were shipped all over China.[46] Today the custom of wearing paper flowers in the hair survives mainly in the countryside.

Liulichang was not only a new year fair but also a year-round symbol of the vitality of Chinese publishing. The thirteen print shops of Ming Beijing had become over a hundred by Qing times.[47] Kovalevsky described shopping for books at Liulichang after a brief walk from the Russian hostel near the Inner City wall:

> The first place to visit and the favorite spot for the walks of our mission members was usually Liulichang; this long street in the Chinese city is almost exclusively occupied by bookshops. Here every bookseller knows the Russians, who enrich our large libraries . . . and acquire for themselves books related to their work. The Russian here is a welcome guest; they seat him, give him something to eat, tell him the news of the city, and offer all the new things printed in the area of sciences and arts. The back rows of the shops are usually crowded with novels, and . . . they are bought here in a huge, amazing number of copies. Few new novels come out; the greatest fame is enjoyed by the old novels, which are reprinted in hundreds of editions and sold at an extraordinarily cheap price compared with the price of books in Europe.[48]

Liulichang was in the Xuannan area south of the Xuanwu Gate, where a literati cultural focus had developed in the Qing era. Beijing's roles as summit of officialdom and site of the highest civil service examinations—plus its importance as a center of scholarship patronized by the throne—made it appealing to the well educated. But the link between scholarship and official life could be problematic, as when the Qianlong emperor used the Four Treasuries (*Siku quanshu*) project of text collection to destroy works that he thought seditious. Literati who clustered in the capital benefited from associating with each other and from lively institutions that served them all, such as the bookstores, native-place lodges, teahouses, and restaurants of Xuannan.[49] By coming together, however, they made themselves more vulnerable to official censorship and control, a dynamic that would outlive the empire.

Greenhouses near the southwestern Outer City wall also attracted the Russians:

> In Beijing every customer is a welcome guest and one is not permitted to leave a good shop without having drunk tea, but in the greenhouses they knew us well, and here they did not ask what we needed to buy, but met us with refreshment, even adjusted to the Russian taste; they gave us not yellow tea, as is the usual custom, but flower tea, always with sugar candy and sometimes with sugar,

which they probably bought from our own servants, since in Beijing it is very difficult to get sugar. The Chinese value it as a medicine for disease of the eyes.

The local gardeners bring their plants to maturity so that they flower for the New Year, because then it is usual to send plants in bloom as gifts and place them in one's rooms, and in February the greenhouses present a beautiful sight. There are very many greenhouses. . . . Chinese gardeners graft the most delicate plants and thus vary the flowers without end and give them a remarkable large size.[50]

Peonies were a new year favorite, and Kovalevsky remarked that he had never seen so many varieties. A Manchu writer around 1900 listed 133 poetically named varieties of the chrysanthemum, a plant valued because it could withstand the fall chill.[51]

Another craft based on natural products that developed extensively during the Qing era was herbal medicine. Famous medicine stores such as Tongrentang, Wanquantang, and Heniantang used secret recipes to develop pills, powders, creams, and ointments with poetic names. Herbal medicines treated colds, sore throats, and other ailments. Many stores had specialties: Shijingzai was famous for its eye medicine, Yuyuantang for its ginseng and creams to treat ulcers. Employees would manufacture medicine at the back of the shop, using ingredients from all parts of China, and sell the finished product at the front. Owners allowed investors to hold stock in their enterprises, and some even had employee shareholders, with a single store employing fifteen to twenty people. The owner, however, would not tell even his loyal employees and shareholders the secret recipe; instead he would wait and pass it on to his chosen successor, usually a son or son-in-law, just before his death.[52] Some medicine stores such as Tongrentang have operated continuously for hundreds of years, keeping drugs in Ming jars bought when they first opened, managing to keep their trade secrets even when taken over by the state in the mid-twentieth century. Some still exist; others have disappeared, along with their secrets.

The Russian envoy also enjoyed attending the theater and watching as avid audiences, at every word and gesture of the best actors, cried out *hao!* (Well done! Excellent!). Although, like the novel, theater had traditionally been considered a form of frivolity rather than serious art, its appeal was great. By the mid-nineteenth century, when Kovalevsky lived in Beijing, there were almost one hundred different troupes in the city, and the nine major ones each had more than a hundred actors. Because women had been excluded from the stage during the eighteenth century, female impersonation became a specialty. From the competition among capital theater troupes there emerged, beginning in the late eighteenth century, the dramatic form later known as Beijing opera (*jingju*), which in Qing times was performed in the Forbidden City itself.

In the Qing era both Inner and Outer cities had numerous restaurants (*zashuaguan*) that included plays and storytelling in the experience offered to customers.[53] Around 1800 in the Outer City there were ten "theater-mansions" (*xizhuang*) that could be rented for parties and theatrical entertainment. Twenty-one Outer City theaters (*xiyuan*), where only tea and snacks were served, were open for programs that lasted all day and into the evening, with breaks for meals. Women did not attend public theaters but could watch performances from the balcony at elite theater-restaurants. Most of those who did so were wives and daughters of Manchu officials, "in full, expensive gowns and headdresses ... with black fiery eyes and a remarkable whiteness of face." Restaurant proprietors would note the women's presence in printed announcements that restricted the balcony to females. The men below betrayed poor manners if they even looked at the women, as Kovalevsky learned from his Chinese host after making that mistake. Women no less than men were devoted to their favorite actors, and Kovalevsky had noticed that during the performance, there was "much more movement, play, and passion in their faces than in those of the men."[54]

Government fears about theater had some basis; without question, the Outer City was a place where officials and common people intermingled. Its way of life cut against the age-old demand that high-status persons, responsible for setting a moral example, avoid rough-and-tumble popular gatherings. Moreover, the Outer City entertainment zone passed by degrees from restaurants, teahouses, and theaters to houses of prostitution, which themselves had many levels. For these reasons, the state reacted negatively to the growing popularity of theaters, especially among Manchus and other bannermen. Imperial edicts prohibited officials from attending plays in the Outer City, although they were permitted to attend performances at the theater restaurants. This rule prompted those who still frequented theaters to wear nonofficial clothing and to remove the hat buttons that showed their rank.[55] When, in 1774, there were nine theaters in the Inner City, the government decreed that no more would be established.[56] In the early nineteenth century, the state also moved against teahouses in the Inner City after plays there criticized officials. At this time the government went so far as to limit the building of new theaters even in the Outer City.[57]

Outer City urban entertainment in the Qing era was comparable to that of cities such as Edo and Osaka in Tokugawa Japan, where similar tensions arose over the uncontrolled association of persons of differing social status (in Japan, samurai warriors and "townsmen") and gender (struggles over women on the stage and in theater audiences). Significantly, both Beijing and Edo—the two largest cities in the world in population around 1800—confined popular entertainment to specific neighborhoods as a way of controlling it. In both cases these constraints were only partly successful. In Beijing even high officials who complied with the prohibition on visiting theaters would invite troupes of actors to their homes to entertain at banquets. On these occasions, listening to musical and theatrical performances, consuming wine and excellent food, presenting gifts, and partying by well-dressed guests and hosts lasted from morning to late afternoon.[58]

Patterns in Daily Life

With its distinct areas marked by variety and both internal and external competition—as of temples, fairs, and shops—the capital's segmented layout was itself a factor in creating the "accommodative strength" of a great city.[59] The Imperial City protected the Forbidden City by separating it from direct contact with the Inner City. The Outer City relieved pressure on the Inner City by providing extensive opportunities for temporary visits, commerce, craft production, and many forms of entertainment. The relative freedom of the Outer City helped to make the tight control of the Inner City possible; it was in the Outer City that tensions caused by the stricter rules of the Inner City could be dispelled.

Banner and nonbanner officials went to the Outer City to enjoy themselves, even though they were not supposed to do so. If they had an early morning imperial audience the next day, they could slip back into the Inner City in the predawn hours through the Qianmen, which reopened briefly for exactly that purpose. Rule enforcement at the gate, like the Stove God's annual report, took human imperfection into account. Similarly, the life of the Outer City was responsive to the wishes as well as the needs of the population. In addition to temples, which also existed in large numbers in the Inner City, the Outer City contained a wide range of commercial enterprises and of goods and pleasures for sale. Some entertainment was free or nearly so; temples and fairs charged no admission, and troupes of actors performed in many social settings besides theaters.

Society in both the Inner and Outer cities included institutions *between* the family and the state: temples, businesses of various sizes, guilds, native-place lodges, and theater troupes. Looking ahead from about 1800, we can see why the role of many of these institutions would grow in the later Qing period. In the nineteenth century, compared to the eighteenth, the Chinese state had too little money to deal with many of its traditional responsibilities. The government would seek to share famine relief or firefighting with groups that had financial resources, such as trade guilds. Moreover, weakening of the Qing state would occur in the context of extraordinary outside challenges to Chinese civilization itself. Urban social institutions such as native-place lodges were equipped to share in the search for politically effective responses, whether the state welcomed their participation or not.

Most people in the Qing capital between 1662 and 1800 found themselves in an ordered and humane setting that permitted spontaneous social life so long as it was not seditious. In the eighteenth century, their world was relatively prosperous and secure, as the 1713 and 1790 birthday scrolls, however idealized, show. In retrospect, it is clear that these favorable conditions began to weaken from about 1800, but high Qing Beijing had flourished to such an extent that even the afterglow lasted for a long time. Kovalevsky's anecdotes of bookstores and pharmacies, greenhouses and craft industry, theaters and restaurants suggest the continuing strength of deeply rooted enterprises and cultural habits well into the nineteenth century. But as that century progressed, industrialization and urbanization gathered momentum in Europe, America, and Japan while the Qing dynasty entered a decline that made it incapable of rapid adaptation. In this new context, Beijing would begin to stand out in world terms not so much for its size, diversity, and organization as for its unique and traditional way of life.

Chapter 4

The City Besieged
and the Last Emperors

THE NINETEENTH CENTURY WAS A TUMULTUOUS PERIOD FOR CHINA, for the Qing dynasty, and for Beijing. The process of dynastic decline—familiar in the historical pattern of successive Chinese dynasties—was compounded by historically unprecedented attacks on China's sovereignty and territory by Western powers. Unable to withstand both external and internal pressures for change, the Qing dynasty collapsed in 1911, and was replaced not by another dynasty but by a revolutionary and republican form of government.

In the Chinese concept of the dynastic cycle, the inevitable waning of a ruling family's power was linked to the declining morality and abilities of its succeeding generations. Inattention to wise and benevolent government would lead to popular uprisings, and the fall of the dynasty would be foreshadowed by floods, droughts, or earthquakes. The experience of the Qing dynasty followed this pattern in practically all respects. From the 1790s until the 1911 revolution, the deterioration of personal abilities of the emperors was abundantly evident. The end of Qianlong's reign was marked by corruption and scandal, and was epitomized by the emperor's own self-indulgent behavior and declining judgment. By granting extraordinary power to Heshen, his much-favored imperial bodyguard, he allowed not only the court but the entire bureaucracy to be corrupted. Qianlong abdicated in 1796, so that his reign would not exceed that of his grandfather, the Kangxi emperor. His son and successor, the Jiaqing emperor, ruled diligently from 1796 to 1820 but was unable to reverse the trends of financial weakness and bureaucratic incompetence. Daoguang, who reigned from 1821 to 1850, inherited these problems and was additionally beset by the Opium War (1839–1842) and Western demands for open ports, trade privileges, and diplomatic relations.

The succeeding emperors of the late nineteenth century literally embodied "dynastic decline." The Xianfeng emperor (reigned 1851–1861), a weak and sickly young man, was totally unable to cope with malicious forces at court, let alone the critical challenges faced by the empire. His death in 1861 at the age of thirty allowed empresses and imperial clansmen to gain power. The last three reigns—Tongzhi (1862–1874), Guangxu (1875–1908), and Xuantong (1909–1911)—were those of child-emperors, largely the creation, as well as the victims, of the empress dowager Cixi, who became the dominant imperial figure from 1861 to her death in 1908. The Tongzhi emperor, her son and Xianfeng's only heir, ascended the throne at age five and died at nineteen. The empress dowager then arranged that her nephew would be the next emperor, a shocking act because it violated the principle of generational succession in order to keep power in her hands. The Guangxu emperor, not yet four years old when he took the throne, died at thirty-seven under suspicious circumstances. The "Last Emperor," the Xuantong emperor (Puyi), Guangxu's nephew and Cixi's grandnephew, was three years old when he ascended the throne; his reign lasted only three years before the dynasty collapsed.

Rebellions, also a sign of dynastic decline, were widespread in the mid-nineteenth century. The largest, the Taiping Rebellion, was eventually defeated by specially recruited regional armies but not without first causing great devastation over wide areas of south and central China and threatening the capital area. At the same time, a growing threat from the West presented itself. China's military defeat in the Opium War led to treaties that opened Chinese ports to trade with the West, allowed residence at certain ports, and gave other privileges to the foreign powers. Trade and residence in turn created other demands and pressures that Great Britain, France, the United States, and other nations continued to exert on the Qing court. Emperors and statesmen succeeded in suppressing the midcentury rebellions, but they were far less successful in dealing with the foreign threat. Although they took some steps toward reform, it was unfortunate for China that the weakest emperors and a generally moribund bureaucracy faced the greatest problems that the dynasty had ever confronted.

Although the first Opium War, which was waged mostly along the southeastern coast, did not directly affect Beijing, the major political and military crises from 1860 until 1911 took place at the capital or nearby. Not only the crises themselves, but the weaknesses of the court's response to them, were known all over China. Whereas previously the emperors had been distant figures who affected few directly, the international crises drew attention to the court and bureaucracy in a way that was unprecedented and nearly always unfavorable. Meanwhile, the emergence of newspapers and popular opinion fostered a growing sense of nationalism. News from the capital no longer took months to reach the south, and newspapers and telegraph permitted an intimacy with daily events that highlighted the external threats while exposing the incompetence and mistakes of the rulers. Beijing became a national political stage upon which the drama of late nineteenth-century China unfolded.

Beijing in the Nineteenth Century

The appearance of the capital from a distance in the nineteenth century was not markedly different from what it had been in earlier times. For Western travelers arriving from Tianjin by water or land, Chinese arriving from the south via the Grand Canal, or Mongols and Russians arriving by camel from the north, the most striking things about Beijing were its massive walls and gates and its many temples and monuments. To all visitors, Beijing was a subject of intense interest and curiosity. John Barrow, a member of the British Macartney mission, recalled that when approaching the capital for the first time in August 1793, they could scarcely contain their excitement at the prospect of entering "the greatest city on the surface of the globe."[1] He was impressed by the density of population in the eastern Inner City and the liveliness of the street scene:

> [He saw different processions] that were accompanying, with lamentable cries, corpses to their graves, and, with squealing music, brides to their husbands, the troops of dromedaries laden with coals from Tartary, the wheel-barrows and hand-carts stuffed with vegetables. . . . All was in motion. The sides of the street were filled with an immense concourse of people, buying and selling and bartering their different commodities. The buzz and confused noises of this mixed multitude, [proceeded] from the loud bawling of those who were crying their wares. . . . Pedlars with their packs, and jugglers, fortune-tellers, mountebanks and quack-doctors, comedians and musicians, left no space unoccupied.[2]

Eighteenth- and nineteenth-century travelers considered Beijing's natural surroundings quite pleasant; in summer and fall, the city seemed park-like. The view from the Western Hills toward the city was of a sea of green, interrupted only by a few yellow-tiled rooftops peeking out from the foliage. Looking west from the Imperial City during his 1849–1850 stay, the Russian envoy Kovalevsky enjoyed the "remarkable view, bright, shining, enchanting. . . . Before us rose the massive indented walls, surrounding a series of palaces" under the "wonderful sky, clear, blue, transparent . . . and the clear aromatic air."[3] Earlier, on first entering the capital through the northeastern Anding Gate, he had found that in Beijing "patterned roofs strike the eye—roofs of gates, houses, temples, everything that has a roof."[4] To the east of the city, the terrain looked barren in winter, and proceeding toward Tianjin, most villages were elevated above the countryside to guard against flooding, but in summer, this area too was profusely green. Robert Fortune, a British botanist who passed through the region in September 1861, remarked on its natural abundance: "Large quantities of Indian corn, buckwheat, sweet potatoes, and soy-beans were here under cultivation. The gigantic egg-apples [eggplants] were very luxuriant . . . and the oily grain [rape] grew to a height of five feet and seemed very productive."[5]

Mid-nineteenth-century visitors were more objective and critical than those of the late eighteenth century had been. To Fortune, the most striking difference between Beijing and other Chinese cities was the breadth and regularity of its major streets, but he deplored their current state:

> The streets of the capital differ much from those of other towns in China which I have visited. They are very wide, straight, and generally run at right angles with each other, so that the stranger has little difficulty in finding his way from one point to another; but they are, for most part, in wretched condition. When the weather is wet they are full of puddles and almost impassable, and when it is dry and windy the dust is blinding and intolerable.[6]

Like Barrow almost seventy years earlier, he was struck by the crowding and cacophony, in this case at the Qianmen, the central gate between the Inner and Outer cities. But some details that caught his attention give the later account a darker tone:

> Inside and outside of this gate, I observed carts in great numbers waiting to be hired, just as we see the cabs in London. Like them, the carts of [Beijing] have their stands in the public thoroughfare. The noise and bustle about this gate was perfectly deafening. Carts were going to and fro, rumbling along the rough stone road, and now and then sinking deeply into the broken pavement. Donkeys, horses, and long trains of camels laden with the productions of the country, were toiling along; a perfect Babel of noisy tongues was heard in all directions; and the dust was flying in clouds and literally filling the air. Stalls of fruit, hawkers of

all kinds of wares, beggars ragged, filthy, and in many instances apparently insane, crowded the approaches to this gate.[7]

Fortune remarked on the variety of consumer and luxury goods available for sale, but he saw no silk or tea for export as he had in the south. He observed that everything stamped Beijing "as a consuming city rather than a producing one." He noticed plenty of food for sale, with many varieties of fruits and vegetables.[8] David Rennie, a physician at the British Legation in the 1860s, also found an abundance of poultry, vegetables, and fish in the Outer City.[9] But when they stepped back from such immediate observations to view the larger scene, mid-nineteenth-century visitors often commented unfavorably on the appearance of the capital. Kovalevsky wrote of his visit to the Imperial City: "The gardens were in a state of neglect; all that nature could support and save from destruction by time was intact, but that for which hands and money were necessary was ruined, like everything existing in China." He contrasted the fresh air on Jingshan, the hill north of the Forbidden City, with the "stinking streets" of Beijing.[10] In 1867 British consular official Nicholas Dennys and his colleagues observed the "universal decay of all that was once beautiful or fine-looking in the way of architecture."[11]

During the nineteenth century, the number of Chinese visitors to the capital apparently increased. As in the past, examination candidates, numbering in the thousands, presented themselves two years out of every three. But now they included not only the candidates from the provinces competing for the highest-level degree, the *jinshi*, but a greater number of those sitting for the Shuntian prefectural examination for the second-highest degree, the *juren*. Unlike other prefectural examinations, the Shuntian examination was open to candidates from anywhere in the empire. It was especially attractive to those who had purchased a degree, a growing trend in the nineteenth century, and since the Shuntian competition awarded a larger number of degrees than elsewhere, an increasing number of candidates chose to go to Beijing to take their exams. During the Qing period, the numbers grew from two thousand to ten thousand, reaching fourteen thousand by the end of the dynasty.[12]

The rapid addition of examination candidates may have been one reason for the increasing number of native-place lodges (*huiguan*) in Beijing in the nineteenth century. There were about 181 *huiguan* in 1788, 329 in 1864, and 395 in 1886 (and 510 in 1929).[13] Beijing was unusual in that its *huiguan* supposedly were primarily for the use of scholar-officials; in other Chinese cities, they served mainly the needs of traveling merchants. But the distinction was not sharply drawn. True, only about 14 percent of Beijing *huiguan* considered themselves primarily for merchants. Yet in the nineteenth century there were more provincial merchants going to Beijing on business than there had been before, and they required lodging. The greater number of *huiguan* also may have reflected the growing desire of localities to have a base in the capital to represent their interests. *Huiguan* continued to exist after 1911, when the traditional scholar-official class no longer existed. All these factors suggest that the functions of the lodges may have shifted gradually to serving everyone in Beijing from a given native-place. They were social centers as well as lodges.[14]

Travel guides were not new—they had their origins in the Ming period—but nineteenth-century guidebooks were oriented toward merchants and had a larger circulation.[15] They always contained an introduction to famous capital sights and descriptions of local customs, foods, dress, holidays, temples, and theaters. They supplied locations of traditional markets for everyday food purchases, but also for luxury goods such as silver, jewelry, and furs. They also identified shops for hats, shoes, embroidered goods, scissors and knives, leather, and factory-woven cotton cloth (*yangbu*). If a visitor wanted to buy sweets and cakes, wines, teas, and other Beijing specialties, the guide told him where to find them.

The most popular guide, *Dumen jilue* [Short account of the capital], was first published in 1845 and went through at least twenty-three editions in the next sixty years. The 1875 edition had a section on "fashionable establishments" including shops for the printing of calling cards, charitable associations, and sellers of Western-style paintings.[16] There was a complete list of *huiguan* and their addresses, as well as of government offices. The guide presented Beijing as a place of many attractions, especially theaters, restaurants, and shops. Yet the tone also was practical and warned the first-time visitor of the difficulty of finding places, the danger of being cheated by local cart drivers and shopkeepers, and the threat of theft:

> Beijing is a flourishing city, its shops and their decorations are the richest in the empire. For example at Dashalar, the Pearl Market, Liulichang, there are jewelry shops . . . , tea shops, shoe stores, open day and night, and they can dazzle the eyes with their colors. The food stores are brightly lit and open day and night. . . . The capital is good at attracting outsiders to gather for feasting and drinking. [But] people from the countryside should take care not to get cheated, or to be tricked into nefarious activities.[17]

Despite the enduring fascination of the capital to outsiders, and the interest generated by new practices and products in the second half of the century, Beijing could no longer, in most respects, depend on the financial and other resources that had made it so formidable in the eighteenth century. While the city continued to be well guarded and managed, its residents, still about a million strong, were not protected from economic hardship and physical dangers. The dilapidated condition of many buildings and streets observed by travelers was only the outward manifestation of political decline and social deterioration.

The situation of the banner families, approximately two-thirds of the city's population, was increasingly difficult.[18] The adaptation of the Manchus to city life had been a Qing problem from the outset. Both the Kangxi and Yongzheng emperors had complained that Manchus were getting too accustomed to urban extravagances. Instead of adopting what the emperors saw as admirably frugal Chinese habits, such as a grain and vegetable diet, the Manchus preferred to eat meat. The Yongzheng emperor had been scornful of their new lifestyle: "They drink and eat until there is nothing left and the whole house is in want. At that point they want to eat something but there is no rice. They want to put something on, but there aren't any clothes. Cold and hunger press in from both sides, but still they boast without regret, 'I once ate fine food and wore beautiful clothing!'"[19]

The emperors also criticized the Manchu bannermen's love of the entertainment found in the Outer City, even though court patronage probably was most responsible for the popularity of "Beijing opera" (a later term) in the nineteenth century. Bannermen loved opera, sometimes to the point of fanaticism, and they even participated as writers or performers.[20] As historian Mark Elliott has observed, by the nineteenth century a "love of opera, more than a love of target practice, was a defining characteristic of Beijing's Manchus."[21] In their taste for opera the banner people followed in the footsteps of their ancestors, the Jin-era residents of Zhongdu who had loved theater so much.

But the fundamental economic problem of banner life was that banner stipends of grain and silver, awarded by rank and fixed at the time of the mid-seventeenth-century conquest, had never been adjusted to meet the realities of later times. As we have seen, the seemingly privileged bannermen were constrained by their status. Underemployed as soldiers, they needed special permission to seek other sources of income, and for more than a century after the conquest even that avenue was not open to them. The economic difficulties of bannermen had been recognized from early in the dynasty, and various measures had been taken to address their plight, but they did not alleviate the essential problem.[22] The eminent scholar Wei Yuan wrote, "Gathered at Beijing are a million who don't govern, who don't farm, who do not labor and do not engage in commerce, do not engage in warfare, but are not ordinary civilians either. Despite the exhaustion of all the empire's resources, there is not enough to support them."[23] In the nineteenth century stipends were often cut or unpaid, further aggravating a difficult situation. In 1865 an imperial decree allowed bannermen to leave the system to seek independent status and employment on their own, but even this explicit policy seemed to have little practical effect, particularly in Beijing, where the banners loomed large in city life.[24]

The bannermen were not the only poor people in Beijing. Beggars, widows and orphans, and other destitute persons were commonplace—although no more so than in many other nineteenth-century world cities. As floods and droughts became more frequent in the nineteenth century, Beijing was increasingly besieged by famine refugees seeking relief. During the huge flood of 1801, officials tried to stem the tide of refugees by trying to let them know that relief was available in local areas. The next spring, when the soup kitchens were extended for another month beyond their usual third lunar month closing, an imperial edict decreed that the kitchens all move their operations outside the city; the edict noted that it would be inconvenient for peasants to come to the city, as the agricultural season was getting busy and the roads would be crowded. The authorities were in fact trying to avoid the social instability that a large influx of refugees would create. In 1823–1824, however, when Beijing and the surrounding region were affected by a serious cholera epidemic followed by tremendous floods, significant quantities of grain were released for reduced-price sales at Beijing.[25]

Vagrancy and begging seemed common in the nineteenth-century capital; the gendarmerie was particularly concerned about "people of unknown background" or "floating population." The demand for famine relief was so great that sometimes people were crushed to death while waiting at soup kitchens, and the police were punished for failing to prevent it. The grave social and political problems that started in the Daoguang period (1821–1850) appear to have changed the emphasis in food security measures from reduced-price sales and gate restrictions, which emphasized price stabilization, to soup kitchens, which emphasized direct relief.[26] Local authorities maintained soup kitchens, normally at temples, but toward the end of the century, more private charitable efforts were seen.[27] In 1890, when floodwaters covered the areas adjacent to the capital and threatened the city itself, several gentry-led groups organized a major relief effort.

Decline in food security was part of a general deterioration in the ability to maintain public order. Starting in the 1820s, gendarmerie documents are full of complaints about policemen late for duty, failing to report crimes, protecting criminals, skipping patrol, and neglecting street repairs. Budget cuts for the gendarmerie in the 1840s and 1850s appear to have exacerbated these shortcomings. From the late 1840s, merchants and other local leaders formed neighborhood associations to undertake some tasks formerly performed by the police, especially in the Outer City. *Shuihui,* or "water associations," fought fires, but also caught thieves, distributed charity, and kept order. In 1861 Rennie saw "hanging out from almost every shop, a small triangular-shaped yellow flag with black letters on it. These, I find, are the insignia of a peace association, which undertakes to do the police of that particular street, expel all troublesome and disorderly characters, and by turns daily furnish members to supervise generally the conditions of the lanes connected with the street." The overburdened authorities encouraged these associations. In the 1880s militia supplemented police in the Outer City.[28] After the tumultuous events at the end of the nineteenth century, even more activities related to local order were undertaken by public organizations as well as government.

The City Besieged

In various ways, both welcome and unwelcome, Beijing in the nineteenth century was no longer the secure fortress that it had been in the previous century. It was periodically besieged by refugees, but at least from midcentury, it was more open to new people (wanted or not), to new products, and, later in the century, to new ideas than almost ever before. The greatest threat to Beijing's security, however, came from attacks by outside forces, first domestic rebels and then foreign powers.

The initial assault was a daring forced entry into the Forbidden City itself in 1813 by about three hundred rebels of the Eight Trigrams sect, a secret religious society with a network of rural believers in the counties surrounding Beijing. With the help of palace eunuchs who were converts to the sect, a few rebels entered the Forbidden City through the Donghua (East Flowery) Gate, and later about seventy or eighty entered through the Xihua (West Flowery) Gate. Once inside, however, they were trapped and had difficulty finding their way around the many pathways, palaces, and internal walls and gates. The Jiaqing emperor, the intended target of the attack, was away at Rehe, but his second son, Minning—the future Daoguang emperor—distinguished himself by using a musket to kill two rebels, and his cousin then shot at least one more. This was probably the last instance when a Qing emperor or future emperor distinguished himself by physical bravery. The skirmishes lasted only a day; the rebels were captured and executed. Their heads were displayed in the Outer City.[29] They had been poorly organized and rather naive in their expectations, yet the event revealed the vulnerability of the court, and it was the first of the major assaults on Beijing in the nineteenth century.

Four decades later a truly dangerous threat came from the Taiping rebels' attempt to attack the capital. The Taiping movement originated in south China; its leader, Hong Xiuquan, after contact with Christian missionaries in Canton (Guangzhou), had decided that he was the younger brother of Christ. He was following the age-old pattern in which antidynastic rebels associated themselves with popular religion, although the use of Christianity rather than Buddhism or Daoism for this purpose was new. By 1853 the Taiping army had swept up to the city of Nanjing on the Yangzi and established a capital there. One branch of the army proceeded northward with the purpose of taking Beijing and extending the Heavenly Kingdom all over China. These forces, originally about twenty thousand soldiers, crossed six provinces and by September had entered Zhili and were advancing toward the capital. The court ordered special preparations for the defense of the capital region, including uncovering and punishing spies, collaborators, and sympathizers within the city itself. Hundreds of cases that were prosecuted show that this was not a simple case of fighting an external enemy. The military defense of the region was assigned to the Manchu general Senggelinqin; his army eventually defeated the Taiping forces, which had been greatly weakened over the preceding months. It was not until March 1855, however, that the Taiping commanders were either captured or killed.[30] The Taiping Heavenly Kingdom at Nanjing was not defeated until 1864.

The Taiping events threw Beijing into a panic. Many high officials and rich families fled. By early 1854 an estimated thirty thousand families had left town. The fear of a Taiping takeover exacerbated existing serious economic dislocations in the city. The troop movements had hindered normal trade along inland routes. At about the same time, the Yellow River changed its course from south to north of the Shandong peninsula, disrupting grain transport along the Grand Canal. Grain prices in the region soared, reflecting both scarcity and panic. There was also a currency crisis in which the value of copper coin—used in daily transactions—became very high relative to the value of silver. The bimetallic monetary system depended on a stable relationship between the two metals; when copper coin became expensive, it pushed up the price of grain and other daily purchases. (The paper money of Marco Polo's time had been abandoned by about 1450, in the early Ming era.) Unable to do business, money shops in Beijing shut down, creating further havoc.[31] Although the Taiping threat was put down by the spring of 1854, its economic effects remained, and "big cash," debased coins issued by the government, continued to cause prices to rise high. The monetary crisis in Beijing in the 1850s had terrible consequences for the city's population, making daily life desperate. The authorities always had taken great care to maintain a stable exchange rate, which they considered just as important as maintaining stable grain prices. With both disruption in grain supply and unstable exchange rates, the normal food and economic security of Beijing's residents was shattered.[32] The situation became so critical that in 1857–1858, for the first time, the authorities extended food relief in a crisis that was not caused by natural disaster.[33]

Just a few years later, in 1860, Beijing suffered an actual invasion by British and French forces and the sacking of the Yuanmingyuan, the preferred residence of emperors when they were in Beijing. This brazen act was the culmination of pressure on China by Great Britain and France for extension of trade privileges and resident diplomatic representation at the Qing court. In 1793 the Macartney mission had failed to gain these objectives. When meeting Qianlong at Rehe, Macartney is said to have refused to follow Chinese court protocol and perform the kowtow, which would have been interpreted as a sign of England's submission to the Qing empire. Many have viewed the failure of this mission as a symbol of a clash of worldviews and as one of the events leading to the Opium War (1839–1842).[34] British victories in the Opium War forced the court to sign the Treaty of Nanjing, which opened five ports to trade, gave the uninhabited island of Hong Kong to the British for use as a base, and granted other privileges. From the British point of view, however, the treaty fell short on several counts, especially the right of the foreign powers to have resident ambassadors at the capital (i.e., to conduct diplomatic relations with China as equal sovereign states rather than as tributaries).

A series of conflicts over treaty revision, the status of the city of Canton, and gunboat skirmishes led to the so-called Second Opium War. In 1858 British forces under Lord Elgin (James Bruce, son of Thomas Bruce, the Elgin of "Elgin Marbles" fame), backed by the French, proceeded to north China, took the Dagu (Taku) forts, and arrived at the port of Tianjin, a mere 129 kilometers (80 miles) from Beijing. Under this direct threat of force, the emperor authorized two high-ranking officials to negotiate the Treaty of Tianjin, which gave the foreign powers practically everything they sought. The next year Elgin returned to China but resisted Chinese suggestions to sign the treaty anywhere except Beijing itself. To both sides, the Beijing locale would give the treaty-signing the greatest legitimacy and importance; this was why the court insisted on another location. (Earlier seventeenth- and eighteenth-century treaties with Russia had been signed in remote border towns, not in either capital.) Now the court required the British to proceed by land to the capital, following the route of tribute missions. Instead, the British tried to proceed up the North River toward Beijing, but they were attacked from the Dagu forts by Qing forces. Taken by surprise, the British lost four gunboats and 89 men, and sustained 434 casualties. They were forced to retreat, and the court abrogated the treaties. Meanwhile, the French decided to support the hard line of the British; the two planned a joint military expedition, and the next summer they returned with a much larger force. On August 25, 1860, they successfully attacked the Dagu forts and took the city of Tianjin. At this point talks resumed, and the Qing commissioners sent by the court agreed that treaty ratifications could take place in Beijing after all. But further complications developed, and Prince Yi, representing the court, ordered the arrest of Harry Parkes and others. Parkes was serving as an interpreter but had acquired a reputation for aggressive and reckless behavior as consul at Canton. His arrest rekindled hostilities, and the British forces continued to advance on Beijing. The Xianfeng emperor, Prince Yi and the court fled to Rehe (Chengde), leaving the emperor's younger brother, Prince Gong, in charge.[35]

On October 5, 1860, British forces reached Beijing and established their headquarters outside the northeastern Anding Gate. Two days later a French contingent reached the Yuanmingyuan, northwest of the city, and started to rampage and loot the buildings. On October 13 Prince Gong acceded to a British ultimatum to open the Anding Gate or allow the city to be besieged. But when the British learned of the losses from Parkes's entourage—nineteen dead and evidence of torture—they burned down the Yuanmingyuan as a "solemn act of retribution" on October 18 and 19.[36] Reflecting later on the options available to him, Elgin said he had chosen the Yuanmingyuan as the best because it was "the Emperor's favorite residence, and its destruction could not fail to be a blow to his pride as well as to his feelings."[37] Just days later, on October 24, the agreement—sometimes called the Treaty of Beijing—was signed, ratifying the Treaty of Tianjin and providing reparations for British losses.

The almost total destruction of Yuanmingyuan was not only a challenge to China's sovereignty and authority but also a symbolic act of violence against the emperor himself. Although foreigners usually called Yuanmingyuan the Summer Palace, this large villa had become the main residence of the Yongzheng, Qianlong, Jiaqing, Daoguang, and Xianfeng emperors. They much preferred the openness of its beautiful gardens and palaces to more confined and formal quarters in the Forbidden City. After spending about three winter months in the latter palace, the emperor and court would move to Yuanmingyuan, returning only for the most formal events; they conducted routine business at Yuanmingyuan. Only in the summer would the court retreat to Rehe, over 300 kilometers (two hundred miles) away and in the mountains, to avoid the heat of Beijing.[38] Like his ancestors, the Xianfeng emperor was attached to Yuanmingyuan, and he was devastated by news of the conflagration there, exactly as Elgin had intended.

The plunder that preceded and followed the burning of the palaces was perhaps even more shocking than the destruction of the buildings themselves. The British said that the first round of looting was the work of French "plunder and wanton destruction." Soon, however, the British were doing more than their share. They ransacked each building, appropriating the contents of all the private quarters and public rooms. Incredible amounts of gold, furs, robes, silks, jades, porcelains, statues, as well as Western clocks and ornaments—some gifts of the Macartney mission or from European contacts of earlier eras—were taken, with some destroyed or damaged in the melee. The burning of the palace two weeks later was accompanied by feelings of triumph, greed, and also awe.[39] Captain Charles Gordon—later to be famous as the leader of the Ever-Victorious Army against the Taiping rebels and still later as "Gordon of Khartoum"— wrote home to his mother and sister that after receiving orders to burn the palace:

> We accordingly went out, and after pillaging it, burned the whole place, destroying in a Vandal-like manner most valuable property, which would not be replaced for four millions. . . . You can scarcely imagine the beauty and magnificence of the places we burnt. It made one's heart sore to burn them; in fact these palaces were so large, and we were so pressed for time, that we could not plunder them carefully. Quantities of gold ornaments were burnt, considered as brass. It was wretchedly demoralizing work for an army. Everybody was wild for plunder.[40]

As soon as these events occurred, conflicting accusations flew: the British saw the French as the initiators of the looting, while the French pointed out that they did not participate in the burning of the palaces. The British had devised their own method for dealing with the spoils of war: they allowed soldiers to do some looting but required them to turn over the goods to a common pool for later auction. The proceeds were then divided among soldiers and officers according to rank. Thus much of the loot reached a public market; items were not necessarily taken home by the individual who had seized them. Many valuable imperial objects ended up in European collections, such as the Victoria and Albert Museum in London. Others were auctioned off at Christie's or other fashionable houses in London or Paris. Still other items were retained by families in private homes all over Europe, but particularly in England. Both the British and French also claimed that local Chinese took advantage of the situation to help themselves to art objects and relics from the grounds of the gardens. Many precious objects showed up in the antique shops at Liulichang, which the British called Curiosity Street.[41]

Although certain small parts of it were repaired, Yuanmingyuan was no longer viable after 1860. The burning of the palaces was virtually complete because the buildings all had been made of wood. Only stone objects, pillars, statues, and the like survived. The European-style palaces that Qianlong had built were seriously damaged, but parts of their stone and concrete structures remained standing in 1860. Yuanmingyuan had been a place where Qing emperors and Jesuit artists and architects had collaborated and where Chinese and European aesthetic tastes had come together in mutual admiration. Its destruction by Europeans marked the eclipse of a more hopeful and culturally open world that had begun to emerge in the seventeenth and eighteenth centuries. Additional damage would be done to Yuanmingyuan in 1900 during the Boxer debacle, with plundering by foreign troops and local vandals. Over time the various stone fragments of buildings and objects that remained were either damaged or removed by various authorities for use elsewhere in Beijing. The ruins of the European palaces, however, continued to serve as a favorite site for outings by Westerners in Beijing. Figure 5 shows French and Russian diplomats and their families in a carefree picnic at the ruins sometime before 1911.

The traumatic events of 1860 caused great alarm within Beijing. When the emperor fled to Rehe, the price of grain in the city doubled, and poor people could afford only spoiled grain. The apparent reason for the price increase was that grain merchants had followed the court, hoping to get higher prices at Rehe. The unstable exchange rates also added to the sense of insecurity, and unfamiliar paper money made things worse. Rennie reported that every morning the exchange shops were "besieged by crowds endeavouring to convert paper money into cash." Even wealthy families were in dire straits: "Provisions are said to be rapidly approaching famine prices, and indications of distress continue amongst the higher classes, judging from the character of the property which continues to be offered for sale at the Legation."[42] Rumors abounded in these months about the emperor's health and when he would return to Beijing; sometimes there were rumors that he already had died. When Xianfeng did die in Rehe in 1861, the return of his body to the Forbidden City was delayed. Although some said he died of heartbreak over the destruction of Yuanmingyuan, it was widely rumored that the true cause was a life of dissipation.

The treaties of Tianjin and Beijing extended privileges to the treaty powers beyond those that they had gained in the Treaty of Nanjing in 1842. These included the opening of more treaty ports for trade, the privilege of foreign residence in some cities, and permission for travel and missionary work in inland China beyond the ports. Most significant for the city of Beijing itself was the agreement permitting treaty powers to establish permanent legations at the capital, a central demand of the British ever since the Macartney mission.

Having gained most of their diplomatic and trade objectives, the British and French turned to supporting the Qing dynasty in its conflict with the Taiping rebels, who in 1860 were threatening Shanghai, which had become the most important treaty port for trade with the West. An era of "cooperation" ensued that lasted for a decade or more, during which Chinese and Manchu officials tried to adjust to the new diplomatic and commercial realities. Prince Gong, who had been left to accept the humiliations of British and French aggression and the ensuing treaty ratification, became for a decade or more the central figure in Chinese diplomacy with the West. While the six-year old Tongzhi emperor was guided by a joint regency of his mother and aunt, the empress dowagers Ci'an and Cixi, Prince Gong and like-minded moderate Manchu courtiers and Chinese statesmen developed a modus vivendi with the foreign powers and their diplomatic representatives. A new institution called the Zongli Yamen served as a Ministry of Foreign Affairs. Previously, relations with oceanic tributary states had been handled by the Board of Rites and relations with Inner Asia had been placed under the Superintendent of Dependencies (Lifan Yuan). Treatment of the Russians had differed from that of all other Europeans; they had been placed in the Inner Asian category and allowed to maintain an ecclesiastical mission in Beijing.

When Frederick Bruce, brother of Lord Elgin, arrived in Beijing in 1861 to present his credentials as British minister, the British were assigned the elegant, spacious mansion of Prince Yi, an act of retribution for the prince's unfortunate role in the events of 1858 to 1860. Located in the southeastern section of the Imperial City, the British Legation was soon joined by others, and the legation area became a focal point for Sino-foreign contacts. For the first time, non-Russian Europeans had permission to reside for indefinite periods in Beijing. In the following decades, they were few in number but highly visible. They included diplomats, their families, and a certain number of men who served the Qing court as advisers or employees. Prominent in the latter category was Robert Hart (later Sir Robert Hart), born in Northern Ireland, who for four decades headed the Inspectorate General of the Chinese Imperial Maritime Customs Service. Hart maintained an efficient and incorruptible customs service employing hundreds of international and Chinese civil servants to collect tariffs from foreign traders. He served the Chinese government loyally, spoke Chinese fluently, and functioned as an important intermediary between the Western diplomatic community and high Chinese officials. Another foreigner who contributed to the spirit of cooperation was W. A. P. Martin, an American Presbyterian missionary, who served as the head instructor at the Tongwenguan, or Interpreters' School, the first modern-style academy to train students for government service. At first the emphasis was on foreign languages, and the students were mostly bannermen. Later, study of science began and Chinese students joined the Manchus. Martin also was responsible for translation of major Western works into Chinese; these included treatises on international as well as French and English law, political economy, natural philosophy, history, physical geography, anatomy, physiology, and other subjects. Martin had a missionary background, but functioned in a secular educational role in Beijing.[43]

The number of foreigners living in Beijing in the late nineteenth century was smaller than that in Shanghai, Tianjin, or other treaty ports, but access to the court and high officials gave them significant roles.[44] On some, though not all, the city exerted a seductive power. A British diplomat wrote in 1865:

[Beijing] has exercised upon foreign representatives a kind of unholy glamour. They have been bewitched. Some have fallen down and worshipped before its scholastic and historical traditions; others have treated the great city and its rulers as a sort of gigantic "curio." If any serious attempt has been made to bring the mandarins into the pale of statesmanship it has been singularly unsuccessful. They remain as retrograde and as hopelessly obstructive as ever.[45]

Proximity to power, particularly rather decadent power, conferred on a few foreigners a kind of authority. While Robert Hart had long experience in China and unquestioned integrity, others were more controversial. George Morrison, the London *Times* correspondent in China from 1897 to 1920, had strong opinions particularly concerning British interests in China, and commanded great attention despite the fact that he never learned to speak or read Chinese. His colleague and rival, J. O. P. Bland, who frequently challenged Morrison's judgments, collaborated with Edmund Backhouse on *China under the Empress Dowager: Being the History of the Life and Times of Tzu Hsi*. This book was long regarded as an authentic view of the late Qing court around the turn of the twentieth century. But it relied on the secret diary of a high-ranking official and imperial relative, Jingshan (Ching-shan), a text that was exposed as a forgery in the 1970s. Although some, especially Morrison, had been suspicious of its authenticity from the beginning, Backhouse's excellent scholarly credentials, including fluency in both Chinese and Manchu, had given the work great credibility.[46] Indeed, by the end of the century, Beijing was a hotbed of diplomatic rumor and social gossip. Martin remarked that Beijing had "risen in the scale of importance to rival Constantinople as a focus of intrigue."[47]

Toward Reform

The decades from the 1860s to the 1890s saw a recovery from midcentury traumas. Despite continued economic hardship for many, local order was largely restored, and daily life resumed its normal rhythms. Yet the opening of the capital to foreign residence also opened it to foreign, largely Western, ideas and technology. Far more conservative and slower to change than the treaty ports, Beijing nevertheless became linked to them through commerce and communication. The opening of Tianjin as a treaty port in the 1870s had a great effect on Beijing. Tianjin was the major port of north China, the center for foreign imports and transhipments from Shanghai and other points both north and south. Western goods now freely entered the north China market, and Beijing in particular with its large population became a major market for foreign cloth, factory cotton, tobacco, kerosene, and other products.[48]

The pace of change was hardly rapid. The telegraph, first introduced to Beijing in 1869, did not actually start operation until 1883, when Beijing first had a direct line to Tianjin. The line soon became critical in linking the capital to the rest of China and to Europe as well. Railroads were introduced in China in the 1860s, but they met much resistance because many saw them as a foreign intrusion that disrupted the rules of geomancy. In Beijing the empress dowager in 1888 allowed a 2-kilometer (1.2 mile) railroad track to be built on the west shore of the Beihai and Zhonghai lakes near the Forbidden City. Given a demonstration, however, she became fearful of the smoke and thereafter did not allow the engine to be used; instead, she ordered a team of eunuchs to pull her car along the tracks. Later there was a toy rail line in the grounds of Nanhai Lake along which the Guangxu emperor allowed servants to push him.[49] Real rail lines were initiated in north China in the 1880s; by 1896 rail connected Beijing to Tianjin, and by 1897 to Baoding, the Zhili provincial capital. But major trunk lines came into operation only after 1905. The important north-south line from Beijing to Hankou, the main entrepôt on the central Yangzi River, was completed in 1906. This line transformed marketing patterns by allowing north China goods, including agricultural products, to be transported easily to central and south China, and it also supplied Beijing with goods from the south. In 1907 the railroad between Beijing and Fengtian in southern Manchuria was completed. Started in 1878 as a line to bring coal from mines at Tangshan to Beitang, it developed into the major link between the capital and Manchuria. In 1909 a line from Beijing northwest to the Great Wall at Zhangjiakou (Kalgan) facilitated trade with Mongolia that previously had been the monopoly of camel caravans. And then in 1911 the important Tianjin–Pukou line tied Tianjin, and thus Beijing, directly to Shanghai by rail.[50]

We have seen how, under the new treaties, Christian missionaries were allowed to establish churches in the interior of China as well as in the treaty ports. France had been particularly forceful in promoting the interests of Roman Catholicism. In Beijing, Catholics were able to reopen churches that had been forced to close and had deteriorated in the late eighteenth and early nineteenth centuries. The Southern Cathedral (Nantang)—on the site of a chapel established by Jesuits under Matteo Ricci in 1605, and rebuilt as a cathedral in 1652—resumed its work. The Northern Cathedral (Beitang), first granted to the Jesuits by Kangxi in 1692 (for curing him of an illness) and dedicated in 1703, had suffered fires and other deterioration. In 1887 the empress dowager desired that property for her own use, and she allocated land at Xishiku, also in the western section of the Imperial City, on which the cathedral could be rebuilt. It still stands there today.[51] The Eastern Cathedral (Dongtang), originally constructed in 1653, was rebuilt in 1884; it stands today in the Wangfujing shopping district.[52] Protestant missionaries, mostly British and American, also began to work in Beijing, but initially their progress was slower in the capital than in other cities and in rural areas.

Unlike the Jesuits of an earlier era, both Catholic and Protestant missionaries in this period made a greater impact on the poor and uneducated than on the elite. In Beijing, as elsewhere in China, the missionaries exercised their greatest influence indirectly through the establishment of schools, charities, and hospitals. In the 1860s the first missionary schools were established in Beijing by various Protestant denominations. The American missionary Eliza Bridgeman opened a school for beggar girls that functioned for thirty years; in 1895 it became the Bridgeman Academy, a secondary school.[53] In 1863 W. A. P. Martin, before his appointment to the Interpreters' College, had started a private school. Numerous other schools followed, but their enrollments were not large, and students were largely from nonelite, and sometimes poor, families whose motives were to secure food and lodging rather than knowledge of Christianity or science. Elite families did not send their children to such schools; they gave their sons a traditional Chinese education so that they could compete in the civil service examinations. Although limited in size, the new schools nevertheless had considerable impact because they were the first to teach biology, geography, history, and mathematics as well as Christianity, Chinese philosophy, and Western languages. They were particularly important in introducing education for girls, who previously had been educated only at home, if at all, and never beyond the age of puberty. These Christian schools later became the basis for universities. Yanjing (Yenching) University, established in 1919, was the outgrowth of Huiwen University (Methodist) and the North China Union College at Tongzhou (Presbyterian and Congregational), and they in turn had grown from a number of Protestant secondary schools founded in the nineteenth century.[54] Medicine was another field for missionary work in Beijing, as it had been in Canton in the early nineteenth century. Starting in 1861 the London Missionary Society and other British and American groups set up hospitals and clinics, which in 1906 united to form the Union Medical and Pharmaceutical Clinic, later to become the Peking Union Medical School; in 1908 a separate women's medical school followed.[55]

In response to the visible and widespread poverty in the city, a greater sense of public responsibility began to develop. The great north China drought famine of 1876–1879 severely affected Beijing, which received, as usual, many refugees from the surrounding area. This event was historically significant not only for its widespread devastation but also for the public response it drew from all over China. Fundraising for the north was spurred on by publicity in Shanghai newspapers and by the initiatives of both Chinese and foreign organizations. Chinese authorities actively encouraged public fundraising to compensate for much-diminished state resources for famine relief. In Beijing, because of the dominance of city affairs by the court and the bureaucracy, local elites were not a strong or well-defined group. In this period more initiatives were taken by "sojourning elites" (i.e., scholars or gentry whose native place was elsewhere but who were residents of Beijing, in some cases for long periods of time). In a book commemorating the flood relief effort of 1890, for example, the preface was written by Pan Zuyin, a native of Suzhou who had served as Shuntian prefect.[56]

Other examples of official and elite cooperation in public activities included the establishment of benevolent associations (*shantang*) that undertook charitable activities. The Hall for Spreading Benevolence (Guangrentang), established in 1880 based on the Tianjin Guangrentang, was the most ambitious of these. It provided shelter for abandoned children, widows, and elderly, all traditionally functions of the state in Beijing. Like other public-private institutions, it also branched out into education, giving practical instruction and preaching sanitation and high standards of conduct. A few charitable schools (*yixue*) had existed earlier, but many more were established in the 1860s to 1880s. A prefect named Zhou Jiamei was active in schools in the Outer City, while a bannerman, Wang Hai, gave generously to set up charitable schools in the Inner City.[57]

Gradually in the 1880s and 1890s there also developed in Beijing a sense of public opinion about national and international events as well as public responsibility for local activities. While Chinese authorities struggled to catch up and to cope, the external threat developed in alarming ways. Aggressive competition among European nations in the late nineteenth century replaced the more "gentlemanly" early nineteenth-century Anglo-French imperialism. Japan began to assert itself as a world power, and in 1894–1895 it surprised the world by winning a war against China and gaining all the privileges there that the European treaty powers already had. Japan also made even bolder demands on China, such as permission to establish factories at the treaty ports. One outcome of the Sino-Japanese war was Japan's annexation to its empire of the island province of Taiwan. Although the advances of Britain, France, Russia, Germany, and the United States into China had been terrible blows, the victory of Japan was even more humiliating because it too was an Asian state, one that Chinese always had considered culturally inferior and marginal to themselves. No other event so dramatically and forcefully brought home to Chinese the weakness of their position in the world as their loss of the war with Japan at this time. With this event, Chinese nationalism fully emerged.

Opinions were formed through traditional as well as modern channels. Although there were official newspapers, especially *Jingbao* (called the *Peking Gazette* by Westerners), independent newspapers did not really develop in Beijing until after 1900. There were, however, other kinds of publications that disseminated new ideas. For twenty years, from 1872 to 1892, Martin and a British missionary published a monthly review called *Record of Things Heard and Seen in China*. It included articles on astronomy, geography, and other scientific subjects; introduced readers to new technology, such as the telegraph, photography, and steam power; and reported on world news and commercial topics. In 1895 the reformer Kang Youwei and others published *Wanguo gongbao* (The globe), later called *Zhongwai jiwen* (News of things foreign and Chinese).[58]

In 1895, however, political opinion in Beijing was formed mainly in networks of scholars who gathered in the capital to take state examinations as well as of those who were more or less permanently in residence, some in office and others pursuing literary or other work related to government. Many were associated with the *huiguan*, the native-place lodges; as we have seen, the lodges had steadily increased in number during the nineteenth century. Before 1860, the *huiguan* were modest in their accommodations and neither played a public role nor sought to do so. By late in the century, however, the *huiguan* were sites of unprecedented political discussion and protest.[59]

Kang Youwei, a young scholar from Guangdong in south China, had visited Beijing in 1888 with the intention of settling there to study government operations firsthand. Discouraged by what he saw, he returned to the south to found an academy in which reform ideas gradually developed. Kang returned to Beijing in 1895 to take the *jinshi* examinations just when the news broke of the Treaty of Shimonoseki, which concluded the Sino-Japanese War. Based in the Xuannan district where most of the *huiguan* were concentrated, Kang drew on a network of like-minded young degree candidates to design the so-called Ten Thousand Word petition. This famous document called on the court to resist foreign aggression and to start a series of reforms so that China could regain its pride and sovereignty. Altogether more than twelve hundred people from eighteen different provinces signed their names. Although never presented to the court, the petition received widespread attention all over China. This was the first time in history that such a petition had been signed, and it marked the beginning of Beijing's role as the national center of political protest.[60] Soon thereafter numerous study societies were formed, representing different reform topics of pressing interest.

For Kang Youwei and his disciple Liang Qichao, Beijing was critical to the birth and growth of their reform movement because of the unique opportunity for lower officials and examination candidates from all provinces to mix in the Xuannan area.[61] They viewed the physical condition of the capital city as a sign of its political decay. Kang Youwei wrote: "No matter where you look in Beijing, the place is covered with beggars. The homeless and the old, the crippled and the sick with no one to care for them fall dead on the roads. This happens every day. And the coaches of the great officials rumble past them continuously; they are as indifferent as are the local officials in the rest of the province."[62]

Subsequently Kang's and Liang's ideas spread to the court itself. The Guangxu emperor had been tutored by an eminent Confucian scholar and statesman, Weng Tonghe, who was receptive to ideas of reform. In 1889 the emperor had turned nineteen, old enough to rule without the empress dowager. He became persuaded that he could lead China into the modern age as an enlightened modern monarch, similar to Peter the Great in Russia or the Meiji emperor in Japan. Over a period of one hundred days in the summer of 1898, he promulgated a comprehensive series of reforms. They included modernizing the government and the educational system on which it rested, developing scientific and technical education that would bring China into the modern age, updating military forces, and, most important, gradually advancing toward a constitutional monarchy. They also included a proposal to move the capital away from Beijing and its entrenched interests to the region south of the Yangzi; Beijing then would become one of nine subsidiary capitals.[63]

But this heady excitement was not to last. The empress dowager Cixi, having been sidelined temporarily, now rushed in—with the support of some courtiers and the backing of a key military figure, Yuan Shikai—to stage the second coup of her lifetime and stop the reforms. The emperor was virtually kidnapped and imprisoned by his aunt, and Kang Youwei, Liang Qichao, and the other reformers fled for their lives. Several, including the younger brother of Kang Youwei, were captured and executed, becoming martyrs of the reform movement. Rarely in life are the forces of good and evil, progress and reaction, so clearly opposed. Rarely in history has a single event been so decisive in the unfolding of subsequent events. It may be argued that such an ambitious program of reforms would not have worked, but within years a similar program was enacted successfully but too late.

Many of the dark events of the late nineteenth century have been blamed on the ignorance, power-hunger, and vanity of the empress dowager. From time to time some seek to rehabilitate her reputation, but it remains clear that her inability to comprehend the nature and seriousness of the challenges that faced China for over four critical decades was astonishing. While the country faced military and financial dangers, she used scarce central government funds to build a new Summer Palace, the Yiheyuan, where she lived much of the time, eating sumptuous banquets—which paying tourists now can order—and watching her favorite operas, sometimes on two stages at once. She also ordered building and renovations within the Forbidden City. When the Guangxu emperor reached his age of majority and she yielded her quarters in the Forbidden City to his young consort, the empress dowager ordered the building of new imperial palaces and gardens in the Nanhai and Zhonghai lake area west of the Forbidden City. It was for this purpose that she had confiscated the original Northern Cathedral and its grounds and also allowed the displacement of about two thousand homes.[64] Photography had been introduced to the court, and the empress dowager enjoyed having a flattering portrait taken of herself on each birthday. (See Figure 6.) The most visible symbol of her folly was the marble boat, a kind of pavilion, at the new Summer Palace; many observed that this vessel did not float and moreover had been constructed with funds badly needed for a modern navy with real ships. Of course, Cixi could not have played such a dominant role had there not been a vacuum of power at the court as well as a conspicuous scarcity of talent and ability. With the exception of Prince Gong, who was forced out of office in 1884, she was surrounded by Manchu relatives of mediocre ability and by conniving eunuchs, the most notorious and hated of whom was Li Lianying, sometimes photographed enacting a Buddhist arhat (perfected disciple) while the empress dowager play-acted a bodhisattva.

The Boxer Crisis

After 1898, events in Beijing unfolded quickly and dramatically. Foreign powers increased their demands on the court, including the so-called carving of the Chinese melon, in which major foreign powers carved out regions for the exclusive rights to development of railways and other interests. Meanwhile anti-foreign incidents proliferated in north China, where Christian missionaries and their Chinese converts were numerous. As anti-Christian violence mounted in the 1890s, so did the foreigners' anxiety. In Shandong Province, two or more popular movements coalesced in the winter of 1898–1899 and by spring 1899 adopted the slogan "Support the Qing, Destroy the foreigners." The origins of the Boxers United in Righteousness were complex: one group from the southwest of the province, the Big Sword Society, was composed of landlords and well-to-do peasants who sought to protect their communities against banditry and outside influences, which included Chinese converted to Christianity. The other group, the Spirit Boxers, was composed of poor and sometimes unemployed peasants, particularly youth, who practiced rituals such as spirit possession or "boxing" exercises said to make them invulnerable to bodily harm. The authorities, including prestigious governors as well as local officials, took different approaches to the Boxers. Some tried to suppress them, while others were more interested in suppressing Christians and foreigners. Boxers began to spread into neighboring Zhili Province, particularly when Yuan Shikai, known to be hostile to the cult, became governor in Shandong. In Zhili, where there were many Christians, several violent incidents occurred, especially at Baoding and Tianjin.[65]

By the early months of 1900 Boxers were entering Beijing itself, apparently unopposed and sometimes undetected. As violence against foreigners and Chinese Christians in the region escalated, the foreign community became alarmed, and their diplomats lodged complaints at the court. The empress dowager and her ministers were deeply divided about what attitude to assume toward the Boxers. According to rumor, the empress dowager was much impressed by a demonstration of the Boxers' pugilistic and magical skills. In late May the diplomats, fearing for the safety of foreigners, called for military assistance from Tianjin. This move decidedly escalated tensions with the court, which withdrew its previous, albeit halfhearted, order to suppress the Boxers. Shortly afterward Prince Duan and other pro-Boxer ministers were appointed to the Zongli Yamen. Violence within the city escalated: on June 10 Boxers destroyed the British summer legation in the Western Hills; on June 11 a Japanese diplomat was killed; on June 13 a large number of Boxers entered the city and began setting fire to churches and foreign homes. The historically important Southern Cathedral was burned to the ground. On June 16 fires spread throughout the area of Qianmen, a major center of commercial activity.[66]

On June 19 the court ordered foreign powers to evacuate their citizens from Beijing and moved toward open hostility with them; some say the precipitating factor was their call for legation guards from Tianjin. The foreign community was divided about what course of action to take. When, on June 20, the German minister (Baron Clemens von Ketteler) was killed by a soldier, perhaps a Manchu bannerman, the Westerners realized how isolated and vulnerable they were and the impossibility of evacuating the whole foreign community. Full-scale hostilities commenced within Beijing; on June 21 the court formally declared war and incorporated the Boxers into Qing forces commanded at the capital by Prince Duan and others. In the meantime, on June 13, the British Admiral Edward Seymour had left Tianjin for Beijing with an international relief column of about two thousand men; on June 18, however, it was repulsed by Qing forces with modern arms and compelled to return to Tianjin on June 26. Communications were impossible, and the foreigners at the capital, not knowing the fate of the Seymour expedition, kept waiting in vain for relief. For fifty-five days, from June 20 until August 14, combined Boxer and Qing forces besieged the British Legation compound, where foreigners and Chinese Christians had sought refuge, and the Northern Cathedral, where another such mixed group was trying to survive the onslaught.

Since the British Legation, a spacious compound of about three acres with twenty-two buildings, was the largest and most defensible of the legations, the diplomatic community turned it into a fortress. Nine hundred civilians and military men crowded into an area usually housing sixty. They established a defensive perimeter around a portion of the rest of the legation area, and they burned down some Chinese homes in adjacent lots to secure a clear line of fire. Across the canal from the legation about 2,700 Chinese Christians were sheltered in the palace of Prince Su. The defenders fortified the entire area and carefully monitored provisions. Men—diplomats and missionaries alike—took up arms to assist the military contingent. Committees formed to manage various aspects of maintaining the compound. Women acted as nurses and cooks. This elite refugee population was multinational—in addition to the British, it contained Americans, Russians, French, Japanese, and Germans—and included a large number of missionaries, sometimes organized into subgroups.[67] Since the dining area was small, Protestant denominations ate their meals in shifts: Presbyterians, Methodists, Congregationalists. There was great fear and lack of information about events on the outside, but the foreigners, when they later wrote about the ordeal, spoke of the bravery and community spirit that had prevailed and praised the British minister, Claude MacDonald, and his wife for their stalwart leadership.[68]

The fighting and devastation were fierce, particularly in the early weeks of the siege. Qing forces soon replaced Boxer soldiers. Chinese guns and artillery killed several foreigners. A major tactic was the use of fires to try to force the surrender of the legation. At one point the Hanlin Academy, adjacent to the British Legation, was torched, and most of its collection of precious books and documents was destroyed.[69] The constant gunfire was intense, although fortunately most bullets missed the compound. Still, there were dozens of deaths and casualties among the guards and officers. Noncombatants also suffered. Several infants died of starvation. As the siege dragged on through the summer heat, some succumbed to illness. Provisions became scarce in the compound, but particularly so in the princely quarters of the Chinese refugees, where many were ill and half-starved. Even more infants died among this group.

At the Northern Cathedral (Beitang), conditions were much worse. Bishop Alphonse Favier had anticipated earlier than had the diplomatic community the possibility of all-out conflict and the danger to the Christian community, and he had made some preparations. A small contingent of about thirty marines had been sent by the French Legation. It was joined by a dozen Italian marines and a volunteer force of Chinese converts. When, on June 13 and 14 all the other churches and cathedrals in the city were torched, Favier directed over three thousand people to take refuge in the Northern Cathedral. Seventy-one were Europeans, including the French and Italian marines, thirteen priests, and twenty nuns. The rest were Chinese Christians, two-thirds of whom were women and children.[70] The Northern Cathedral was more isolated than the British Legation, and its defenders fought off a relentless barrage of artillery, firearms, and eventually projectiles coming from thousands of Boxers under the command of Prince Duan himself. Food and medicine were insufficient. Some converts, no longer able to bear their hunger, left the compound only to be slaughtered. In the end 400 died, including 166 children, but the cathedral and most occupants survived.[71]

The epic siege finally ended on August 14, when an eight-nation expeditionary force of twenty thousand soldiers (half were Japanese; the others, Americans, Russians, British, French, Germans, Austrians, and Italians) reached the capital and ended the hostilities. The next day the empress dowager and her court escaped in humble disguise to Xi'an, the ancient capital to the west. China had lost a war against the foreign powers, and its great capital of Beijing was under foreign occupation.

Western witnesses who kept detailed diaries and memoirs recorded the violence during this crisis. Widespread slaughter, beheadings, and torture were common throughout the city, with Christian converts the major target of the Boxers, but there was random destruction too. Nearby Tianjin, with its foreign settlements and numerous Christian churches, suffered terrible ruin; the foreigners there had been liberated a few weeks earlier than the Beijing legations. From Tianjin to Beijing, all the towns were devastated, and most surviving occupants fled. Exactly thirty-nine years after Robert Fortune had observed flourishing crops in this area, the countryside was desolate, with houses burned down and corpses floating downriver.[72]

In Beijing, much destruction and flight had occurred when the Boxers began to enter the city. According to the missionary Arthur Smith, between the Boxers and the army, "the city was reduced to an acute pitch of misery. . . . Many families were extinguished, and in others only one or two out of eight or ten members remained alive. Hundreds of house doors were walled up entirely, which often meant that there was no one left." After the siege was lifted, the full extent of the loss was revealed. Dead bodies were everywhere.[73] In the legation area, only the British and American legations, the Hong Kong Bank, and the Hotel de Pekin were left standing. As far as the rest of the city was concerned, an American war correspondent observed: "When we entered [Beijing] we found the city swarming with foreign troops but deserted by the Chinese. Evidence of shot and shell and fire were to be seen on all sides. Acres upon acres of a once thickly populated city had been burnt to the ground. Temples and palaces were pierced with shells or destroyed, and miles upon miles of houses had been sacked of all things they once contained."[74] Boxers escaped, disappearing into the countryside if they could. Those who were caught could consider themselves lucky if they received a formal execution, as in Figure 7, which depicts a Boxer being led to the Caishikou execution ground. Many were slaughtered without any formalities. Some innocent Chinese and Manchu families fled their homes; others, fearing the worst from the Western forces, took their own lives.

The perpetrators of violence were not only the Boxers and Chinese military forces. In the year or more after their entry into the city, the Eight-Power United Army celebrated their triumph in many actual and symbolic ways. First they staged a triumphal march into the Forbidden City itself, now devoid of rulers, which was similar in symbolism to the vandalizing of the Yuanmingyuan in 1860, but without the physical destruction. To the conquerors, unrestricted access to the dreaded and mysterious *forbidden* city was thrilling. American soldiers set up camp. (See Figure 8.) Some of the Europeans were disappointed to find only the smallest of rooms outfitted with furniture and settings of a distinctly faded nature.[75] Objects were stolen from the Forbidden City and from buildings all over Beijing. Looting was commonplace; compared to what had occurred in 1860, it was not localized but widespread, and of longer duration. As historian James Hevia writes, a "loot fever gripped the armies and Euroamerican population in Beijing, and a wild orgy of plunder ensued." Lady Claude MacDonald filled eighty-seven cases and said she had not really begun to pack. Chinese residents tried to protect themselves by fashioning flags of different nations and declaring they had already been marauded.[76] Violence was directed against Chinese people themselves, not just the rulers as in 1860.[77] Missionaries participated in looting, to the shame of a few. Some European newspapers and journals noted with dismay the extent of plunder by Western and Japanese armies. Violence and marauding spread to other towns in Zhili and lasted through the winter of 1900–1901. Punitive expeditions set out to avenge missionary deaths in Baoding. In the course of these missions, foreign soldiers presided over the executions of Boxers in Chinese fashion, decapitation with a sword.[78]

Foreigners rationalized violence against Chinese and Chinese property as revenge for atrocities against Western and Chinese Christians. Many took an apocalyptic view of recent events that included a visceral hatred of the empress dowager. W. A. P. Martin, who had worked at the highest levels with Chinese and Manchu scholar-officials for forty years, wrote:

> She has made war not without provocation, but wholly unjustifiable, on all nations of the civilized world. Allying herself with the powers of darkness, she entered into diabolical conspiracy and sanctioned unheard-of-atrocities in order to keep her people in ignorance and shield her family from the competition of superior light and knowledge. It is one more exhibition of . . . the eternal war between the spirit of darkness and the God of Light.[79]

Another difference from the events of 1860 was that the siege of the legations in 1900 had been closely followed by millions worldwide. With telegraph and newspaper communication, news of the siege, and the anti-Christian violence generally, flashed around the world. In mid-July it was erroneously reported that the entire Western community in the legations had been slaughtered. For weeks people believed that all were dead; obituaries were printed and memorial services held. The sensationalism and horror that this real and imagined event evoked in Europe was like that after the 1857 Sepoy Mutiny in India. In both cases, East and West, Christian and Heathen, were pitted in a "clash of civilizations."

The Boxer Protocol negotiated in September 1901 imposed on China extremely harsh terms: punishment of the responsible officials, a diplomatic mission of apology, a crippling indemnity of 450 million taels ($333 million), to be repaid over the next thirty-nine years with interest, a suspension of the civil service examinations for five years in cities where Boxers had dominated, and a Legation District to be legally defined and defended by Western guards—all further restrictions on Chinese sovereignty. For China it marked new depths of subjugation and humiliation. That the terms were not still harsher was due to the wise intervention of a few Chinese (not Manchu) statesmen serving as governors of the southern provinces, who had disregarded the court's declaration of war on the foreign powers and kept the conflict confined to the north and particularly to the capital area. The Boxer uprising—with all its enormous national and international consequences—was thus at some level an intensely localized, Beijing-centered, conflict. The empress dowager's worldview was narrowly court-centered, not China-centered. Not until Boxers entered Beijing and foreign powers started to send troops into the city did she actually decide on war. The direct threat to her and the court, not the threat to the nation, had prompted her to make a desperate and misguided choice.

End of the Old Regime

In most ways the year 1900 was much more of a turning point for Beijing than 1911, the year the dynasty was toppled by revolutionary forces.[80] In the fall of 1900 the physical infrastructure of the city was shattered. Not only the rulers but much of the ordinary population had been dislocated, at least temporarily. Foreigners and not a few Chinese participated in widespread looting. The normal sources of urban security and imperial authority had been removed, and in their place, for a year or more, a multinational foreign occupation sought to run the city along with collaborators. Yet out of this frightening and uncertain situation emerged a Beijing that was fresh in many ways, with new and reconstructed buildings, roads, transportation, and a difference in spirit. It was as if the breaches in the walls and gates of the city by both Boxers and foreign troops had opened the capital not only to violence and destruction, but also to positive foreign influence and reform. New ideas, new institutions, and a significantly new way of life now were layered on top of old customs and structures.

Western influence took many forms. Signs in Western languages, including advertisements for lessons in English and other tongues, appeared everywhere. One ad promoted "YMCA Reading, Writing, and Coffee Rooms." Foreign funds soon financed rebuilding of churches, cathedrals, legations, and other structures.[81]

The various rail links to other regions of China were completed. Earlier the terminal for the Tianjin line had been at Lugou Bridge (Marco Polo Bridge), well outside the city walls. In 1900 the rail tracks breached the city wall for the first time. A hole was blown in the wall of the southern city and tracks laid all the way to the Qianmen area, just outside the Inner City.[82] (See Figure 9.)

The major developments in the city, however, were not the direct result of exposure to the West but rather a continuation of initiatives begun (but suppressed) in the 1880s and 1890s reform era. The catalyst for these changes was the court itself. With plenty of time to contemplate her limited options while exiled in Xi'an, the empress dowager returned to Beijing in January 1902 hardly a new woman, but definitely a more realistic ruler. Even before the court returned, it began to issue a series of decrees that put into force essentially the same bold reform program that the Guangxu emperor and Kang Youwei had proposed, and that Cixi had halted, in 1898. The New Policies included the restructuring of the government with creation of ministries instead of the old Six Boards, the reform of education and the abolition of the centuries-old civil service examinations, the creation of a modern army, and eventually the recovery of economic rights granted to foreign powers. As these reforms took effect over the next few years, the rising tide of public opinion all over China pressed the court for acceleration of its timetable for a national assembly and a constitution. Reformers and moderates like Kang Youwei regarded a constitutional monarchy as their main hope of achieving political modernization while maintaining Chinese tradition. In the meantime revolutionary forces were advocating the overthrow of the dynastic system.

At the capital the New Policies had an electrifying effect and permitted the growth of seeds planted earlier. The founding of Beijing University is one major example. In the 1898 reform period, the Imperial or Metropolitan University (Jingshi daxuetang)—as it was then called—had been formed by incorporating the Interpreters' College (Tongwenguan) that had been so important in introducing Western scholarship to the capital. Sun Jia'nai was the chancellor, and W. A. P. Martin was head of the Western Studies division. The university had difficulty getting started, however, and its activities were suspended in 1900 during the Boxer upheaval. In late 1902 the university was revived, with Zhang Baixi as chancellor and Wu Rulun as head of studies. (See Figure 10.) The original emphasis of the curriculum was "Zhongti, Xiyong," from the slogan "Chinese learning as the foundation, Western learning for use," but the new curriculum was more progressive than the slogan. It included sciences, mathematics, law, foreign languages, and other subjects. In 1910 it had eight divisions: classics, liberal arts, law and politics, medicine, science, agriculture, engineering, and commerce. The university was seen as the pinnacle of a new nationwide system of public schools; the best students from each province would be privileged to attend the university. As such, it was still a training school for future government servants; yet its broad curriculum signaled new educational objectives in place of the intense and almost exclusive mastery of the Confucian classics that had been required for the civil service examinations, which were finally abolished in 1905. In 1912 the name of the new institution was changed to Beijing (Peking) University.[83]

Major reforms in the management of the city of Beijing took place in the decade between the Boxer Uprising and the 1911 revolution. The maintenance of public order was taken over from the six nations that had carved the city up into six police districts—English, American, French, Italian, German, and Japanese. In 1902 a joint bureau for police and public works was created under Prince Su (Shanqi), a member of the imperial clan and head of the old gendarmerie. At first confined to the Inner City, the bureau's jurisdiction was later extended to the Outer City as well; its responsibilities included firefighting, prisons, public health, and regulation of temples, theaters, markets, and other public establishments. It was also responsible for road construction, lighting, telegraph wires, and other aspects of the physical infrastructure of the city. A police academy was established on the Japanese model, which was much admired. When a national Ministry of Police was created in 1905, the Beijing police was included within a hierarchical structure that became the Ministry of Civil Affairs a year later. Nevertheless, the police retained a fair degree of local autonomy.[84] Although the new force did not entirely displace the old gendarmerie, which survived until 1924, it was more professional and more concerned with civil administration. This coexistence of old and new institutions was characteristic of the Qing practice of multi-layered and overlapping authorities in Beijing.[85]

Modernization of the city's physical infrastructure was considered a vital aspect of the new administration of the city. Even before creation of the Office of Public Works in 1909, there was a great effort to pave the major roads in the Inner and Outer cities, install street lighting and telephone wiring, clean the streets, and improve the sewer system. Many foreign technical experts consulted with local officials on these projects. Foreign settlements in various treaty ports and Japan served as models for Beijing. The result especially impressed foreigners, who had not been shy in their complaints about Beijing's dust, dirt, and smells. George Morrison, the correspondent for the London *Times*, had described Beijing as "the filthiest city in the world," but returning in 1911 after a few years, he saw modern facilities and services including telephones and mail delivery an astounding eight times a day. Another, Dutch colonial official Henri Borel, wrote that in Beijing

> one can see . . . how much reform has been achieved in a few years, especially during the last four years. The streets used to be full of puddles in which one risked breaking his neck: in the evening they were scarcely lighted by the paper lanterns, and very often unsafe as well. Everywhere there was dirt and water and a population hostile to the foreigner and to all foreign novelties. Now they are busy macadamising the roads, steam rollers are everywhere at work, the entire city has electric light, telephone wires are hung.[86]

Martin remembered: "Over forty years ago, when I exhibited the Morse system to the astonished dignitaries of [Beijing], those old men were amused but thought it would never work in China. Now electricity is transforming lives." He added: "The provinces are now covered with wires. Governors and captains consult with each other by wire. . . . The people, too, appreciate the advantage of communicating by a flash with distant members of their families."[87]

Another important development in this decade was the introduction of public health and sanitation measures. Officials supervised public places such as markets. In 1906 two large covered marts were established, one at the Dong'an Gate of the Imperial City and the other at the Guang'an Gate of the Outer City. Another set of regulations concerned safety and sanitation at hotels. Yet another dealt with houses of prostitution. Authorities closely watched two public hospitals and pharmacies. They checked that vaccinations were given, and in 1910–1911 they formed sanitation brigades to combat and contain an outbreak of plague. The gendarmerie compiled statistics on causes of death in relation to city areas by keeping track of corpses carried through the gates for burial. (Burial was not permitted inside the city walls.) Other measures included quarantine of tuberculosis, leprosy, or syphilis patients.[88] It is difficult to say how widely such rules were enforced or to measure their impact, but their existence indicated a new public consciousness about health and sanitation.

These rapid changes in the management of the city and in its physical appearance show the impact of the New Policies on Beijing. There were three dimensions of change: the centralization of administrative authority, now mostly Chinese, not Manchu; a view of Beijing as one city, not Inner and Outer cities; and the transformation from military to civil administration.[89] One aspect of the government-sponsored reforms was the encouragement of local self-government and the creation of chambers of commerce. In this, as in so many other areas, Beijing, because of its close identification with the central government, was slower to develop than Shanghai and Tianjin. Two municipal government public welfare associations were established in 1906, and in 1910 a municipal council and assembly were to be elected, according to the reform agenda for local self-government. But these plans were cut short by the revolution.[90] Beijing had begun to develop a sense of local autonomy in this decade, but most of these developments were still tied to the imperial government's reform initiatives.

All these changes, however, stimulated an urban consciousness, an awareness of something that might be called the public good. It was not until after 1900 that Beijing had its first independent newspapers, decades after Shanghai and other cities had dailies. In 1901 *Jinghua bao* (Capital talk) was published every ten days; it ceased publication and returned as the daily *Jinghua ribao* (Capital talk daily). Covering local, national, and international news, it also ran editorials, satirical cartoons, and advertising; it was the first to use photographs in its stories. The paper was written in vernacular Chinese (*baihua*) for a popular audience. In this period there were also literary, foreign-language, commercial, and school newspapers. Newspapers especially for women began; the first, *Beijing nubao*, was published in 1905. A dynamic genre of pictorials, or illustrated newspapers, *huabao*, which had existed as early as 1884 in Shanghai and other cities, was introduced to Beijing only in 1902. Using woodblock prints and vernacular Chinese, these papers also commanded a wide audience.[91]

Among the illustrated papers, *Xingshi huabao* (Awakening the world pictorial), first published in 1909, reveals a great deal about Beijing life and attitudes in the early twentieth century. Cartoons by artist Li Juchai depicted street or domestic scenes; names were not mentioned, but specific locations (such-and-such *hutong*) were. Each drawing depicted some social situation and provided sarcastic or mocking commentary. Two young ladies standing by a doorway were joking and talking in loud voices: the comment said that such behavior "lacked education." A couple quarreling and gesticulating inside their home showed bad manners: "Is this called freedom of expression?" said the comment. The couple quarreled when the wife came home late one day; she said it was an era of freedom and equality, and she could do what she liked. He replied that this was shameful behavior and could not be called "freedom." (See Figure 11.) In another illustration an official is at home smoking an opium pipe while a friend tries to persuade him to quit smoking. The comment says: "Smoking is closer than one's flesh and blood. This man says that even if he lost his position, his daughters could support his habit by singing opera, but a poor person would even sell his daughter to get opium." These drawings depict a kind of street or *hutong* life in which private behavior comes to public notice. The commentator has a conservative view of appropriate decorum, but rather than invoke Confucian morality to condemn unseemly behavior, he speaks of lacking education or public virtue. People are still in traditional family settings, but they have rather sharp tongues and untraditional kinds of freedom. Men and women are still in nineteenth-century garb; men have their queues, and some women are shown with small (bound) feet. Yet women are seen outdoors, not cloistered indoors in a traditional way. They are out walking, taking rickshaws, conversing with each other, and talking to men in public.[92]

⊷≈⊶   ⊶≈⊷

Historians long will debate whether the reforms were too much too soon or too little too late. By finally assuming leadership in the cause of reform, the Qing court was, of course, hoping to save itself. But ironically, the reforms only strengthened the forces that led to its demise. Despite his persecution by the empress dowager, Kang Youwei and other moderates had hoped to preserve the monarchy, in constitutional form, in order to provide an orderly transition to a modern nation-state. The new forces of nationalism, however, reacting to the Sino-Japanese War, the terms of the Boxer Protocol, and other forms of foreign encroachment, proved impossible to contain. The revolutionary movement had emerged in Guangdong Province in south China in the 1890s. After an uprising at Canton in 1895 failed, its leader Sun Yat-sen (Sun Yixian) had to flee China. He built up revolutionary support and funding overseas in Japan and later in Europe and the United States. Shanghai was another center of revolutionary activity—benefiting from vibrant sources of information and freedom afforded by the International Settlement there. Central China was a third locus of revolutionary organization. Many revolutionaries also found refuge and support in Japan, where Chinese students had gone for higher education. Although the victor in the recent war against China, Japan had become a model for Chinese revolutionaries and reformers alike; Japan demonstrated how an Asian nation could modernize successfully; in 1905, after the Russo-Japanese War, it also showed how an Asian nation could defeat a European power.

The forces of revolution were gathering everywhere but Beijing, which as the imperial capital was the focus of revolutionary attention. The fact that there was almost "no there there" was unfortunate for the monarchical cause. After

November 15, 1908, even the despised empress dowager was gone. And by a curious coincidence, the young Guangxu emperor died the day before, November 14. It was said that the empress dowager made sure that her nephew would not survive her. Reginald Johnston, who later became the last emperor's tutor, claimed that Guangxu had indeed been sickly and died a natural death, but he was one of the few to think so.[93] The empress dowager, age seventy-three, did die a natural death, but she had arranged that the successor to the throne would be Puyi, a nephew of the Guangxu emperor. As Puyi was only three years of age, his regent would be his father, Prince Chun. Barely thirty years old himself, Prince Chun was described by Johnston as "well-intentioned," but in the next two critical years he vacillated on key issues and, instead of appeasing anti-Manchu sentiment by sharing power with Chinese officials, he appointed mostly Manchu princes to the newly created cabinet. Johnston wrote that Prince Chun "shrinks from responsibility, is disastrously deficient in energy, will-power and grit. . . . He is helpless in an emergency, has no original ideas, and is liable to be swayed by any smooth talker."[94]

The Qing rulers inspired contempt because they had failed to show courage and intelligence in the face of the relentless foreign threats to China in the late nineteenth century. If there had been a Kangxi or Qianlong on the throne, perhaps his broader view of the world and greater skill would have made a constitutional monarchy seem more attractive to Chinese popular opinion, but this was not the case. The very fact that the Manchus were not Han Chinese became a major component in the nationalism that emerged in this decade. "Nation" became defined not just in terms of the political nation-state but also in ethnic terms as the Han nation. Historical and cultural differences between Manchu and Han, little discussed since the late seventeenth century, were magnified and Manchus demonized in racist propaganda. The revolutionary martyr Zou Rong wrote that the Manchus were just another one of a series of barbarian tribes that had existed on the periphery of Chinese civilization: "Their tribes . . . fundamentally are of a different race from our illustrious descendants of the Yellow emperor. Their land is barren; their people furry; their minds, bestial; their customs savage." Cutting off the queue that the Manchus had required all Chinese men to wear as a sign of submission now became the badge of loyalty to the revolutionary cause.[95]

Thus, when the Wuchang uprising took place in central China on October 10, 1911, the will to resist was not very strong. Within a few months province after province submitted to the revolutionary tide. It was not a bloodless revolution, but it was not a protracted war either. Sun Yat-sen returned to China from the United States and accepted the provisional presidency, but Yuan Shikai, the major military figure at the time, played a critical role in arranging for the Manchu surrender and was selected as the first president of the republic.

The last emperor, the six-year-old Puyi, received what was regarded as a generous settlement that allowed him to remain in the rear section of the Forbidden City (what used to be called the inner court). He had been raised in a pampered, feminine environment, and his sheltered childhood continued under the direction of remaining eunuchs, loyal retainers and, from 1919 until 1924, an English tutor, Reginald Johnston. Having little serious business to attend to, as a young man he learned to ride a bicycle, play tennis, and indulge in idle pleasures. He was the center of many restoration plots, and the riches of the Forbidden City that he occupied were systematically pilfered by the remaining staff. In 1923 the Palace of Established Happiness (Jianfugong), which had been a favorite place of the court ladies and where, as a young child, he had been photographed with them, burned to the ground. (See Figure 12.) The fire was thought to be the work of eunuchs who were covering up for their theft of valuables there.[96] Shortly afterward Puyi ordered the expulsion of all but fifty eunuchs from the Forbidden City.

The prosperous Manchu family shown in Figure 13, possibly from the imperial clan, exemplifies the happier survivors in the new era. Although neither the family nor the date is given, we can see the characteristic Manchu headdress and clothing of the women. Seated is the matriarch of the family; the man to her left may be her son or son-in-law; he wears a sword. At the rear the young women of the family, sisters and cousins, stand with their servant girls between them. The boys seated on the ground in the front appear still to have queues, which suggests that the picture was taken before 1911, or shortly thereafter.

The ordinary Manchu banner population also received relatively favorable treatment. In Beijing they numbered about half a million in the late nineteenth century and constituted more than half of the population of the Inner and Outer cities together, slightly less than half if suburban figures are included.[97] By the early 1920s banner people accounted for about a quarter of the Beijing population.[98] Although their lives were no longer formally defined by banner status, they continued to receive some stipends for a while after 1911. Most remained in Beijing to find their own living, but they were poorly equipped to do so. They were no longer despised for being Manchu, but they were often discriminated against because of their poverty and because they tended to find the most menial work, such as pulling rickshaws.[99] Yet, oddly enough, over the next few decades Manchus and their descendants would achieve a kind of culturally iconic status, self-identified and seen by others as the essential "Beijingren," or Beijing people.[100]

Chapter 5

"Old Beijing" and Republican China

THE FIRST HALF OF THE TWENTIETH CENTURY WAS A PERIOD OF MANY changes for Beijing but also many paradoxes. No longer the imperial capital after 1911, capital of the struggling republic only until 1928, and not yet the capital of the unified communist state as it would be after 1949, the city in some ways developed a more independent urban identity. Yet again and again, contending warlords and political parties sought to control Beijing and to limit the growth of political autonomy. Many aspects of the city's infrastructure became modernized, as happened during this era in Shanghai, Tianjin, and China's other treaty ports. Yet urban modernity was only partial, and much of daily life for ordinary people continued in the patterns and rhythms of the past. Republican-era Beijing was also the birthplace of an intellectual movement that led to mass public demonstrations—seemingly a sign of an emergent civil society—but this trend was ultimately halted by government repression and Japanese occupation. After 1911 there was a new Beijing supposedly free of the constraints of tradition, yet paradoxically the Beijing that people today remember best—and regret the loss of—is "Old Beijing."

Although the centers of political activity leading to the 1911 revolution had been in central and south China, Beijing and north China were the stronghold of the dominant military power holder, Yuan Shikai. Finding excuses not to go to Nanjing, where Sun Yat-sen and his supporters wanted to establish the new capital, Yuan insisted that the capital of the republic remain at Beijing. The dependence of the revolutionary forces on the military balance held by Yuan was one indication of the weakness of the new Republican government. Sun Yat-sen, widely acknowledged as the predominant leader of the revolutionary parties, could only step aside to allow Yuan to be the first president. In addition to promising military stability, Yuan was a figure well known to the foreign powers, and many argued that they would more readily support a new government strong enough to guarantee their treaty rights.

Yuan provided stability and gained diplomatic recognition, but his commitment to republicanism proved to be ephemeral. In fact, his presidential inauguration took place in the Forbidden City in the Taihedian (Hall of Supreme Harmony).[1] As new political parties engaged in an electoral process, Yuan moved against them in brazen ways, including assassination of the rising political star Song Jiaoren. Revolutionary forces gathered again in 1913 and challenged Yuan in an unsuccessful uprising known as the Second Revolution. Yuan persisted in undertaking the annual imperial ceremonies at the Temple of Heaven. (In Figure 14 he is seen en route.) In 1915 Yuan, on the advice of an American political science professor, sought to restore a monarchical system with himself as emperor. With popular forces reeling from these events, it was fortunate for history, and perhaps also for Yuan, that the new would-be emperor died a natural death in 1916.

Yuan's was not the last attempt to revert to imperial government. Thoughts of a restoration of the Qing dynasty were very much alive in Beijing in the years after 1911. After all, the boy-emperor Puyi still occupied the private sections of the Forbidden City, and thousands of imperial clansmen, palace officials, eunuchs, and hangers-on clung to the hope of a restoration. The capital was full of rumors and schemes. After Yuan's death, the warlord Zhang Xun briefly controlled Beijing and restored Puyi to the throne in July 1917.[2] Less than two weeks later, however, a powerful coalition of warlords drove Zhang Xun out of Beijing, ending the brief restoration. Only in November 1924, when warlord Feng Yuxiang forced Puyi out of the Forbidden City for good, did hopes of restoration fade.

After Yuan's death Beijing (now generally called Beijing, Northern Capital, rather than Jingshi, Capital City) continued to be the national capital, but the central government's control over the provinces was weak at best. A succession of warlords and their cliques fought for control over various regions and particularly for control of Beijing itself. Whoever dominated Beijing ran the legitimate government of China, conducted foreign relations, and maintained treaties concluded since the nineteenth century. These "unequal treaties," which would remain in effect until 1943, contained foreign privileges that infringed on Chinese sovereignty. In return, the presence of the foreign legations in Beijing ensured the safety of the city from military attack. Because the Boxer Protocol of 1901 protected the district now called the Legation Quarter, the warlords avoided attacking Beijing itself. The transition from one regime to the next in the period 1916–1928 was generally peaceful with little military presence inside the city.[3]

Yuan's successors were known as the Beiyang clique because they had been trained at his Beiyang Military Academy. But the warlords soon split into factions and constantly switched alliances among themselves. The three main factions in the north were the Anhui clique of Duan Qirui, the Zhili clique (including Cao Kun, Feng Yuxiang, and Wu Peifu), and the Fengtian clique under the "Manchurian warlord" Zhang Zuolin. Initially there was still the nominal structure of a constitutional government, but in 1923 Cao Kun became president by bribing the parliament. In 1924 Feng Yuxiang, the "Christian warlord," with Zhang Zuolin's support, took Beijing, breaking the hold of the Beiyang warlords. In 1926 Zhang Zuolin and Wu Peifu drove Feng from Beijing. In June 1927 Zhang Zuolin dissolved the standing cabinet and established his own military government in Beijing, which lasted a year until Nationalist troops entered the city in June 1928.[4]

The Nationalist Party (Guomindang) had regrouped in south China after the failure of electoral politics and the party's defeat by Yuan in 1913. After the early death of Sun Yat-sen in 1925, Chiang Kai-shek (Jiang Jieshi), head of the Whampoa Military Academy near Canton that trained Guomindang officers, became party leader. In the following year he led the Northern Expedition, which reunified most of south China and defeated or co-opted most of the northern warlords. In 1927, the Nationalist Party established its capital at Nanjing on the Yangzi River, ushering in a decade of rule from this major city in central China, relatively close to the more Westernized treaty port of Shanghai from which Chiang had received much support. To the Nationalists, Nanjing seemed the appropriate place to build the modern capital of a strong and reunified state. Beijing appeared to them as an exotic and dusty relic of earlier eras, with too much Manchu and Mongol influence and too many camels. They associated Beijing with political conservatism, warlord corruption, and imperial decadence.[5] Thus from 1928 until 1949 Beijing lost its status as national capital. It was called not Beijing (Northern Capital) but Beiping (Northern Peace), a name that had been used in the early Ming dynasty when the southern city of Nanjing was sole capital and the Yongle emperor had not yet taken the throne.

Although its municipal government fell under the jurisdiction of the Nanjing-based central government, Beijing itself (we continue to use this name rather than Beiping or Peiping) was still the object of contention by warlord forces that jockeyed for power in north China. Chiang's power in the north was weak; he relied on warlord cooperation, which was not easy because they continued to scheme not only against each other but against him. In 1930 the warlord of Shanxi, Yan Xishan, withdrew his support from Chiang and briefly established a new government at Beijing, but Zhang Xueliang, son of the Manchurian warlord, regained the city for the Nationalist government. The northern warlords, loosely supportive of Chiang Kai-shek but still wielding independent military power and motivated by personal ambitions, also had to deal with Japanese encroachment in Manchuria, a process that had begun at the turn of the twentieth century and had grown more dangerous over time. For Chiang, the warlords, and Japanese alike, Beijing was the most important city in north China and a prize to be controlled.

In 1931 the Mukden incident, an explosion on railroad tracks caused by junior officers of the Japanese army but blamed by them on the Chinese, precipitated the Japanese takeover of Manchuria. The puppet state of Manchukuo had as its emperor none other than Puyi himself, with a "throne" at last. Japanese forces threatened Beijing, but the Tanggu agreement of May 1933 kept the Japanese army north of the Great Wall, leaving Beijing and Tianjin as a demilitarized zone. In 1935, the He-Umezu agreement led to another military truce, but also created a North China Autonomous Zone, including Beijing, where Japanese interests were recognized. Throughout the late 1920s and 1930s, the Japanese continually made overtures to the northern warlords, several of whom were known to be sympathetic. Finally, in July 1937, following the clash of troops southwest of Beijing at Marco Polo Bridge on the seventh of that month, the Japanese took over north China and occupied Beijing. This Japanese move inside the Great Wall, into the historic homeland of the Chinese people, was the signal for full-scale war. The occupation would last more than eight years, until August 1945.

Municipal Governance
and Self-Governance

Although shifting political struggles determined Beijing's physical security in the years from 1911 to 1949, there was a notable change in the city's governance as well as a degree of urban autonomy. During the Qing, its administration had been subject to the complex and deliberately overlapping jurisdictions of the Imperial Household Department, banners, Censorate, gendarmerie, Shuntian Prefecture, and two counties (Daxing and Wanping)—all of which had offices within the city itself. The capital of the surrounding province, Zhili (called Hebei after 1928), was located nearby in Baoding. After 1912 the central authorities continued to play a dominant role in municipal government, but there were fewer conflicting and deliberately redundant lines of authority. In 1914 the Metropolitan District (Jingzhao) replaced Shuntian Prefecture. Containing numerous counties, the Metropolitan District served mainly the countryside around Beijing rather than the city itself. Nevertheless, there was still much administrative confusion. In 1921 sociologist Sidney Gamble observed:

> The Government of [Beijing] is a Chinese puzzle. Many different boards and agencies, including the National Government, with its President, Cabinet and Parliament, the Metropolitan District and two of its 20 hsien [counties], the Military Guard under the Board of War, the Municipal Council and Police Board, both of whom are responsible to the Minister of the Interior, are all functioning in the city. The powers of the various boards are determined by custom rather than by law, so it is practically impossible to describe their relationship under all conditions.[6]

Although national and local offices coexisted, the city of Beijing had become a single administrative entity, no longer split into Inner and Outer cities and no longer spatially defined by city walls, especially after 1928. At first the city government was still a function of the central government and was not locally chosen. In 1914, however, a Municipal Office chiefly responsible for public works—including streets and public spaces, utilities, and public health—came into existence. The initiative for its creation came from Zhu Qiqian, minister of the interior, who suggested to Yuan Shikai the importance of local governing bodies. Having served as police chief in Beijing, he saw the need for a municipal institution separate from the central government. In the opinion of historian Shi Mingzheng, this was one of the most significant institutional changes in the history of the city. The Municipal Office itself was more like a city hall than an elected deliberative body; its officers included engineers and architects as well as clerks and secretaries. All were well educated, and they functioned together effectively.[7]

Before 1914 the Municipal Police Board had been the de facto governing authority in the city. After 1914 the new Municipal Office took charge of overall city planning and construction while the Police Board focused on maintaining order, collecting taxes, reporting census data, fighting fires, and regulating commerce. The two agencies cooperated and together exerted considerable influence on urban life.[8] Creation of a new police force had started in the late Qing era under Prince Su, who led the way in formation of a Japanese-style police academy. The modern Japanese police had in turn been based partly on French, Prussian, and British models. Most of the new police were recruited from among bannermen seeking gainful employment. There were ten thousand men in the police force in the late 1910s, more per capita than in other major world cities: twelve per thousand residents, compared with London, Paris, or Berlin, with only two or three per thousand people.[9]

Beijing, Gamble wrote in 1921, "has well been called the best policed city in the Orient. Any one visiting the city is struck by the large number of traffic officers on the streets, one every few hundred yards on the busy thoroughfares, while those who live in the city are constantly amazed at the extent and efficiency of the work done by the police." He considered them efficient, well trained, and knowledgeable about Beijing's streets and neighborhoods.[10] David Strand's study of 1920s Beijing emphasizes the large role of police in maintaining peace and order. The policeman was supposed to know his beat so well that he would be able to prevent crimes. The *Rules of Policework,* a guide for new recruits, asked: "What sort of person is a policeman? He is a man of learning. A learned man is diligent night and day in accordance with his official responsibilities. A policeman is also sharp of eye and ear and quick-witted. When he comes across something, he can take one look and decide whether it is important or insignificant, trivial or weighty." The policeman was not merely supposed to apprehend criminals but to mediate disputes while they were still at an early stage.[11] He was expected to show far more discretion and intelligence than might be expected based on his pay and social status.

The early twentieth century Beijing police were more proactive than the Qing-era gendarmerie had been, but the rapidity with which a modern force emerged was related to the city's long experience with premodern bureaucratic policing. Financed in part by the continuation of banner stipends, the gendarmerie itself survived until 1924. This was the organization that Gamble called the Military Guard. It operated from its old Inner City headquarters and worked together with the new police (Gamble's Police Board) in patrol, arrests, and enforcement of regulations. On occasion the Military Guard even took the lead in controlling the city, as in responding to the demonstrations of May–June 1919 (on which see below). Thus the seemingly instant emergence of the modern Beijing police occurred in a context in which the gendarmerie was still a daily presence, though reduced in size. Gendarmerie legal experts lectured at the new police academy, and numerous individuals took high-level roles in both institutions, in some cases simultaneously.[12]

As the country's most modern police force, Beijing's was a model for those emerging in many large Chinese cities. Indeed, one aspect of Chiang Kai-shek's approach to social control was modernization of police throughout the land. The police, he said, should be the "nannies" of the people. Chiang's vision of the "nanny" role was decidedly authoritarian, and under the Nationalists after 1928 there was a close connection between control of the police and military-political leadership. Zhang Yinwu, Beijing mayor from 1929 to 1931, was commander-in-chief of the garrison as well as head of the police.[13] Much of police instruction came to involve indoctrination in the ideology of Chiang's New Life Movement—moral training plus Confucian-Christian puritanism—which he launched in 1934 to compete with the asceticism and discipline of the Communist Party.[14]

The expanded functions of the police in the 1930s also were a response to the greater sense of insecurity within the city. As the military situation in the region became more dangerous because of ongoing Japanese aggression to the north, more refugees entered Beijing, the number of jobless and homeless people rose, and crime increased. To some it seemed that newcomers and perfect strangers became the norm, and one's neighbors were not likely to be old-timers. A new Peace Preservation Brigade maintained public security; a thousand men on bicycles or motor tricycles patrolled day and night. Neighborhood police stations replaced old sentry boxes. More like offices than sentry boxes, they collected data on household registration, "bad elements," and unusual disturbances.[15]

Though modernized in their functions, both the Municipal Office and the police continued to be tied to central authority. The only public institution that had any democratically elected component was the Chamber of Commerce. The late Qing court, in an effort to bring merchant leadership into cooperation with the government, had mandated the establishment of chambers of commerce as part of its reform program. In Shanghai the chamber got an early start in 1902 and, together with its Chinese city council, proceeded to form a basis for local self-government. In Beijing, however, business interests were much weaker and official interests overwhelming. Consequently, the Beijing Chamber of Commerce appeared only in 1907. Even in 1919 it represented only 4,600 economic units in the city, ranging from banks and modern companies to traditional "native" banks and exchange shops; small food, grain, and meat shops; tea stores and pharmacies; and purveyors of luxury apparel, cloth, furs, and shoes.[16] As long as the list seemed, these shops constituted only 17 percent of all stores in Beijing; most did not belong to the Chamber of Commerce, and the city had few modern industries.[17]

The Chamber of Commerce had absorbed some guilds into its membership even though they were a premodern form of craft, commercial, or professional association. Among the craft guilds were carpenters, house painters, cloisonné designers, and tailors. In the commercial group were retailers, grocers, and restaurateurs; in the professional group actors, barbers, water-carriers, and storytellers.[18] Membership included masters and apprentices, owners and employees. Guilds were intended to settle internal disputes within the line of trade, and to a large extent they limited competition among members.[19] They also provided social services and support by operating charities, providing for burials, and organizing religious observances of devotion to a patron deity.[20] Like native-place lodges (*huiguan*), guilds (*hanghui, gongsuo*) were a traditional—though much older—form of association that had proliferated in the late Qing period.[21]

Chambers of commerce had a broader set of concerns than guilds, and dealt more extensively with the local authorities, but in Beijing the local was always tied to the national. Thus even this relatively democratic and open chamber, which was supposed to represent the interests of local society against those of the government, was strongly buffeted by national politics. Author David Strand illustrates this process by relating the story of An Disheng, president of the Beijing Chamber of Commerce from 1918 to 1920. An was a native of Xianghe County in Zhili Province, close to Beijing, and had scored so well on the civil service examinations that he served the Qing government as a scholar in the Hanlin Academy, the most prestigious appointment to which a young graduate could aspire. He then served in a number of local and metropolitan posts both before and after 1911. In addition to his scholarly and official background, An also became a successful entrepreneur in the jewelry business. After his election as president, he took the Chamber of Commerce in a politically assertive direction, first opposing state monetary policies and then organizing merchants to oppose the government's position at the Versailles Peace Conference by mounting a boycott of Japanese goods. In 1920 he was easily reelected president, but a short time later he and his vice-president were charged with embezzling funds and arrested. Although he was acquitted and released that same year, it was clear that his organized protest against policies of the Anfu warlord clique had led to reprisals. His successor, Yuan Baosan, was a traditional banker who decided to defer to the constituent guild interests in the Chamber of Commerce and not assume a broader type of leadership. Hoping to win reelection in 1922, An Disheng championed the cause of local self-government and urged the Chamber of Commerce to become more independent of the Municipal Office and its central government sponsors. Expected to win because he was a popular figure, An instead lost narrowly to Sun Xueshi, owner of a Beijing duck restaurant chain, who served until 1926.[22]

The story of An Disheng illustrates the stirrings of self-government and electoral politics, as well as the severe limitations of both, in the Republican era. Self-government became a popular cause in the 1920s—in 1922 there were over forty self-government associations in Beijing—though in the long run it would lose out to yet stronger forces.[23] Nevertheless, popular opinion and political democratization did develop. Local leadership and socially progressive initiatives appeared. Beijing generally lacked an elite with strong local roots. Almost everyone of importance, politically at least, came from all over China. An Disheng was exceptional because he was a native of a nearby county; yet he too returned to his home after his troubled career. In Shanghai, where most leaders were not natives either, they at least came from the cities of the surrounding lower Yangzi region, such as Ningbo or Suzhou. In Beijing, leaders—in this period mostly warlords, officials, or intellectuals—were from all the provinces of China, not just the city's hinterland. Among the many academic and literary figures who were identified with Beijing in the 1920s and 1930s, almost none was originally a Beijingren. When out of work or favor, former courtiers, warlords, and their followers often took refuge in Tianjin, where the foreign-controlled areas at the treaty port could provide legal and economic sanctuary.[24] In fact, that is where the emperor Puyi fled in 1924; out of work, he sought sanctuary in the Japanese concession.

One exemplary local figure was Xiong Xiling, born in 1870 and a native of Hunan Province. A brilliant young scholar, Xiong received the *jinshi* degree at the unusually young age of twenty-four and was appointed to the Hanlin Academy in 1894. At the capital he associated himself with the 1898 reform movement but survived to serve both the Manchus and the new Republican government. In 1913 he held the office of premier, but his "first-caliber cabinet" did not survive Yuan Shikai's hatchet. Although widely respected and often consulted, he did not hold major office afterward. Instead he remained in Beijing and became an important philanthropist. In 1917 he headed the national commission for relief and reconstruction after the massive flood of the Hai River basin, which affected Beijing, Tianjin, and the entire region. In 1918 he founded a school and orphanage for child victims of the flood and in 1920, a school for poor children and orphans located in the Western Hills, the Xiangshan Ciyuyuan. Soon he changed the school's goal to providing all stages of education: elementary and middle school as well as a normal school for training teachers. His plan to add a college was never realized, but the school attracted much favorable attention, and by 1949 it had educated more than six thousand students.[25] Xiong was a prominent leader in many other organizations, a traditional-style local elite member but also a modern philanthropist. The family portrait taken in 1929 shows Xiong with his wife, their son seated in front, and two daughters with their husbands and children. (See Figure 15.) They look prosperous and happy, befitting this type of portrait. One young couple is dressed in Western-style clothing, while the other wears Chinese-style clothing (with Manchu-derived *qipao*) although the woman (Xiong's daughter) wears her hair stylishly bobbed. This was as close to a local elite family as one could find at that time, and yet they were not of local origin, and eventually moved to Shanghai and Hong Kong during the war with Japan. Moreover, Xiong's local prominence started with his national reputation.

Public Spaces and Structures

In its physical appearance and material life, Beijing witnessed significant but not radical transformations from the 1910s through the 1930s. New Western-style buildings, parks, and shops gave the central areas of the city a modern appearance, but homes and residential neighborhoods remained largely unchanged.

Beijing was not as westernized or cosmopolitan as the major treaty ports. Yet for either Chinese or Western visitors, its attractions were not limited to its imperial palaces and gardens. The 1924 edition of *Cook's Guide* spoke of the pleasant natural surroundings, not just the attractions of history and culture. Beijing "is all that is characteristically Chinese in the superlative degree." Not only did art and workmanship attain the " highest level of excellence" there but the city had "the most efficient native police force . . . , the best and largest universities, the finest art collections, the richest temples, the most magnificent palaces; the most vigorous people physically. . . ." In addition, "the city enjoys the healthiest climate in the lowlands of China," and "cleanliness is attainable." During the Boxer period, *Cook's* wrote, Beijing was "a city of smells. Now there is certainly no city in China, under purely Chinese administration, with better streets and a more wholesome atmosphere."[26] For other foreigners, it was the magnificent sights and historic atmosphere that still enchanted. According to Juliet Bredon, author of the best

English-language guide to Beijing's historical monuments in the 1920s, the view from the Qianmen was especially impressive:

> This view is indeed the key to the whole city, and the visitor . . . commands the wonderful prospect of the Palaces, the leading feature in every view of [Beijing], so that the eye is always returning to rest upon them. Because of the vast sweeping lines of their roofs, they look larger even than they are—look mountainous. Their yellow tiles shining against the dark background of the hills remain the supreme memory of the capital—a picture changing, yet ever beautiful, beneath every caprice of hour and light, whether the noonday sun shines down on them so heavily that it seems to raise about them a swimming golden halo, or they lie under a blanket of glittering snow—whether the moonlight softly touches them with silver figures, or the storm wraps them in copper clouds. A symbol of the colourful past, they dominate the city, and always will, however much may change about them with the times.[27]

But lowering her eyes below the rooftops, even Bredon could see that all was not the same. At the very gate where she was standing, major changes already had occurred. She decried "the hideous railway stations" and "the masses of ugly foreign-style buildings." Both the outer and inner towers of the Qianmen and the curved walls that joined them had been destroyed by foreign artillery during the Boxer uprising. (Each of the gates into the city had been constructed this way. Invaders might breach the first gate, but it could be closed to entrap them within.) Soon afterward both towers were rebuilt—the first historical reconstruction since the Qianlong period, but actually designed by a German architect.[28] Later the circular walls around the towers were removed to facilitate the flow of traffic of both traditional and modern vehicles. Across the wide boulevard on the southeast stood the main railway station that brought passengers to Beijing from Tianjin and beyond.

With the introduction of railways into the city, the protective walls of all three important gates on the southern wall of the former Inner City were breached, Xuanwu and Chongwen as well as Qian (Zhengyang). In 1916 a local rail line circled the city connecting the main gates with the Beijing-Fengtian rail line at the Dongbian Gate near the southeast corner of the Inner City. To accommodate a new north-south street, an additional entrance, called Heping Gate, was created between the Xuanwu and Qian gates. By 1927 all the walls of the Imperial City had been torn down to accommodate new streets and traffic patterns.[29]

Street construction was a major focus of the municipal government, and the number of paved roads and streets greatly increased. The expansion of major streets through the city demanded further breaks in the walls. Chang'an Boulevard, the major east-west thoroughfare south of the Forbidden City, was widened and extended; by 1937 it reached beyond the city walls.[30] Street widening and paving opened the way to streetcars starting in 1924. By 1943 there were seven routes connecting major points. Trolleys greatly facilitated transportation within the city, but they were not heavily used because the cost was high for the working class and many people lived at or near their workplaces. Most trolley passengers were government officials, students, and visitors.[31]

Rickshaws, however, greatly benefited from road construction. Imported from Japan in the late nineteenth century, they rapidly became the most common form of transportation. Although seen as old-fashioned and backward—the Japanese term *jinrikisha* means "human power vehicle"—rickshaws actually were a product of modern technology. Crudely constructed at first out of wooden wheels, they later used thick rubber tires, which gave a smoother ride. The expansion of paved streets allowed runners to pull more efficiently, while the vehicles' small size and flexibility also worked well on the unpaved back streets and *hutong*. Rickshaws were popular with Beijing's middle class, for whom they became the most common mode of transportation. In the 1920s sixty thousand rickshaw-pullers collected a half million fares daily in a city of one million, and one of five families in Beijing depended on rickshaw-pulling for its income. So characteristic were rickshaws of life in the 1920s city that Strand dubbed it "Rickshaw Beijing," the title of his book.[32]

In an era of transition, the new did not simply displace the old. Instead, old and new coexisted in a casual mélange. Almost every mode of transport could be found on the streets of Beijing: automobiles, trolleys, rickshaws, bicycles, animal-drawn carts, and, on the back streets, cargo-laden camels. Photographs taken by Donald Mennie about 1920 reveal that most of the city still had unpaved streets, traditional shops, and traffic unchanged in appearance from the past. One shows a dusty city boulevard with decorative arch (*pailou*), crumbled pavement stones, carts of various kinds, and pedestrians. (See Figure 17.) An overhead view of a "street in the Tartar City" gives an impression of the roofs of shops and residences, which as in Qing times were rarely taller than one storey. Camels and rickshaws are visible, but overhead electrical wires are a sign of change. (See Figure 18.) In front of the Qianmen, by contrast, the street is paved and clean, but the traffic consists largely of rickshaws, carts, and porters. (See Figure 19.) Although the Qianmen area was usually congested, the environs of some of the other city gates and walls could be deserted and dusty. Another picture shows workmen eating a noonday meal beneath an Outer City gate. (See Figure 20.)

New Western-style buildings clustered in central areas. Unlike Shanghai, Tianjin, or other treaty ports, where Western banks, hotels, and businesses dominated the downtown architecture, Beijing's Western-style buildings did not affect the traditional architectural unity of the capital. Except for the Northern, Eastern, and Southern cathedrals, which had an older history, most of the Western-style buildings housed significant new institutions in Republican-era Beijing.

One architectural design popular after 1900 was the Western-style facade, in which a grand doorway, archway, or gate would be superimposed on a traditional Chinese-style building. Some were found on the entrances to conventional *si-heyuan* compounds.[33] The ornate facades of shops in the Dashalar shopping district were outstanding examples. One of the best was the Ruifuxiang Silk Store, built in 1901, with another branch in 1903. These shops still stand today, and are more representative of the era than the buildings of entirely Chinese-style emporia, such as the Tongrentang Pharmaceutical Shop, whose business originated in the Ming dynasty. Figure 21 shows the archway, ornate decoration, and frieze above the Ruifuxiang entrance.

Public buildings of the 1920s and 1930s were usually in a Western architectural style. The railway stations were the first of these. The station at Qianmen, with its characteristic arched roof and clock tower, still stands today, although it no longer serves as a station but houses shops including Kentucky Fried Chicken. The Ministry of Foreign Affairs and other government offices also had Western-style edifices. The Legation Quarter, rebuilt after the Boxer destruction of 1900, contained some of the leading examples of Western architecture, including the British, American, French, and Japanese embassies, residences, and grounds. Many still survive, but serve different functions. Now as then, they are hidden behind high walls and not easily visible from the street. International banks also erected imposing buildings: the Hong Kong and Shanghai Banking Corporation, Banque de l'Indochine, Chartered Bank of England, Australia, and China, and the like. The National Bank of New York was housed in a monumental neoclassical structure, complete with Greek columns, designed by the American architect Henry Killam Murphy, who designed similar buildings in the treaty ports of Hankou, Tianjin, Shanghai, and Canton. The international hotels, including the earlier Wagon-Lits Hotel (Liuguo fandian) and the original Peking Hotel (Beijing fandian, originally Hotel de Pekin, built in 1907 and expanded to a seven-storey new building in 1917) also were notable structures.[34]

Missionary schools established in the late nineteenth century were built in Western style. When Qinghua (Tsinghua) University developed from a secondary school, it acquired a large piece of property at Changchunyuan, previously the Kangxi emperor's retreat in the Haidian district. There, following the advice of Murphy and other Western architects, the university constructed between 1914 and the 1930s an American-style university campus, with classrooms, assembly hall, and sports fields. Its imposing entrance gate had Greek columns, pedestal, and archway. Today this is still Qinghua's south gate. (See Figure 27.) The signature campus building, its central auditorium, was a close replica of Thomas Jefferson's classical, neo-Palladian style rotunda at the University of Virginia. The campus had some Chinese landscaping in a few areas, but the architecture was predominantly Western.

By contrast, the campus of the American missionary-sponsored Yanjing (Yenching) University, adjacent to Qinghua, employed largely Chinese architecture and landscaping in an American-style college campus. The man-made Nameless Lake (Weiming hu) was encircled by willow trees and pathways, with a pagoda overlooking the scene. All the classrooms, library, and public buildings were designed in traditional Chinese style: tiled roofs, red-painted pillars and woodwork, and some buildings clustered in courtyard fashion, though they were constructed with modern engineering techniques and materials. John Leighton Stuart, Yanjing University president from its founding until 1946, later wrote:

> We had determined from the outset to use an adaptation of Chinese architecture for the academic buildings. Graceful curves and gorgeous coloring were designed for the exteriors while the main structures were to be constructed throughout of reinforced concrete and equipped with modern lighting, heating, and plumbing. Thus the buildings were in themselves symbolic of educational purpose in preserving all that was most valuable in China's cultural heritage.[35]

The thirteen-storey pagoda—which still stands as the most recognizable structure on campus—housed a water tower. After 1949 Yanjing University ceased to be an independent entity, and this beautiful campus became the home of Beijing University.

For most Beijing residents, however, Western-style banks, embassies, and campuses were inaccessible and not part of daily life. For them the important public spaces were temples and their fairs, markets and shops, and public parks. The last were new in China's cities, and several opened in Beijing in the 1910s and 1920s. The Central Park was located on the grounds of the Altar to Soil and Grain just west of Tiananmen. Beginning in 1914 this park, with its restaurants and pavilions, became a favorite spot for relatively well-off citizens of Beijing. After 1928 it was called Zhongshan Park to honor Sun Yat-sen, who was best known as Sun Zhongshan. Northeast of the city wall the grounds of the Altar to Earth were transformed into Capital Park, which had lecture and exhibition sites as well as recreational facilities. Other public parks were established at former imperial altars (temples) to Heaven, Agriculture, Sun and Moon.[36] (See Map 6.)

Markets, however, were still the most important locations for social interaction and daily commerce. They ranged from humble neighborhood shops and itinerant peddlers to newly created centers. Temple fairs and markets remained important in the lives of ordinary people, especially lower-middle-class families. Temple fairs, operating weekly or twice weekly, consisted of outdoor stands that sold hand crafted household goods, such as utensils and baskets. As before, they were neighborhood gathering places. In the Republican period, temple markets may have increased in number and become more permanent than periodic ones, and the commercial functions of temples became, in many cases, more important than their religious ones.[37]

In the past, commerce within the Inner City had been restricted to fairs or smaller markets, while trade in luxury goods and entertainment of various kinds flourished in the Outer City. The area near Qianmen in the Outer City had been the main center for all kinds of commodities, restaurants, and entertainment. Nearby Dashalar housed clothing stores, medical outlets, and more restaurants. Liulichang, adjacent to Dashalar, was an important emporium for books, artwork, antiques, and curios. After 1911, when the traditional restrictions of the Inner City were removed, the Qianmen area became less central for the luxury goods market, which was drawn into the Inner City. It remained, however, a hub for ordinary goods, and Dashalar and Liulichang retained their more specialized markets. In the 1930s photographer Hedda Morrison captured a street scene with tobacco shops and restaurants in the Qianmen area. In another photo, shoppers at Liulichang inspect scroll paintings at the new year's fair. The men wear long gowns and cloth shoes. The Western hats and the electrical wires overhead are the only signs that these pictures were taken in the twentieth century. (See Figures 22 and 23.)

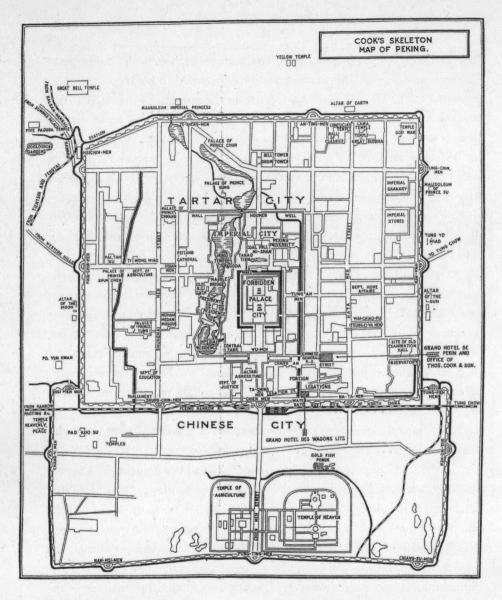

Map 6. Beijing in the Republican Period. *Source:* Peking, North China, South Manchuria, and Korea. *5th ed. Peking: Thos. Cook & Son, 1924*

Chien Men – Qianmen

Di Wong Miao – Lidai diwang miao

Hsi Chin Men – Xizhi Gate

Lama Temple – Yonghegong

Old R. C. Cath – Old Northern Cathedral

Pai Tah Su – Baitasi

Pao Kuo Su – Baoguosi

Peitang Cathedral – Northern Cathedral since 1887

Po Yun Kwan – Baiyunguan

Tung Yo Miao – Dongyuemiao

Wai-Chiao-Pu – Ministry of Foreign Affairs

Wangfujing became the principal center for modern shops, particularly for those selling Western goods. Close to the Legation Quarter, it attracted the city's foreign community as well as more prosperous Chinese customers. Wangfujing resembled the stylish shopping streets in most treaty ports, and boasted storefront windows, fashionable women's clothing, men's tailors, hairdressers, drugstores, and drycleaners. Attached to Wangfujing was the Dong'an Market, where old style market stalls and entertainment as well as new shops appealed to a wider range of customers and tourists. Unlike the traditional markets, they all were enclosed in a large shed-like structure that protected them from the elements. Shops were open on a daily basis, and the market itself was organized not by temples but by the police. At Xidan and Dongdan, traditional markets located on the western and eastern sections of Chang'an Boulevard, outdoor stalls were replaced by permanent, enclosed shops. These new shopping districts served the needs of wealthy and middle-class customers, who found them more attractive than older markets or fairs. Removal of the walls of the Imperial City benefited business because it allowed traffic to flow more easily.[38]

Serving the common people of Beijing was the popular Tianqiao ("Heavenly Bridge"), a market area stretching to the west of the Temple of Heaven southward as far as the Yongding Gate. When the Temple of Agriculture, adjacent to the Temple of Heaven, opened as a public park in 1917, the government designated Tianqiao as a new market area. The streets were cleaned and trolley lines designed to terminate there. People came from all over the city to shop, eat, and be entertained. The atmosphere was raucous; it had the feel of a carnival, but was as accessible as a market and required no tickets. One could view peepshows as well as wrestlers, magicians, acrobats, storytellers, and medicine dealers, whose work was a cross between business and entertainment. The shops at Tianqiao sold a variety of goods, but secondhand and recycled items made it extremely popular with the working class in particular. Tianqiao cast a spell over ordinary Beijing residents. For them it represented hope, freedom, and a sense of belonging. "Tianqiao is the epitome of Beijing; it is a microcosm of life there," wrote one observer. Tianqiao was critical to the "formation of Republican Beijing's identity," historian Madeleine Dong maintains.[39] Such a market was like the street, "the poor man's great show; and also his education."[40]

Life and Death in Beijing

Beijing's population expanded rapidly between 1912 and 1949. In 1912 the population of the Inner and Outer cities together was reported as 725,000 people; in

1917, 812,000; in 1925, 1.2 million; in 1935, 1.1 million, and in 1948, 1.5 million. If the population of the immediate suburbs is taken into account, the number reached 2 million by 1948. And if the surrounding counties are included, the population exceeded 4 million in 1948. This growth was caused by immigration from the countryside, not by changes in birth and death rates. The demographic situation in Beijing was fluid, with many newcomers but also many people leaving the city. After the 1911 revolution, some of the Manchu banner families left for Manchuria to make a living. But even greater numbers of poor people came in from the surrounding countryside in Hebei and Shandong to seek a living in Beijing. This immigration was pronounced during major floods, such as those of 1917, 1924, and 1949, but warlord military activity and later Japanese invasion caused even greater numbers to seek shelter within the city. Especially after July 7, 1937, when the Japanese invaded and occupied north China, conditions in the countryside became desperate, and peasants sought food and safety.[41] Unlike large-scale transfers of population at the start of the Yuan, Ming, and Qing eras, most of the immigration in the Republican period was neither mandated nor controlled, and it consisted predominantly of the rural poor.

Around 1920, pioneering social scientists Sidney D. Gamble and John S. Burgess organized a team of Chinese researchers, mostly university students, to survey the neighborhoods of Beijing. The data compiled between September 1918 and December 1919 formed the basis for *Peking: A Social Survey* (1921)—a groundbreaking source for studying the city's society. According to their survey, Beijing had a population of 812,556, of whom 63.5 percent (515,535) were male and 36.5 percent (296,021) were female. The high male-to-female ratio probably was true in the Qing period as well but had not been verified until this study. Gamble and Burgess explained the imbalance by pointing out that the population was largely made up of immigrants coming to the city at a young age (between fifteen and thirty) in search of "education, business training and official position." This group included some already married men who chose to leave their families at home while seeking employment. Of the younger males coming to Beijing some were university students and others were unskilled laborers looking for work. The ratio of males to females seemed to be highest in the former Outer City, where Beijing's workshops and factories were concentrated and where out-of-town employees were numerous. In the strictly residential neighborhoods elsewhere in the city, males and females were more evenly balanced. University students, even if married, would generally leave their wives in their hometowns, and officials seeking appointments left their families at home, at least until they established themselves. Remarkably, one informant estimated that there were 100,000 to 125,000 "expectant officials" in the city, but only five to six thousand positions. Although it is not clear that this was literally so, it conveyed the mixture of hope and despair that those coming to the capital must have felt.[42]

The standard of living for most in Beijing was not high, and a police survey found about 12 percent of the population, close to 97,000 people, were either "poor" or "very poor."[43] Another study from 1926 found conditions to be even worse, with 16.8 percent of the population destitute and 9.2 percent poor. In this survey 47.3 percent of families were "lower middle class," 22.4 percent "comfortable," and another 4.3 percent well-to-do.[44] In 1928 the mayor and head of police estimated that more than 100,000 people were destitute and another 100,000 unemployed in Beijing.[45] In short, by most measures roughly a quarter of the population was below, and about half were just at, the subsistence level. A study of Manchu and Chinese families found that the median annual income was $90 to $109, which was considered more than enough for a family. The greatest share of the family income, about 83 to 68 percent, went for food; the very poorest spent as much as 90 percent on food. For the poor, cornbread and turnips were the staple fare.[46] The amount of grain—coarse grains, such as millet or corn—consumed by Beijing families varied according to their incomes, but only up to a certain point, after which a greater portion of their food budgets would be spent on vegetables, meats, and condiments. On average, working class families consumed 1.2 catties (1.6 pounds) of grain per person per day but aimed for 1.5 catties. Although nutritional needs varied according to occupation, gender, and age, such a diet was just about at the subsistence level.[47] Fine grains (rice or wheat), meat, chicken, or duck—for which Beijing is so famous—were at this time beyond the reach of a large segment of the population.

The Manchu banner families were the largest and most characteristic group among Beijing's poor. The situation of most bannermen, except the highest ranking, had been pitiable throughout the nineteenth century. After the revolution their formerly privileged situation, with stipends of grain and silver as well as guaranteed housing, deteriorated increasingly over time. Grain stipends were suspended, and by the 1920s cash stipends were issued only on three major holidays. Because the Manchu population constituted 20 to 25 percent of Beijing's total population, its distress meant that a considerable number of people were unemployed or barely employed.[48] The common opinion was that the former bannermen were either unable to work or unsuited to it. Even Gamble subscribed to the latter view: "Long years of living on the government bounty have unfitted most of the Manchus for earning a living; and now many of them would rather starve than go to work."[49] The poverty and misplaced pride of the bannermen became the subject of satire. In a typical scene the bannerman buys the cheapest sesame bun in the teahouse and spends hours eating it while pretending to practice calligraphy. One day his son comes to the teahouse, saying "Baba, go home right away. Mama wants to get up." The father says, "So let her get up. What do I have to go home for?" The son replies, "You're wearing her pants. If you don't get home, she'll have nothing to wear."[50] That this story was not merely a joke is suggested by a 1930 survey of low and middle-income families, about 75 percent of the population: "Only one-fourth of these people had anything to wear when they washed their summer clothes, and less than one-fourth had anything to wear when they washed their winter clothes. Those who did not had to borrow clothes from other family members on wash days."[51]

Two lines of work became associated with bannermen: rickshaw-pulling and policing. Bannermen made up a large portion of the rickshaw-pullers in the city. In 1920 about three-quarters of ten thousand policemen were bannermen. Students and actors also pulled rickshaws. For them rickshaw-pulling was seen as a kind of downward mobility that went with craft or trade jobs; for others rickshaw-pulling was a step up the social and economic ladder.[52] A policeman had to be literate, but his job did not carry status or high pay. Sometimes off-duty policemen moonlighted as rickshaw-pullers at night; some were still so poor that they ate at soup kitchens in the winter.[53]

In the past the truly destitute and homeless had resorted to begging. According to one estimate, in 1878 there were over twenty thousand naked beggars in the city. Most beggars tended to congregate just outside Qianmen. On the roads to the city during the Qing era, begging had been organized by a Beggars' Guild with a "king," who would direct the territorial distribution of beggars, and levy "taxes" on shopkeepers and even wealthy families. Under the republic, however, begging was banned although it continued in more modest fashion.[54] More widely accepted, however, was operating soup kitchens for the poor. This traditional practice expanded in the twentieth century, and as before it was seasonal, lasting during the cold months, usually from December to mid-April. There were twelve centers run by the police or the military. People would gather daily, each clutching a bowl or other receptacle. No questions were asked; all who came were assumed to be deserving. Gamble described the careful routine:

When the time comes for distribution, the outer gate is closed so that there may be no chance for any repeating and those who are in the courtyard, numbering anywhere from seven hundred to three thousand, are lined up single file. First come the children, then the women, and finally the men. The long line goes slowly by the large tubs of steaming porridge where each person . . . is given a big dipperful of hot food [a porridge of seven parts millet and three parts rice]. No one is allowed to eat his porridge in the courtyard; so those in charge see to it that every one leaves as soon as he is served. Once outside the gate, it does not take long for the porridge to disappear.[55]

According to records, 550,000 to 640,000 meals a month were dispensed at these twelve soup kitchens; in one particular month, as many as 700,000 meals were served. Thus on average 20,000 meals were served per day when the kitchens were in operation. During the winter of 1925, a time of military crisis, another source said that soup kitchens served 30,000 people per day. These numbers exceed those fed in the later Qing, and suggest that there was greater poverty in the Republican period.[56]

Other social services were available to the poor and abandoned in Beijing, but they were far from sufficient for the city's needs. Writing just before 1920, Gamble characterized these as experimental institutions. They included foundling homes, such as Xiong Xiling's, orphanages, and a few old-age homes, one started in 1895 by "ladies of the foreign community." Each of these establishments stressed cleanliness and discipline.[57] In general, the spirit of social reform inspired such new institutions of the late Qing and early republic. Another example was the Beijing Model Prison established in 1912 as part of a legal reform movement. Authorities saw prisons as places for rehabilitation rather than punishment. Prisoners were given a full day's work, which often included printing and bookbinding. Prisoners under eighteen years of age received two hours of classroom work a day. Lectures on religion and morality, some by Christian missionaries, were heard by all. Although the Beijing prison was a model imitated elsewhere in China, and appeared successful, many prisoners still returned to a life of crime when released.[58]

Despite general poverty in the Beijing population and limited opportunities for a person to improve his economic status, Republican Beijing was a relatively healthy place to live. "The health of [Beijing] is on the whole very good," wrote Gamble. He attributed this to the effort expended by the police in cleaning up the city and also to the work of forty-six hospitals and about a thousand doctors, 10 percent of whom had some Western medical training. The influential Peking Union Medical College, established by the Rockefeller Foundation, was training a generation of Chinese medical students.[59] Evidence of improved health conditions appeared in surveys taken at a demonstration health station in the Inner City—a project jointly run by the Peking Union Medical College and the municipal government. Their data revealed that mortality rates had improved and life expectancies were higher. At the age of five, life expectancies were 54.1 years for men and 47.1 years for women. By contrast, records of imperial lineage members from 1644 to 1740 show life expectancies at age five of only 37.9 and 35.2 years, respectively.[60]

Increases in life expectancy occurred as the result of public health interventions, not higher living standards, according to sociologist Cameron Campbell. Death rates from common infectious diseases, such as typhoid, dysentery, cholera, smallpox, diphtheria, and measles declined steadily from the early 1910s.[61] Improvements in the city's water supply and sewage system may have helped to reduce the occurrence of disease. The quality of drinking water always had caused dissatisfaction. Because Beijing was not located near a major river, most households had relied either on shallow wells in their own courtyards, which had bitter-tasting water, or on fresh water from the Western Hills sold by peddlers. In 1908 the Beijing Waterworks Company began using Western technology to set up water treatment plants and a system of pipelines through the city. The system was expensive, however, and as late as 1930 only about 10 percent of Beijing's population enjoyed scientifically treated running water.[62] The city's ancient sewage system was even more of a problem. Not only were the sewers open, but by the twentieth century many were in disrepair and had not been regularly cleaned out. People routinely threw their garbage into the streets, which must have contributed to the spread of disease. In the Republican period, the city tried to rebuild the sewer system, not replace it, focusing mostly on the commercial and wealthier residential districts of the Inner City. Although much remained to be done, this progress too may have contributed to improved sanitary conditions.[63]

In the first decades of the twentieth century, many city governments in China took initiatives to raise the level of public consciousness about sanitation and public health (*weisheng*), which they considered an important aspect of a modernizing nation.[64] After 1928, under the Nationalist government, public health campaigns increased in Beijing and were reinforced by an intrusive police force. Campaigns for improvement of personal hygiene included emphasis on eating habits, tooth brushing, and cleanliness. Those for public sanitation included not spitting or urinating in the streets, cleaning up waste matter, and eliminating flies; officials lectured schoolchildren on these topics. Between 1934 and 1937, as part of the New Life Movement, there were annual city hygiene campaigns in parks, streets, and neighborhoods, with booths offering various types of information and advice. There was also the "healthy children competition" that offered free vaccinations and public talks and demonstration. A public health inspection squad was mobilized to inspect shops, hotels, restaurants, and other public facilities. Policemen also visited various districts to check on compliance.[65]

Despite the undeniable poverty in the city and the genteel shabbiness of many of its inhabitants, Beijing held its attractions for people of all classes. Nothing captures the bittersweetness of Beijing better than the famous novel *Camel Xiangzi* (*Luotuo Xiangzi*), sometimes translated as *Rickshaw Boy*. The author, Lao She, is the writer most identified with Beijing in this period, renowned for his ability to capture the lives of ordinary people amid social changes in the city. Born in 1899, Lao She (the pen name of Shu Qingqun) was a true Beijingren of Manchu background; his father was a palace guard killed during the 1900 allied occupation. Although his family was very poor, he was able to get free education, room, and board at the Beijing Normal School. After graduation he became the principal of a primary school in the city, studied at Yanjing University, and taught Chinese in Beijing and Tianjin. He studied English at Beijing University and in 1924 went to London to teach Chinese at the School of Oriental and African Studies, where he read Dickens and other English authors. His experience in Britain made Lao She a sharper observer of his own society. Returning to China in 1930, he soon devoted himself entirely to writing. *Camel Xiangzi* was published initially in serial form in 1936–1937.

Xiangzi is a young man from the countryside who goes to Beijing to find work. Rickshaw-pulling attracts him because there are few barriers to entry and because, being tall and strong, he is exceptionally good at it. Renting a rickshaw to pull, he works with little rest and few luxuries and is generally liked by his customers and fellow pullers. After three years he manages to save enough money to purchase his own rickshaw, the culmination of his dream of independence. Shortly afterward, however, he is conscripted by soldiers and loses his rickshaw. Escaping, he manages to steal three camels—the source of his nickname—which he trades for cash to return to the city. Reaching Beijing, barely able to walk, he is tempted to kiss the earth beneath his feet. He loves

> the medley of horses, the cacophony of sounds, the stench of dust. . . . He had
> no parents or brothers, no relatives at all; the only friend he had was this ancient

city. It had given him everything. So even if he starved here, he loved it better than the countryside. Here there were things to see and things to hear, light and sound everywhere. As long as he worked hard, there was money past counting here. Endless good things too, more than he could eat or wear. Here even a beggar could get soup with meat in it, whereas in the countryside there was nothing but maize flour. When he reached the west side of Gaoliang Bridge, he sat down on the bank and wept for joy.[66]

Twice more Xiangzi saves money to buy a rickshaw, only to lose it again. He works for one family that treats him well, but other employers are not so humane. He ruins his physical health through overexertion and his emotional health through disappointment and frustration. His only source of human comfort is "Tigress," the tough daughter of the owner of the rickshaw company, who offers marriage, but she dies in childbirth. Later a young woman who likes him commits suicide after she is sold into prostitution. Xiangzi loses his hope and his integrity as well, learning to cheat and betray. Disappointed, embittered, and weary, at the end Xiangzi is without a rickshaw and gets along by hiring himself out to participate in wedding and funeral processions. But still he could appreciate how

the sudden warmth seemed to awaken the city from its spring drowsiness, people roused themselves to seek amusement, their enjoyment blossoming in the warmth in step with the flowers, grasses and trees. The young, green willow branches and sprouting reeds of the Nanhai and Beihai Lakes attracted youths playing mouth organs, couples rowed small boats into the shade of the weeping willows, or drifted among the young lotus plants, humming love songs, their eyes kissing. . . . .

Fun, bustle, colour and clamour everywhere. The sudden warmth of early summer seemed to bewitch the ancient city. Death, disaster, and poverty receded, its many inhabitants mesmerized into dreamily singing its praises. Dirty, beautiful, dilapidated, bustling, chaotic, easy-going, and charming, this was the great city of Beiping in the early summer.[67]

Xiangzi's story can be taken to represent the plight of all of China. Proud, hardworking, and decent, China and Xiangzi both meet a disappointing end. Lao She seemed to be expressing the view that individual effort alone could not overcome a hostile society and implying that some kind of collective effort was needed.[68] Yet the story has a unique and specific setting—a Beijing that was still easygoing, charming, and "a great city."

The New Culture Movement
and Beijing's Intellectuals

In the Republican era young scholars and writers were drawn to Beijing not so much by its ancient charm as by its intellectual dynamism and by the opportunity to work for a modern China. The new universities—particularly Beijing, Qinghua, and Yanjing—attracted students from all directions. They recruited the most talented individuals, many from the Shanghai, or lower Yangzi, region, to their faculties. Some intellectuals came to Beijing to serve the government, but this was much less prominent a motive than it had been in imperial times. In the past, aspiring scholars had prepared for the civil service examinations close to home and then moved up to the county, prefectural, and provincial capitals to take their examinations. In the new era they came to Beijing—as well as Shanghai, Tianjin, and a few other major cities—for their higher education, not for examinations.

For the intellectual elite, it was idealism and service, not position or profit, that were the primary motives for moving to Beijing. The best and the brightest concentrated in the city particularly during the decade between 1916 and 1926. Cai Yuanpei can be considered the senior figure of this intellectual era. Born in 1868, a generation older than most of the others, he had received a classical education, achieved the highest degree in 1890, and even served in the prestigious Hanlin Academy. He later became interested in modern education, including that of girls, and participated in anti-Qing revolutionary activities in Shanghai. He was minister of education under both Sun Yat-sen and Yuan Shikai. After a period of time in Europe, he was appointed chancellor of Beijing University (known as Beida from *Beijing daxue*) in 1916. More than anyone else he is credited with building the university to be the foremost institution of higher education in China. He hired dozens of faculty members able to teach a curriculum that introduced Western philosophy and science but still respected traditional Chinese learning. His character, integrity, and great prestige as a scholar inspired others to such an extent that Cai completely changed the reputation of the university.[69] From its origins, the school had drawn mostly office-seekers, not scholars; both faculty and students had indulged in gambling and prostitution. The university had been called the Brothel Brigade and other unflattering names.[70] But under Cai's leadership, there developed a new spirit known as Beida *xuefeng,* or the "Beida winds of learning."[71]

Among the Beida faculty of this era were some who would play pivotal roles in the search for a more modern China. Chen Duxiu served as dean of the college of arts and letters from 1917 to 1919, a crucial period in the growth of the New Culture Movement; he was one of the founders of the Chinese Communist Party in Shanghai in 1921. Li Dazhao, another founder of the party, served as librarian and professor at Beida for ten years, 1918 to 1927. He was responsible for introducing Marxism to Chinese intellectuals, most significantly to Mao Zedong, who was employed in the library for a few months during 1918 and 1919. (The young Mao could not afford to be a student at the university.) Hu Shi, who had studied with John Dewey in the United States and would become one of the most important Chinese intellectuals of the era, was recruited to teach philosophy while still in his twenties. He was associated with Beida for almost thirty years, with several interruptions to go overseas; from 1946 to 1948 he served as president of the university. Other well-known intellectuals, such as the writers Shen Congwen and Zhou Zuoren (brother of the writer Lu Xun, whose real name was Zhou Shuren) taught at Beida off and on through the 1930s and 1940s.

The New Culture Movement was born in 1917 in Beijing in the intellectually vibrant environment of Beida. Under the encouragement of Cai Yuanpei, many publications and student discussion groups—all concerned with the future of China—flourished. All agreed that there were aspects of traditional society that needed to be changed before China could become a strong, progressive nation able to withstand foreign aggression. Most important was the need to break the intellectual stranglehold that classical learning had on progress; the years of study required to master classical Chinese meant that writing and literature were still in large part an elite monopoly. To extend literacy to ordinary people, Hu Shi advocated the use of vernacular Chinese in writing; in other words, people should write in the same way that they spoke. This was roughly comparable to saying that books should be written in English rather than in Latin. Chen Duxiu, dean at Beida, supported Hu Shi by publishing his articles in *New Youth*, a magazine that he had started in 1915 at Shanghai. Chen moved to Beijing when Cai Yuanpei assumed the presidency at Beida in early 1917. *New Youth* itself, and other publications like *New Tide*, were themselves written in vernacular Chinese, which was called *baihua*. The journal was immensely popular among students because it contained frank and open discussion of timely topics. Students could not wait to buy each new issue. "It came to us like a clap of thunder which awakened us in the midst of a restless dream," recalled one reader.[72]

"New Culture" meant replacing the philosophy and social system of the old culture, Confucianism, with an ideology of individualism and freedom. For intellectuals and students, the old culture stood for conservative reverence for antiquity and enslavement to the family system. The very term "New Youth" expressed the idea that youth was something to be valued, whereas the Confucian system esteemed old age. The old way valued being old and even acting old. "He's young but he acts old" had been a high compliment. Instead, argued the editors of *New Youth,* being young and thinking and acting young should be praised. Filial piety had led people to be subservient. Also, women should be respected; the new culture particularly attacked old customs such as arranged marriages. Women's education was promoted, and more women attended universities. (See Figure 24.) Above all, the New Culture urged that a spirit of science and rationality rather than custom and prejudice be applied to problems. In government, democracy should prevail. For simplicity, Chen Duxiu characterized these goals as "Mr. Science" and "Mr. Democracy."[73] Such iconoclastic ideas were popularized by the short stories of Lu Xun, who became China's best-known writer. In "The True Story of Ah Q" (1921) and other works, he depicted tragicomic characters who had all the traits of false pride, ignorance, and slavishness that he thought the Chinese possessed. His stories conveyed concisely and effectively the message of the new culture.

The influence of foreign ideas on the New Culture Movement was profound. Study overseas was an important experience that these intellectuals shared. Especially after the civil service examinations were abolished in 1905, thousands of young people had sought education abroad. In the first decade Japan was the most common destination because of its proximity to China and the similarity in written language. As the Asian nation that had adopted Western technology and learning most rapidly, Japan played an important role in supporting the revolutionary cause before its own imperial ambitions tarnished its reputation in Chinese eyes. Both Lu Xun and his brother Zhou Zuoren studied in Japan prior to 1911. Hu Shi went to the United States on a Boxer Indemnity Scholarship. He began at Cornell University but found his true calling in studying with the eminent philosopher and educator John Dewey at Columbia. He maintained his association with the United States throughout his life and from 1938 to 1942 was Chinese ambassador in Washington. Cai Yuanpei studied in Germany before and during his presidency at Beida, and also had traveled to France and the United States. The poet Xu Zhimo studied in the United States and then in England, where he met famous writers of that period such as Katherine Mansfield. For these scholars and writers, overseas education was not just casual tourism or personal improvement but an experience that deeply influenced their views of Chinese society. Others, including future leaders of the

Communist Party such as Zhou Enlai and Deng Xiaoping, went to France in the 1919–1921 period to join a work-study program.

Personal ties as well as fascination with China drew important foreign intellectuals to Beijing. Hosted by his student Hu Shi, John Dewey spent two years lecturing in various cities; students eagerly absorbed his ideas on ethics, education, and social philosophy.[74] The British philosopher Bertrand Russell spent almost a year in China, from the fall of 1920 to the summer of 1921, lecturing on economic, social, and educational reform.[75] Margaret Sanger gave talks on family planning in 1922. The Indian poet and Nobel Prize winner Rabindranath Tagore, with his imposing height and white beard, drew the most attention. Focusing on a common Asian experience, Tagore's interest in traditional Chinese philosophy and literature found a devoted following in Europe and among some Chinese, but it also drew criticism from liberal intellectuals. These visits always had their focus in Beijing, where intellectual life was especially lively in the 1920s. (See Figure 16.)

Tagore's interpreter and companion in China in 1924 was the young poet Xu Zhimo. A gifted poet and charismatic personality, Xu was perhaps the central figure in a circle of highly creative intellectuals. His personal life, which he did not hide, enhanced his celebrity. Like most men of his generation, Xu had been married by family arrangement to a local girl, whom he left at home when he went to study in the United States and England. Soon Xu was attracted to Lin Huiyin, then only sixteen, who was accompanying her father, Lin Changmin, in England. Lin Huiyin was well educated and cosmopolitan; she also was considered a great beauty. Her father, however, already had arranged her engagement to Liang Sicheng, the son of Liang Qichao—originally a disciple of Kang Youwei and now Republican China's most prominent intellectual. During the Tagore visit, Xu Zhimo was able to spend time with her, but she remained true to Liang Sicheng (and her father). Xu soon fell in love with another woman, somewhat older than Lin Huiyin and well suited to his intellectual interests and experience. She was married to someone else, but after a few years the couple did marry—an event scandalous to some and romantic to others. After 1927 Xu split his time between Shanghai and Beijing. He died tragically in a plane crash in 1931.[76]

Xu Zhimo's brief life illustrates the glamorous and daring side of Beijing's intellectual elite in the 1920s. Lin Huiyin and Liang Sicheng's story illustrates the early idealism of the intellectuals and their later disappointments. Lin and Liang went together to the United States in 1924 to study architecture at the

University of Pennsylvania, and Liang spent another year at Harvard. Upon receiving their degrees, they married and returned to China via a wedding trip through Europe, where they viewed important monuments. Back in China in 1928, Liang Sicheng taught at universities including Beida and Qinghua; in 1946 he became chair of the architecture department at Qinghua. In these years he concentrated on documenting the history of Chinese architecture. On many field trips, Liang and Lin sketched the remains of ancient temples. Their goal was to help preserve China's architectural tradition while drawing on the best of their Western training. Today Liang is revered for advocating a plan for Beijing after 1949 that would have preserved the historic city and created a new capital alongside it. In the current nostalgia for "Old Beijing," Lin Huiyin and Liang Sicheng are seen as a beautiful couple, marked by learning, sophistication and integrity.[77] (See Figure 26.) In 2004, on the hundredth anniversary of her birth, Lin Huiyin's life was celebrated in numerous biographies.

Student Movements and Wartime Beijing

The New Culture Movement was strongly linked to political events at the capital, and particularly to popular reaction against the warlord government's weakness vis-à-vis Japan. During World War I, Japanese aggression had increased, taking advantage of a power vacuum created by the withdrawal of the Western powers' attention from China as they waged war in Europe. In 1915 Japan had submitted to the Yuan Shikai government the infamous Twenty-one Demands, which included serious economic and political concessions. The Japanese also put the next government under considerable pressure, and President Duan Qirui had accepted loans from the Japanese and made deals with them that were unknown to the public. At the Versailles Peace Conference in 1919, Great Britain, France, and Italy, later joined by the United States, agreed to recognize Japan's claim to Shandong Province, previously under German domination. (Both China and Japan had sided with the Allies.) The Chinese delegation was about to sign the peace treaty when news of this and other secret understandings with the Japanese reached China. On May 4, amid general outrage, student demonstrations erupted in Beijing. More soon followed in other Chinese cities, and over the next month great popular pressure was brought to bear on both the government in Beijing and the delegation at Versailles. In the end China did not sign the peace treaty because Chinese students in Paris physically prevented the delegates from leaving their hotel for the signing ceremony.

The May Fourth incident was a Beijing event of enormous significance in Chinese history. On the afternoon of May 4, 1919, about three thousand students gathered at Tiananmen. Thirteen colleges and universities participated, but the Beida group was largest and took the lead. Students had prepared leaflets and signs and composed a manifesto: "This is the last chance for China in her life and death struggle. Today we swear two solemn oaths with all our fellow countrymen: (1) China's territory may be conquered, but it cannot be given away; (2) the Chinese people may be massacred but they will not surrender. Our country is about to be annihilated. Up, brethren!"[78] At about two o'clock, they marched toward the Zhonghua Gate between Tiananmen and Qianmen. They particularly targeted three high officials who had been active in arranging concessions to the Japanese and who, they believed, were meeting in Beijing that very day. At the Legation Quarter, they called on the U.S. ambassador and left cards for the British, French, and Italian ministers. Then they marched to the home of Cao Rulin, one of the three targeted officials, near the Foreign Ministry. Told that he was not at home, when in fact he had escaped out the back door, students stormed into Cao's house and set it on fire. Others found Zhang Congxiang, their second target, and beat him up. Throughout these events the demonstrators had the sympathy of onlookers and even of police. Eventually one student died of wounds sustained in the melee. Only late in the day did police officers step in and arrest thirty-two students.[79]

The May 4 demonstration marked the first major movement organized by students that gained support among all classes in Beijing and beyond. It also drew sympathetic international attention. Although there would be protests and strikes in other places afterward, the May 4 incident itself could not have occurred anywhere else. Only in the atmosphere of academic freedom and debate fostered at Beida by Cai Yuanpei and Chen Duxiu could such an event have developed at this time. And only in the capital, with the hated warlord leadership in sight, could the vigorous ideas of the New Culture Movement be combined with political activism in such a powerful way.

After 1919 the New Culture Movement was sometimes called the May Fourth Movement; thus the May 4 incident gave its name to the broader trends that had produced it and that continued for several years afterward. Although there continued to be widespread agreement on social changes that needed to occur, there was considerable disagreement among intellectuals about participation in political action. Hu Shi urged scholars to focus on the world of ideas and not become involved in debates about "isms," all-embracing systems such as socialism. He believed that democracy could come about only gradually as the general level of education of the Chinese people rose. After 1919, however, other intellectuals, including Chen Duxiu and Li Dazhao, focused on one particular "ism," Marxism, that claimed both to explain China's dilemma and to offer a concrete plan for political action. Sun Yat-sen's original vision of a Western-style parliamentary republic had not worked in China; the republic had degenerated into warlordism. The 1917 Russian Revolution offered an alternative model. In early 1920 the Comintern (Communist International), seeing potential in the May 4 demonstration, sent Grigori Voitinsky to attract activists to its revolutionary cause.[80] The Chinese Communist Party was founded in 1921 in Shanghai, where Chen Duxiu had fled after brief imprisonment following May 4. Shanghai's International Settlement and French Concession offered protection from Chinese authorities. The Communist Party operated secretly from Shanghai, but after 1927 the Nationalist government forced it out of the city and into the interior provinces of Hunan and Jiangxi, where the Communists created guerilla bases.

In Beijing political action continued. Soon after the May 4 demonstration, a flurry of activities led on May 19, 1919 to a general strike that quickly spread to the whole nation. At Shanghai, students built important alliances with merchants and workers, and activists' focus shifted to that city.[81] In Beijing on June 3, at a demonstration of more than 1,000 students, the police and military arrested 178 and beat some of them badly. Over 400 were imprisoned in a building on the Beida campus and denied food. Still, thousands of other students appeared on the streets in the next days. On November 29, 1919, students again demonstrated to protest Japanese killing of seven students involved in a boycott in Fuzhou in southeastern China. (See Figure 25.)

Six years later, a major mass demonstration and strike took place in Shanghai on May 30, 1925, after Shanghai police killed twelve protesters who were demonstrating against the killing of workers in a Japanese textile factory. This event sparked massive rallies in Shanghai and other cities that had far more participation and organization than the May 4 demonstration of 1919. In Beijing students from all the universities launched a strike and other actions; on June 3, 1925 (a memorable date from 1919), 8,000 students, including women and children, marched all day around the city. At Tiananmen a crowd of 50,000 students and citizens gathered shouting "Strike, strike." One group marched to the Chamber of Commerce to demand that merchants call a general strike. On June 10 a crowd of 100,000 people—including representatives of fifty-seven organizations—gathered at Tiananmen. Not only was the scale larger than that of May 4, but the marchers' route stretched into the Outer City.[82]

As these mass movements in Beijing intensified, the forces opposed to them also became stronger. On March 18, 1926, another large demonstration gathered at Tiananmen, this time to protest the warlord government's capitulation to Western demands to remove certain military fortifications at Tianjin. When the protestors gathered at government offices, guards and soldiers unexpectedly shot into the crowd and charged with bayonets. Fifty demonstrators were killed and 200 wounded; most were students, but some were ordinary citizens. The "March 18 incident" was the most violent of the 1920s demonstrations.[83] The atmosphere in Beijing was charged; the new warlord regime under Zhang Zuolin even tried to intimidate and destroy the student movement by undermining Beida itself—denying funds to pay faculty and splitting the university into different administrations. At this point many professors and students left Beijing for Shanghai and elsewhere.[84] Some, such as Zhou Zuoren, felt remorse over having allowed their students to endanger themselves. Others, such as his brother Lu Xun, were enraged by the bloody events.[85]

After the Nationalist government established its capital in Nanjing in 1927, it still kept a close watch on Beijing. Following a familiar pattern, it directly appointed the key municipal officials and exerted its own forms of social control, such as a tougher police force. The Guomindang's hold on the north was tenuous, however, because it depended on the cooperation of the defeated warlords and on appeasement of Japanese aggression. Chiang Kai-shek's base of support was in central and south China, and throughout the Nanjing decade (1927–1937), his principal goal was to exterminate the Communist movement in its base areas in the interior provinces while barely holding off the Japanese in the north. He famously said, "The Japanese are a disease of the limbs, but the Communists are a disease of the heart." After the Japanese occupied Manchuria in 1932, turning it into the puppet state of Manchukuo, the situation of north China and Beijing was perilous indeed. Public opinion all over China favored a tougher Nationalist stance against Japan, and Beijing residents lived in continual apprehension. In Beijing and elsewhere students organized a Resist Japan National Salvation Association. As the Nationalist Party itself became the target of student agitation, the movement took on a leftist tinge, causing the authorities to suppress it harshly for almost three years between 1932 and 1935.[86]

In the spring of 1935 Japanese demands intensified, and the He-Umezu agreement foresaw the removal of all resistance to Japan in Hebei. It seemed that

Figure 1. Confucian Temple. *Credit: Haili Kong*

Figure 2. Bell and Drum Towers. *Credit: Stephen F. Dale*

Figure 3. Hall of Supreme Harmony (Taihedian). *Credit: The Palace Museum, Beijing*

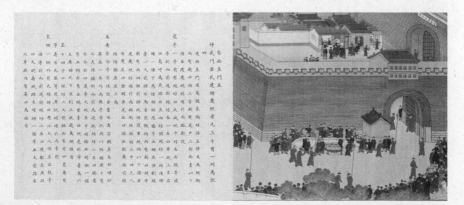

Figure 4. Xizhi Gate and Calligraphy, section of Kangxi sixtieth-birthday scroll *(Wanshou shengdian)*. *Credit: The Palace Museum, Beijing*

Figure 5. (above) Picnic at the European Palaces at Yuanmingyuan, dated before 1911. (Photo by Théophile Piry.) *Credit: Collection Charles Blackburn, Neuilly, France*

Figure 6. (right) Empress Dowager Cixi, 1903. *Credit: The Palace Museum, Beijing*

Figure 7. Boxer about to be executed at Caishikou, 1900. *Credit: Forbidden City Press, Palace Museum, Beijing*

Figure 8. Ninth U.S. Infantry in the Forbidden City, 1900. *Credit: Library of Congress, Prints and Photographs Division*

Figure 9. (left) Railroad cut through city wall, ca. 1900. *Credit: Arthur H. Smith,* China in Convulsion *(1901), Vol. 2, Front*

Figure 10. Imperial University (later Beijing University) deans and students, 1902. *Credit: Library of Congress, Prints and Photographs Division*

Figure 11. (left) Couple quarreling, Illustration from *Xingshi huabao*, ca. 1909. *Credit:* Jiujing "Xingshi huabao": wan Qing shi jing baitai *(2003)*

Figure 12. (below) Puyi, the child emperor, and court ladies in the Palace of Established Happiness (Jianfugong). *Credit: Forbidden City Press, Palace Museum, Beijing*

Figure 13. Manchu banner family portrait. *Credit: Forbidden City Press, Palace Museum, Beijing*

Figure 14. Yuan Shikai en route to perform imperial sacrifices at the Temple of Heaven. *Credit: Collection of Kong Family*

Figure 15. Xiong Xiling (back row, center) and family, 1929. *Credit: Beijing City Haidian District Archives*

Figure 16. Rabindranath Tagore (front row, center) in Beijing, 1924. Photographed at the home of Reginald Johnston, the deposed emperor Puyi's tutor (with white hair and mustache, standing in the back row). Standing just to Tagore's right was Lin Huiyin, the young woman who served as his interpreter, and standing at the extreme left of the second row was the poet Xu Zhimo (wearing a Chinese gown and glasses). *Credit: The Palace Museum, Beijing*

Figure 17. Street with archway (pailou). *Credit: Donald Mennie,* The Pageant of Peking *(1920)*

Figure 18. "Street in the Tartar City" showing rooftops and a camel train in foreground. *Credit: Donald Mennie,* The Pageant of Peking *(1920)*

Figure 19. (left) Qianmen (Zhengyang Gate). *Credit: Donald Mennie*, The Pageant of Peking *(1920)*

Figure 20. (below) Workmen resting in front of unidentified gate. *Credit: Donald Mennie*, The Pageant of Peking *(1920)*

Figure 21. (left) Ruifuxiang silk shop in Dashalar, 2005. *Credit: Lillian M. Li*

Figure 22. (below) Shopping street with many signs (photo by Hedda Morrison). *Credit: Hedda Morrison Collection, Harvard-Yenching Library, Harvard University, Copyright President and Fellows of Harvard College*

Figure 23. (left) Liulichang, men viewing scrolls at the New Year's Fair (photo by Hedda Morrison). *Credit: Hedda Morrison Collection, Harvard-Yenching Library, Harvard University, Copyright President and Fellows of Harvard College*

Figure 24. (left) Women students at North China Women's University (photo by Sidney D. Gamble). Women students studying in the library of the North China Union Women's College in 1919. Founded in 1864 by Eliza Bridgeman as a school for beggar girls, it joined with Yanjing University in 1920. *Credit: Sidney D. Gamble Foundation for China Studies*

Figure 25. (below) Student demonstration, November 29, 1919 (photo by Sidney D. Gamble). *Credit: Sidney D. Gamble Foundation for China Studies*

Figure 26. (right) Liang Sicheng and Lin Huiyin on the Temple of Heaven, 1936. *Credit: Courtesy of the estate of Wilma Fairbank*

Figure 27. (below) Qinghua students at South Gate, 1958. *Credit: Collection of Kong Family*

Figure 28. Family in front of *hutong* home, 1958. *Credit: Collection of Kong Family*

Figure 29. Same *hutong* with bicycles, 2006. *Credit: Collection of Kong Family*

Figure 30. Mao and Red Guard, September 8, 1966. *Credit: Bettmann/CORBIS*

Figure 31. Tiananmen, April 5, 1976. *Credit: Li Xiaobin*

Figure 32. Petitioner, 1978. *Credit: Li Xiaobin*

Figure 33. Democracy Wall, 1978. *Credit: Li Xiaobin*

Figure 34. (right) Private enterprise: Tea stand, 1980. *Credit: Li Xiaobin*

Figure 35. (below) House in *hutong* selected for demolition, ca. 2004. Character "chai" means "tear down." *Credit: Yue Shengyang*

Figure 36. (above) Dancing at Jingshan Park, 2005. *Credit: Stephen F. Dale*

Figure 37. (left) Salsa dancing, Beijing University, 2005. *Credit: Stephen F. Dale*

Figure 38. (above) Jianguomen street, 1958. *Credit: Beijing Jiucheng (The Old City of Beijing), by Beijing shi chengshi guihua shijiyuan. Beijing: Yanshan chubanshe, 2003.*

Figure 39. (above) Jianguomen intersection, 2006. *Credit: Haili Kong*

Figure 40. (left) Wangfujing shopping street, with Dong'an Market, 2006. *Credit: Haili Kong*

Figure 41. Xizhi Gate light rail station, 2006. The station is located in the Xihuan Guanchang, a multi-use business and commercial development. Two of its three distinctive buildings are shown here. *Credit: Haili Kong*

Figure 42. Hall of Beijing City People's Congress, 2005. *Credit: Haili Kong*

Figure 43. The Great Hall of the People and the National Grand Theater, 2005. *Credit: Haili Kong*

Figure 44. "Time Line." Artist Zheng Lianjie and son holding a 1957 family portrait in Tiananmen Square, 2000. *Credit: Zheng Lianjie*

Figure 45. Dongyue Temple pailou with man, 1912. *Credit: Musée Albert-Kahn—Département des Hauts-de Seine*

Figure 46. Dongyue Temple pailou with skyscrapers, 2005. *Credit: Lillian M. Li*

Figure 47. Hong Kong visitors at the Temple of Ancient Monarchs (Lidai diwang miao), 2005. *Credit: Lillian M. Li*

Figure 48. "Jimmy Jing's Bed and Breakfast" in a *hutong*, 2004. *Credit: Lillian M. Li*

Figure 49. Shooting a TV commercial in *hutong* in the Houhai district, 2005. *Credit: Lillian M. Li*

Figure 50. Ruins of European palaces at Yuanmingyuan Park, 2005. *Credit: Lillian M. Li*

nothing now stood in the way of Japan's occupation of all of north China. In an atmosphere of alarm bordering on panic, students once again began to organize protest. This time the leadership originated at Yanjing and Qinghua universities, not Beida. On December 9 students from all over Beijing headed toward the headquarters of General He Yingqin, minister of war, near the Xinhua Gate of the Zhongnanhai compound. But the Yanjing and Qinghua students were prevented from entering the city by closing of the Xizhi Gate. Other students marched toward the Legation Quarter. All along the march, students chanted anti-Japanese slogans and passed out leaflets to onlookers. That evening all agreed on a general strike. On December 16, a week later, 7,800 students participated in a well-planned demonstration.[87] Proceeding from different points of the city, marchers converged at Chang'an Boulevard, then proceeded to Qianmen and south to Tianqiao. When they approached the Foreign Ministry, where they hoped to present their demands to authorities, they were fired on with blanks.

Like the May Fourth and May Thirtieth movements, the December Ninth Movement affected actual events. In the short run, the Japanese plan to move to a five-province "autonomy" structure was thwarted, and the Nationalist military commander continued to resist Japanese demands. Public opinion did matter, and pressure on Chiang Kai-shek to fight the Japanese continued to mount. Then, in the Xi'an incident in December 1936, Chiang was kidnapped by one of his warlord followers; on emerging a few days later he committed the Nationalist Party to a united front with the Communists against Japan. The two parties had cooperated for a few years in the mid 1920s, so this would be the second united front.

The December Ninth Movement may have originated as a spontaneous student demonstration, but it is fairly certain that its development after December 9 involved "professionals," i.e., Communist organizers. American journalist Edgar Snow claimed that the student leaders were "mostly Christian or Christian-trained youths. . . . There was not a Communist among them." But most Chinese scholars have agreed that "without Party leadership, the December Ninth Movement would have been unable to spread so broadly, penetrate so deeply, and maintain itself for so long a time."[88]

The December Ninth Movement postponed but could not stop the Japanese takeover of north China. On July 7, 1937, a skirmish between Japanese and Chinese troops at Marco Polo Bridge marked the outbreak of full-scale war. The Japanese army secured its hold on key points in the north and took Beijing. In the fall they moved on to the Chinese city of Shanghai and its hinterland (leaving the foreign settlements alone until just after Pearl Harbor in 1941). In December 1937 Japanese forces took the Nationalist capital of Nanjing, wreaking horrific destruction on both soldiers and civilians. By late 1938 the Nationalist government had retreated westward to the city of Chongqing, which became its wartime capital.

Japanese forces entered Beijing on August 8, one month after the outbreak of war. Although fighting had sometimes been fierce, the city did not experience the level of violence seen in central China. Beijing became the site of the Japanese-controlled Republic of China Provisional Government, which, despite its name, was a regional administration with jurisdiction only over several north China provinces. Throughout the war Beijing and Nanjing had separate Chinese administrations and Japanese military commands. In 1940, however, the Beijing government's name changed to North China Political Affairs Commission to signify that the "puppet" government under Wang Jingwei in Nanjing was the higher authority, but this was only a nominal change. The city administration was directly appointed by the provisional or regional government, a pattern long known in Beijing's history. In terms of organization and structure, there was almost no change except that Japanese "advisers" were added to the personnel already in place. The mayor, initially Yu Jinhe, served concurrently as chief of police, also an arrangement known in the past. The top levels of Chinese and Japanese authorities, including the key collaborators, were all outsiders, yet another familiar pattern. Although it could be harsh and repressive, the occupation left space for negotiated or mediated behavior. Occupied Beijing was not "an impenetrable fortress" but "more like a mesh net, restrictive and yet full of holes," as historian Sophia Lee puts it.[89]

The social history of Beijing under Japanese occupation from 1937 to 1945 has not been well studied. More than sixty years later, the war of resistance against Japan (its common designation in China) is most often described with reference to its military events and the suffering of the entire Chinese people. In Beijing the occupation was a difficult and frightening period, but the relative stability of the situation and the continuity in daily life can be attributed to accommodation, i.e., collaboration, as well as to sheer repression. After the war the principal collaborators, those Chinese who had held office under the Japanese authorities, were tried and punished. Chief among them was Wang Kemin, who had been head of the provisional government. He had served various warlord regimes in different capacities and also had been a banker. The most sympathetic collaborator was Zhou Zuoren, who had served as dean at the wartime Beijing

University (an amalgam of various universities in the city) and later minister of education during the occupation. Of all the well-known May Fourth intellectuals, he was one who had chosen to remain in Beijing. Japanese-educated, fluent in the Japanese language, and married to a Japanese woman, Zhou must have thought that he could serve as a useful mediator between Chinese citizens and Japanese authorities, as long before Liu Bingzhong and Hong Chengchou had worked with Mongol and Manchu imperial invaders.

Since Japanese advisers were relatively few, the authorities also relied on a political organization, the Xinminhui (People's Renovation Society), to exercise social control. Based on a model already used in Manchukuo, the Xinminhui was a way to recruit Chinese community leaders to join in the implementation of propaganda, food rationing, social services, and surveillance of teachers and students. Its many branches penetrated neighborhoods. Membership in the Xinminhui was useful for individuals and families; it gave them access to opportunities and protection from further interference. The Xinminhui had a Confucian ideology that emphasized a common East Asian heritage. In all these ways—ideological, political, and social—the Xinminhui sought to build a mass social base, as did the Guomindang during the New Life Movement of the 1930s or the Chinese Communist Party after 1949.

War and occupation made every aspect of daily life much more difficult. The city's population continued to grow as a greater number of rural people sought protection in the city. Occupied Beijing was a far safer place than the countryside, where Japanese army savagery reached its height during the mop-up campaigns of 1940 to 1943, which had the slogan "Kill all, burn all, loot all." Including the immediate suburbs, the population rose from 1.4 million in 1932 to 1.7 million in 1941. Within the city, the Japanese civilian population grew rapidly from about 2,400 in 1937, to 22,000 in 1939, and 60,000 in 1940. Many Western residents remained in Beijing until Pearl Harbor in 1941, after which they either left China or were interned in a few camps. A few high-profile Westerners, such as Yanjing University president John Leighton Stuart, were kept under house arrest. Residents experienced many uncertainties, but the rising cost of daily goods was their biggest problem. By July 1941 grain prices had risen to 3.7 times their level in April 1937; by March 1944 prices were 19.7 times higher. Food rationing and antihoarding measures were imposed in 1942. Under these circumstances crime rates rose, including crimes associated with drug trading.

After the Japanese surrender in 1945, the Nationalist Party gained control of Beijing and held it until late 1948. All over north China, however, the Communist base areas that had developed before and during the war remained independent, and a bitter civil war soon erupted between the two sides. Thus in Beijing wartime conditions were not improved by the removal of the Japanese. Over the war years Japanese authorities had improved the physical infrastructure of some parts of the city, especially the western sections where they maintained their offices and residences. But other parts of the city had been neglected, and after the war their deterioration continued. Food and basic supplies were still in short supply, and there was much social and political unrest, which the Communists were able to exploit. In spring 1947 a popular movement protested against hunger and the civil war.[90] Much discontent was caused by the Nationalist Party's treatment of intellectuals and students who had remained in the city during the war. Thousands of students fleeing Communist advances in Manchuria camped out in public places, such as the Temple of Heaven. When, in July 1948, many marched to the Municipal Council to protest their condition, several were shot and killed and many more wounded.[91] Returning to Beijing in 1948, American scholar Derk Bodde found it "a much sadder and more impoverished city than the one we had left eleven years before." He observed that the city was impoverished not just physically but spiritually.[92] In January 1949 the Communists' Red Army liberated "Beiping." (See Color Plate 11.) On October 1, 1949, Communist leaders declared the founding of the People's Republic of China and renamed its capital Beijing.

In his play *Teahouse* (*Chaguan*, 1957), Lao She depicts the declining fortunes of a Beijing teahouse in 1898, 1917, and 1945. The owner Wang works hard to keep his teahouse open but in the end has nothing. Similarly, the promise of the reform movement of 1898, the revolution of 1911, and the defeat of the Japanese in 1945 have led only to disappointment. In the introduction to the third act, one character chants:

Eight years the Japanese occupied
Old Beijing, old China's pride.
The people suffered without relief,
Their only choice was death or grief;
But the Eighth Route Army won their hearts
As it drove the cruel invaders out.
And they gazed with hope at the stars and moon;
Victory promised a new life soon.
Humph! Now the Kuomintang are in Beijing,
Outdoing the Japs in everything.

Troubles galore plague Proprietor Wang;
Neither he nor I'll be around too long.
The old teahouse is a pretty sad case,
But nothing seems to work these days.[93]

Old Beijing and New China

When people in China today look back on the eventful and complicated years from 1911 to 1949 in Beijing, it is neither the growth of various aspects of modernity nor the suffering of wartime that they remember. What they recall is Beijing's special identity as a fading imperial capital with quintessential cultural charm and magic. The fond memories of "Old Beijing" are in fact images of the city in the Republican period, not the truly old Beijing of the Ming or the Qing.[94] In recent years veritable torrents of books have been published with photographs of the residences of famous Beijingren or loving drawings of the traditional *hutong* life. Photo collections and biographies now emphasize the "beautiful people" of the May 4 period, including Xu Zhimo, Liang Sicheng, and Lin Huiyin.

The contemporary wave of nostalgia and regret repeats on a larger scale the nostalgia and regret that were felt in the Republican period itself. Then too there was an explosion of books about Beijing's past by Chinese scholars who recorded every detail of every street and alleyway, every story about every famous monument, every fact about what Beijing people ate and how they celebrated their holidays. As Madeleine Dong points out, these works highlighted "the specificity of 'place' and the uniqueness of local culture."[95] These writers felt they must record all the details before the old way of life disappeared. Yu Qichang wrote, "I am getting old, and the capital city is not the city it once was anymore. . . . I am so lucky to have lived in this capital city of six hundred years with great culture. I have seen its glory, its decline, and its destruction."[96] Western residents of Beijing, some with considerable experience and expertise, also began to record the details of a charming place that was in danger of destruction. Hedda Morrison, a German photographer, created a visual record of temples, street life, and craftsmen in many trades. Her photographs appear in many current Chinese publications about Old Beijing, almost always without attribution.[97] In 1935 L. C. Arlington and William Lewisohn, foreigners long in China, published a guidebook to Beijing's monuments, *In Search of Old Peking*. As the title suggests, they feared that the old city was vanishing and decried the ubiquitous neglect and ruin of historic structures. "To all of us who have lived long in Peking and love it, this neglect is closely related to tragedy."[98]

Regret for the old Beijing and the old way of life had been associated with a conservatism that was characterized as Jingpai, the Beijing way of doing things, as opposed to Haipai, the Shanghai way, which was progressive and Westernized. Yet as the Japanese threat developed in north China in the 1930s, the old capital itself came to symbolize the new nation. Preservation of old Beijing customs, speech, and culture became identified with preserving the national heritage, and hence the nation itself. The Beijing accent became the national standard for Chinese speech, as the pronunciation of the BBC is for English. The national language, *guoyu*, was in fact Beijing Chinese; Westerners called it Mandarin. And Beijing opera, *jingju*, became identified as a uniquely Chinese cultural form, known as *guoju*, or national opera.[99] When the famous opera singer Mei Lanfang—trained to sing women's roles—toured the United States in 1930, Beijing opera represented to the outside world the essence of Chinese culture.[100] In these ways, once again what was local—customs, people, culture—was inextricably tied to what was national. And in these ways, things that were old were tied to things that were new.[101]

Chapter 6

Mao's Beijing and
Socialist Transformation:
1949 to 1976

FOR THE CITY OF BEIJING AS FOR THE REST OF CHINA, THE YEAR 1949 was a momentous turning point. The establishment of the People's Republic of China meant an end to over a century of foreign oppression as well as of internal unrest and rebellion. For the first time since the eighteenth century, China had a strong government, and now it also had leaders who were committed to creating a more egalitarian society.

Although Marxism had been introduced to China by way of Russia and the Bolshevik Revolution of 1917, the triumph of the Chinese Communist Party in 1949 owed more to the hard struggle of the party over thirty years—in guerrilla warfare in remote base areas in central and northwest China, in war against the Japanese, and then in civil war against the Nationalist Party—than it did to Marx's vision. Living in the already industrialized Western Europe of the late nineteenth century, Karl Marx had envisioned a class struggle that would eventually result in the triumph of the working class, or proletariat, over the capitalists and an even more distant utopian dream of communism under which the state would wither away. Instead, China's revolution had adopted a rural strategy, in which the peasantry's struggle against landlordism and other inequities played a much larger role than the proletariat's struggle against capitalists. Coming to power in 1949, Mao Zedong and other party leaders could bask in the triumph of having achieved national consolidation, but they had to move quickly to stabilize the rural scene while trying to transform China's overwhelmingly agrarian economy and small industrial base into a wealthy and powerful modern state.

In the early and mid-1950s, the party leadership shared a strong consensus about policy directions, but in the late 1950s, significant divisions emerged. Mao became sensitive to criticism from intellectuals, many of whom were party loyalists and revolutionary comrades, and he targeted them in the anti-rightist movement of 1957. Increasingly Mao emphasized the use of ideological campaigns to motivate "the masses" to continue class struggle while working toward greater productivity. Other leaders, particularly Liu Shaoqi, focused on economic planning, education, science, and technology. Although the party line emphasized both "redness" and "expertise," increasingly it was better to be "red" than "expert." The campaigns, as well as the internal power struggles of the party leaders, threatened the very stability and security that they had begun to achieve. Until Mao's death in 1976, Beijing as well as China careened from consolidation and growth to mass movements, political chaos, and economic crises.

The selection of Beijing as capital was natural, inevitable, and deliberate. No other city could better symbolize the legitimacy and authority of the new regime. While retaining the Forbidden City at its center, Beijing under Mao experienced many physical transformations, most prominently the creation of new public spaces and buildings and most controversially the destruction of major gates and walls. The boundaries of Beijing were extended well beyond the familiar Inner and Outer cities, and Beijing became the first municipality to be placed directly under the jurisdiction of the central government, bypassing any provincial-level administration. Much of the newly incorporated territory remained predominantly rural, and throughout the Mao era the essentially urban part of Beijing was still concentrated in the area of the former Inner and Outer cities. The growth of Beijing population from two million in 1949 to more than eight million in 1976 was caused mostly by immigration from other parts of China and a higher birth rate, but some of it could be attributed to enlarged administrative boundaries.

Social transformations in the city, though less visible, were equally fundamental. Following the Communist victory in 1949, hundreds of thousands of party and government workers were transferred to Beijing. This demographic shift was almost as dramatic as the Ming emperor's transplantation of thousands of families in the early fifteenth century or the expulsion of Han Chinese from the Inner City by the Manchus during the Qing reorganization of Beijing in the 1640s. The newcomers were in effect the Communist elite; their children and grandchildren are among those who now identify themselves as Beijingren or particularly *xin* (new) Beijingren.

Socialism transformed the daily lives of both old and new Beijing residents. The organization of work, the pattern of markets and commerce, and the assignment of residences affected most of the population. For some in old neighborhoods in the Inner and Outer cities, private family life and familiar Beijing customs survived alongside the new social and political realities. Yet Beijing as a whole had more than ever become a public stage, the place where every major policy change of the new People's Republic was formulated and announced. In the many ensuing mass campaigns, especially the Cultural Revolution, the people of Beijing became the model for entire movements and were, for better or worse, the vanguard of the nation. One dynamic of a campaign was to warn the millions by making an example of a few; thus Beijing residents with their greater visibility were also among the leading victims of mass politics. For all intents and purposes, particularly for the outside world, Beijing *was* China.

Physical Transformation of Beijing

On January 31, 1949, without a single shot being fired, the first of about 200,000 soldiers of the People's Liberation Army—fully armed and accompanied by tanks and artillery—marched triumphantly through the Xizhi Gate after the Nationalist surrender. Three days later, on February 3, a grand parade through the Yongding Gate toward the Qian Gate began a formal celebration that lasted eight hours. (See Color Plate 11.) The new rulers took over an almost intact city. Advisers told Mao that there were three possible choices for a capital: Nanjing, Xi'an, and Beijing. The southern city of Nanjing had been a capital of regional dynasties *ca.* 220–589, but its use by more recent regimes—the Ming and the Nationalists—had been brief. Xi'an had a glorious past and great historical significance as capital of the Han and Tang dynasties, but it was far from China's coast, where modern industries now were concentrated. Beijing, however, had been chosen as capital by several dynasties, and its imperial architecture was far better preserved than that of the other two cities. Moreover Beijing, given its Ming and especially its Qing history, was the symbol of a strong and unified state. It was located in the north, where the Communists had gained great strength during the war of resistance against Japan, and it was the antithesis of the Guomindang capital at Nanjing as well as of capitalistic and westernized Shanghai. Yet there also were deep ironies in the Communists' choice of Beijing. Revolutionary leaders whose experience had been forged in the countryside, and who had explicitly condemned the corruption of both urban life and traditional society, especially in the treaty ports, now selected as their capital the city that most symbolized imperial authority and traditional urban grandeur.

On October 1, 1949, a celebration of the founding of the People's Republic announced to the world that Beijing had regained its status as national capital. When Mao proclaimed the founding of the People's Republic of China on the balcony at Tiananmen, thousands cheered with tears and smiles at the same time. A high-ranking official at the ceremony recalled, "My little daughter asked me why so many people were cheering, and I told her that she would understand it better when she grew up. For me, this was the day I had waited for and worked toward for decades."[1] Many people later especially remembered Mao's declaration to the People's Political Consultative Conference on September 21: "The Chinese people have now stood up." As one exclaimed, "How could we not be excited? Just look at Chinese history: the people never could stand up either to their own rulers or to foreigners."[2] On October 1, 300,000 overjoyed listeners on the square shouted "Long live the People's Republic of China!" "Long live Chairman Mao!" The phrase "long live" (wansui) literally means "ten thousand years" and had been used to wish longevity to emperors, but this was the first time that Mao had received such a tribute at Tiananmen. Years later some veteran revolutionaries admitted that when they heard the crowd shouting words that put Mao on the level of an emperor, they had a sense of foreboding. At the time, however, most people were ecstatic, full of pride and optimism.

Born in a prosperous Hunan peasant family in 1893, Mao Zedong had been one of the founders of the Chinese Communist Party in 1921. Unchallenged as its leader since the mid-1930s, he had charted Communist strategy through war and civil war. Strong-willed, militant, and resilient, he had spent years in austere conditions in his wartime base at Yan'an in the northwest. In October 1949 Mao was hailed as a national hero, and figuratively Beijing became the preeminent place where the red sun of socialism was expected to rise. Looking out from the Tiananmen balcony, he remarked in all seriousness that in the near future he wanted to see factory smokestacks everywhere in the capital. With their base no longer in the countryside, the Chinese Communist leaders viewed the vast farm sector as a source of economic surplus for investment in industrialization. The farmer's surplus would feed the workers and, by means of sale abroad, provide foreign exchange for imported heavy machinery. The new rulers wanted to reconstruct Beijing not only to meet the demands of the central government, but also to increase the city's industrial capacity and to enlarge and satisfy its working class.[3]

Mao appointed Peng Zhen, who had been a leading party organizer in north China and Manchuria, to head the Beijing Municipal Government. Mao, Liu, and Premier Zhou Enlai made all key decisions regarding Beijing, and Peng implemented them. Beijing's new status as an independent municipality benefited the city, but it also cut off any possibility of autonomy. The central government interfered in almost all important municipal decisions, including those on city planning, which had to be approved by Mao himself. He and other leaders provided principles for the reconstruction and industrialization of Beijing to the Capital City Planning Commission founded in May 1949; this group was composed of city government officials, military commanders, experts, and Soviet advisers. It took more than four years for the commission to submit a proposal in November 1953. Major inter-related areas of disagreement during its deliberations included whether to locate the central government offices inside the city, whether to demolish the old city wall, and whether to limit the size of the city.

One of the most distinguished participants in these discussions was the widely respected architect Liang Sicheng, trained at the University of Pennsylvania, who strongly advocated preserving the old Beijing. In December 1948 he had provided Communist leaders with a list of the most valuable structures in the city, urging the army to protect them when moving against Nationalist forces. In Liang's eyes, Beijing was an architectural treasure that belonged to the world, not just to China. It should be a political and cultural center, not an industrial one. At experts' meetings even before the commission was founded, he twice made vigorous proposals to build a new administrative center outside the city. He argued that the old city was itself a museum and should be preserved to the maximum; large-scale construction of new administrative buildings would destroy its artistic unity. Liang suggested that the central government be located in the western suburbs, where the Japanese had built their military headquarters during the war. State ministries and commerce-related government organs could be built in the west. For the old city, his plan included a new east-west horizontal axis—today's east and west Chang'an Boulevard—crossing the old north-south central axis in order to meet modern traffic needs. Liang further argued that a city must satisfy popular demands not only for working and commuting but also for residence and recreation. He insisted that the city wall be preserved and suggested its use as a public "ring park," where people could spend their leisure time. (The walls were wide at the top and there was ample space for walking.) Later he invited Chen Zhanxiang (Charlie Cheng), an internationally acclaimed architect trained in England, to join the Commission. Chen fully supported Liang's ideas, and together they wrote the Liang-Chen proposal on the location of the central government (February 1950).[4]

Critics of the Liang-Chen proposal argued that the state administration should be inside the old city because construction expenses would be saved and also because Tiananmen Square should be the literal as well as the symbolic center of the nation. Soviet experts commented that precisely because of the historical importance of the city, the new capital should be built on the foundation of the old one. For his part, Mao apparently never considered living or working outside Beijing. As early as December 1949 he had said that the government should be inside the city and only some less important organs located outside it. Not long afterward Mao and other party leaders moved into the Zhongnanhai compound just west of the Forbidden City, part of the imperial Western Park of the Qing era. The Liang-Chen proposal appeared doomed; ominously, its authors had been excluded from the group that prepared the final commission document in spring 1953.[5]

Soon both Liang Sicheng and his rivals in the architectural debates learned that the reconstruction of Beijing actually had begun before they had reached any conclusions. In some locations demolition of the Outer City wall had begun in 1950. Mao had decided that the demolition of the city wall was a major priority, the central government had settled the matter, and city officials had begun to take action accordingly. Thus Mao brushed aside controversy in an autocratic manner reminiscent of the Yongle emperor of the Ming dynasty. To Liang, the city wall was a great treasure, a beautiful "national necklace." To the victorious Communist revolutionaries, it symbolized the rotten old society and the authority of the privileged ruling class whom they had just defeated.

Liang and his followers were concerned with preserving the beauty of the city and all the historical insight that its structures could yield about the past; the new leaders focused on political symbolism and industrialization. A 1958 Beijing report to the central government requested that the city wall, as an artifact of the old society, be demolished completely within ten years. Parts were torn down at that time, and following a seven-year interval caused by natural disasters and a retrenched budget, the remnants fell during subway construction in 1965. The army demolished the city wall without hesitation, and only a few gates survived. Zhang Bojun, minister of transportation in the early 1950s, commented that the attitude of some leaders had been that they did not "have yesterday, so there was no need to preserve yesterday. Therefore, many great things that remained from yesterday, such as the city wall and archways on the streets, of course were worthless."[6] It was a view opposite to that of Liang, who once said that "architecture is history made of stone."[7]

Politicians sought architectural grandeur that would project an impressive image of the capital and the People's Republic.[8] New buildings primarily reflected their wish for centrality and splendor: office complexes, conference halls, and hotels were built to be monumental to the eye and modern/traditional hybrids in style. Soviet experts recommended that state office buildings be constructed along the new east-west Chang'an Boulevard. To allow parades including tanks and cannons to pass through during celebration of the first anniversary of the People's Republic in 1950, the boulevard was enlarged to be 90 meters (295 feet) wide, and two beautiful old three-arch commemorative *pailou* were torn down. The general idea was to highlight the sharp contrast between the old imperial palace compound and the modern socialist governmental complexes.

In 1958 the central government decided to complete ten grand construction projects in Beijing as a visible demonstration of socialist achievements for the celebration of the tenth anniversary of the People's Republic in 1959. These projects were the Cultural Palace of Nationalities, the Military Museum of the Chinese People's Revolution, the Hotel of Nationalities, the National Agricultural Exhibition Hall, the Museum of Chinese History and Revolution, the State Guest House at Diaoyutai, the Beijing Workers' Stadium, the Overseas Chinese Hotel, the Beijing Train Station, and the Great Hall of the People. In design they all were visually spectacular compared to the low residential housing in Beijing, and they all combined the Soviet style with traditional Chinese features. These serious, imposing constructions, over which Liang Sicheng designed traditional Chinese big roofs with protruding eaves, were typical of public buildings of the 1950s. Decorative elements were minimized so as to avoid criticism of the structures as bourgeois. Statues of workers, farmers, and soldiers in front of the buildings replaced the traditional pair of stone guardian lions; confident and optimistic, socialist man looked to human rather than mythological agency for his protection. Major streets were broadened and entrance gates made high and wide; the layouts inside were straightforward and predictable. Architecture expressed the idea of serving the masses as well as the power and authority of those who now ruled in their name.

Like dynastic rulers of the past, the Communist state had unlimited power to mobilize labor; thus completion of the ten projects took only about a year. Among the ten, the design and construction of the Great Hall of the People (see

Figure 43) may be the most important, although many Chinese architects consider the Cultural Palace of Nationalities the best. Construction of the Great Hall on Tiananmen Square involved experts from Beijing and from many of the provinces, as well as 300,000 local volunteers, working in spare time after their regular jobs. The Great Hall could hold more than ten thousand people for meetings and five thousand in one huge dining room for state banquets. Since its construction, almost all important state-level meetings, such as the People's and the party congresses, have been held there. At the time, Premier Zhou Enlai told architects and engineers that the "most important issues in the structure of the Great Hall are safety and durability. This Great Hall should last longer than the Forbidden City and Zhongshan Park [near the southwest corner of the Forbidden City], at least 350 years!"[9] Zhou thus envisioned that the Great Hall of the People and the Communist regime would last at least eight decades longer than the 267 years of the Qing dynasty.

An even more critical construction project not included in the group of ten was the second expansion of Tiananmen Square, which began in November 1958. Mao ordered that the square become the largest and most spectacular such space in the world; it would reflect the greatness of the Chinese people and honor the birthplace of the People's Republic. The new square was intended to hold more than a half million people. Mayor Peng Zhen required that Chang'an Boulevard between Tiananmen and the square be strong enough to allow the heaviest tanks to pass through without damaging the surface of the road.

After ten months of round-the-clock work, the reconstruction of Tiananmen Square—for which a labor force of more than one million had been organized—was completed in August 1959. The expanded square covered an area of 40 hectares (99 acres). Combined with the 15 hectares (37 acres) occupied by the Great Hall of the People, the whole square measured 55 hectares (136 acres). The square itself was more than 2.5 time larger than after its first expansion from 1949 to 1954.[10] More than ten thousand houses and other buildings that had surrounded the area were torn down in order to make room for the Great Hall, the square, and the Museum of Chinese History and Revolution. Newspapers and other media reported nothing about the physical and emotional difficulties of moving displaced residents. Nor were any public laments heard when the Zhonghua Gate (built in the Ming dynasty, known earlier as the Daming [Great Ming] and Daqing [Great Qing] Gate) was demolished during the project. Qianmen (the Qian Gate) of the old Inner City survived and was preserved as a significant structure along the city's main north-south axis.

Tiananmen Square, modeled on Red Square in Moscow, became an essential icon of both new Beijing and new China. It was the place where the May Fourth Movement had begun in 1919, the place where students and scholars of the time had chosen to voice their political views. In contrast to the Forbidden City, enclosed within high walls and moats that symbolized the power of emperors, Tiananmen Square opened up a massive space to represent the power of the people and the revolutionary spirit of socialist China. As art historian Wu Hung pointed out, "Tiananmen Square itself had to be transformed from an insulated imperial quarter into an open space for political activity and visual presentation."[11] Tiananmen became a political space and public showcase for both the people and the rulers. During the Mao era the latter annually held two great celebrations in Tiananmen Square. Generations of Beijing residents remember traveling to Tiananmen with their classmates for mass rallies on International Labor Day (May 1) and National Day (October 1). Although they did not always understand the significance of the events that they witnessed, those students chosen to participate in the parade were honored and excited.[12]

The Monument to the People's Heroes was erected in 1958 in the center of Tiananmen Square, directly on the north-south axis, with Mao's words "Eternal Glory to the People's Heroes" inscribed on its north side. The intention was to legitimize the regime by showing the revolution's broad popular base.[13] The granite monument, almost fourteen feet (4.2 meters) taller than Tiananmen, symbolically overpowered the nearby palace complex. As historian Hou Renzhi and architect Wu Liangyong noted, "The old architectural complex of the Forbidden City . . . receded to a place resembling the 'backyard' of the square; it had been relegated to a secondary status."[14] The front of the monument faced north rather than south, reversing the auspicious orientation according to traditional geomancy. This reversal suggested the direct challenge of the monument to the monarchical past that was prompted by Mao's romantic ideas and daring spirit.

When Yuan Dadu had been built in the thirteenth century, a center marker for the entire city, roughly equidistant from the four major external walls, had been placed along the central axis in the center of the palace city. According to Chen Gan, a major architect of the early 1950s, the imperial palace had been the traditional zero point on the central north-south axis, but after the founding ceremony of the People's Republic, "everything in the city would have to divorce itself from the old zero and align itself with the new zero."[15] The new flagpole in the square briefly became that location; after 1958, however, the Monument to the People's Heroes replaced it as the zero point for both the square and the city.

One reason for placing the central government inside the city had been that it would be less expensive than building entirely new complexes outside it. Finding spaces for many agencies in the old city was not as difficult as it might at first appear. Most religious institutions had been ordered to shut down, native-place lodges (*huiguan*) forced to disband, and buildings that had been used by the Nationalists were empty. From the early 1950s the Public Security Academy occupied the Dongyue Temple (Dongyuemiao) and the National Buddhist Association claimed the Guangji Temple (Guangjisi); *huiguan* sites became government offices, schools, and factories. The Forbidden City remained the Palace Museum, but adjoining areas on its eastern and western sides became public parks. Ministries and government organs made their offices in former princes' courtyards. The Ministry of Health occupied a courtyard complex of six spacious quadrangles at No. 2 Guoxian hutong. Important ministries were hidden along obscure narrow alleys. As we have seen, Mao and a small group of party and state leaders took the lake and garden compound in Zhongnanhai—which only fifty years earlier had been one of Empress Dowager Cixi's favorite places—as their office and living space. Since 1949 this large compound, encircled by a high wall, has become a new Forbidden City. As in the old one, much of what happens there is not visible to the people and is the subject of constant speculation in Beijing and throughout China.

Most new office buildings for state ministries were built west of the old city wall, as Liang had suggested. Only a handful of office buildings of important ministries—such as Defense, Public Security, and Foreign Affairs—were built inside the city wall. Whether inside or outside the wall, these huge office buildings too were Soviet in style. They were enclosed within their own high walls, entered through imposing guarded gates, and surrounded by spacious gardens that placed them at a distance from major streets. Visitors to mid-twentieth-century Beijing often complained about the inconvenience of walking along the endless walls of these complexes to reach bus stops or public shopping areas.

During the Mao era, Beijing was on its way to becoming the nation's second largest industrial base after Shanghai, and industrialization brought additional physical changes to the city.[16] In the course of the first five-year plan (1953–1958), the sum of 950 million *yuan* was invested in capital construction of industry in Beijing. The electrical engineering industry was the most remarkable: 21 new factories were built, and 104 existing factories were expanded. Most of the electrical factories were located together in the Jiuxianqiao district northeast of Beijing. The largest and most expensive single project of industrial construction was the Beijing Shijingshan Steel Factory, a major iron and steel producer west of the city that had beginnings as early as 1912. By the 1990s the total number of factory workers in Beijing had reached 2.1 million.

Transformation also came to the Haidian district of northwest Beijing, where the Qing emperors had built summer villas and Republican-era academic institutions had established themselves. This area became a new national center for education and technology. After 1949 the government reorganized existing colleges. Furen University, originally Roman Catholic, became a state-owned and state-run college in 1950, as did Yanjing University in 1951. In 1954 the Ministry of Higher Education decided to designate only six institutions as key national universities; and of these, five (Beijing, Qinghua, People's, and Beijing Agricultural universities, and the Beijing School of Medicine) were located in the capital, the first four in the Haidian district. Eight specialized colleges were expanded, including the College of Forestry and the Aeronautical Engineering Institute, and several new colleges opened, including the Beijing Film Academy, the College of Diplomacy, the College of Posts and Telecommunication, and the Beijing Foreign Languages Institute. The Chinese Academy of Sciences, located next to Beijing University in Zhongguancun, was founded in 1957 as a national center for advanced scientific and technological research. By 1960 there were sixty-nine institutions of higher education in Beijing. No other Chinese city received the resources to compete with Beijing in this rapid growth, and the capital more than ever became a place for cultivation of scholars and experts in all fields.

Because of urban reconstruction and expansion in the 1950s and after, modernization of transport became a necessity. There was much to be done: a woman from Shanghai who had studied in the capital in the early 1950s remembered that at that time, Beijing did not seem to be a "city" at all compared to Shanghai. The first sounds that she heard after awaking on the day after her arrival on a college campus were the neighs of horses and brays of donkeys, and the first sights were several camels and donkeys strolling down the street. Indeed, vehicles drawn by horses and donkeys appeared on major boulevards near the Forbidden City not only in the 1950s, but even in the 1960s and 1970s. There were fewer than two hundred working buses and trolley buses in service in Beijing in 1949 but more than twenty thousand rickshaw-pullers. Rickshaws actually were more useful than other forms of transportation because they could move about more easily in the narrow *hutong*. Major intersections, such as the one at Jianguo Gate, resembled those of a small town rather than a major city, as shown in Figure 38, compared to the present-day Jianguo Gate intersection in Figure 39.

Transportation choices gradually increased. Between 1949 and 1952 the city government reconstructed 248 kilometers (154 miles) of streets inside the city and widened Chang'an Boulevard. By the end of 1952 the number of buses and trolley buses had grown to 372 and included a bus company that the city government had transferred from Nanjing to help manage the system. The number of rickshaws began to decline because rickshaw-pulling seemed out of place in the new society, and bicycles played an ever greater role in daily life. The bicycle became a multi-functional family caravan for transportation to and from office, shops, and schools. Visitors were amazed to see thousands of bicycles packing most of the ten lanes of Chang'an Boulevard during rush hour. Hundreds of thousands of residents developed virtuoso bicycle skills, such as riding one bicycle while leading another. Aided by the flatness of the terrain, "Rickshaw Beijing" was becoming "Bicycle Beijing." The bicycle filled a pressing need: rickshaws were disappearing, but automobile taxi service was almost nonexistent. All passenger cars were owned by the government and by work units (*danwei*); only officials of certain ranks had cars and drivers. Riding in a car was not only a luxury but an indicator of social status. For common people, owning a bicycle was itself a luxury, not only because bicycles were expensive (more than one hundred *yuan* per bicycle, about two to three months' salary for a college graduate) but also because of shortages. The government began to distribute ration coupons for bicycles to work units in the 1960s. A retired professor recalled that it took him many years after college to acquire his first bicycle in the early 1960s; decades later he still remembered the thrill of the freedom and mobility that it gave him.

In the earlier Mao era—despite construction in Tiananmen Square, destruction of the city wall, industrialization, educational expansion, and development of new forms of transportation—many places in Beijing retained a feeling of continuity with the past and even with the previous century. A Japanese writer who lived in the capital for more than twelve years between 1958 and 1969 remarked: "Our visitors all admired the quietness of our home. Although it is [in] the center of the city, it is absolutely quiet if without wind. When the wind blows, the sound of *sha-sha* made by the scholartree branches in the yard can be heard. I could even clearly hear the noise made by woodpeckers." It was only after the Cultural Revolution began in 1966 that all kinds of noise finally invaded the street where he lived as well as the whole city.[17] In literary works and personal memoirs, it is surprising to find not only the Beijing of the 1930s and 1940s but also that of the 1950s and early 1960s described as a quiet and peaceful city where most of the tree-lined streets and narrow alleys are never crowded.

Socialist Transformation and Daily Life

Population

In the first decade of the People's Republic, more than 400,000 people were transferred to Beijing. The capital's population reached close to seven million in 1959, three times the population of 1949. Most of the transferred were military personnel, administrators, and professionals. They usually lived in newly constructed complexes or college campus dormitories; they spoke Mandarin (standard Chinese, called *guoyu* or *putonghua*) with the accents of their birthplaces. Because their social status in the new system was higher than that of most local residents, they were generally respected and welcomed. Although population growth slowed after the mid-1960s, there were still about eight million residents in Beijing in 1976.

In addition to massive immigration, another reason for the growth of Beijing's population was the government's 1950s policy of encouraging large families. The state and party promoted the Soviet image of the "glorious mama" who gave birth to many children. In particular, the new government wanted party and Red Army veterans to produce more children as trustworthy revolutionary successors. The government paid for a nanny for each newborn child of a veteran military officer of certain ranks. These policies helped to create a generation of Chinese baby boomers in the 1950s. Even ordinary families such as the He's, who lived in a rather crowded *hutong* courtyard house near the Forbidden City, often were large. Mr. He, a senior civil engineer, and his wife had eight children, of whom five were in a photo taken in 1958. (See Figures 28 and 29.)

In a report to the central government in January 1957, city administrators noted population growth and pointed out that the largest portion of it came from the continuing flow of transferred officials.[18] One such official usually brought along five or more other people, including family members and a maid. High-ranking officials also might bring in bodyguards and a personal secretary. In the early 1950s the government introduced on the national level both a residential registration (*hukou*) system and a food rationing policy. These practices contributed to state control of food supply and also to security.[19] The system required that every resident register with the local police station and that only registered persons be eligible to receive ration coupons for items such as matches, soap, eggs, pork, beef, cooking oil, rice, and wheat flour. By the 1960s these regulations made it extremely difficult for people from other parts of the country to move to the capital, and immigration dropped sharply—from 560,000 in 1959 to only 61,000 in 1966.[20]

Population growth of the city through the birth of more children was a different story, because family planning and birth control were not recognized by party leaders as issues at that time. Mao ignored the 1957 city report and criticized the "bourgeois" advocacy of population control by Ma Yinchu, an economist and president of Beijing University until 1960.[21] Especially after the Great Leap Forward began in 1958, Mao firmly believed that China could achieve miracles partly by *using* its huge population, then estimated at about 600 million.[22]

Large-scale immigration into Beijing in the 1950s led to significant changes in city living conditions and lifestyle. In some ways the old slow-paced Beijing life began to give way to fast-paced collectivized mass movements and close-knit work units. The old residents carefully watched and learned from the newcomers how best to live and speak under the new authorities. By doing so they hoped to avoid making unnecessary errors or bringing unwanted troubles on themselves and their families.

Housing: Dayuan

Many high-ranking officials and celebrities, members or nonmembers of the party, were assigned the spacious courtyard houses of the former Manchu princes or nobles. These were distributed according to a hierarchical ranking created in the early 1950s along with the salary system.[23] Even famous intellectuals holding key positions received elegant courtyard houses with rents subsidized by the state. Mao Dun, novelist and minister of culture, lived in such a house, now the Mao Dun Museum. Zhang Bojun, chairman of the China Democratic League (a token non-Communist group) and minister of transportation, enjoyed a seventy-nine-room courtyard house in the area of Di'anmen, north of the Forbidden City. Should the occupant fall out of favor, however, he would be evicted immediately. Because housing assignments directly reflected the political status of the assignees, change in one usually was registered promptly in the other.

The majority of cadres and intellectuals—such as professors, scientists, and other experts—did not qualify for spacious courtyard houses. Instead they were assigned to live in clusters of newly built apartment buildings. These residential areas were called *dayuan* (large residential and office complexes), and they were designed, constructed, and managed by individual work units (*danwei*), such as ministries, universities, and military offices. Because of the shortage of land inside the city, most *dayuan* were suburban. Compared to the *dayuan* of relatively low-status colleges and research institutes, the *dayuan* of powerful units such as high-tech universities or military offices were well guarded and enclosed by walls. Although similar *dayuan* could be found elsewhere in China, they were a distinctive feature of Beijing because the city had such a high concentration of high-ranking officials and key governmental and military units.

The culture of the privileged *dayuan* was quite different from that of commoners who lived in twentieth-century *hutong* or factory workers' apartment buildings.[24] The *dayuan* provided a convenient and safe environment in which the *danwei*'s employees and their families lived and worked in a campus-like privileged community. A *dayuan*'s residents all knew each other because they worked together in addition to living as neighbors. Most of them were transferred cadres and professionals rather than old Beijingren; their children quickly adapted and spoke standard Beijing Mandarin, but without extensive use of local slang. Particularly those living in high-level *dayuan* had a sense of superiority to local people because of their revolutionary experiences and intellectual abilities, as well as material privileges such as central heating, internal dining halls, stores, post offices, public bathhouses, nurseries, and even elementary schools. In addition to the low rent, which could be as little as ten *yuan* per month, another advantage was the ease of raising children in so controlled an environment. Privacy was minimal, however, because all residents were from the same work unit and their children attended the same schools.

Yang Rae, a diplomat's daughter, offers a vivid description of her childhood and youth in a very privileged *dayuan* in the western suburb of Beijing, near the Summer Palace, beginning in 1957:

> Our new home was located in a huge yard [*dayuan*], many times larger than Nainai's (grandma's) compound (a courtyard enclosed on four sides in a *hutong*). People called this place a *jiguan* [leading organization]. . . . Later I learned that the *jiguan* we lived in was the Ministry of Investigation under the Central Committee of the Chinese Communist Party. In other words, it was the Chinese CIA. . . . Outside the yard were acres and acres of rice and lotus fields. . . . The big yard was guarded by fully armed People's Liberation Army soldiers twenty-four hours a day, seven days a week. Anyone who wanted to come in or go out had to show a pass with their photos. Even children were no exception.[25]

As in Yang's case, many high-level *dayuan* were located in a rural setting although they were considered part of the city. Armed guards at the front gate not only made entrance difficult for outsiders but also inconvenient for residents. Yet having a pass to enter a guarded *dayua*n may have given young children a sense of privilege and superiority over those who were not allowed to enter:

> Only we often forgot to bring the passes. When this happened, we would try to slip through the gate, among a crowd, or behind the guards' backs. Sometimes we succeeded. If we got caught, the soldiers would send us into the reception room, a brick house behind their sentry box. The old man there was very kind. He knew everybody's parents. When we came in, he would ask us how our parents were lately and then ring the bell. This time the soldiers would have to let us go in.[26]

"Enclosedness" was one of the main features of *dayuan* culture. D. Jin, six or seven years younger than Yang Rae and the son of a military doctor, remembered that he only played with children from the same *dayuan* when he was growing up south of Beijing. They all knew each other's families and shared a similar background; more important, they had enough space and facilities to play inside the *dayuan*. After entering graduate school and moving to the United States, he married an old *dayuan* friend.

As Yang recalled, "Looking back on it, I think a sense of superiority already existed among students who were from the [*dayuan*]."[27] How could they not have such feelings? Ten percent of the students from her elementary school would go to Beijing 101 Middle School, the most prestigious elite middle school in China, from which more than 90 percent would be admitted to colleges. They had much easier access than did ordinary residents to many resources, such as special libraries, bookstores, museums, and even the Children's Palace, where children could learn scientific subjects at an early age. Thus the distinctive isolation of *dayuan* life created a special environment for the new generation. As Lisha Chen, who grew up in a *dayuan* outside the Yongding Gate in the early 1960s, recalled: "We didn't usually mingle with the kids outside of *dayuan* to play after school mainly because we didn't often find common interests. We did notice the difference between us, but didn't really think further about why it was so. For people in Beijing then, living in a *dayuan* was also an indicator of social status," she added, "therefore it was natural that *dayuan* kids had a feeling of being 'better' than the others who lived outside." D. Jin said "I knew how to ride a bike at seven and had my own bike at twelve in the early 1970s. After that I rode my bike to and from school. Of course, *hutong* kids usually didn't have their bikes until much later."

The new China was supposed to be an egalitarian society, but as in the Soviet Union and Eastern Europe, a privileged class developed rapidly. The sons and daughters of veteran revolutionaries, most of whom grew up in *dayuan*, belonged to the most trusted class. Seeing them as successors who one day would carry on the revolution into the future, Mao praised them as the "morning sun." Compared to other people their age, they were well informed and well connected. As they matured and mastered Marxist vocabulary, they referred to ordinary residents as "petty city dwellers" (*xiao shimin*), a pejorative label for those who supposedly were concerned only about themselves and had no grand vision, political or otherwise. It was almost a synonym for "petty bourgeoisie." In the long run the *dayuan* way of life had mixed outcomes. It produced a new generation that was to play a leading role in the destructive Cultural Revolution and then be "sent down" to the countryside. It also would produce an only slightly younger generation that would use freedom resulting from chaos and neglect to educate itself and, when the opportunity came, to envision a very different Beijing after the death of Mao.

Housing: Hutong

In contrast to residents of the *dayuan*, *hutong* dwellers usually enjoyed relative privacy because their housing arrangements had nothing to do with their work units. *Hutong* life more closely resembled that of the old days in Beijing. Most residents lived in the same place for generations. Geographically, most poor people lived in the south in the former Outer City. The majority of the courtyard dwellers could not afford a courtyard per family as in earlier times. Many were workers, restaurant chefs or servers, low-ranking office clerks, and school teachers. Their work units usually did not have apartment compounds for their employees. Because of the continuing shortage of housing in Beijing as the population rose, several generations of the same family often had to share the same courtyard. The situation worsened further in the 1960s when most civilian construction stopped because of economic constraints. Courtyard life became even more crowded than it had been in the 1930s-era conditions depicted by Lao She in *Camel Xiangzi*. An entire family of two or even three generations would be packed into *every room* adjacent to the central courtyard. Often five or more families shared one or two water faucets. Day or night, residents had to leave the courtyard to use nearby public latrines built in these neighborhoods; often they had to wait in line to do so. As culture critic Zhang Yiwu, who lived in such a courtyard as a child, recalled:

> The *hutong* needs to change because it does have inconvenient aspects. One is running water. The whole courtyard compound usually only had one faucet. Once winter arrived, the faucet in the open air easily froze. I remember when I was little, at about nine o'clock every night, all families were reminded to fetch

water and save it in a big container, and then the water was shut off until the next morning. Furthermore, every family had to share one faucet for washing clothing and preparing dinner, which often caused conflicts and fights among neighbors.[28]

In socialist Beijing, everyone had to be accounted for and registered. Work units took charge of all employees and their families, providing or at least assigning housing, health care, and schools. They even regulated personal matters, such as the timing of marriages and births. In addition, from the 1950s to the 1990s, a network of neighborhood committees ruled daily life for everyone, both those in work-unit housing and those outside it. By causing the residents to watch each other, the neighborhood committees extended police power, and in fact they worked closely with local police substations. The committees' daily chores could be as minor as distributing ration coupons, offering help with domestic problems, and caring for the old and the young when necessary; they could be as major as watching the neighborhood and reporting any unusual activities or unregistered strangers to the local police. They particularly helped city authorities to ensure that *hutong* areas with mixed residents from different social backgrounds received adequate attention.

Shopping

One consequence of the collectivization of business ownership in the 1950s and 1960s was a sharp decrease in numbers of neighborhood markets and peddlers in the streets and *hutong*. Starting in the early 1950s, the government pressured business owners to transform private ownership to joint state-private ownership. Small businesses, such as tailor shops and shoemakers that had fewer than three employees and funding of less than two thousand *yuan*, were merged into co-ops, while bigger enterprises, such as the locally famous Chinese pharmacy Tongrentang, were required to set up a joint state-private system. By January 1956 almost eighteen thousand private enterprises had come under joint ownership. Increasingly, a system of state stores operated all commerce from the neighborhood food markets to the larger co-ops and more elaborate department stores. At the same time the state monopoly of major products and commodities (including grains) began under the socialist planned economy. Department stores had only limited goods to display, and small businesses hardly got enough to sell. The total number of neighborhood markets and convenience stores was more than 31,000 in 1957, but that figure was less than half of what it had been in 1952. State-run department stores were established in the major business districts; the best known opened at Wangfujing in 1955. These stores were intended to replace both the high-end Western shops of the Republican era and the traditional markets filled with a great variety of vendors and peddlers, but the changes occurred at the expense of enjoyable aspects of the old Beijing way of shopping. The Dong'an Market, just opposite the new Wangfujing Department Store, continued to offer customers more variety of local food and specialties at lower prices. After the socialist transformation began, however, bargaining was no longer allowed. All prices were fixed, shortages of supplies were common, and salespersons had little motivation even to sell, let alone bargain, because the sale had no effect on their income.

Food

In the 1950s the city government transferred to Beijing chefs and managers from five nationally acclaimed regional restaurants and opened up five new state-owned restaurants under their original names: Tianjin's Islamic style in cuisine could be found at Hongbinlou, Shanghai's southern delicacies at Laozhengxing and Meiweizhai, Guangzhou's Cantonese flavor at Datong jiujia, and Sichuan's distinctive regional flavor at Sichuan fandian. These high-quality regional restaurants entertained important visitors and cadres newly transferred from other parts of the country, helping them to overcome homesickness. They also enriched Beijing life and benefited the local residents. Although these establishments were relatively expensive and most people could enjoy them only once in a while, they soon became part of local life. One memoirist writes that he never could forget the "*shuijian bao*" (a kind of Shanghai-style dumpling stuffed with meat)[29] at Meiweizhai, not far from his childhood home on Jiaojia *hutong* in the 1960s. At the same time, formerly famous local restaurants, which were always more popular and affordable, remained open under joint state-private ownership in the mid-1950s and then under state ownership in the 1960s.

In the past the most memorable local food had been sold by street-alley peddlers. They provided tasty, convenient, inexpensive delicacies and basic food to common people: candied haws (small red hawthorn fruits) on sticks, deep-fried dough cakes, fresh hot soy-bean milk, and baked sweet potatoes. They could be found at the corners of *hutong* daily from early morning to late at night as well as at temple fairs, in traditional market districts such as Tianqiao, and at train and long-distance bus stations. These familiar scenes gradually disappeared by the end of the 1950s. Particularly after the Cultural Revolution started in 1966, it was hard to find any peddlers on streets or alleys. The main reason was political and ideological: privately owned business, however small and humble, was considered shameful in the late 1950s and almost illegal and even antisocialist by the late

1960s. The hidden agenda of the city government was that it would be much easier to control and manage society without floating populations such as unregistered, or even registered, street peddlers. Also, in socialist Beijing, the slow pace of
famous local teahouses was no longer appropriate because the leisure class was disappearing. To be sure, the teahouses were still there, but the customers were
mainly retirees who could afford the time to chat with friends for hours over tea.
These changes meant loss of tradition and variety in Beijing life.

Dress

After 1949, people's clothing and hairstyles changed with the new social and political order. Although no dress code was ever decreed, Beijing residents, especially new
cadres, progressive intellectuals, and white-collar workers, had to consider what kind
of clothing would now be politically appropriate and socially acceptable. In the
1920s and 1930s, Shanghai had taken the lead in setting fashion, but now that dress
had taken on political meaning Beijing as the new capital showed the way.

Almost without exception in the 1950s, most male government officials wore
old Communist army fatigues or solid blue or gray "Mao jackets," a modified version
of the Republican-era "Sun Yat-sen jacket," with four big pockets in front. Only
diplomats wore Western-style suits with ties and dress shirts. Men's long gowns,
which formerly had been standard for the educated and wealthy, faded away. At a reception held by the city government in 1950, Duanmu Hongliang, a writer just returned from Hong Kong, wore a brand-new Mao jacket but Hong Kong-style
pointed leather shoes. On the same occasion, the writer Lao She, who had once
lived in London and had just returned from the United States, wore a neat suit and
tie and carried a walking stick, just "like an English gentleman."[30] Others present
immediately noticed the inappropriate dress and remembered the scene years later.

For girls and women changes in style were more gradual, but Soviet fashions
were very popular and also politically stylish. Soviet cloth was imported in great
quantities to be made into skirts and blouses, and one-piece Western-style dresses
(which were not common before). Another Soviet-inspired garment, known as the
"Lenin suit"—with double-breasted jacket, pointed collar, and sash belt—was almost a uniform in the 1950s for female cadres, clerks, and teachers who wished to
project the image of progressive, socialist woman. In the Yan'an era, masculine
clothing had already become popular.[31] In the 1950s, however, women still had
permanent waves, and girls and younger women still wore their hair in two
braids—but a single braid was considered very stylish. Slacks became more common, although skirts were sometimes worn, and even the traditional qipao could

seen on special occasions. High heeled shoes were infrequently worn, but low heels (called "half-high heels") were common.

Starting in the late 1950s, however, women's clothing became much plainer and less colorful. The Great Leap Forward and the Sino-Soviet split cut off the ample supply of imported cloth, and, more importantly, political pressures restricted options. Simple blouses and solid-color slacks became the norm. In the 1958 photo of Qinghua University students, all the male students wear Mao jackets except one who has a Western sport coat. The two female students are simply dressed in pants, as modestly as workers or peasants of that time. (See Figure 27.) By the time of the Cultural Revolution in the late 1960s, women and girls alike cut their hair short and kept it straight. They rarely wore skirts. And plain greys, dark blues, and browns became almost universal. In these ways, people used appearance and dress to show their political conformity.

Dancing

Informal ballroom dancing had become popular at Yan'an during wartime. In Beijing, dancing was a new kind of social gathering that expressed liberation from a traditional social ethic. It also demonstrated commitment to the equality of men and women. On weekends Beijing officials, intellectuals, college students, soldiers and factory workers attended dancing parties. Young people, male and female, were particularly encouraged to participate in order to meet new friends and establish close relationships. Where parents formerly had arranged marriages for their children, *danwei* managers assumed the responsibility of finding matches for young people in their units. In contrast to the old commercial dancing halls that had entertained only the leisure class and white-collar workers before 1949, the new dancing parties were free of charge and organized by work units and schools.

The enthusiasm for social dancing, however, led to problems, such as an increase in family crises and divorces. A Japanese observer commented:

> I remember that during my first visit to new China in 1952–53, dancing parties were very popular. In addition to the International Club and Beijing Hotel, all the government units held dancing parties every Saturday night. Once I was invited to a dance organized by the Peace Promotion Committee. I felt very embarrassed and it was hard to handle this situation, because I never have liked dancing. The young interpreter tried to persuade me [by saying] enthusiastically, "In new China, you would not be able to find a marriage partner if you knew neither dancing nor singing."[32]

Although the people at large lost their dancing parties in the 1960s, Mao and other top leaders at Zhongnanhai did not. According to the memoirs of Mao's physician Li Zhisui, there was a weekly dance at Zhongnanhai on Saturday nights in the 1950s, which Mao and other leaders attended regularly, and to which many young actresses and dancers, often physical education students, also were invited. These continued and Wednesday nights were added in 1960, although the economy suffered a serious setback that year.[33]

For many local residents in the 1950s, Beijing was an "ideal capital" (*lixiang shoudu*) because the city was clean, well disciplined, and publicly upbeat. All the brothels, gambling houses, drug traffic, and gangsters seemed to disappear soon after the People's Liberation Army entered Beijing. Even petty thieves and pickpockets were rare. In May 1953 the municipal telephone company placed its first public phone booth in Zhongshan Park in central Beijing. Anyone could use the phone by putting money in an open and unwatched box. After a month, the sum collected exactly matched the number of times the phone had been used.

The slogan of socialist equality was everywhere, and class differences were supposed to be minimized, if not entirely abolished. The new salary system started in the early 1950s, and differences in pay among factory workers, office clerks, intellectuals, and high-ranking cadres were not large. A skilled worker earned about 180 *yuan* per month, a top-level university professor over 300 *yuan*, and Mao himself only 610 *yuan*. Starting salaries for male and female college graduates were the same. Ordinary residents, especially vendors or restaurant servers, still earned salaries much lower than those of intellectuals or government and party cadres. Average annual salary per working person in 1957 was 748 *yuan*, an average of 250 *yuan* per family member.[34] Ration coupons for food and cloth limited the amount families could purchase, and government-subsidized housing and medical care reduced the need for cash. Nevertheless, the focus in the 1950s was on the advance of equality: the privileges of landlords and Manchu princes belonged to the past and those of the new elite were either not known or not yet seen as a problem.

Mao's Mass Campaigns and Their Impact on Beijing

By the late 1950s it was clear that Mao was not satisfied with gradual progress in either production or equality of distribution. One of his favorite sayings was

"Trees would like to be quiet, but the wind never stops blowing." By the wind that "never stops blowing," he meant class struggle. He constantly warned cadres that "if the east wind [socialism] doesn't overpower the west wind [capitalism], the west wind will overpower the east wind." For him, especially as he aged and his thinking grew more rigid, there was no middle way, no compromise; everything had to be "red," not "expert." The younger Mao who had been able to hold those poles in dynamic tension, realizing that both were necessary, slipped away. The aging Mao more than ever felt the need to overpower his enemies, whether real or fabricated.[35]

As early as 1927 Mao had written that a "revolution is not a dinner party . . . it cannot be so refined, so leisurely and gentle. . . . A revolution is an insurrection, an act of violence by which one class overthrows another." The rise of the Communist Party had occurred in the crucible of national unification, war, and civil war as well as social revolution. A "rectification" campaign at Yan'an in 1942 had subjected intellectuals not only to criticism in mass forums but also to physical abuse, driving some to suicide. Land reform in 1949–1950 had encouraged confrontations resulting in an estimated 1 million deaths in landlord families.[36] But even internal "enemies" who survived were not safe. The party classified some citizens (such as former landlords, capitalists, and Nationalist officials) as not yet belonging to "the people." In the early 1950s these individuals could be imprisoned or subjected to programs of intensive "thought reform," or both. They and their families suffered official discrimination for decades because of their "bad" backgrounds. Thus the mass campaigns of the 1950s and 1960s developed themes of class struggle and patterns of violence that had played a role in earlier revolutionary experience.

In 1955 Mao suddenly ordered the arrest of the literary critic Hu Feng, the writer Lu Xun's most prominent disciple, and launched a campaign to curtail intellectual freedom. Next, in 1956, he seemed to encourage people to express their opinions about state and party policies (the "Hundred Flowers" campaign). He followed this with a large-scale "anti-rightist movement" in 1957 that attacked as "rightists" more than ten thousand liberal Beijing intellectuals who had responded to his earlier invitation to speak. Mao soon dismissed most from office and sent them to frontier labor camps, where many remained for more than twenty years.

Soon after the anti-rightist campaign, Mao began the "Great Leap Forward," a movement to speed economic growth that pushed the whole country to the edge of collapse. He decided to reorganize all the working-living units into huge "people's communes." Beijing became an experimental site for urban communes. Starting in 1958 the city established five of these: at Shijingshan, Chun-shu, Beixinqiao, Erlong Road, and Tiyuguan Road; in 1960 the central government decided to promote the concept further and ordered Beijing authorities to build thirty-three new communes. The size of the urban commune was actually based on the preexisting neighborhood units, and the result was that everyone living in the area concerned now worked for the commune. Factories, administrative organs, schools, shops, and residents in the commune were administered as a whole. Even peddlers, vendors, housewives, retirees, and children found themselves mobilized and controlled. The communes also were encouraged to run small factories and schools, though with insufficient funds and technical support. Many public dining halls were established to serve commune populations. Intended to replace individual family kitchens, the dining halls also were meant to eliminate any private spaces, possessions, or occasions—basically, family life itself. Everyone was supposed to see himself as primarily part of the commune and only secondarily part of the family.

With real parents cast aside, the party secretary of the commune or of smaller units within it became the new collective parent who made decisions about virtually everything. Besides the transformation of social structures, Mao and his government gave highest priority to the manufacture of iron and steel, considered the most important index of national economic modernization. Everyone in the commune was mobilized to contribute every scrap of metal from home and recycle it to make iron and steel. People were called on to volunteer to build stoves and to make iron without any technical assistance. At the same time, the dining halls served free all-you-can-eat meals to everyone to advertise the commune system.

The consequences of the government's misguided policies and of the blind optimism, trust, and enthusiasm of the people were more severe than anyone could have anticipated. Because of the concurrent anti-rightist movement, most cadres and intellectuals dared not express their opinions and had to conform to the party line. The architect Liang Sicheng did not even have enough power to protect his loyal city-planning associate Chen Zhanxiang, who was labeled a rightist in 1957. How then could he protect the city wall? The Outer City wall and half of the Inner City wall were almost completely demolished by mobilized commune volunteers during the Great Leap Forward. Another consequence of the movement was hunger and famine. By June 1960 the Beijing food supply ran dangerously low with stored food adequate for only seven days. Hunger stalked even the *dayuan:*

Pork, chicken, fish, cookies, candies, nuts, canned goods, fruit, vegetables—in short, all edible things—vanished from the store shelves. Afterwards [more] ration coupons were invented, all kinds of them: grain coupons, cooking oil coupons, meat coupons, fish coupons, egg coupons, tofu coupons, pastry coupons, sugar coupons, cigarette coupons, cotton coupons, cloth coupons, and many more. . . . Suddenly money lost its magic power. . . .

The coupons, moreover, differed from one place to another. . . . With a ration coupon, an adult in Beijing was allowed to buy around thirty pounds of grain each month at a subsidized price. Children's rations varied according to their age. In addition, each person got up to a half-pound of meat, half a dozen eggs, four ounces of cooking oil, and some tofu [each month].[37]

Many officially reported achievements in the Great Leap era were terribly inflated and unforgivably fake; for example, the iron produced by urban commune volunteers was useless. Local officials feared Mao and reported to their superiors what they thought he wanted to hear, thus causing the state and party to make faulty decisions based on incorrect data. More than thirty million people died of hunger nationwide, and Beijing became desolate and despondent at the end of the Great Leap Forward around 1960. Finally, in the face of undeniable failure, Mao agreed to step down temporarily from the front line and let Liu Shaoqi and Deng Xiaoping lead national retrenchment.

Liu Shaoqi, head of state, had been educated in the Soviet Union in the 1920s. A labor organizer and party leader, he was the author of *How to Be a Good Communist*, which was instrumental in training party members and promoting their loyalty and discipline. Deng Xiaoping, secretary-general of the party, was the son of a Sichuan landlord family; he had joined the party while on a work-study stay in France in the 1920s. Now Liu and Deng swung the pendulum back to the "expert" pole from the "red" one. They abolished radical policies by dissolving urban communes and their subordinate units, such as dining halls; returning woks and other tools to help families reequip their own kitchens; and giving people back some freedom and privacy. Although China recovered from the Great Leap Forward in a relatively short period, Mao grew increasingly angry because he was afraid of losing face as well as authority.

As Mao found that his authority indeed had been shaken, he suspected the disloyalty of the Beijing Municipal Government as well as of the party's Central Committee. Preparing his attack, he sent his wife, Jiang Qing, to Shanghai to contact sympathetic party radicals there. Mao encouraged the publication of an article of literary criticism by Yao Wenyuan on November 10, 1965, even revising it three times. This article accused Wu Han, deputy mayor of Beijing and the author of a recent play set in the Ming dynasty, *Hai Rui Dismissed from Office*, of using the drama to show sympathy for Peng Dehuai. Peng was a recent minister of defense who had been dismissed because of his criticism of the Great Leap Forward in a private letter to Mao. Yao asserted in print that Wu Han and his group within the party were trying to reverse the verdict on the dismissed defense minister in order to attack Mao. According to Mao, Peng Dehuai and his followers also opposed the party and the revolution itself.

Mao became furious when Mayor Peng Zhen and other leaders in Beijing refused to reprint Yao's article in major national newspapers; they considered it arbitrary, groundless, and unjustifiable, and they feared that it might hurt innocent people. Peng Zhen told a Japanese visitor, "It is not a political issue, but an historical play. Chairman Mao says it is a political issue. How troublesome!"[38] Mao decided to destroy the disobedient Beijing Municipality. With the support of Lin Biao, the new defense minister, and of military forces, Mao dismissed several top party leaders in early 1966; first among them was Mayor Peng Zhen. Mao's real target was Liu Shaoqi, but he had started his attack with the Beijing Municipal Government. There was almost a clean sweep of major and minor officials in that bureaucracy. Many veteran party leaders committed suicide.

In 1965 Mao's intentions initially were mysterious even to those close to him, but soon it became apparent that his goal was to attack those who had criticized and sidelined him since the Great Leap Forward, or even earlier. He accused his former revolutionary comrades of treating him "like a dead ancestor," of kicking him upstairs. Linking them with the party leadership and machinery, he decided to destroy the very organization that he had led and shaped through decades of revolutionary struggle. The purge focused on Beijing because that is where top party figures were concentrated. Mao apparently considered Beijing unsafe and feared a coup. A special task force, the Capital Work Team, was charged with making the city militarily secure. Command of two armed police divisions was transferred to the Beijing Garrison, which itself was expanded to four divisions. After returning to Beijing from Shanghai in July 1966, Mao did not dare to reenter the Zhongnanhai leaders' compound, but resided instead at Diaoyutai, the state guest house on the west side of the city.[39]

Mao's purges might have remained secret had he not then sought to turn the internal power struggle into a mass campaign. In a sign of the importance of Beijing University to the political leadership, he took his first fateful step there. In May 1966 Kang Sheng, probably Mao's top "enforcer" during the Cultural Revolution, sent a secret investigation team headed by his wife to uncover political dissent at the university and to purge its top administrators. Some Beida "leftists" distrusted Peng Zhen, and one of them, Nie Yuanzi, party branch secretary in the Philosophy Department, became an informant and aide to the investigation team. She was partly responsible for a big-character poster denouncing the president of the university and two other administrators for subverting the Cultural Revolution in Beijing. A huge uproar ensued, and a battle of posters began. Kang Sheng sent a copy of the Nie poster to Mao, who was in Hangzhou; Mao declared that its content should be publicized all over the country. This broadcast signaled the true beginning of the Cultural Revolution as a nationwide mass movement. In Beijing all the universities and schools were immediately thrown into turmoil, and a period of violence ensued.[40]

Unlike earlier political campaigns, in which Mao had depended mainly on the party and those who came from poor and uneducated backgrounds, he now shifted his trust to the "morning sun" generation, those who had been born and raised in the new China. When the rumor that Mao's authority had been threatened spread among the *dayuan* complexes, the privileged children of the veteran cadres agitated to do something to protect him. On May 28, 1966, a group of Qinghua University High School students secretly gathered and formed an organization called the Red Guards (*hong weibing*) whose goal was to protect Mao and his power. At the beginning, only high-ranking revolutionary cadres' sons and daughters were allowed to join the Red Guards.[41] On June 24, 1966, Qinghua University High School Red Guards mounted a poster headed "Long Live the Rebellious Spirit of the Proletarian Revolution," which declared "Revolution is rebellion, and the soul of Mao Zedong Thought is rebellion. . . . The revolutionary should emulate the Monkey King [a character of popular literature], brandishing his staff and using his mystical powers to shatter the old world and to send everyone and everything into chaos, the more chaos the better."[42]

As long as Liu Shaoqi could control the Cultural Revolution in Beijing, he tried to suppress the new student organization and label it illegal, even counterrevolutionary. Liu was following the pattern that Mao himself had used to handle turbulent mass actions by cracking down on any units led by the masses rather than by the party. Surprisingly, Mao took the opposite position in a letter dated August 1, 1966, to the Qinghua Red Guards. He wrote: "Your posters of June 24 and July 4 state clearly your anger and reprimand toward the landlord class, imperialism, revisionism, and their running dogs in their exploitation and suppression of workers, peasants, revolutionary intellectuals, and revolutionary parties. . . . I want to extend to you warm support."[43] Refusing an appeal to control the chaos that was developing, Mao declared, "Beijing is too civilized! . . . There is not a great deal of disorder. . . . Now is not the time to interfere."[44] As he had written nearly forty years earlier, a revolution is not a dinner party.

Mao's letter was a signal from the top. When it circulated widely, hundreds of Red Guards units organized not only at high schools, but also at colleges and even at elementary schools in Beijing. Soon there were thousands of such groups throughout China. On August 18, 1966, Mao and other leaders held a mass rally celebrating the Cultural Revolution at Tiananmen Square. In the imperial era, ceremonies in the Forbidden City just beyond Tiananmen were often held at dawn to appear more impressive and awe-inspiring. Now more than a million Red Guards and faculty from Beijing and elsewhere gathered in the early light for Mao's review. The Red Guards were wearing used army uniforms and red armbands printed with three yellow Chinese characters saying "Red Guards" in Mao's style of calligraphy. Even Mao himself, with a Red Guard armband given to him by a student on his left arm, was wearing a brand-new army uniform. This departure from his usual dress implied his fighting spirit and reasserted his irreplaceable position as revolutionary commander in chief. The historic scene began:

> About 5:00 a.m. on August 18, 1966, shortly after sunrise, Mao Zedong, followed by Lin Biao and Zhou Enlai and clad in a grass-green People's Liberation Army uniform with a red star emblem on the cap, walked over the Jinshui bridge beneath Tiananmen . . . smiling and waving to the crowds, shaking hands and moving among the people for a while. Then, waving to the people with his military cap clutched in his hand, he returned to the bridge. Recapping himself, he proceeded toward the gate. In an instant, the sea of red flags covering Tiananmen Square became an ocean roaring with the sounds of "Long live Chairman Mao!"[45]

From that moment, only seventeen years after Mao had first been hailed with the words *wansui!* (ten thousand years!) at the founding of the People's Republic in the same square, he became a "living god." Mao connected himself to the "morning sun" generation by making his appearance at sunrise and at a short distance from them. He effectively fanned passion and blind worship among the

Red Guards, who kept waving their arms with little red books (*Quotations from Chairman Mao Zedong*) in their hands and shouting slogans with tears on their cheeks. Mao's personal review legitimized the Red Guards and their rebellious actions. They felt invincible and charged with fighting spirit. They had tasted the thrill of mass politics but had no idea of its dangers or even of the true motives of the idealized authority figure who—miraculously it must have seemed—had reached out to them. (See Figure 30.)

From August 19 on, thousands of Red Guards appeared on almost every major street in Beijing and began a movement to destroy the "Four Olds" (Old Ideas, Old Culture, Old Customs, and Old Habits). Since the Four Olds was an ambiguous concept, almost everything on the street could be destroyed in the name of revolution, from old hairstyles to the names of streets and local stores. The young Red Guards literally checked every passerby on the street and used scissors to cut women's long hair, Western jeans, and colorful shirts, which they consigned to the Four Olds category. The signboard of the Quanjude, the famous roast duck restaurant, was smashed because the old name had connotations of "Confucius" and "moral," and many old street signs were destroyed or covered with new, revolutionized names. Chang'an (Long Peace) Boulevard became East-Is-Red Boulevard, Wangfujing (Prince's Palace Well, the business area) became Preventing-Revisionism Street, and Dong'an (Eastern Peace) Market changed to East Wind Market. The Red Guards even proposed changing the name Beijing to East-Is-Red City.

On August 22, Beijing radio stations highly praised the Red Guards' actions and cheered at their victory over the Four Olds, encouraging them to continue. The following day's major newspapers, local as well as national, repeated these supportive tones. Emboldened, the Red Guards, mainly teenagers, created more turmoil. The local authorities, including the Beijing Municipal Government and the public security officials, seemed confused and paralyzed by these lawless and moblike Red Guards who somehow were honored in the highest places. They either did nothing to stop them or cooperated with them.

The Red Guards started ransacking temples, churches, and important historical places and relics in Beijing. They destroyed religious idols; burned Bibles and other religious books; dug up the remains of "counterrevolutionaries," capitalists, and missionaries from graveyards and tore down their tombs; and publicly tortured and humiliated monks, pastors, and religious believers. The well-known Biyun (Azure Cloud), Wofo (Reclining Buddha), and "Lama" temples (Biyunsi, Wofosi, Yonghegong), Islamic mosques, and many more religious institutions absorbed the wrath of the Red Guards. Statues of the Buddha at the Tanzhe (Oak Pool) and Jietai (Ordaining Terrace) monasteries (Tanzhesi, Jietaisi) were destroyed, as were many stone stelae and inscriptions at Tanzhesi.[46] Red Guards tore down the more than three-hundred-year-old tomb of the Jesuit missionary Matteo Ricci.[47] According to the statistics of the Municipal Bureau of Cultural Relics, among almost seven thousand cultural relics selected for preservation in 1958, nearly five thousand were damaged by Red Guards between late August and mid-September 1966.[48] The architectural remains and grounds at Yuanmingyuan, once sacked by the British and French, were now the object of Red Guard violence, and walls, trees, and stones were removed.[49] Only the timely intervention of Premier Zhou Enlai saved the Palace Museum in the Forbidden City from the Red Guards; it would be off-limits throughout the Cultural Revolution.

Red Guards held mass rallies to torture intellectuals, former landlords and capitalists, and even their own high school teachers and principals, many of whom were beaten to death. The Red Guards were "resplendent in their military fatigues, army belts, and red armbands," as described in writer and musician Liu Sola's autobiographical novel, *Chaos and All That*. They went through thousands of *hutong* to search for hidden counterrevolutionaries and undiscovered Four Olds in private homes, with the acquiescence of local police stations and neighborhood committees. They ransacked randomly chosen houses and interrogated and even beat the people they found there. Twenty-four hours a day, seven days a week, the Red Guards could appear banging on anyone's door. They would enter shouting slogans and obscenities and start looking for financial papers that the residents (suspected by the Red Guards of being former landlords) had concealed.[50] One-third of the city's homes were ransacked and more than seventeen hundred people beaten to death by Red Guards during the campaign against the Four Olds. In the Red Terror, as it was called by the Red Guards themselves, Beijing was left not only naked, chaotic, and helpless, but a "living hell."

At several secondary schools, the Red Guards set up centers for interrogation of teachers and staff. After the news broke that the principal of Beijing Number One Girls High School had been beaten to death by Red Guards, the Red Terror immediately spread out to the whole of Beijing. Wen Jierou,[51] a senior editor and translator, described her mother's death:

It was already nine o'clock when I left the office on the night of August 27. . . . I had just reached the gateway to the compound on Douzui Lane when I was caught off guard by a "Halt!" and surrounded by a band of ruffians. . . . They shoved me into the main courtyard of No. 30, Alley Eight, and force me to stand at attention facing Mama's dwelling. . . .

One of the thugs smacked me on the back with his fist and bellowed, "The old spy alienated herself from the people and hanged herself to avoid being punished. . . . Get your ass over there and look at her!"

When I entered her room, dear Mama had already been taken down and parked on her cot, . . . I had been told that a person's face becomes contorted and purple after death by hanging, but Mama in death was as serene and composed as if in a deep sleep; any expression of terror had vanished. . . .

In a deafening roar, the ruffians all shouted at once that I must swear out loud, "She deserved to die! This rids the world of a piece of rotten flesh!"

Could people be any crueler, any less human than this, anywhere in the world?[52]

Wen's mother, who was the wife of a former Nationalist diplomat and the sister of a Nationalist military officer killed by the Communists in the early 1950s, had decided not to tolerate false accusations, physical torture, and endless interrogations anymore. She chose to kill herself to maintain her dignity and self-respect.

Wen's experience was typical in Beijing during "Red August." Another case was that of Lao She, the novelist and playwright who had been invited to return to China from the United States in 1950 and who had been honored as "People's Artist" by the government. In August 1966, however, the author of *Camel Xiangzi* and *Teahouse* became a target of the Red Guards. Along with about thirty other intellectuals and Beijing Opera performers, including the writers Duanmu Hongliang and Xiao Jun, Lao She was dragged by a group of high school Red Guards to the Confucian Temple. In the courtyard of the temple, the Red Guards built a bonfire to burn traditional opera props that they had consigned to the Four Olds.

All had their heads shaved; some had black ink poured over their heads. The Red Guards ordered them to kneel around the fire, used branding irons on them, and beat them with the theatrical props and the brass buckles of leather belts. In the oppressive summer heat, sixty-seven-year old Lao She . . . was severely beaten and lost consciousness. He was then dragged to the Beijing Municipal Literary Federation, where he was greeted by several hundred Red Guards shouting slogans.[53] He was hit with leather belts and fists, kicked, and spat on. . . . In the early hours of August 24, when his wife Hu Jieqing took him home, he was ordered to carry a placard labeling him as "active counterrevolution-ary" and to report to the Literary Federation that morning. At home, Lao She took off his shirt to show a body wracked and bloodied beyond decency. . . . Early that morning, Lao She left his home carrying the placard. He did not go to work at the Literary Federation; instead, he went alone to the edge of Taiping Lake outside of Desheng Gate in the western part of the city, where he sat for the entire day, hardly moving. In the darkness of the night, he drowned himself in the lake.[54]

Like Lao She and Wen's mother, many other innocent people showed their indignation and protest by ending their lives during the Red Terror of August 1966. That same month brought disaster to Liang Sicheng, the professor of ar-chitecture who had lost his battle to save the city wall and other historic struc-tures. His first wife and collaborator in field research, Lin Huiyin, had died of tuberculosis in 1955, and Liang had remarried in 1962. His second wife, Lin Zhu, later described events of summer 1966 in the Department of Architecture at Qinghua University, where she also worked. At the time, Liang already had been criticized publicly as a rightist:

> I didn't dare to think about it, but I had a premonition that they'd never let Sicheng go. Finally the thing I had most feared came about. That day I was reading a big-character poster in front of my department and suddenly someone was pushed out the door. A huge black placard was hanging on his chest on which were written some white characters: "Reactionary Academic Authority, Liang Sicheng" with a big cross over his name. The crowds in front of the de-partment burst out laughing. Stooped over, he tripped and almost fell but forced himself onward. I raised my head and for a moment our eyes met. My god! I cannot describe the expression of utter humiliation and shame in the eyes of that upright scholar whom I loved so much. Even now, if I were given a chance to re-live my youth in exchange for looking again into his eyes at that moment, I would say no. . . . That day when we got home we almost didn't dare to talk for fear of striking the other's wounds. From then on, whenever he left home he had to put on that black placard.[55]

In 1966 and after, Liang and Lin Zhu underwent many searches of their home, confiscations of their property, and public struggle meetings. Liang's salary was cut off, his bank accounts frozen. Weakened by illness that had been exacerbated by a forced move to small, cold quarters in 1967, abandoned by many who may have feared to associate with him, Liang died of illness in January 1972 at the age of seventy.

In 1966 Red Guards even controlled the Beijing Railway Station, checking passengers in and sending "hidden" landlords or "counterrevolutionaries" out of Beijing. By the end of September, they had driven 85,000 people out of the city.[56] More than 114,000 families were searched and forced to give up their private collections of calligraphy and paintings as well as gold and savings in foreign currencies.[57]

From August 18 to November 25, Mao reviewed Red Guards at Tiananmen Square eight times; these occasions involved at least eleven million Red Guards and other students from all over the country and further established his personality cult. As thousands more students traveled to the capital in order to experience Beijing and to be reviewed by Mao, Red Guards from the capital began to travel to other parts of the country to speed their rebellion. As a result, the whole nation saw Beijing Red Guards as representatives of Mao, the Party Central Committee, and Beijing. Such were Beijingren in the eyes of many Chinese citizens in 1966.

With Mao's approval, all trains and long-distance buses were free for Red Guards and students to ride, and those from other places were offered free food and temporary accommodations in Beijing. With Mao's support, Xie Fuzhi, minister of public security, told police leaders in Beijing and the provinces that "we cannot do things according to ordinary practice, and we cannot follow criminal statutes. If you detain people who beat up other people, you will make mistakes. . . . Should the Red Guards who kill others be punished? My view is that if people are killed, then they are killed; it's no business of ours."[58] Because the Red Guards appeared to have approval from Mao, no one seemed to be able or willing to stop their violence. The vulnerability of Beijing and of China to a disastrous decision at the top by an aging leader too long in power resonated with earlier history. Residents of Beijing at least in their mid-eighties in 1966 might have recalled that in 1900, the worst Boxer violence began after such a signal from Empress Dowager Cixi, and that the city gendarmerie thereafter did not try to contain it.

The Red Guards were organized loosely and never had any unified authoritative leadership, although they all claimed that they were Mao's protectors and that his thoughts guided their actions. But Mao's thoughts were full of internal contradictions. As has been suggested, the Red Guards had no idea of his true agenda in the Cultural Revolution. Early Red Guards in Beijing were mainly sons and daughters of veteran revolutionary cadres. They were as merciless and as brutal to former landlords, ex-capitalists, and intellectuals as their parents had been to "class enemies" during the pre-1949 revolutionary era. To protect itself, the party had tried to turn the Red Guards toward attacking intellectual and cultural figures, teachers, and the Four Olds. But Mao also wished to even the score with the party. When his target shifted to the high-ranking cadres themselves, many Red Guards felt betrayed and disillusioned by seeing their own parents become "class enemies" to be criticized, tortured, and even jailed. This sudden switch of class identity—from trusted revolutionary cadre to class enemy—traumatized a large group of Red Guards and made them rethink their susceptibility to Mao's cult of personality and to his manipulation of ideological categories. Words such as "bourgeois," "proletarian," "the people," and "class enemies" gradually had lost any meaning—they meant whatever Mao said they meant *today*. Maoist stress on *thought* as opposed to objective social and economic circumstances—the original Marxist focus—made it possible to reclassify anyone as an "enemy" at any time.

Even to Mao and the Party Central Committee, the mass movement had appeared increasingly out of control in 1967, especially among energetic students who had no classes to attend and no job except for destruction. College-age Red Guards fought factional battles on campuses, including those of Beijing and Qinghua universities, that involved thousands of people and the use of guns and machine guns. Some of the weapons were stolen and others were obtained from the army. With more campuses becoming scenes of endless fighting, with Mao constantly shifting his favor from one faction to another, with party policy ever changing, the Red Guards' enthusiasm for the Cultural Revolution finally began to wane, and the "morning sun" generation had to face a new day.

At the end of 1967, elementary and secondary schools as well as colleges were ordered to reopen after a year-and-a-half shutdown. Students all were ordered to go back to the classroom. At the same time, the city government sent more than ten thousand workers and eight thousand army officers into schools, including colleges, to supervise and lead school administration and ensure that teaching was on track. But when Red Guards had to give up the power they had recently gained to teams of workers and military officers, violent resistance and confrontation often took place. In a directive of December 22, 1968, Mao finally moved to send young people to be re-educated by peasants and to become new, educated farmers. With the exception of a small number of high school graduates from military families who joined the army to avoid being sent to the countryside, there was no escape. By June 1971, a total of more than 415,000 Beijing high school graduates were sent to remote provinces and frontiers as well as to the suburbs. At long last, the Red Guard Movement ended.

In the meantime, according to *People's Daily* on October 5, 1968, Mao decided to streamline his bureaucratic machine, including all the state ministries and the Beijing Municipal Government, by sending thousands of cadres to special rural schools, called May Seventh Cadre schools, where they could do physical labor and study Mao's works. Beijing immediately sent six thousand cadres. Eventually more than 8,500 Beijing Municipal Government cadres were "transferred down" to the countryside, and their Beijing residence permits were cancelled, meaning that they might never be allowed to return. Thirty percent of medical workers—with their family members, more than ten thousand people in all—were moved out of the city to the northwestern provinces of Gansu and Ningxia. In 1969 a total of 308,000 residents left Beijing in a single year,[59] in most cases against their wishes. Beijing became much quieter than it had been for some time, with no Red Guards on the streets and most of the *dayuan* almost empty.

The children in *dayuan* were freer than ever because both their parents and elder siblings had been "sent down." Many young children were left by themselves or were cared for by their grandparents. They had no homework to do or simply refused to do any because schools were still chaotic and anarchism prevailed. As vividly represented in Jiang Wen's film *In the Heat of the Sun* (1995), the post-Red Guard generation in the *dayuan* became troublemakers at school and street-fighters in society.[60] They were generally detached from the mainstream and cynical toward life and politics. Those who grew up in the late 1960s often were ignored by both parents and society; they had to educate themselves. They were nurtured by foreign music and literature that they found on their own in libraries or their parents' locked bookshelves (concealed because of the Cultural Revolution). They looked at the Beijing cityscape in their own ways with their own value system and their own vision of space and time. With little or no authoritative guidance, they were able to go wild and stretch their imagination. People of this age group later became a dynamic force in reshaping Beijing in the 1980s and 1990s.

When Mao's chosen successor, Lin Biao, suddenly fled and died in a plane crash on his way to the Soviet Union in September 1971, all China was shocked. Lin Biao was accused of planning to assassinate Mao as part of a secret conspiracy to usurp state power. Reflecting on this bizarre turn of events, people soberly rethought the absurdity of Maoist politics and the destructive path of the Cultural Revolution. Mao, then in failing health, decided to unfreeze China's relationship with the United States and to open the door to negotiate with President

Richard M. Nixon; a meeting between them occurred in February 1972 in the Great Hall of the People. (It was at this meeting that Nixon told Mao that he had "moved a nation" and "changed the world." Mao replied, "I have not been able to change it. I have only been able to change a few places in the vicinity of Beijing."[61]) Although Mao's intention was to employ a more flexible foreign policy to resist the Soviet threat, Nixon's visit became a milestone that helped China reconnect with the West, though at first in a limited way.

After Lin Biao's death, Premier Zhou Enlai became a symbol of moderation and passive resistance to Mao's radical policies. In 1974 Jiang Qing, Mao's wife, and other leading radicals initiated a campaign to criticize Confucius and Lin Biao, which really targeted Zhou. This campaign, which some called a second Cultural Revolution, did not involve violence but it was a sign that the radicals were still in power.[62] Both Liu Shaoqi and Deng Xiaoping had fallen from power early in the Cultural Revolution. Liu died from illness and mistreatment in 1969, but Deng survived to return to leadership, not just once but twice. In 1975 Mao decided to reappoint him as first vice premier. The resolute Deng turned out to be not only a supporter of Zhou, but capable of acting boldly. He quickly shifted the focus from class struggle to economic modernization. Although Deng was once again attacked by the radicals, he re-emerged as party leader after Mao's death.

The year 1976 was a pivotal one for China. In January Premier Zhou Enlai died of cancer. Mao did not attend the funeral and ordered that public mourning be minimized. Jiang Qing remarked that even though Zhou was dead, she still wanted to fight him to the end.[63] The people, however—from cadres and intellectuals to ordinary commoners—had respected Zhou and appreciated his behind-the-scenes efforts to contain the damage done by the Cultural Revolution. They too had associated him with Confucius, not negatively but with the great tradition of Confucian morality. Now he was gone. In the first entirely voluntary demonstration since the founding of the People's Republic, more than a million people stood or even knelt on both sides of Chang'an Boulevard as the hearse took Zhou's remains to the crematorium. They created a ten kilometer (more than six mile) long funeral procession to say farewell.[64] A boulevard that had been widened for government-orchestrated parades now accommodated a spontaneous expression of popular feeling. The unmistakable implication was that a regime that had based its legitimacy on speaking in the name of the people might have to listen to them.

Beginning on March 19, Beijing residents continued their spontaneous mourning for Zhou by setting up a wreath at the base of the Monument to the People's Heroes in Tiananmen Square. Hundreds more soon appeared there but were removed by the police. Angry citizens kept sending bigger and heavier wreaths to the monument to express their sorrow; the authorities kept removing the wreaths after midnight and sending more plainclothesmen and militiamen to discourage people from leaving any more tributes. On March 30 more than twenty army officers sent wreaths to Tiananmen. Two soldiers, claiming to be following their conscience rather than orders, prevented the removal of wreaths that day.[65]

The tug-of-war continued and intensified until April 4, which coincided with the traditional Qingming festival of homage to deceased ancestors. On that day, over two million mourners spontaneously poured into Tiananmen Square with wreaths and flowers; they also brought banners and placards on which they had written poems, eulogies, and slogans. Besides mourning, people expressed their anger toward Mao's wife, Jiang Qing, and her radical associates. Later that evening, after most of the mourners had gone, more than two hundred official trucks and their crews came to remove the wreaths; police detained fifty-seven mourners who tried to protect them. On the next day, April 5, the mourners returned and a violent confrontation occurred. Angry mourners burned the car of the commanders in charge of the removal of the wreaths; later they also broke into the square's militia headquarters and burned straw stacked inside. In response, fifty thousand militiamen, three thousand policemen, and five battalions of garrison troops were ordered to enter the square with clubs in hand to suppress the people there. [66] Within about ten minutes, more than two hundred victims lay seriously injured. After initial questioning, they were escorted to Zhongshan Park and elsewhere, where they were searched and further interrogated; 388 people were handcuffed and sent to prison.

In the April 5 Tiananmen incident, individuals risked their lives to express their thoughts. For the first time since 1949, the people had made themselves heard in the "People's Square." Yet by doing so they put themselves in considerable jeopardy. One man bravely talking about Zhou's death was promptly arrested when he finished. (See Figure 31.) Although the immediate outcome of the April 5 incident was that Deng was stripped of all his official positions for a second time, the event clearly signaled that the people's tolerance of Maoist politics and the Cultural Revolution had reached its limit.

On July 28, 1976, a major earthquake, traditionally an omen of great change, occurred in Tangshan, about a hundred miles (161 kilometers) from Beijing; hundreds of thousands of people died. Seismic waves reached the capital immediately, causing hundreds of deaths and thousands of injuries. Most Beijing residents, except those living in one-storey houses, had to move into temporary tents or camps for about six months. On September 9 Mao died of multiple afflictions, including amyotrophic lateral sclerosis and heart disease.[67] Less than a month later, the so-called Gang of Four—including Mao's wife, Jiang Qing, Yao Wenyuan, and two other radical leaders—was arrested. Hearing of the arrest, many people silently held up five fingers, knowing that this was truly the end of the Mao era. Full understanding of the ten-year ordeal that had caused the Chinese people so much needless suffering would be the work of future decades; for the moment it was enough that the Cultural Revolution was over. Millions voluntarily attended a three-day celebration of the arrest of the Gang of Four at Tiananmen Square. Then they went home to enjoy dinner with family and friends and set off firecrackers. In this way, in October 1976, the residents of the capital awoke as from a nightmare.

Chapter 7

Economic Reform
and Cultural Fever:
1976 to 1989

THE DEATH OF MAO ZEDONG BROUGHT A SENSE OF RELIEF BUT ALSO created great uncertainty about the future. During the next two years, however, potentially destructive struggles over the leadership were averted. Under the new party head Deng Xiaoping, China moved forward along relatively pragmatic lines that had been suppressed during Mao's lifetime. At top-level meetings in December 1978, the party announced a program of Four Modernizations—in agriculture, industry, defense, and science and technology. Soon decollectivization of agriculture changed the face of rural China; meanwhile international trade and investment as well as new industrial and manufacturing enterprises transformed cities. China had begun to open its door even under Mao; Nixon's 1972 visit and the resulting joint communiqué by U.S. and Chinese leaders had signified a real shift. Under Deng, the door opened much wider. Business and academic exchanges involving Chinese citizens, overseas study by the best university students of the People's Republic, joint industrial ventures—all were new departures justified by the need for economic development.

Chinese leaders recognized that the Four Modernizations required a full-scale restoration of higher education, which had been dormant for more than a decade. Colleges had reopened in 1972, but prospective students needed to have politically clean family backgrounds and nominations from their work units. The university entrance examinations of 1977, the first since the beginning of the Cultural Revolution, once again made academic ability and achievement the main criteria for entrance. Rehabilitated faculty members were free to resume their teaching and research. Although there were still ideological constraints, the new openness encouraged lively debate. What some intellectuals regarded as the "spiritual isolation" of China during the Cultural Revolution came to an end. Indeed, fresh ideas from the outside world that came through the open door ignited a "cultural fever" (*wenhua re*) that stimulated critical thinking about values for the individual as well as the nation. The new market-oriented, commercialized urban life also fostered artistic expression ranging from avant-garde films to popular music. A more tolerant and relaxed social atmosphere encouraged cultural pluralism. As the country's preeminent academic and media center, Beijing was at the forefront of all these changes.

The new policies of the late 1970s and 1980s emanated from the capital and affected its citizens in greater measure than they did people elsewhere. Beijing's intellectual circles generated ideas at a heated pace. Yet it was also in Beijing that tensions between economic reform and a one-party political system first became apparent. The new economy was partly capitalistic, but it had to operate within the bureaucratic state system. The new culture could be liberal, but political authority could not be challenged directly. It was in Beijing that corruption and growing economic inequities aroused the most dissatisfaction and anger. It was in Beijing that a movement boldly advocating a "Fifth Modernization"—democracy—took root among university students, who tried in a series of demonstrations at Tiananmen Square to persuade party leaders to accept their views. And it was in Beijing in the early morning hours of June 4, 1989, that hundreds—perhaps thousands—of innocent citizens lost their lives when the party called in the army to repress the movement by force.

The Mao Zedong Memorial Hall
and Tiananmen Square

Placement of Mao's remains in an imposing new mausoleum in the center of Tiananmen Square symbolized the end of the Mao era. Hua Guofeng, Mao's designated successor, intended to enhance his own authority by honoring Mao in this way. But Tiananmen Square, though created by the state, could be used both by the state and by the people, as the incident of April 5, 1976, had shown even before Mao's death.

After much debate, the Memorial Hall for Mao was built at the site of the former Zhonghua Gate (demolished in 1958), between the Monument to the

People's Heroes and Qianmen. It thus became part of the long north-south axis that extended from the southern end of the old Outer City through the Forbidden City and beyond as far as the Bell Tower. This had been the processional route to the imperial throne, what some described as a sacred way, and the new mausoleum affected its symmetry and balance. The Ming and Qing emperors all had been buried in the hills northwest and northeast of the capital; for Mao to be enshrined in a crystal casket kept on public view was not in keeping with traditional burial or mourning practices. Those who made this decision had in mind a different precedent. In Red Square in Moscow, the remains of Lenin since his death in 1924 had been treated in a manner similar to that used for venerated monks of the medieval Russian Orthodox Church, whose bodies had been preserved for centuries in catacombs.

The Memorial Hall, completed in August 1977, also changed the spatial arrangement of the square itself. In connection with the project, the state further increased the size of the square so that its capacity grew to 600,000 persons. Many buildings on both east and west sides were demolished, and the square became fully rectangular in shape. The Monument to the People's Heroes, which since its erection in 1958 had been the center of the square and of the city, had been placed so as to symbolize opposition to the imperial past, represented by the Forbidden City.[1] But the mausoleum stood facing the portrait of Mao himself at Tiananmen, destroying any sense of symbolic confrontation of historical eras. In any case, the Memorial Hall soon fell into the background of both events and the square itself. Mao's legacy was entombed along with his body, even as Tiananmen Square continued to attract those who wished to express dissent.

Economic Reform in Beijing: The Second Revolution

Beijing residents had been quick to ridicule Hua Guofeng's promise to carry Mao's thought forward by means of the two "whatevers": he pledged to "obey *whatever* Mao had said and continue *whatever* Mao had decided." After returning to power for a third time in 1977, the far shrewder Deng Xiaoping backed away from Mao's legacy but without publicly repudiating Mao's ideology. Deng focused on practical solutions rather than rhetoric. In the late 1970s his indifference to "redness" as a criterion for state policy was welcome to a people weary of ideological battles. His most characteristic remark was a folk saying: "It doesn't matter if the cat is black or white as long as it catches mice." He invoked familiar

Maoist slogans, such as "practice is the sole criterion of truth," as support for the new policies. In this way he skillfully moved beyond Hua's "two whatevers." Recognizing that reform required both bold change and some measure of continuity, Deng asserted that China could develop "socialism with Chinese characteristics" and create a "socialist market economy."

Economic reform in the cities had three main aspects: encouraging international trade and investment, transforming the troubled state-run companies, and establishing small-scale private enterprise. The government implemented each of these policies first in Beijing and then expanded it to the whole nation.

A new approach to foreign trade made it possible for China to buy and sell goods in international markets without ideological limitations. The purpose of trade became solely the economic one of meeting the demands of the market. Imported goods came not only from socialist countries but also from capitalist ones, such as Japan and Germany, and they no longer were limited to heavy machinery and "high-tech" factory equipment. They included televisions, recording devices, refrigerators, and many other consumer products that would have been considered too "bourgeois" before 1976. During the Mao era Beijing stores rarely had been able to stock sufficient goods to sell, but by the end of the 1980s they had not only enough but also an unprecedented variety of offerings.

Investment from the West returned to China for the first time since 1949, and businesses set up joint ventures based on a mutual interest in profits. In Beijing the first luxury hotel, the Jianguo, which opened on east Chang'an Boulevard in 1982, was funded and run jointly by the People's Republic and Hong Kong. The Jianguo's lobby and bar were popular with Westerners, and the hotel played a major role in accommodating the first wave of post-1949 international tourists and business travelers. The main reason for its success was not the architectural layout, which featured duplex suites and up-to-date equipment, but rather new management methods aimed at the achievement of an "international standard" (a frequently invoked though often mocked phrase in this period). Such a goal had a positive impact on hotels in the capital because it effectively challenged the practices of stagnant socialist management.

In 1984 the first U.S.-China automobile joint venture by American Motors and Beijing Jeep started manufacturing passenger vehicles for both city and country, even though at the time there were almost no privately owned cars in Beijing. A significant symbolic gesture was the choice of locale for the contract-signing ceremony, which was held in the Great Hall of the People on May 5, 1983. This hall rarely had been the scene of nonpolitical events, let alone of one partly sponsored by an American company. In the long run many signing ceremonies occurred there; after three or four years of negotiations, executives of foreign companies usually were impressed by the invitation to come closer to the center of Chinese power. In addition to their wish for access to a huge market, American and European firms saw doing business in China as a bold and future-oriented move.[2] By 1988 Beijing had 261 joint ventures and total foreign investment reached US$1.64 billion.[3]

The internal reform of state-run enterprises took a major step forward by focusing on management systems and the role of retained profits. After conducting experiments in Beijing's larger state-owned factories in 1979, the authorities decided to implement a system of "contractual responsibility" in 475 such enterprises. The new system gave individual units more flexibility in managing production and deciding on uses of retained profit, such as improving equipment and distributing bonuses or incentives to employees. This reform reduced the responsibility of the state or the city while offering more freedom for enterprises to manage themselves. Within a short time, productivity increased. For example, the Capital Iron and Steel Plant at Shijingshan increased its annual profits by 20 percent between 1981 and 1985. Some employees, however, felt threatened by the disappearance of guaranteed employment (the "iron rice bowl"). The sheer momentum of the old-style management of a centralized planned economy, combined with the mentality of conservative leaders still in government, caused the reform to stall. Capital Iron and Steel had to stop its "contractual responsibility" experiment in 1995 when the contract expired.[4] But the system worked well for most small-scale companies. In general, highly centralized enterprise management began to loosen.

City construction projects became more efficient and competitive because state-run Beijing companies no longer monopolized all projects. After January 1988 all large projects were obliged to select and contract with construction companies by means of a bidding process.[5] Thereafter, both Beijing and provincial companies entered bids for projects that they wanted. This practice also helped to minimize construction budgets. Bribery sometimes influenced results of public bidding, however, and this became a major issue. Another complication was that provincial companies, if selected, caused Beijing's floating population of migrant workers to increase sharply.

After 1986 small or medium-size state-run enterprises in financial trouble were auctioned off to private individuals or to collective, partially state-funded enterprises. This transfer released the state from responsibility and gave the new owners a chance to revive the companies and make them profitable. Most such transactions were quite successful, confirming the need for management reform. Party hard-liners, though, harshly criticized this reform as a process of creating new capitalists.

A few of the new owners did become wealthy capitalists, the kind of people whom Mao had attacked repeatedly. Yet they were exactly the kind of people whom Deng wanted to cultivate. In China as elsewhere, communism had made the mistake of undermining individuals' motivation to work and strive. With the slogan "to get rich is glorious," Deng welcomed the growth of private enterprise, and he approved of pioneers who quit secure jobs in government or in state-owned enterprises, joined the private sector, and became rich in a relatively short time. They exemplified a trend called "jumping into the sea" because of its uncertainty and dangers. True enough, some pioneers with social and political connections had special access to highly controlled materials, such as iron and steel, and to resources, such as foreign investors and trading companies. The fast-growing wealth of the new capitalists was troubling to many, and participants in the student movement of the mid-1980s accused them of profiteering along with corrupt officials.

The city government particularly encouraged the growth of small-scale private enterprise, which it considered the best solution to unemployment. By the end of 1979 there were 400,000 young unemployed Beijing residents, most of whom were returned "sent-down" youth. (The term sent-down, literally "downward transfer" (*xiafang*) refers to people forced to move from city to countryside during the Maoist era.) The city government, in addition to encouraging street and neighborhood committees to expand collectively owned businesses in 1979, allowed people to start privately owned small businesses for the first time since 1949. The government licensed food stands, bicycle repair shops, and hairstyling salons. Small business owners also were allowed to hire a limited number of workers. This reform began, appropriately, in the Chongwen district in the eastern part of the former Outer City, which had been a commercial and craft-industry area from imperial times. But the idea immediately spread to the whole city, and within a year 123,000 of the formerly unemployed had jobs. In August 1979 twenty-five young people borrowed a thousand *yuan* and set up a tea stand in the Qianmen area. They started selling tea at two cents per serving to passersby. (See Figure 34.) Several years later they owned a trading company worth more than ten million *yuan*.[6] By the end of 1983 there were 36,000 business units based on self-employed individuals in Beijing alone.

Because different types of ownership and patterns of management coexisted, the relations between supply and demand began to change. The state monopoly of raw material had to loosen to allow for the very existence of the private sector. Starting in 1985, the system of state *monopolies* became one of state *contracts* for purchase and marketing of grain and cotton. In addition, prices for all farm produce, as well as for meat, eggs, poultry, and fish, were allowed to float. Exceptions were made for pork and Chinese cabbage—the most common meat and vegetable consumed by Beijing residents—because the city wanted to ensure that the new floating prices would not cause social and political unrest. Actually the result was just the opposite. Watermelons, the most popular summer fruit, always in the past had seemed to be in short supply and normally had been rationed for Beijing residents. In summer 1986, however, the state monopoly on watermelon purchase and sale was lifted. Beijing markets received more than twice as many watermelons to sell than they had before, simply because the number of sources of watermelons from state, collective, and private business had expanded greatly. Floating prices and wider sources of supply allowed business owners in all categories to focus on consumer demand and competition in a dynamic market.

Restaurants also became newly capitalistic ventures. Unlike the state-mandated transfer of several representing major regional cuisines to Beijing in the 1950s, diverse restaurants funded and managed by cross-provincial joint ventures were established in Beijing in the 1980s. As a result, 150 new provincial restaurants opened and greatly changed the gastronomical status quo in the capital. Because of intense competition, these enterprises had to demonstrate their strengths to survive; as a result, the quality of food, service, and management rose noticeably. Hostile or indifferent servers and menus with most items "unavailable"—commonplace in the Mao years—disappeared.

At all levels, both suppliers and consumers now had access to better and more varied foods. In one instance, a young boy from Anhui in central China, following along with his older brothers, walked almost 1,300 kilometers (over 800 miles) to Beijing carrying his corn-popping cylinder and portable coal stove. His ambition was to make more money than he could earn as a farmer back home. At the capital his hostel cost him the equivalent of about thirty U.S. cents per night. He said:

[In Beijing] I make over two *yuan* a day—over four on a good one. We carry our gear to outside an apartment block and shout "Fresh popcorn!" Once you start popping you draw a crowd. One explosion works a lot better than a dozen shouts. They bring their own corn—all I do is pop it at twenty cents a time. For that I'll pop them a whole sack of corn—much cheaper than the price at the state shops."[7]

Enterprising people set up movable food stands where they sold traditional cooked foods, such as deep-fried pancakes, on streets near residential areas and on college campuses. Thus mobile street vendors once again became an insepara-ble part of Beijing daily life, as they had been before 1949.

Economic Reform and Social Change

The reform program of the 1980s envisioned Beijing as a political and cultural center but no longer emphasized its role as an industrial city. This was a signifi-cant change from the ideas of Mao, who above all had wanted to see smokestacks when he looked out from Tiananmen. Instead, a "General Plan for Beijing City Construction" prepared by the Capital City Planning Commission in 1982 fo-cused on the importance of Beijing as a center of science and technology that would support the Four Modernizations. The new plan also discussed control of urban expansion and environmental hazards. It created a context for progress in construction, transportation, tourism, and historic preservation.

Housing construction aimed to improve daily life for Beijing citizens by eas-ing overcrowded conditions. Thousands of politically rehabilitated university fac-ulty and cadres, in addition to sent-down youth, were returning to the capital; the city accordingly sped up the construction of simple apartment compounds where they could live. Unlike the *dayuan,* which housed people from a single work unit (*danwei*), the new *xiaoqu* (small residential district) had living spaces that were assigned by different work units to those who were in need of housing. Another major distinction from the *dayuan* was that a *xiaoqu* was open rather than walled or guarded, offering its residents private space that allowed them to live in a much less collective style. Most residents of a *xiaoqu* did not know each other, but this actually was appealing to many who earlier had lived in commune-like arrangements whether they wanted to or not. In 1978 high-rise apartment build-ings of this kind appeared south of the Qianmen area and provided homes for more than seven thousand families. These residential high-rises, even taller than existing hotels and office structures, changed the formerly flat cityscape of Bei-jing. The buildings, constructed on a limited budget, were simple and crude; ele-vators stopped only at every fifth floor.

At the same time, several luxurious and spacious apartment complexes were built especially for recently rehabilitated high-ranking cadres and well-known intellectual figures or their widows. The Muxidi high-rise complex outside the Fuxing Gate on the west was the most famous of these structures. It was dubbed the widows' building because widows of several persecuted state leaders lived there, including the wife of former president Liu Shaoqi. As symbolic compensation for past cruelties, several writers—including Hu Feng, arrested by Mao's order in the early 1950s; Ding Ling, a woman writer who won the Stalin Prize for Literature; and Cao Yu, an equally famous playwright—also lived in this luxury building, where an apartment with five or six spacious rooms had running hot water and elevators that stopped at every floor. Several similar guarded complexes around Beijing were ironic reminders of Mao's political campaigns and the privileged hierarchy that had coexisted with the drive for equality in that era.

New apartment buildings were of great interest to the population but were not the most celebrated constructions during the 1980s. In 1988, to mark the fortieth anniversary of the People's Republic, two major Beijing newspapers identified the ten best local construction projects of the 1980s by means of a public vote. Those chosen were the New National Library, the International Exhibition Hall of China, the Central Color Television Center, the Terminal Building of the Capital Airport, Beijing International Hotel, Grand View Garden (with a design based on the novel *Dream of the Red Chamber*), the Changcheng [Great Wall] Hotel, the China Theater, the National Museum of the Chinese People's Anti-Japanese War, and the Dongsi Shitiao Subway Station. Unlike the structures chosen on the tenth anniversary in 1959, the buildings were selected mainly for their architectural merit, not their political significance.

New housing and major projects like the "ten best" led to further development of transportation. The construction of ring roads was a key part of the 1982 city plan. In addition to thirteen major north-south and east-west roads, the plan projected four ring roads[8] surrounding Beijing to improve traffic conditions and connect the city with suburban and rural districts. These planned ring roads were cyclic beltways designed for automobiles, not bicycles. By the end of 1981 the first already was complete; it was called the Second Ring Road because it followed the line of the wall of the former Inner City. The first ring was considered to be the line corresponding to the wall of the Imperial City that had been removed in the Republican period.

The growing number of motorized vehicles was the major theme of multiple changes in transport. Bus and trolley bus service already had increased to almost thirty times the amount available in 1949. Starting in 1984, minibuses with higher fares were added to regular public transportation; they offered convenience by stopping and taking passengers when hailed spontaneously along a fixed route. By 1987 there were two subway lines in full operation and a third under construction. Subway lines carried more than 800,000 passengers daily, or 8 percent of all the passengers on public transportation. In the mid-1980s taxicabs became yet another alternative, and there were more than twenty thousand taxi drivers and more than two hundred taxi companies in the city. The increase in automobiles, buses, and minibuses, combined with the ring roads, began to reduce the role of bicycles. Although bicycles still dominated traffic during rush hours and were especially well suited to navigating the narrow *hutong*, the direction of change clearly was not in their favor. Private passenger cars were still rare, but motorcycles became an affordable, more powerful replacement for bicycles. Across many centuries of Beijing history, choices for moving about the city never before had been so numerous, so fast, and so widely available.

As Chinese and foreigners traveled to the capital more often and more easily, the government saw the potential economic importance of preserving significant older structures. Of twenty-four Chinese cities that the state designated as historical and cultural centers, Beijing was the most important. Many sites there—especially temples, mosques, and churches—began to be restored; the Yonghegong, a Qing princely palace that became the Lama Temple, welcomed visitors in fall 1981. The Palace Museum, which barely had survived the Cultural Revolution, reopened. The pent-up interest of the outside world in China presented an opportunity to earn foreign exchange urgently needed for modernization. As early as 1987, Beijing's annual tourist revenue reached about US$550 million, twenty times that of 1978.[9]

Historic restoration and tourism benefited the small, privately owned businesses—barber shops, restaurants, small convenience stores, and many others—that the state already favored as a solution to unemployment. As a consequence of Mao's drive for collectivization both urban and rural, there were only 15,000 such business sites in the capital in 1978; there had been 57,000 in 1949. Residents and visitors often complained that it was hard to buy a quick lunch or get a haircut. By the end of 1988 about 100,000 sites had been added, more than three-quarters of them privately owned. Many urban people remembered how to run a small business, just as in rural areas many farmers remembered how to run a family farm.

Intellectual Liberation and Cultural Fever

For people with a university education—the group that had been called intellectual elements (*zhishi fenzi*) during the Mao years—the greatest change in the reform era was the rehabilitation of almost all of those who had been labeled "rightists" in 1957. This amounted to a great liberation of thousands of individuals from arbitrary constraints on their education and employment. For high school graduates, especially those who had been sent down to be reeducated in rural areas, the greatest change was the restoration of college entrance examinations in 1977. The state abandoned the political background check in the process of college admission that had denied, or sharply limited, higher education for those from "bad" families (descendants of landlords, capitalists, or Nationalist officials). Even surviving former landlords, capitalists, and Nationalist officials themselves were treated by the government as ordinary citizens for the first time since 1949.

Deng Xiaoping's goal was to free people from Maoist ideological shadows so that they could develop their individual talents along state-approved lines and contribute to the Four Modernizations. In the Beijing area alone, 128,500 young people from eighteen to thirty years old, including many who had been sent down earlier, took the college entrance examinations in December 1977. Sixteen thousand gained admission to college in Beijing to fulfill their lost dreams of higher education. Internationally recognized film director Zhang Yimou, who had a "bad" family background but under the new rules was admitted to the Beijing Film Academy in 1977, recalled during a recent interview: "For me, what was most important about my time at the academy was not what I learned, but the fact that I had changed my life and escaped from the predicament in which I had been trapped. At the time, acceptance by a university was a symbol that you had freed yourself from the terrible circumstances of the past. It meant that you had taken a brand-new path in life, a path that opened up a new world of opportunities."[10] The generation of students that came together in Beijing after entrance examinations were restored not only changed their own lives but in the long run made tremendous contributions to society.

From the late 1970s the Chinese government began to send professionals and scientists to study abroad at state expense, usually on programs of scholarly exchange, more rarely as candidates for advanced degrees. After policy changes in the 1980s, however, more and more young people went abroad for graduate degrees on the basis of private funding or scholarships generously provided by foreign institutions. Their most common destinations were the United States, Canada, Japan, Australia, and Europe. For political and economic reasons, most of these students decided to remain in their host countries rather than return to China. But the so-called brain drain that continued until the late 1990s was not entirely a one-way street. Those who settled overseas remitted funds to their parents, following an established Chinese practice, and for many families, having an adult child overseas was a badge of pride and a source of hope.

The majority of students, however, did not leave China and the strongest graduates in the first several reform-era college classes were assigned to work in Beijing. (Well into the 1990s, the state still followed its former practice of assigning college graduates to jobs.) Unlike Mao, who had distrusted "intellectual elements," both Hu Yaobang, then secretary general of the party, and Zhao Ziyang, premier of the State Council, called on think tanks to help formulate new policies. In the 1980s many scholars, writers, artists, and merchants from the provinces chose to go to Beijing and stayed there as long as they could, even though the residential-registration and food-rationing systems were still in place. With so many highly capable participants in discussions both public and private, 1980s Beijing became an arena in which the most important political and cultural questions arose.

Many educated people focused on the question of "what next?" for China. The Cultural Revolution had destroyed any possible optimistic interpretation of Maoist socialism and the dictatorship of the proletariat. Seeking other ideas to fill the vacuum left by discredited ideology, liberal-minded scholars inside the party looked back to Marx's works, many aspects of which had played little or no role in Maoism. Zhou Yang, a former propaganda chief who had been purged by Mao at the beginning of the Cultural Revolution, emphasized Marx's early humanism in an article published in 1983.[11] He rediscovered the Marx who had looked to a future socialist society to make possible the optimal development of the human personality. Under communism, people would not be limited to one job or function, but would go fishing in the morning and write poetry in the afternoon, contributing to society according to their abilities and receiving its goods according to their needs. Zhou also called attention to Marx's concept of alienation, a state of mind that occurs in capitalist society because exploited workers are estranged from the objects of their labor. Making a point that in 1983 was readily apparent to his audience, he added that alienation also occurs under socialism, as when conditions such as a personality cult and the abuse of power get out of hand. People of Zhou Yang's generation were sufficiently inculcated with Marxism to look to this nineteenth-century system for new insights. Younger people were attracted to more recent Western thinkers. Existentialism, especially the thought of Jean-Paul Sartre and Martin Heidegger, came to China in the reform era and struck a chord among intellectual elites in Beijing. Indeed, the meaning of life and the significance of being and time had become haunting questions for the survivors of Maoism.

Philosophers and critics such as Beijing-based Li Zehou and Liu Zaifu emphasized subjectivity over objectivity and hence the subjective self over the collective in writings during the 1980s. This way of thinking had significant Chinese antecedents, especially in Daoist philosophy, poetry, and landscape painting. Writers and artists in Beijing—including Liu Xinwu, Wang Meng, and Bei Dao—published works in various forms that expressed their feelings of alienation and their view of the absurdity of politics. Performance of modern plays, such as *Absolute Signal* (1982) by Gao Xingjian, attracted thousands of young people but irritated conservative party officials. Perhaps they might have contained their ire had they known that Gao later would be awarded the Nobel Prize for Literature (2000). Hard-liners launched an "anti-spiritual-pollution" campaign to attack Zhou's humane interpretation of Marx as well as to shut down most of the independent literary magazines of modernist poets and exhibits by avant-garde artists. But this short-lived campaign failed to ruin the liberal atmosphere for intellectuals in Beijing.

Among thousands of newly translated works, Gabriel Garcia Marquez's novel *One Hundred Years of Solitude* was widely read in Beijing literary circles as well as on college campuses. Magic realism—the effort to understand reality by considering dimensions of imagination such as magic, myth, and religion—fascinated Chinese writers. Alex Haley's *Roots* also may have led Chinese to think more about their own past. By the mid-1980s their attention had shifted to questions of history and culture. Why had China fallen behind the rest of the world in the nineteenth century? Were defects in Chinese civilization to blame, and if so, what could be done about them? From about 1984 a new generation of writers and film directors explored these fundamental questions, and a spontaneous literary movement produced perspectives both powerful and subversive. Its Beijing products, including Chen Kaige's film *Yellow Earth* (1984), Zhang Yimou's film *Red Sorghum* (1987), and Su Xiaokang's television series *River Elegy* (1988), were perhaps most representative. They challenged conventional Chinese ways of thinking about history, and they enlightened the public by reconsidering the image of China. Artists held up a mirror to reflect that image in a way that was critical rather than sentimental or nostalgic. In many ways these works echoed the May Fourth Movement of the 1920s, except that the 1980s search for national identity focused on China's past rather than on Western thought. Although the participants in these artistic efforts were all urban, they became extremely interested in rural life, farmers' speech, and folk culture because these topics were related to deep historical themes. Seeking roots (*xungen*) could take many forms given China's long and complex past.

For most people a movement even better known than the one seeking roots was the irresistible emergence of popular culture, which began in the early 1980s and reached its peak by the end of the decade. Tape recorders brought pop music and love songs from Hong Kong and Taiwan to every street corner day and night, from *hutong* to college campuses and even to Tiananmen Square. Like a strong gust of wind, they blew away both propagandistic revolutionary songs and Soviet light music. The songwriter Jia Ding first heard the difference in the work of the female Taiwanese singer Deng Lijun (Teresa Teng): "The first time I heard Deng Lijun's songs was in 1978. I just stood there listening for a whole afternoon. I never knew before that the world had such good music. I felt such pain. I cried. I was really very excited and touched, and suddenly realized that my work in the past had no emotional force."[12] People, especially the young, found in Deng's songs a power that came naturally through her "soft, sweet, often whispery and restrained" voice. Listeners appreciated the way Deng expressed her feelings through a personal, intimate, and feminine sound that had been missing from mainland music since 1949.

Social dancing, no longer considered a bourgeois activity, became popular again in the 1980s. Dancing now was not just a way of socializing but also a means of self-expression. The fast rhythm of disco had great appeal. Like Deng Lijun's songs, disco dancing is personal and expressive; it fits the desire of young people to vent their emotions. Young disco lovers usually preferred to go to public spaces, such as Yuanmingyuan, or more remote areas. Many commercial dance halls soon opened to the public. Famous hotels, formerly available only to foreign guests and domestic officials, opened space for the dinner and dancing parties of ordinary people. During weekends the Friendship Hotel, located near several college campuses, the Hotel of Nationalities on Chang'an Boulevard, and the Heping (Peace) Hotel in Wangfujing attracted so many young people for dancing that local police grew nervous and newspaper reporters became inquisitive.

Both state and privately owned salons and cafés, rather than teahouses, appeared in Beijing to satisfy people's increasing demand for more enjoyable places to "hang out." College students, intellectuals, and professionals liked having such spaces to discuss contemporary issues and their personal academic projects while eating and drinking. This Westernized form of gathering, reminiscent of intellectual circles in prewar Shanghai, was novel and stimulating for Beijing residents.

Reopened churches and temples provided another important public space for people who dared to show their curiosity about religion. Deng's program of Four Modernizations had the moral purpose of lifting the entire Chinese people out of poverty, but "to get rich is glorious" was simply inadequate as a philosophy of life. The discrediting of Marxism had left a spiritual vacuum. For many Beijing residents, religion was a way of dealing with their anxieties and painful memories. Some looked to the ancient Chinese philosophical schools of Confucianism and Daoism. Buddhism and Islam, as well as Christianity and Biblical studies, also attracted attention. On Christmas Eve in 1979 a Methodist church near Dongdan was so full of believers and visitors that some local people had to wait outside the church, and some even climbed over a fence to get closer. At that time churchgoers were either older believers who had been forbidden to pray during the Cultural Revolution or younger ones who were eager to learn Western religions and convert to Christianity. Few middle-age people appeared at churches, perhaps because of fears of changing official policies.

A hybrid of "root-seeking" and Western rock music, the *xibeifeng* (northwest wind) fad swept into Beijing's cultural scene in 1986. This was a style of folk song associated with northern Shaanxi, a region that was one of the ancient cradles of Chinese civilization. The rock singer Cui Jian initiated the fad when he stepped onto the stage of the Capital Workers' Stadium in April 1986 with his guitar and sang his soon-to-be famous song "Having Nothing."[13] As described in a recent study,

[The song] combined the folksy characteristics of the northwest with a strong, fast modern disco/rock beat. . . . In contrast to the stepwise melodies and the soft, sweet, restrained, and highly polished singing style of most *liuxing/tongsu* [popular] songs of the time, *xibeifeng* songs are loud and forceful, almost like yelling, in what many Chinese writings describe as a bold, unconstrained, rough, and primitive voice. The new style was a kind of musical reaction against the style of songs from Taiwan and Hong Kong. . . . The new style combined the most primordial elements of the backward, desolate rural areas of northwest China with the most modern rhythm. It was a combination of something quintessentially Chinese with something very modern. In this, it represented the revival of Mainland creativity in the new modern, cosmopolitan era.[14]

This was exactly the motivation of the "root-seeking" movement. Writers, film directors, and singers were inspired by the idea of reviving the dynamic power of the five-thousand-year-old Chinese civilization. This power would come from rediscovering and promoting the unrestrained, primitive, and wild spirits of northwest China's barren yellow plateau. The force and fire of "Having Nothing," with both its musical beat and expressive lyrics, were so striking that it circulated widely in Beijing as well as the whole nation:

> I have endlessly asked when you will go with me
> But you always laugh at me having nothing
> I want to give you my aspirations and also my freedom
> But you always laugh at me having nothing . . .
> The soil under my feet is moving, the water beside me is flowing
> But you always laugh at me having nothing
> Why do you always laugh, why do I always have to chase
> Do you really mean to say that before you I will always have nothing
> Oh oh oh oh oh oh, when will you go with me . . .[15]

The song was supposedly based on Cui Jian's personal experience. It sounded like a love song that described how an emotionally troubled young man expressed his disappointment about losing his girlfriend. Cui Jian himself said, "To me, 'Having Nothing' is nothing extraordinary, just a love song; but it turned out to be a milestone."[16] This strong sense of loss and nothingness, of frustration and sadness, found a lasting sympathetic response among young audiences, even though it aroused official disapproval almost immediately after the concert.

When Cui Jian performed at Beijing University later in the year, he also created a sensation. Liu Jianmei, then a freshman, recalled: "The appearance of Cui Jian was so much fun, so fresh, and so original. We all enjoyed Deng Lijun's songs, but Cui is different. Cui's musical language is not only Chinese and creative, but more important, unique and rebellious. His song, 'Having Nothing,' reflected exactly what I felt. That is to say, Cui's music is personal and individualistic, and represents our generational feelings of anger, confusion, and anxiety. That was why Cui Jian was so much welcomed in the 1980s." A male student offered similar remarks, "We really liked the song, and we could really identify with it."[17] The sense of nothingness spoke to the disillusionment and frustration of the confused young generation born in the mid- or late 1960s. They had witnessed only a little of the chaos of the Cultural

Revolution in their early childhood, and they had grown up in the transitional post-Mao era. This generation felt that they "had nothing" during the era of cultural fever—no history, no beliefs, and no identity. Cui's "nothingness" told of a negation; it distrusted and refused history, reality, and everything except the lost self. Cui said, "I was indeed searching for self from the very beginning."[18] As cultural critic Nimrod Baranovitch pointed out, "'Having Nothing' introduced into post-revolutionary China a whole new ethos that combined individualism, nonconformism, personal freedom, authenticity, direct and bold expression, and protest and rebellion, in short, the essence of Western rock culture."[19]

Cui Jian introduced powerful rock music and a cool "hippie" style; Wang Shuo, about ten years younger, started a new trend called hooligan literature and openly described himself as a vulgar person writing to make money. Wang grew up in a Beijing *dayuan* and belonged to the post-Red Guard generation. His extensive use of Beijing slang and humorous expressions, his cynical tone and lack of restraint won immediate attention from readers as well as critics, and his novels and "sit-com" television series became popular in the late 1980s. Wang's "hooligan" literature represented the Beijing of the era through vivid description of the boring and empty character of aimless young people's lives. Sometimes Wang transformed serious social issues into a light-hearted farce or laughter. He deliberately explored social margins and "hooligan"-type people, exposing ethical and political aspects of city life that urbanites often see but to which they seldom pay attention. Wang's rebellious nature appeared in his sarcasm and irony. He was perhaps the first truly commercial writer of the 1980s, and his work especially offered perspectives for readers on social problems in contemporary Beijing.[20]

Overall, the thirst for Western culture in translation, the literature of "root-seeking," Cui Jian's rock-and-roll and pop music, and Wang Shuo's "hooligan" literature together sustained a new cultural fever that affected students and other Beijing residents, old and young, in a profound way. As a college student of the 1980s said, "People my age were greatly influenced by the cultural fever, the way of thinking, and even related behaviors. The most significant change for me was the shift of focus from the political to the cultural, from the collective to the individual. We began to ask questions about the meaning of life. We were so eager to express ourselves." Another student added, "The cultural fever helped people to make choices based on personal experience. This individualism and the spirit of openness gave me self-confidence, and I realized that I was capable of doing things for myself."[21] The nature of the cultural fever was not unitary or monotonous, but plural and diversified. Both elite and popular audiences had the chance to enjoy the coexistence of multiple cultures and the freedom to make choices. As the rich, spontaneously launched movements mixed with translated Western ideas, impatient younger people demanded faster reforms in all fields, while the officially sponsored cultural discourse of the mainstream gradually lost its monopoly position. Sooner than anyone in the 1980s thought possible, these two broad forces would collide.

The Democracy Movement and the Tiananmen Crisis

Reform brought many positive changes to Beijing, but there were still many old unsolved problems as well as new ones. Unlike academic figures and celebrities, ordinary people wrongfully treated in the Mao era were not necessarily rehabilitated in a timely manner. Thousands of petitioners from all over China managed to come to the capital, and beginning in 1977 Beijing residents often saw provincial petitioners outside Xinhua Gate, the main entrance to Zhongnanhai party headquarters. They were waiting for a response after submitting their petitions for redress. "Petitioner," taken by photographer Li Xiaobin between Tiananmen and the Wu Gate in front of the Forbidden City in 1978, caught the helpless, anxious expression of the man, who wore three large Mao badges to confer maximum legitimacy upon his request. (See Figure 32.) Although permitting people to petition at the capital level was in itself a step forward, it meant that the government had to deal patiently with seemingly endless embarrassing scenes that easily could become something much worse.

Tiananmen Square, a short walk from Zhongnanhai, became a focal point for bearers of petitions. When the Party Central Committee in November 1978 decided to reverse Mao's verdict on the April 5, 1976, Tiananmen incident, what had been called an anti-revolutionary movement suddenly became a revolutionary one. The 388 people who had been arrested as "counterrevolutionaries" were declared innocent and released immediately. This reversal gave new sanction to popular political expression in Tiananmen Square and by extension in other public spaces. The Monument to the People's Heroes thus acquired a different meaning: it became an open space where people could voice dissent. The nearby mausoleum was a reminder of another legacy from the past now open to new interpretation: the Maoist message that "to rebel is justified."

In 1978–1979, new kinds of events began to occur in Tiananmen Square. On December 17, 1978, a group of twenty-eight young petitioners went to the square to protest economic conditions in rural southwest China; they claimed that they spoke for fifty thousand people who had been sent down to do farm work in Yunnan. In January 1979 several thousand sent-down youths returned to Beijing and demonstrated in Tiananmen Square with banners that read "We don't want hunger" and "We want human rights and democracy."[22] Later that month about thirty thousand sent-down youths, some with their very young children, came to Beijing to petition for help. Faced with successive mass demonstrations, the state sped up its decisions on young people of urban origin still remaining in remote areas; in the early 1980s, it finally allowed most of them to return home.

The same months in late 1978 and early 1979 that saw demonstrations in Tiananmen Square marked the birth of "Democracy Wall." Beginning on October 30, 1978, with four young workers from Guizhou Province in the southwest, people began putting up big-character posters on a wall in Xidan, a business district on the western side of Zhongnanhai. As a photo by Li Xiaobin shows, the wall looked like a familiar scene from the Cultural Revolution, but the content of these posters concerned unsolvable personal cases and unjust persecutions still in progress. (See Figure 33.) Many young people—especially avant-garde artists and poets, military veterans, and returned sent-down youth—called for more freedom in art and more democracy in politics. They began to circulate self-edited and self-funded unofficial liberal magazines, such as *Chinese Human Rights, Today, Exploration,* and *Beijing Spring.* The big-character posters whetted the appetite of the participants for spontaneous group discussions in Tiananmen Square, which became a kind of open forum on the national future.

When political discussions on Democracy Wall and on the square began to challenge the existing system, and especially when in 1978 Wei Jingsheng, a former soldier, openly called for the "Fifth Modernization: democracy," the authorities' tolerance finally snapped. The city government arrested some of the activists and ordered Democracy Wall moved from the central Xidan area to a relatively quiet and more out-of-the-way place, Yuetan (Temple of the Moon) Park. In March 1979 Deng emphasized that in order to realize the Four Modernizations, the whole nation must adhere to four cardinal principles: the socialist path, the proletarian dictatorship, the leadership of the Communist Party, and Marxism and Mao's thought. Chen Yun, a conservative senior party leader, added the metaphor of a bird cage: the market economy was like a bird that always should be kept in a socialist cage to prevent it from flying away. In other words, although Deng was leading reforms that moved away from Maoism, reforms that were abandoning centralized planning and replacing it with a market-oriented economy and a decollectivized society, he had no intention of changing the political system.

Even though they were sympathetic and supportive of Democracy Wall, most college students and faculty did not participate in the pro-democracy movement of the late 1970s, mainly because a normal academic system and social order had only just been restored, and intellectuals in general were optimistic and confident about Deng's leadership. A decade later the situation had changed. Inflation caused by the transition to the market had become hard to control. Because of the privatization of ownership and trade, a small group of people had become wealthy, and the gap between rich and poor had widened. Hard-liners and reform factions within the party continually clashed; Deng tried to balance the two sides, with the result that his policies vacillated and were often ambiguous. He confessed that there was no model at all to follow. According to rumor, he once said, "We had to cross the river by feeling for the submerged crossing stones. Take one step at a time. And each step counts as one." As leaders in much of the Communist world were learning in the 1980s, there was no map of the path from the planned economy to the market.

The very success of reform caused people to be impatient with problems and eager for further reform. The still-existing bureaucratic system and its privileges not only became obstacles but also nurtured a powerful new class, the "clique of crown princes and princesses." These offspring of high-ranking party veterans were in key positions in government or were taking advantage of the economic reform to set up profitable private enterprises. At the same time, some cadres engaged in official profiteering (*guandao*), speculative buying and selling in order to benefit from the dual price system that had developed as state-owned and privately owned business competed for resources.[23] Although a new election method had been introduced at local and county levels to begin a gradual development toward a democratic system, voters often complained about unfair manipulation of prepared slates of candidates.

In the face of all these social and economic problems, college students once again called for political reform. In so doing they invoked not only the Fifth Modernization, democracy, but also the May Fourth Movement's slogan of "science and democracy," stressing the interdependence of the two. The new movement started in the south, including Shanghai, and soon aroused a reaction on Beijing campuses. The students' demands included an end to corruption, more freedom of speech, a fairer electoral process, and sufficient funding for college fa-cilities. First, wall posters reappeared on campuses; then street demonstrations and rallies followed at Tiananmen Square on December 23, 1986. These gather-ings ignored an order from the Beijing municipality on November 1, 1981, stat-ing that work units and individuals were not allowed to hold parades, rallies, and lectures or to post pamphlets of any kind in the square.

The small-scale demonstration of December 23 did not last long, and no serious confrontation took place. But only three days later the Beijing city gov-ernment announced even stricter rules for public demonstrations. And seven days later Deng told senior leaders and cadres that the students' demonstration was a serious matter and any "bourgeois liberalization" must be firmly opposed. Several liberal-minded and outspoken intellectuals and cadres, including the Beijing-based journalist Liu Binyan, were expelled from the party. Even Hu Yaobang, Deng's hand-picked successor and a key reformer, was forced to re-sign from his position as secretary-general of the party. Deng's view was that China should look to the West for technology, methods of enterprise manage-ment, and investment but reject "bourgeois" political ideas, such as democracy. In early 1989 Deng told foreign guests that "China at its current stage needs to concentrate its attention on economic development. If we seek for democracy in [political] form, the result will be that we would gain neither democracy nor economic development. The only consequence would be chaos."[24] To Deng and his listeners at this time, the word "chaos" (*luan*) meant first of all the Cultural Revolution.

The eventful year of 1989 became another important turning point in Bei-jing history. Young students who had been nurtured by the atmosphere of cultural fever on campus had a passion for idealism and justice. Liberal intellectuals and teachers had inspired them with ideas of democracy. The journalist Liu Binyan's principle of loyalty to people, as well as his sharp criticism of official profiteering and abuse of power, set a model for young students to follow. In this context, a sudden and unexpected event triggered another wave of the student movement: on April 15, 1989, former party secretary-general Hu Yaobang suffered a fatal heart attack. Regarded as a liberal and efficient leader who had removed many political shackles and ideological taboos, he had played a role in the abolition of the family-background check for university entrance and in the rehabilitation of almost all the victims of Mao's campaigns. Students also respected Hu as a hero in the struggle against party and state corruption. It was widely believed that, un-like most top leaders, neither Hu nor his relatives had any link to corruption. For all these reasons, Hu's forced and premature resignation, followed by his sudden death, aroused sympathy and anger on Beijing campuses. As in the case of Premier Zhou Enlai's death in 1976, dissenters used official mourning as an opportunity to make themselves heard.

Three days after Hu's death, more than two thousand students from Beijing University went to Tiananmen Square, gathered to listen to speakers in front of the Monument to the People's Heroes, and submitted to the government a petition with seven demands. They included a reevaluation of Hu Yaobang; a cancellation of the "anti–spiritual pollution" and "anti-bourgeois liberalization" campaigns and rehabilitation of those criticized; a battle against corrupt officials; freedom of the press and public expression; increased funding for education; abolition of the ten articles on public demonstrations issued by the Beijing city government; and an open apology for past wrong policies and decisions of the government. On the same night, more than eight thousand students—mainly from Beijing University, People's University, and Beijing Normal University—came to protest at Xinhua gate, the front gate of Zhongnanhai.

On the early morning of April 22, when the state funeral for Hu was held in the Great Hall of the People, about thirty thousand college students came to Tiananmen and insisted on submitting a petition to Premier Li Peng himself. (Li, an engineer educated in the Soviet Union, had become acting premier in late 1987.) Several student representatives walked up the steps of the Great Hall of the People and knelt near the top, attempting to submit a rolled-up petition reminiscent of those used by petitioners in imperial times. Thousands of students behind the representatives chanted "Dialogue, dialogue, we demand dialogue." Their request was rejected. At one o'clock that afternoon, students voluntarily left Tiananmen but decided to call for class boycotts and a student strike as a united action all over China.

The situation heated up quickly and became increasingly confrontational. On April 23 student representatives from twenty-nine colleges founded the Beijing College Student Autonomous Association. This new group immediately announced that the original seven demands must be accepted and that the student movement was a patriotic and pro-democracy one. As a matter of fact, founding any organization without government approval was a serious political offense and doing so was absolutely forbidden under the People's Republic. On April 26 the *People's Daily,* the party's official newspaper, declared that the student movement and its activities were causing "turmoil" (*dongluan*) that had the goal of fundamentally negating the party's leadership and the socialist system.

Rhetoric used in the editorial, such as "turmoil" and "anti-revolutionary conspiracy," made students even angrier than they otherwise would have been. As Liu Jianmei, who had attended Cui Jian's concert as a freshman and in 1989 was a senior at Beijing University, recalled:

> All we wanted to do was to help, not at all to overthrow, the government, to speed up the reform and fight against graft and corruption. We were all shocked by the editorial from *People's Daily* and felt we were totally misunderstood and wrongly accused. We had to express and defend ourselves. A dialogue was badly needed. But we didn't have anywhere to air our views and feelings, not to mention [any idea] how to arrange a dialogue. I felt taking to the streets was the only way we could find to let people know and let the Party Central know what we felt.

Indeed, students were upset because they felt that their patriotic intentions had been ignored, and their sense of betrayal was overwhelming. The party's use of the term "turmoil" pushed the student movement to a second stage, from peaceful petition to angry protest.

On May 2 a new student petition with twelve demands asked for a dialogue between government leaders and student representatives; this petition too was rejected. On May 4 more than twenty thousand students from fifty-six colleges in Beijing and beyond held another large demonstration at Tiananmen.[25] They chose the date to mark the seventieth anniversary of May 4, 1919—a highly significant date because the Chinese Communist Party traces its origins to the May Fourth Movement. The year 1989 also marked the fortieth anniversary of the People's Republic of China and the bicentennial of the French Revolution. Zhao Ziyang, secretary-general of the party who had just returned from a state visit to North Korea, expressed views different from those of Premier Li Peng and the *People's Daily* editorial when he told foreign bankers: "There should be no big turmoil. They [the students] are not against our social system. We must be calm, rational, tolerant, and disciplined. The issues should be solved in a democratic and legal way."[26]

In addition to college faculty, more than half a million Beijing residents openly supported the students. They lined the streets and offered food, water, and encouragement; some of them even marched alongside the students. Among them were reporters and editors of journals, television and radio stations, and major newspapers who on May 19 submitted their own petition demanding a dialogue with party leaders in charge of mass media. Print and other journalists ignored government restraints and covered student demonstrations as accurately and comprehensively as possible, which won yet more sympathy for the students.

The Beijing Workers' Autonomous Federation, formed on April 20, joined in the fight against official profiteering and corruption. Even though workers subsequently became a highly visible part of the movement, their agenda differed from that of the students. While the latter in general believed that the reforms had not gone far enough, protesting workers—for the most part employees of state-owned enterprises (electronics, steel, automobiles)— thought that they already had gone too far. They perceived the urban economic reforms as directly responsible for their own declining standard of living and for new levels of governmental corruption.[27] Nevertheless, with the participation of workers and people from all walks of life, the movement belonged to the whole city.

In yet another tactic to have their petition accepted and their voices heard, student volunteers began a sit-in and hunger strike in Tiananmen Square on May 13. It lasted seven days, with more than three thousand students participating. In a land that had known hunger and famine, in a city that still rationed food after a decade of reform, among volunteers who appeared to have little weight that they could afford to lose, a hunger strike had distinctive emotional reverberations. And the strike was successful because it attracted more attention from the city, the nation, and the world. Many college faculty and staff, local residents, and government cadres as well as medical workers came to Tiananmen and offered assistance; they brought medicines and other supplies. Three years earlier the student Liu Jianmei had felt that the song "Having Nothing" expressed her own feelings. In May 1989, however, when she passed through Chang'an Boulevard while marching with other students toward Tiananmen, she was moved by the masses of supportive spectators: "I felt a special thrill in my heart and felt we had the support of the whole city." The sense of local and national solidarity may have been particularly intoxicating to young people who deeply feared "having nothing." Thousands of students were sitting at the square, occasionally singing and dancing, clad in youthful clothing. Hong Kong donors sent dozens of colorful tents for those who stayed overnight. Many flags, representing different schools and work units in the square, were fluttering in the warm, gentle wind. Emergency medical vans and trucks with food and water sat nearby. (See Color Plate 12.) The weather was unusually fine in May that year, and in the sunshine the fully packed square looked festive and dynamic.

On May 16 a long-scheduled state visit to the capital by Soviet president Mikhail S. Gorbachev attracted many international media crews, which immediately made Beijing the focus of world interest and the students at Tiananmen the focus of Beijing. The drama of the hunger-strike held everyone's attention. Meanwhile the Chinese government suffered the humiliation of not being able to entertain its state guest according to plan because the main square of its capital city had become a forum for unending dissent. Zhao Ziyang himself went to Tiananmen and urged students to terminate the hunger strike and find a mutually acceptable solution. A majority favored accepting his offer, but a minority opposed it and prevailed.[28] Zhao's emissaries, Bao Tong and Yan Mingfu, as well as the writer Dai Qing, tried to mediate a settlement, but all were rebuffed. Almost at the same time, Premier Li Peng visited hospitalized hunger-strikers; later he held a meeting with student leaders at the Great Hall of the People, but in both visits communication between the two sides thoroughly failed. Meanwhile, in response to these Beijing events, similar demonstrations broke out throughout China.

On May 20 Premier Li Peng on behalf of the Party Central Committee and the State Council declared martial law in Beijing; the city government carried out this order in seven districts around Tiananmen. After an unsuccessful attempt to dissuade his colleagues from making this decision, secretary-general Zhao Ziyang was dismissed from all of his official posts. The declaration of martial law and the fall of Zhao precipitated the third and final stage of the student movement.

The demonstrators and their supporters did not appear to be intimidated. The hunger strike ended on May 20, and students returned to more moderate forms of protest. In the following days, between May 20 and June 3, more and more demonstrators and local residents—including cadres, workers, professionals, and even high school students—went to Tiananmen Square to show their support. Many volunteers among city residents set up barricades along Chang'an Boulevard to stop military trucks from entering the city; they also gave soldiers food and flowers. It was the first time since 1949 that armed People's Liberation Army soldiers had been called into Beijing. People surrounded the soldiers and treated them as sons and brothers; the young recruits, some from distant areas, hardly knew how to respond.

On May 30 a group of students from Beijing's Central Arts Academy placed a thirty-five-foot-high white plaster and Styrofoam statue of the "goddess of democracy" directly in front of the gate at Tiananmen. Although no one explained its intended meaning, this huge symbol seemed to reinforce the determination of those in the square. The sudden appearance of the statue sent a silent message to the authorities and raised the level of the confrontation between the two sides.

Two weeks after martial law had been imposed, leaders ordered a crackdown. Armed troops with tanks forced their way to Tiananmen Square on the night of June 3. The delay apparently had been caused by Deng's consultation with other authorities both in Beijing and elsewhere in China. Despite daily government warnings to clear the square that had begun on May 20, thousands came out on the streets on June 3 to see what would happen. Some tried to block the army's movement with barricades but tanks smashed all these hastily built structures. Many in the crowds had to run away to avoid being shot. The carnival-like mass rallies suddenly turned into a terrifying and bloody massacre. Along Chang'an Boulevard city residents, including passersby and spectators, could not believe that soldiers of the people's army were shooting real rather than rubber bullets at the people. This outcome may not have been an act of deliberate policy; it may have resulted from a kind of "spontaneous combustion" that occurred when the army met unexpected violent resistance, when citizens took some weapons from soldiers, and when pipe bombs and Molotov cocktails were thrown at the troops. The combination of tanks and heavily armed soldiers entering a city in which emotions ran high in favor of the demonstrators proved to be lethal.[29]

On the evening and early morning of June 3–4, 200,000 men from twelve group armies and three military regions were ordered to retake the square. The exact number of casualties in the wake of the suppression is still controversial, and may never be known. Outside reports of civilian deaths have ranged from two to seven thousand. Later, Chinese government sources put the number of deaths at three hundred. Those who died are known to have included ordinary Beijing residents crushed by tanks that were rolling toward the square; thirty-six students in the square; and several dozen soldiers and police.[30]

Tiananmen Square was taken over by armed soldiers and cleared after the last groups of student demonstrators withdrew in the early morning of June 4. Mass arrests for what the party called a "counterrevolutionary rebellion" followed. That verdict still stands.[31] As Deng put it just afterward, the crux of the matter was a conflict between the set of four principles—the socialist state, the proletarian dictatorship, the leadership of the party, and Marxism and Mao's thought— and bourgeois liberalization. In 1991 the Chinese government confirmed more than 2,500 arrests in connection with the May-June disturbances.[32] Several dozen activists managed to leave the country and went into exile with the help of foreign sympathizers. Two elements in the student movement that had been especially threatening to the authorities were the workers' autonomous organizations and the great number of supporters and sympathizers among party members and state cadres. China's leaders had learned lessons from Eastern Europe and understood the mortal threat to a regime based on dictatorship of the proletariat when the proletarians themselves—the industrial workers—publicly oppose it, as had happened in 1980 in Poland. In Beijing, the workers' autonomous organizations were immediately broken up and their leaders arrested, but relatively few cadres known to have sympathized with the movement and only about 4,000 of almost 650,000 party members known to have supported the students were punished.[33]

On June 6 Beijing mayor Chen Xitong congratulated the martial law troops on their "initial victory" in "the struggle to quell counterrevolutionary rebellion." Three days later Deng himself, in his capacity as chairman of the Central Military Commission, spoke publicly on the Tiananmen crisis: he praised the troops highly and called the dead soldiers martyrs. "Actually," Deng explained, "what we faced was not just some ordinary people who were misguided, but a rebellious clique and a large number of the dregs of society." These opponents, he said, intended to overthrow the Communist Party and topple the socialist system.[34] At the same time, Deng reaffirmed the importance of economic development. "Without reforms and openness, how could we have what we have today? There has been a fairly satisfactory rise in the standard of living, and it may be said that we have moved one stage [forward]." He also said that "what is important is that we should never change China back into a closed country."[35]

The 1980s reform had moved the planned economy a long way toward a "market plus plan" system. Greater economic opportunity had led to more open cultural expression. In this atmosphere it was all but inevitable that the wish for political freedom and pluralism would become stronger. Tiananmen grew out of a paradox: forsaking orthodox Marxism, the party was staking its legitimacy on economic growth, but to achieve that growth, it had to free people in many ways, to liberate individual talents and motivations to work hard in the economic and academic realms. Yet it drew the line at those same wishes for freedom in the political realm. Years later a former participant reflected, "I have always considered that the '80s of the twentieth century were a romantic era, transient, vulnerable but very individualistic and exciting."[36]

The Tiananmen crisis was a shocking and indelible series of events with many historic dimensions and grave consequences for the immediate future.

More than ever Beijing was on the national and international stage, and Tiananmen was the literal and symbolic location of that stage. The Monument to the People's Heroes was its center. Unlike previous major events in China that had remained hidden behind "the bamboo curtain," the events of mid-April through June 1989 received worldwide television and news coverage. Each day's events were broadcast to millions all over the world and to millions within China. Under the clear blue skies of May, in the openness of Tiananmen Square, amid the high spirits of so many people, anything seemed possible. Commentators on U.S. television described it as one of the most important developments anywhere since World War II. Dozens of other cities held demonstrations and parades to express solidarity with the students. In Beijing the whole city rallied behind them. At first even the soldiers seemed to be sympathetic to the movement, which was much more inclusive and extensive than May Fourth and other earlier demonstrations had been. The people of Beijing were heroic. In the end, more Beijing citizens died on the night of June 3–4 than students.

Economic reform and the opening of China had led to demands for political reform. But Deng Xiaoping had firmly put economic reform before political reform. Gorbachev and political reforms in the disintegrating Soviet Union were the negative example. In using military force, Deng had gambled that the sheer success of economic reform in the long run would trump the intensely negative immediate reaction at home and abroad. Deng won this gamble when within a few years most Beijing people, caught up in material improvement in their own lives, forgot about political reform. Repelled by the violence of 1989, they repeated the government line: Russia had made a mistake by putting political reform before economic reform, but China had succeeded by putting economic reform first. The events at Tiananmen that had seemed so shocking—the end of all hope—turned out to be a minor distraction on the road to globalism in the Beijing urban setting.

Chapter 8

Beijing Boom, Urban Crisis, and the Olympic City: 1990s and Beyond

BEIJING WAS UNUSUALLY QUIET IN THE MONTHS AFTER THE TIANANmen crisis. While victims' families were dealing with their losses, the authorities removed all traces of the demonstrations, sit-ins, and crackdown from Tiananmen Square and the Monument to the People's Heroes; only the ruts made by tank tracks on Chang'an Boulevard remained as visual reminders of what had occurred. As the 1990s unfolded, however, the capital underwent an extraordinary economic boom. Shining skyscrapers sprouted along the boulevard; business complexes and hotels with revolving rooftop restaurants attested to Beijing's new role as a center of international trade and finance. Modern plazas and malls carried foreign brands, most of them manufactured in China. Globalization also fostered a glamorous lifestyle for the rich, and by the turn of the century a new middle class was enjoying better housing, a family automobile, and excellent restaurants. A high-tech culture began to redefine Beijing, and even laborers and street vendors were seen using cell phones.

Globalization, consumerism, and rampant growth also had a negative side. The city itself seemed to be for sale as large chunks of urban real estate were claimed by developers. Within the "Old City," the area of the traditional Inner and Outer cities, neighborhood after neighborhood fell to the bulldozer. Highrise residences and shops replaced the familiar *hutong* and courtyard houses. Multiple ring roads that were meant to ease transportation gradually encircled the city, but instead they brought more cars, traffic jams, and pollution. Beijing's selection to host the 2008 Olympics stimulated even more construction, but it also raised public consciousness about gridlock and environmental dangers. Conflicts between urban modernization and tradition, though not new, had become more complex than ever.

The Beijing Boom: Changing Ways of Life

Structural and legal changes designed to promote economic growth facilitated Beijing's new ways of life in the 1990s. The household registration (*hukou*) system that had loomed so large in restricting migration to Beijing and other cities, and also in keeping people under surveillance, became less important after rationing was abandoned in 1993. Migrant workers, entrepreneurs, artists, and others now could come to Beijing without concern for their legal registration status; as long as they had money, they could rent or even purchase housing, buy food, and find jobs. For college graduates, the end of the work-assignment system meant farewell to the "iron rice bowl" in return for the more highly valued chance to find employment anywhere. In general, the change particularly benefited those who were eager to leave their home areas, usually small towns or poor rural villages, without official approval. As a major center of the new global economy, Beijing in the 1990s attracted untold numbers of migrants in search of opportunity.

Housing

Privatization of housing and a real estate boom were central to changing ways of life in the capital from the early 1990s. Housing reform was a bold move toward a market economy because the state used to control and manage housing through work units (*danwei*). With the exception of people who had lived in Beijing before 1949, most residents were assigned to their living units based on seniority and rank. Housing assignments were an indicator of power and status. But as early as spring 1988, Premier Li Peng commented at a meeting of the People's Congress that housing should be just another market commodity, like refrigerators or bicycles. Popular reaction to the possibility of housing for sale was ambivalent at first; city residents thought about how much money they could possibly have or borrow from banks, and how safe it would be politically to own a private living space.[1] (Communist ideology had taught that the desire to own private property was reprehensible and "bourgeois.") At the beginning, the projected house sales included two categories: "subsidized houses," living spaces previously assigned by work units to their employees to rent and now sold to them at a low price subsidized by the government, and "commodity houses," more expensive housing, newly built to a higher standard, for which no subsidies would be provided.

The initial experimental subsidized housing sale occurred in the suburbs. The transactions converted renters to owners of dormitory apartments. In 1989 the new state-run Beijing Real Estate Exchange Company prepared to help residents exchange, buy, or sell their houses. In February the first group of employees from the Number Six Beijing Construction Company bought the houses in which they were living and received property deeds issued by the government; these deeds acknowledged the owners' legal property rights in the house, even though they did not own the land and had to be aware of certain restrictions on exchange or resale. With extensive subsidies based on employees' seniority and rank, the prices were affordable. People who bought houses at this time had to pay maintenance fees to designated agencies to cover any necessary repairs or cleaning of public areas. These fees were higher than the rent that they had paid before. But the buyers still were pleased to own their living quarters and have the freedom to remodel their homes at will. The bond between employees and work units loosened, and people became more mobile because they could exchange their houses.

Faced with accumulated issues left over from the previous housing system, Beijing city government decided that state-run work units no longer would assign housing to their employees after June 15, 1998. Instead, people either could rent or buy houses on their own. In 1999 the municipality further ruled that state-owned housing would be sold only at cost prices; and the cost price of newly built housing in eight suburban areas was set at 1,485 *yuan* per square meter (about US$18.56 per square foot). Thus, by the end of 1999, most Beijing residents who used to live in work-unit assigned housing owned their living quarters. Calculations about real estate—when and where to move—became an obsession for Beijing's *danwei* generation, who grew into a new middle class.

The unit price of luxury apartment high-rise buildings in downtown Beijing rose, with this boom in commodity housing, from several thousand *yuan* per square meter in the late 1990s to well over 10,000 *yuan* in 2006. Many new single-home developments appeared, particularly in northern Beijing, which was widely believed to have better *fengshui*. (A century earlier, the three "superior banners" had been quartered in the northern part of the Inner City.) Gated communities were built well north of the Old City. For the very wealthy, there were the exotically named Napa Valley, Orange County, Vancouver Forest, and Heidelberg Village, often designed by foreign or foreign-trained architects and located between the Fifth and Sixth ring roads; buyers needed one or two private vehicles to live in these areas, which lacked public transportation. (See Map 7.) Each well-designed and spacious single house was priced at five to ten million *yuan* (US$600,000 to over one million), affordable only for a handful of private entrepreneurs, movie and music stars, or individuals with money from unknown sources. According to official statistics, the average annual income of a Beijing urban resident was slightly more than 10,000 *yuan* in 2000 (ten times more than in 1986[2]) and about 15,000 *yuan* (less than US$2,000) in 2005.[3]

New mid-to-high-cost gated housing compounds, mostly in the suburbs, were walled and guarded. Living in these compounds changed lifestyles; sports and other facilities—tennis courts, swimming pools, gyms, and gathering places—were available to residents in a community center. Such compounds in the more crowded central city also offered indoor parking spaces. Residents soon came to regard these amenities as necessities rather than luxuries. In addition, several novel ungated housing developments appeared in downtown Beijing. On the east in the embassy area was Xingfucun (Happiness Village), a huge residential complex designed by several foreign architects, in which high-rise apartments were integrated with offices, shops, restaurants, and an art gallery.

Migrants

As Beijing residents were adopting new ways of living, subcommunities were forming and integrating themselves into a capital that was becoming cosmopolitan in ways quite different from the past. In addition to tourists, merchants, and diplomats from around the world, newcomers from within the People's Republic itself continuously flowed into the city, creating a large floating population. Most intended to stay in Beijing temporarily, but many remained year after year. According to official statistics, their numbers reached four million in 2003, among whom three million had been in the city more than six months.[4] The number who "floated" into Beijing averaged 15,000 on any one day in 1965, 300,000 in 1978, 900,000 in 1985, and more than 1 million in 1987. Thirty percent of them left Beijing on the same day they arrived; but about 70 percent stayed for more than one day. More than 50 percent consisted of construction workers and female domestic servants from the countryside.[5] The migrants offered the city a cheap

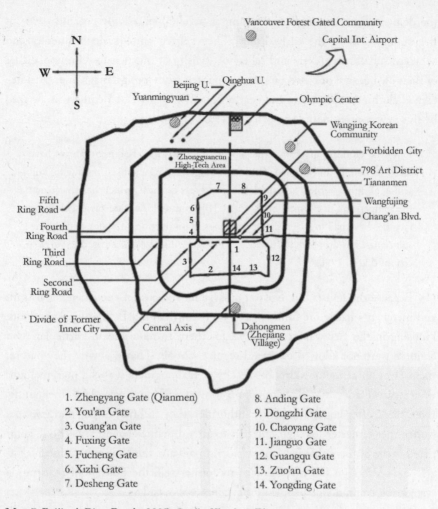

Map 7. Beijing's Ring Roads, 2005. *Credit: Xiaodong Zhang*

1. Zhengyang Gate (Qianmen)
2. You'an Gate
3. Guang'an Gate
4. Fuxing Gate
5. Fucheng Gate
6. Xizhi Gate
7. Desheng Gate
8. Anding Gate
9. Dongzhi Gate
10. Chaoyang Gate
11. Jianguo Gate
12. Guangqu Gate
13. Zuo'an Gate
14. Yongding Gate

labor force, but at the same time their presence caused problems in housing, education, transportation, crime, and social stability.

A typical example was Zhejiang Village at Dahongmen, five kilometers (about three miles) south of Tiananmen, where migrants mainly from Wenzhou in Zhejiang Province in southeast China lived together and operated fabric workshops and tailoring establishments. These southern entrepreneurs had anticipated the demand for more modern clothing as people increasingly became aware of the outer world in the early 1980s. They started small-scale businesses and achieved success as makers and sellers of stylish but inexpensive clothing, either of their own design or based on patterns pirated from foreign magazines. A state-owned clothing company in the nearby Xuanwu District of Beijing was amazed by this new competition. It reported in 1995:

> Since the clothing market further opened in 1991, non-Beijing residents have come to Beijing and formed Zhejiang Village. They have been producing and selling all kinds of new stylish clothing in great quantity, which has sharpened the competition in clothing markets. . . . [By contrast] the state-owned clothing factories have had to face difficult situations in production and sales, and as a result capital has dropped drastically. . . . Production in 1994 decreased to 77 percent of that in 1990.[6]

Because the household registration system still existed, the Zhejiang artisans and merchants had more limits placed on them than did Beijing local residents. Housing in the city was not available for them to rent, and in particular their children were not allowed to attend regular schools. That was why they had set themselves up at the outskirts of the city at Dahongmen: it was a marginal area where surveillance and discrimination against migrants were less threatening. Even there, after negotiation with authorities, they still had to pay 680 *yuan* per student per semester for their children to attend public elementary school, compared to the 80 *yuan* that local city residents paid and the 40 *yuan* that local farmers paid. Although but a shadow of its former self, the household registration system still could divide people into insiders and outsiders.

With increasing demands for housing in Dahongmen, rent there increased by a factor of ten within a decade. In 1993 Wan Xianjie, a real estate developer from Zhejiang, rented a third of an acre of land for six years and built his own walled *dayuan* with efficiency rooms to rent to migrants. This proved so lucrative that other developers followed suit. In Ma Village alone migrants rented twenty seven hectares (sixty-six acres) of land on which they constructed *dayuan* for their people. The annual rental turnover was about two million *yuan;* by 1995 there were forty-six similar *dayuan* in this area.[7] There were only 10,000 farmers in or near Dahongmen, but in 1992 there were 80,000 migrants plus 200,000 temporary residents. The total value of the area's trade, mainly in apparel, reached thirty billion *yuan* annually, which was 54.5 percent of the total trade in clothing in all of Beijing. Local people, most of them farmers, secured salaried jobs, lived on rents they received, and moved into five-storey apartment buildings. The town was booming.

In June 1995, however, Beijing city government decided to tighten its control of the floating migrant population and keep their total number under three million. Zhejiang Village became a major target, probably because it not only contained many people living outside the household registration system but also posed a major threat to state-owned clothing factories. In November the government mobilized six hundred armed police and two thousand others (work-team members from nearby work units) to "clean up" Zhejiang Village, demolish *dayuan,* and expel the migrants. By the end of the month, 89 percent of *dayuan* housing had been demolished by force and twenty-two of the *dayuan* evacuated. Most people returned to the south or went elsewhere in nearby Hebei Province, where they were welcomed to live and establish businesses. The government's action was not popular, except perhaps with managers of state-owned clothing factories; other local residents regretted the loss of the jobs and additional income that these enterprising migrants had contributed to the city.

The Zhejiang Village story was not over, however. The migrants returned in April 1996, and this time they took pains to establish a close and explicit collaboration with local people. Together they built compounds with both residential and office space that they called *gongsi* (companies). Local and Zhejiang businessmen spent two million *yuan* renting the nearby former state-owned Beijing HQ Rubber Factory that had gone out of business; they converted the old factory to a *dayuan* called HQ Leather Jacket Factory, and maintained minimum pay for the 150 laid-off rubber factory workers. Economic ties and mutual interest finally caused Zhejiang Village to be accepted as part of Beijing; the city even planned to make it a stop on a projected new subway line. The significance of the tale of Zhejiang Village, as sociologist Wang Hansheng argued, was that it not only greatly challenged the state-owned apparel enterprises but also successfully introduced fresh concepts of marketing and management.

Foreigners

New international residential communities also emerged in Beijing at the turn of the twenty-first century. In addition to the mostly Western business and diplomatic populations in the embassy area, South Korean communities were of particular interest. By 2006 there were more than 100,000 Koreans living in Beijing. (See Map 7.) In Wangjing, northeast of the city, 60,000 Koreans ran schools for their children, operated grocery stores and restaurants where all the signs and menus were in Korean, and worshipped at their own Christian churches. Korean-language newspapers were published there, and Korean news websites had more than 50,000 participants. Traffic signs in Wangjing were to be replaced with signs in Chinese, English, and Korean before 2008. Friendship, marriage, assimilation, and joint business partnerships were all factors keeping Koreans in Beijing. Like Chinatown in New York or San Francisco, Wangjing was the "Korea Town" of Beijing.

A second Korean settlement at Wudaokou, an academic district, developed rapidly in the mid-1990s. Most of the Koreans there were college and graduate students living in high-rise apartment buildings. Most decided to stay in China after their studies, working either for Korean companies or joint ventures. Younger bilingual Koreans there spoke Chinese better than their white-collar compatriots in Wangjing, and they felt fortunate to be experiencing the dramatic transformation of the capital. In 2002 the joint-venture Beijing Hyundai Automobile Factory broke ground; only six months later the first Hyundai cars manufactured there were rolling down the streets, a source of pride for Koreans in Beijing.

Many other foreign nationals who lived and worked in Beijing for long periods chose to live near their compatriots: Russians clustered near the Chaoyang Gate and Temple of Heaven areas; Germans near the Yansha shopping center at the northeast corner of the Third Ring Road; and Japanese around Changfu Palace just outside Jianguo Gate on Chang'an Boulevard. Some long-term Western residents, especially those who were married to Han Chinese, liked to live in traditional *hutong* neighborhoods and mingle with neighbors. It became commonplace to see people of different nationalities almost everywhere in Beijing. The government even decided to experiment by issuing identity cards to permanent residents to help deal with growing numbers of potential foreign immigrants. With the exception of Hong Kong, no other Chinese city had so many diverse subcommunities.

Consumerism

Wealth, housing, and cars were the basic elements in a new lifestyle that featured consumerism and leisure. The purchase of every newly constructed apartment or house required the owner to finish the interior walls, lay flooring, install plumbing, select appliances, and buy furniture and drapes or blinds. The customer had bought only the house structure, not a finished house. Every new owner became an expert on heating, ventilation, and other aspects of house construction that in the United States were left to the builder. Hundreds of retail and wholesale outlets developed to meet these new needs. Specialized stores devoted to kitchen and bathroom fixtures were concentrated in one neighborhood; those specializing in heating and cooling were found in another. One emporium on the Fourth Ring Road in the Chaoyang District, about the scale of a two-storey Wal-Mart, sold nothing but drapes and curtains from domestic and foreign manufacturers. Within this structure, each company had its own retail shop enclosed on three sides and open to a corridor at the front. After shopping, customers placed an order, and drapes and curtains were made to order, delivered, and installed within a week. There were also gigantic new shopping centers, such as Golden Resource New Yansha Mall—with a parking capacity of ten thousand cars—near the northwest corner of the Fourth Ring Road, and several IKEAs and Wal-Marts. IKEA was vastly popular; probably every new house or apartment contained at least one IKEA computer table and lamp. Wholesale clubs built in recent years around the greater Beijing area resembled those in the megacities of developed countries.

For everyday shopping, the majority of Beijing residents went to a supermarket. One chain called itself Hyper-Market, adapting a European term for supermarket. Another popular supermarket chain was the French Carrefour (well rendered in China as *jia lefu,* or Happy Family), which had several successful outlets in the city. When shopping was a family outing, as it often was, it was easy to stop on the way to have a bite to eat. In the Carrefour in the Zhongguancun area, the market occupied two underground floors, while the ground floor contained restaurants and boutiques. Although there were some neighborhood markets in walking distance, many of the larger ones required a car or taxi to reach, adding to the general congestion. The large supermarket chains had their own store vans that picked up shoppers from certain neighborhoods. They also distributed weekly color circulars featuring the specials of the week. Many shopping patterns common in the United States became a normal part of Beijing life.

Much consumerism centered on children, especially because after 1982, state population policy allowed each urban couple to have only one child. This rule appeared to be so thoroughly accepted in cities like Beijing that young couples did not even wish to have a second child; they preferred to save their money toward a better life for the small family that already existed. Thus a typical child had, in addition to two devoted parents, four doting grandparents who, if they had had only one child themselves, focused on their one grandchild. The child easily could become spoiled and/or overweight from eating all the new foods now available; boys suffering from this syndrome were known as Little Emperors, and Little Empresses were not unknown.

Leisure

Another new lifestyle, a reflection of changing moral ideas and values, was that of married couples who chose not to have even one child but instead gave priority to leisure activities and travel. Younger people, particularly white-collar employees, enjoyed independence and freedom, and might remain single or constantly postpone marriage. The number of unmarried men and women between thirty and fifty years old in Beijing was 100,000 in 1990, but it was three or four times more in 2006. The divorce rate in Beijing was the highest in the nation, higher than that of Japan, South Korea, and Singapore.[8] It was quite common that neither wife nor husband liked to eat and cook at home. Young couples loved to gather for weekly parties or dine out.

Most women were required to retire at age fifty-five and men at sixty. Many retirees used continuing education programs to learn about a topic in which they were interested; often they found dancing a pleasurable way to remember past eras. Older people liked to apply colorful makeup and perform *yangge*, a rural folk dance popular during the war of resistance in the Yan'an area. Those who were young in the 1950s and 1960s enjoyed ballroom dancing on streets or in public parks, as in Jingshan Park on a crisp November morning. (See Figure 36.) Retiree dances have become a common sight in Beijing. Young people, of course, were interested in other kinds of dance. Students at Beijing University signed up for salsa lessons, perhaps dreaming of a spicier way of life. (See Figure 37.)

The explosion of cell phones and the Internet in Beijing—and practically everywhere in China—allowed new lifestyles to blend more easily with older patterns. Relatives and friends stayed in close touch even as they moved into distinct residential subcommunities. People caught in traffic, a daily occurrence in Beijing, could telephone or send a message to say that they would be late. Taxi drivers who could not find an address called the destination to ask directions. Even people who could not afford a land line could buy a cell phone. Instead of carrying their home keys around their necks as in the old days, elementary school children wore colorful cell phones so that they easily could call home and friends. The Internet opened up previously narrow daily lives to the world in a way that was truly revolutionary. The censorship of politically sensitive material was not a problem for most people, who used the Internet mainly to send personal messages and to obtain information. True, new subcommunities sometimes created barriers similar to the old walls, but two trends cut across these barriers: mass consumerism, meaning that anyone with money could browse and shop anywhere, and communication networks widely available by means of cell phones and the Internet.

Globalization and Commodification: Beijing for Sale

In the 1990s, not just real estate and consumer items but the very structure and foundation of the city seemed to be for sale. Huge neon-lit commercial advertisements for beauty aids and other commodities appeared at some of the most visible spots in the capital, places where for decades only political messages had been seen. Public buses carrying colorful advertisements for foreign and domestic products appeared on the streets for the first time in January 1993, signaling a new wave of commercialization. Bankrupt state-owned factories and their attached facilities were for sale or rent, and even the most precious land of the city was open to foreign investors and developers.

Deng Xiaoping's 1992 policies promoting a "socialist market economy" made possible great changes in the coming decade. The most striking case may have been the megaproject of redeveloping Wangfujing. Beginning in 1992, Wangfujing, the iconic commercial center of Beijing located just a few blocks east of the Forbidden City and Zhongnanhai, began a metamorphosis. The state-run Wangfujing department store, built in 1955, opened up control of its management, prices, hiring, and distribution to stockholders and interested buyers. McDonald's (Maidanglao) opened its first location at the corner of Wangfujing and Chang'an Boulevard in 1992, attracting forty thousand customers seeking a "taste" of America on the first day of business.[9] Partly because of controversy, it took five years for a Beijing–Hong Kong joint venture to demolish the eighty-seven-year-old Dong'an Market at Wangfujing and rebuild it to reopen in 1998, as well described by Anne-Marie Broudehoux. At a cost of US$300 million, this traditional market was converted into an international shopping mall arranged in a twelve-floor, multi-use modern complex. (See Figure 40.) In appearance, the complex was supposed to fit in with other new structures built under the leadership of Mayor Chen Xitong. These large boxlike buildings were topped with small pavilion-like towers. The guideline for the renovation was to create a commercial center where Chinese could see the world and foreigners could learn about China.[10] It sounded reasonable, but many thought that its real purpose was to promote consumerism and business. The huge interior space was equipped with several escalators and elevators to connect multiple shopping floors and looked stylish and postmodern. There was almost no trace of the former Dong'an Market. The new market excited consumers who loved novelty and fashion, but it disappointed others who missed the more modest routine and fun of shopping in the traditional way. They also regretted the loss of personalized services that had been offered by businesses too small to make the transition to the sleek new structure.

No matter how many complaints the municipal government received, the grand redevelopment projects did not stop with Wangfujing. Another, even bigger commercial complex, Oriental Plaza, was to extend from the southern end of Wangfujing to Dongdan along Chang'an Boulevard. According to its promoters, this complex of shopping malls, luxury apartments, hotel space, and offices would play a central role in the overall Wangfujing area. Mayor Chen Xitong put this piece of the most valuable central land in Beijing on the market and sold it in 1992 to the Hong Kong tycoon Li Ka-shing, who held a 52 percent stake in Oriental Plaza.[11] Even with the investment funding in hand, it was more difficult to complete this project than the New Dong'an Market. In addition to demolishing an entire block and leveling the homes of twelve thousand people, the municipal government had to pay US$12 million to relocate McDonald's flagship store to the first floor of the New Dong'an Market, where it would be much less visible than at its former location. The project eventually cost US$2 billion.

Controversy over the site as well as the size of Oriental Plaza plagued the project. Battles over different phases of the work continued throughout the 1990s. In 1994 city planners and historical preservationists managed to halt construction by reporting that the design violated building codes in the capital: It "exceeded the 30 meter height limit set for this historically sensitive area . . . and [had bypassed] the rule stating that any building worth more than 50 million *yuan* must be submitted for acceptance to the Central Planning Bureau." Soon Premier Li Peng interrupted the project until it could go through "proper procedures and comply with established regulations."[12]

In 1995 Mayor Chen, who had been responsible for the sale of the right to use the land for Oriental Plaza and had insisted on carrying out the project without proper procedures, was reportedly involved in a financial scandal and accused, along with his associates, of receiving US$37 million from Li Ka-shing. Soon afterward Vice-Mayor Wang Baosen committed suicide. Chen himself was dismissed as mayor, and in 1997 he was sentenced to sixteen years in jail for "fraud and dereliction of duty."[13] Mayor and party chief of Beijing for twelve years (1983–1995), he had been one of the leaders who urged Deng to crack down in the Tiananmen crisis of 1989.

After Chen's downfall, many protested to the authorities about the Oriental Plaza project. The environmentalist Liang Congjie, son of the architect Liang Sicheng who had tried to save the city wall in the 1950s, was among the opponents. In a 1995 letter he asked rhetorically: "Here in Beijing, who will bear the historical responsibility for allowing such a colossal building as Oriental Plaza, built with Hong Kong capital, to stand among symbols of the people's political power, such as Tiananmen, Zhongnanhai, and the Great Hall of the People . . . and to be taller than these buildings, so that it towers over all the other buildings in the area? It would be unlawful to allow such a thing to happen."[14]

Only six months after Liang wrote his eloquent letter, the State Council approved the Oriental Plaza project after some modest adjustments. Work on the foundation began in December 1997, five months after Britain returned its former colony of Hong Kong to China. With thousands of army laborers working day and night, construction was completed before October 1999, in time for celebration of the fiftieth anniversary of the People's Republic. Although both Oriental Plaza and the New Dong'an Market were realities with which Beijing residents had to live, there were many lingering questions. Why was Oriental Plaza needed when the New Dong'an Market already had provided so much modern commercial space? Why was the gigantic plaza built in the heart of the overcrowded Old City, with little consideration of the needs of local residents or of historical and cultural factors? One critic commented that the Oriental Plaza project "epitomized the Chinese people's lost sovereignty over their own environment as wealthy outsiders increasingly dictated the way their cities are transformed. For many, 1997 had brought Hong Kong's takeover of China, not the opposite."[15]

Another dimension of Beijing's development was the expansion of the Zhongguancun area into a center of the new "cyberworld." High tech had long been emphasized as fundamental to the Four Modernizations and an inseparable part of business and daily life. Beijing contained a national high-tech center located at Zhongguancun in the neighborhood of the Chinese Academy of Sciences, Qinghua University, and Beijing University. Zhongguancun started down the path of becoming China's Silicon Valley in 1980 when Chen Chunxian, a scientist at the Chinese Academy of Sciences, left the laboratory and set up the first private high-tech enterprise in this area. Many private enterprises followed suit, producing and selling calculators, phones, and computers in the 1980s and, more recently, cell phones. These enterprises began to cooperate with the nearby advanced academic institutions, thereby doubling and tripling their business. Then the prestigious scholarly institutions themselves began to change, inventing corporate and marketing approaches to management of their own affairs. Before long Zhongguancun—originally a muddy narrow road with jostling traffic of trucks, bicycles, and horse-drawn vehicles—became a dynamic "street of electronics" famous throughout China. More recently, as one of the busiest districts of Beijing—full of high-rise buildings, stores, and restaurants—it has been promoted to "electronic city." Its contributions to the nation included promoting computer applications; developing, producing, and selling hardware and software for electronic devices; and pioneering new corporate patterns for research institutions and commercial companies.

The globalization and commodification of Beijing also extended to the art world. During the remaking of Beijing in the past fifteen years, a new art district has developed in Dashanzi, in the Jiuxianqiao area of northeastern Beijing. In the time of Mao and Deng, this area was occupied by the developing electronics industry. Because some of the plants belonged to the defense industry, factories bore numbers rather than names. For example, Joint Factory 798 had more than ten thousand workers and several subfactories. By the early 1990s, however, most of the subfactories had stopped production because of financial problems, and more than 60 percent of the workers had been laid off. Soon the entire compound of Joint Factory 798 sat empty. Before any real estate developers expressed interest, the discarded factory site, with its generous space and low rent, attracted a group of avant-garde artists who had lived together near Yuanmingyuan and elsewhere from 1984 to 1993.

The group of urban bohemian artists, politically marginal and socially semi-reclusive, began to return to the city in 2000 and rented Dashanzi's sprawling workshops and huge warehouse platforms designed by East Germans in the 1950s. They converted these spaces into stylish art galleries and spacious living quarters. Other artists and business people from China and beyond were attracted to invest in the area. Even the local government grew convinced that the city should have such an art district. By 2005 the 798 Dashanzi Art Area had filled up with domestic and international avant-garde painters, sculptors, photographers, fashion designers, music composers, experimental performing artists, and writers. The new occupants creatively turned outdated remnants of the old factories—Soviet-made machines or fading *Long Live Chairman Mao* slogans on the wall—into artistic decorations or bittersweet nostalgia. In 2005 there were at least forty art galleries and many artists from all over the world at 798. Because the taste for contemporary avant-garde art was still undeveloped in China, buyers included a disproportionate number of international foundations, galleries, and private collectors. The 798 area itself was a global market: several exotic and trendy restaurants and bars as well as high-end tailor shops opened up there; a Chinese version of the American teenage magazine *Seventeen* had its editorial office in a converted former workshop, with fashion shows occurring regularly; and companies such as Sony, Christian Dior, and Toyota held galas there to launch new products.

The development of theme restaurants was another response to market opportunities in the 1990s. They appealed to the wish for novelty and nostalgia for the past. Xiangyangtun (Sun-facing village) Restaurant, located between the Summer Palaces and Beijing University, resembled a wealthy landowner's house before the Communist revolution swept landlords away. Its interior was a traditional opera theater with a high, decorated ceiling and dozens of small opium den–like rooms on three sides. A stage at the front was used for performances while customers were dining. In almost every corner of the house were cultural artifacts such as "little red books" of quotations from Mao, Red Guard armbands, old propaganda posters, and a sent-down youth's farming tools. The show onstage was a comic dialogue accompanied by folk music from northeastern China. Similarly, a restaurant called Black Soil was run by a group of former sent-down youth; it attracted people who shared that experience and also perhaps an ability to recall it in a mood mellowed by the passage of time. Another theme restaurant, Red Capitalist, operated by an American since 1999, offered imitations of Zhongnanhai cuisine, including Mao's and Deng's favorite dishes. It was reminiscent of the Imitations of Palace Food restaurant in Beihai Park in the 1920s after the last Qing emperor had left the Forbidden City.

Theme restaurants had begun to ebb by 2005, but the bar culture appeared to be more lasting. It was easy to understand why many bars in Sanlitun, the diplomatic district, had been popular for years. But more recently a string of bars lined Houhai (Back Lake), a scenic area of the former Inner City with the best preserved courtyard houses in the capital. Civilizations seemed to meet as Zen Bar and Buddhist Bar sold Jack Daniel's and Budweiser. Behind the bar area were several beautiful courtyard houses that had been converted into bed-and-breakfasts. (See Figure 48.) Pedicab tours of the aged *hutong* alleys by day and of the colorfully lit exotic bars by night created an artificial Beijing image; they made the historically significant Houhai area seem commercialized and tourist-oriented.

Urban Crisis

At the beginning of the twenty-first century, the Old City had expanded vertically while the entire city had extended itself horizontally. According to a newspaper report in 2005, the size of the newly developed area outside the Second Ring Road already was equal to one and a half times that of old Beijing (everything within the Second Ring Road).[16] The surrounding counties, once predominantly rural, had been incorporated into the city as districts (*qu*) that could take the initiative in development and governance. New houses and communities had risen from farm fields. A city that was beautifully designed and developed as a work of art marked by symmetry and balance seemed to have degenerated into a free-for-all.

Anticipating the Olympics, Beijing authorities built a sleek Beijing Planning Exhibition Hall at Qianmen. With four marble storeys and state-of-the-art exhibitions, conference rooms, and shops, this hall met the highest international museum standard. Within it, interpretive displays explained stages of Beijing's growth, plans proposed since the mid-twentieth century, and futuristic ideas for various districts. Intended as a monument to rational city planning, the museum served instead as an ironic reminder of visions that have been worked up by earnest architects only to be ignored by power holders. The seemingly uncontrollable sprawl that had overtaken Beijing can be explained in part by the city's position as a national capital where party leaders and top bureaucrats had a stake, often a highly personal one, in urban development.

By the turn of the century, the Beijing boom in lifestyles and real estate had led to an urban crisis of serious proportions. For people with a sense of history and an appreciation of the old Beijing, the rapid disappearance of traditional residential areas in the Old City was the most controversial and heartbreaking aspect of this crisis. In the Qianmen area, for example, because the city planned to convert the main north-south street into a pedestrian-only avenue, seven new streets had to be built to carry other traffic. As a result thousands of courtyard houses and other structures, including old and famous emporia like the Qianxiangyi silk store, were doomed to destruction. District authorities designated courtyard houses in this vicinity as "dangerous and dilapidated," a label that, according to city law effective in 1990, allowed developers to tear them down. Indeed, 1990 is now considered by some experts as the turning point for old Beijing.[17]

Some officials described the Qianmen area as a typical slum with more than 57,000 residents, of whom almost 10,000 were over sixty years of age and almost 1,000 were handicapped. But as reporter Jiang Weiwei commented, it was sad to realize that this cultured commercial street and area of historical sites, including many former *huiguan* (native-place lodges) and houses of celebrities in the Qing and Republican eras, was about to disappear forever. Many elderly residents complained that the compensation given them for their apartments was not enough to cover the cost of new housing out on the Fourth or Fifth Ring Road. A younger resident said, "Even if I could afford it, I still don't want to move out. How could I tolerate three to four hours a day commuting back and forth to work, not to mention taking my kids to school every day?"[18] Remarking on the authorities' false claims that the houses were dangerous, another resident said, "Living in such an old courtyard, who doesn't know the importance of preventing fire? During the several decades that I lived here, I didn't see any fire until the recent removal started." An older man who had lived in the area for sixty years made artificial limbs for handicapped people. As a self-employed small business owner, he said, "I will definitely lose my income if I move. Old customers won't be able to find me in the suburbs. Neither can I open a new business in a strange place at my age."[19] Reporters, college students, and experts constantly came to take photos or videos to catch the last moment of the disappearing site, and most of them expressed their sympathy; some even published articles or took up the residents' cause with the government. But all was in vain. It took bulldozers a few hours to demolish the residents' memory-laden homes.

Ian Johnson, former *Wall Street Journal* correspondent in Beijing, reported the case of a Wangfujing resident who lost his home to the Oriental Plaza project in 1994: "During the 1990s, the city confiscated a hundred thirty-eight billion *yuan* [roughly US$15 billion] in real estate. More than two hundred thousand people in the Old City lost their homes. They got practically nothing in compensation." Mr. Feng's home of thirty years was sold to the developer for $125,000 and he was compensated with "a small apartment on the tenth floor of a housing silo . . . that probably cost a tenth of the $125,000 to build. The local government pocketed the balance, in violation of laws that require fair compensation."[20] Mr. Feng first filed a lawsuit against the developers and the district government; this soon failed. Then he and his friends managed to get 23,000 participants to sign and file a 1998 mass lawsuit; it too was rejected.

Attempts at government regulation were rational and admirable, but they were largely ignored. Destruction of *hutong* was permitted by the very authorities and district governments who were supposed to enforce the regulations. The Capital City Planning Commission was unable to enforce the rules that had been enacted, while four districts in the Old City—Xicheng, Dongcheng, Xuanwu, and Chongwen—became powerful and benefited greatly from development. Money and land transactions involved collusion between government officials, especially at the district level, on one hand, and developers, on the other. The latter generally hid their identities because these transactions were so controversial. In fact, most of the developers in Beijing either had close ties to bureaucrats or once had been bureaucrats themselves. They appeared to have a kind of "feudal" right to dispose of the land. The general perception was that permissions for purchase of the right to use land rarely were put up for bids on the open market. Instead, they were handled in secret transactions involving kickbacks and turnovers in complex pyramid schemes that obscured legal ownership. Critics suggested that when a developer argued that a project would be profitable, the state was motivated to ensure that other state offices did not create obstacles to his plans. Because the government simultaneously was managing and regulating large parts of the economy, corruption and mismanagement were exceedingly likely to occur.[21]

Real estate was widely regarded as the most corrupt area of development. A few argued that such transactions were not really illegal but merely took advantage of the weakness or underdevelopment of property rights and laws. According to one estimate, a total of over 10 billion *yuan* (or US$1.25 billion) was misappropriated during the 1990s. As Johnson wrote, "To put it in context, during the 1990s, developers had ripped the city off the equivalent of an entire year's worth of economic output, as if every man, woman and child, all 11 million Beijingers, had simply given away everything they produced in one year."[22]

The large scale of real estate development helped account for the massive, clumsy, and even outlandish appearance of so many of Beijing's skyscrapers. A Western architect with twenty years of experience in Beijing believed that the question of scale was the key explanation of poor design. Real estate was "sold" (with leases of fifty to seventy years) to developers in large blocks, reflecting their previous use by institutional *danwei*. Corruption was rife because the "seller" of the land "rights" was the government itself, with bureaucrats in different offices and ministries controlling those "rights." Development on such a large scale of such valuable real estate led to maximizing usable space by building the tallest possible buildings.

Mayor Chen Xitong was not the last high city official to be charged with corruption and abuse of power, dismissed, and sentenced to jail. Not long after the city declared that the Beijing Olympic Organization Committee would be the cleanest possible, Liu Zhihua, Vice-Mayor of Beijing, suddenly was dismissed from all his positions for "leading a dissolute and decadent life." Liu had been a key person in the city government and was in charge of city planning, construction, housing reform, demolition of dangerous houses, redevelopment of the Old City, and traffic and communication; his role on the Olympic Organization Committee, however, had been his most important. Although the official announcement provided no details, rumor had it that the main reason for Liu's downfall was corruption and abuse of power; if the bribes he received exceeded a certain amount, he could face a severe penalty.[23]

The demolition of old *hutong* seemed inexorable. According to journalist Wang Jun, there were about seven thousand *hutong* in 1949 and nearly four thousand in the 1980s; almost six hundred *hutong* have disappeared annually since the late 1990s.[24] The word *chai*, "to be demolished," could be seen painted on buildings everywhere, even on some that were in good condition. (See Figure 35.) The Wangfujing project alone wiped out four thousand homes.[25] According to a *New York Times* report in August 2005, the city had about eight thousand construction sites.[26] Former native-place lodges (*huiguan*) that had survived in other uses since 1949 have been torn down in the Xuannan real estate boom.[27] No wonder Shu Yi, son of the writer Lao She, once sighed, "Ah, Beijing is now indeed a concrete forest!"[28]

Another aspect of the urban crisis arose from rapid growth of motorized transportation. In November 2003, when the Fifth Ring Road was completed, the construction of the Sixth already had begun. After two decades of road building, Beijing was surrounded by five ring roads that were supposed to smooth traffic flow and connect city districts. (Figure 39 shows the Second Ring Road at the Jianguo Gate intersection. This may be contrasted with the same location in 1957 in Figure 38.) Although by this time most industry had been moved out of the city, thousands of vehicle muffler pipes continued to spew pollution into the air. By 2004 there were more than seventy thousand legal, and a considerable number of illegal, taxicabs on Beijing streets. Car sales in 2003 reached 408,000, with more than 69 percent to private individuals. Bicycle Beijing had become Automobile Beijing. The clear azure skies for which the city once had been known were rarely seen.

The sheer scale in the capital could be dehumanizing. Major streets had three or four lanes in each direction, and ring roads divided one neighborhood from another. Often neighborhoods and communities were arbitrarily split by large roadways. To get from one side of the campus of Beijing Foreign Languages University to the other required crossing about ten lanes of traffic with only limited pedestrian underpasses available. The pedestrian definitely did not have the right of way, and the concept of "yield" was unknown. Leisurely rhythms of past daily life could not continue; parents or grandparents had to pick up children at school because it was unsafe for them to cross streets by themselves.

The ring roads seemed to be nooses choking the city rather than beltways allowing it to function smoothly. Except for late-night hours, they almost always were jammed with thousands of cars and super-size trucks. Traffic jams on the Second and Third Ring roads were even worse than those on streets in the city. It took almost two hours to drive via ring roads to Beijing University (northwest of the city) from Tiantan (Temple of Heaven) Park (in the southeast part of the city). Yet by a straight route through the city in reasonable traffic, such a trip would have taken only about forty minutes. Many Beijing residents said that the only efficient transportation was the subway, yet during the 1990s there were only two subway lines in the city. A train station at Xizhi Gate connected the subway line to a new light rail system that extended to Zhongguancun, Qinghua University, and many gated communities in northern Beijing. (Figure 41 shows the new station at Xizhi Gate.) As the city prepared for the Olympics, seven new subway lines were under construction.

If life for the emerging middle class presented difficulties as well as opportunities, the underclass found even more formidable obstacles. The gap between rich and poor yawned wider and wider. Since the late 1990s, thousands of workers had lost their jobs in state-owned factories that either moved out of the city or went bankrupt. Most of these workers had no skills beyond the operation of specific machines; moreover, most were in their forties and fifties, too old to learn another skill yet too young to retire. These "40–50" people usually were both raising children and taking care of their own parents, according to a special report published in *Workers Daily* in 2005. On Bajiao Street of Shijingshan district, "40–50" people accounted for 40 percent of 1,100 laid-off workers. They only received about 1,000 *yuan* per month but had to support a family of four or five in a society that had become more expensive: city residents often needed cash where before subsidized housing or medical care had sufficed. According to a survey in *Beijing Statistical Report 2005,* only 9.3 percent of laid-off "40–50" people were likely to be rehired.[29]

Petitioners were a transient part of the underclass. Even at the turn of the century, they continued to come into Beijing from the provinces to seek redress for their grievances. For a while they sought shelter in houses scheduled for demolition near the train station south of the former Outer City. On one chilly night in December 2005, hundreds were forced to evacuate. Soon, however, dozens of them settled outside the Supreme People's Procurate near the old Legation Quarter to wait for their cases to be reviewed. They set up tents on the sidewalk nearby, creating in effect a new "petitioners' village" in the heart of Beijing.

"New Beijing" and Olympic City

The "New Beijing" of the twenty-first century had an appearance that was strikingly different from what it had been at any time in the past. The public parts of the city boasted an international look that bore little evidence of imperial-era architectural styles. Consensus on this result had been reached only gradually. Once it had seemed imperative to retain some traditional Chinese architectural features even in modern buildings. Most leaders thought that as the capital, Beijing should look "Chinese." But especially after they lost their bid to host the 2000 Olympic Games in 1993, they chose to stress the city's international and modern side.

During his years in office as Beijing mayor and party secretary, Chen Xitong championed the idea of "Chineseness" to an extent that many ridiculed. He required that all new high public buildings have one or even two pavilion-shaped structures on the top as a Chinese stylistic element. A typical example was the office building of the Beijing Municipal People's Congress, the top of which resembled the Tiananmen balcony (see Figure 42). No matter how critical the comments on such structures by Beijing architects, this kind of detail could be viewed as an ironic mark of the Chen era that was imposed on Beijing. Some called the tops of these buildings "putting on a Chinese hat" (*gai yige Zhongguo maozi*).

A certain reconception of Tiananmen Square was the strongest indication of a new way of thinking about the city's public appearance. After the 1989 Tiananmen crisis, authorities wanted to downplay the square's political significance. For this reason, cultural elements surrounding the square were emphasized. Song Xiaolong, who as head of the City Planning Institute has long been in charge of square planning, commented that this latest reconstruction[30] in the late 1990s did not transform the spatial or functional arrangement of Tiananmen Square. In his view, it was the building of the National Grand Theater in 1997 that first altered the formal and solemn atmosphere of the square. Then came the expansion of the National Museum on the east side of the square, the controversy over whether the Ministry of Public Security should leave Chang'an Boulevard—it did not—and even suggestions that the Mao Memorial Hall and the Great Hall of the People be removed from the square.[31] These unlikely removals did not occur either.

Nevertheless, when the theater's strange ellipse-shape building, a "shiny egg of glass and titanium encircled by a large pool and entered through an underwater tunnel,"[32] gradually emerged on the west side of the Great Hall of the People in 2004, public controversy erupted. The birth of the National Grand Theater was both changing and challenging the conventional view of Tiananmen Square. As early as 1958 Premier Zhou Enlai had declared that a national theater should be built near the square, though the project was not approved until the late 1990s. In 1998 the State Council for the first time invited international bidding, and a highly competitive selection process took more than a year. The winner was a project designed by acclaimed French architect Paul Andreu in collaboration with Qinghua University.

Andreu refused to conform to Chinese tradition. He explained that almost all the buildings around Tiananmen Square were symmetrical in style, but that he "would like to add a new chapter onto this history, which is to cut off from history. For the sake of preserving an ancient culture, the best way is to push it toward a margin of crisis."[33] It was a quintessentially un-Chinese idea, and many Chinese did not accept it. If an observer took a bird's-eye view from either the Tiananmen balcony or the top of Jingshan (Prospect Hill), the National Theater looked unharmonious and asymmetric among the buildings on either side of the square. Some even thought that the ellipse shape resembled a traditional grave mound.[34] (See Figure 43.) People also questioned why it was necessary to spend vast sums to hire Western architects to design a significant national building. The giant egg-shaped complex cost nearly US$372 million. But many others, most prominently Jiang Zemin, the party leader since Deng's death in 1997, saw the National Grand Theater design as a symbolic gesture acknowledging China's membership in the global family and the relationship of Beijing architecture to postmodern culture, both points that had been in question as recently as the early 1970s.[35]

Zhou Qinglin, head of the planning and design section of the National Grand Theater Project Committee, commented that the decision on the theater delivered a strong futuristic signal and the "direct impact was that the National Grand Theater broke the shackles and made more avant-garde architectural designs possible later, such as the new headquarters of Chinese Central Television (CCTV) by Rem Koolhaas, and the 'Bird's Nest' high-tech National Stadium for the 2008 Olympic Games by Herzog and de Meuron."[36] These foreign designers' architectural structures were considered three grand constructions in Beijing for the new millennium. Differences from both Chinese tradition and the Soviet style of the 1950s spoke volumes. As Liang Sicheng and Lin Huiyin had written in a Republican-era article about the Beijing suburbs, "No matter whether you come across a towering ancient city gate or an abandoned palace foundation, all are silently telling you or even singing out to you the unbelievable changes wrought by time."[37]

Why did internationally renowned architects of the twenty-first century find it so exciting to work in Beijing? Rem Koolhaas, the designer of the daring new CCTV building, told a reporter that he valued the youthful outlook of the Beijing authorities who managed his project. He noted that at New York's Whitney Museum and Los Angeles' Modern Art Museum, the average age of the decision maker was between seventy and eighty, but on the CCTV project he never dealt with anyone older than forty-five. In addition, Koolhaas welcomed the opportunity to influence new architects at Qinghua University's design school.[38] For their part, officials and developers in Beijing considered young Chinese architects insufficiently advanced to handle major projects. They also perceived that hiring famous world architects like Koolhaas and Andreu conferred a kind of international prestige on Beijing.

Most of the monumental buildings of the last decade have been designed by "offshore," including Hong Kong, architects. This echoed earlier eras. Although the city planning and architectural influences on Beijing in past times were principally Chinese, the great khan Khubilai drew on architects and builders from many lands when Yuan Dadu rose in the thirteenth century, and the Qing emperors employed Jesuit artists, especially in construction at Yuanmingyuan. Chinese gardens and pavilions were fashionable in eighteenth-century Europe. In the 1920s and 1930s U.S. architects such as Henry K. Murphy profoundly influenced new architectural styles in Beijing and other cities. China's opening to the outside in the current global economy is reminiscent of links with other civilizations that go back many centuries.

China's successful Olympic bid in 2001 only strengthened the resolve of its leaders to make the "look" of Beijing international and contemporary. The government had spared no effort to present China as an open and progressive nation. Its failures in previous bids had been due in part to the international outcry after the Tiananmen crisis of 1989. The most recent campaign had included an extraordinary operatic event on June 23, 2001, in the Forbidden City. The performance of three world-renowned tenors—José Carreras, Plácido Domingo, and Luciano Pavarotti—created a strange and unusual atmosphere, a mixture of the ancient and the exotic. This memorable concert seemed to intensify the eagerness of many to see Beijing host the 2008 Olympics. Less than a month later, on the evening of July 13, 2001, Chinese leaders learned that Beijing had been selected. The whole city was overjoyed. Amid a flurry of text messages on cell phones, more than ten thousand people spontaneously went to Tiananmen Square to celebrate, the first such occasion since the 1989 crisis.[39]

Soon, in almost all corners of the capital, huge advertisements for the Olympics seemed to appear overnight. The Beijing Olympic Organization Committee immediately began to set the tone for the event, though the slogans "Humanist Olympics," "Green Olympics," and "Technological Olympics" all seemed to focus on remaking Beijing rather than on the games themselves. The authorities appeared to be responding to public criticism of traffic and pollution caused by cars and construction. Befitting the "green" theme, the designs for the two major Olympic stadiums resembled a bird's nest and a cube of water. To symbolize the "humanist" idea, the Olympic logo depicted a figure running, but it also embodied the shapes of three well-known Chinese characters: the character "jing" for Beijing, the character "wen" meaning civilized or cultured, and the character "ren" for human person. (See Figure 40.)

The design of the new National Stadium was a topic of much comment. Renowned Swiss architects Jaques Herzog and Pierre de Meuron, who designed the Tate Modern in London, noted the "openness to audacious projects" in China. Discussing the bird's nest stadium, Herzog reflected with remarkable candor: "They have the most radical things in their tradition, the most amazing faience and perforated jades and scholar's rocks. Everyone is encouraged to do their most stupid and extravagant designs there. They don't have as much of a barrier between good taste and bad taste, between the minimal and expressive. The Beijing stadium tells me that nothing will shock them."[40] The stadium, covered with bands and beams of steel stretching in all directions, was markedly avant-garde. Its design, even though difficult and costly ($300–400 million), was more acceptable to most Chinese than that of the National Theater.[41] With a capacity of 91,000 people, it was designed to host the opening and closing ceremonies of the games.

The stadium appeared to be a monumental landmark for twenty-first century Beijing and a symbol of China's new global role. Herzog and de Meuron sincerely wish that the National Stadium "might do for Beijing what the Eiffel Tower, itself erected for a temporary exposition, has achieved for Paris."[42]

In addition to the two major stadiums, Beijing must build or renovate seventy-two sports stadiums and training facilities, lay asphalt for fifty-nine new roads, and complete three new bridges by the time of the opening ceremony.[43] The city also must provide housing for twenty thousand Olympic participants and guests. In the run-up to the event, Olympic frenzy has stimulated more redevelopment projects and contributed to the tendency to demolish more of old Beijing. Moving from slogans to action, the city has taken several steps to control pollution, in addition to the construction of new subway lines. As early as 2000, Beijing Municipality auctioned off the rights to use nine pieces of land inside the city formerly occupied by state-owned factories. In March 2005 the government announced that the iron and steel factory at Shijingshan, with 120,000 workers (a sixth of the total number of workers in the city), would move out of city limits by the end of 2010. These decisions also contributed to the "green" theme.

A senior Chinese reporter for *Chinese Youth* said ironically, "It seems to me that this all belongs to a 'face' project, the face of Beijing as well as that of China." To him, the 2008 Olympics showed the world's acceptance of China, and for that reason it could be a milestone in China's renaissance as a nation. That, he suggested, was why the appearance of Beijing was of such great importance. Total investment in the Olympics was about US$12 billion, with half from the Chinese government and the other half from abroad.

The millennial capital of China was being transformed into a hybrid global megacity. Even with all the new additions—the Wangfujing commercial center and international trade district, the high-tech area in Zhongguancun, the 798 art colony and the avant-garde National Stadium—Tiananmen Square still retained its position as the center of the city. Like many other visitors, performance artist Zheng Lianjie thought that this was the best place to mark his father's death by first holding an old family photo in front of Tiananmen and then having a new one taken including his son, too young to have appeared in the older picture.[44] Tiananmen was the point where the past, the present, and the future met as well as the local and the global. (See Figure 44.)

All the monumental structures around the square—including the palaces of the Forbidden City, Mao's Great Hall of the People, and the National Theater—stand today as witnesses to history. As early as 1994, a huge clock with a digital timer went up on the west side of the National Museum. Its purpose was to show the public when Hong Kong, which had become a British colony after China's loss of the Opium War in the nineteenth century, would be returned to China in 1997. More recently, a similar digital timer for the 2008 Olympics attracted photographers in the square. The difference was that this clock was a reminder of the future rather than the past, of the promise of the twenty-first century rather than the humiliations of the nineteenth. Even though the clock does not really tick, it still reflects the mental rhythm of contemporary Beijing, hasty and impatient to reach the Olympics, yet anxious about the uncertain future. Some social critics noted that in the 1980s, when Beijing was poor, people were charged with idealism; later, when Beijing became rich, people lived on without idealism. But this formulation was perhaps too simple. As the achievements and resources of Chinese tradition flow together with science, technology, and international cultural influences in the twenty-first-century city, these elements will combine and the strands will intertwine in ways that cannot be predicted.

Epilogue

Preserving the Past:
The City as Museum
and Showcase

APPROACHING BEIJING TODAY, THE FIRST-TIME VISITOR WILL NOT experience the thrill of the clear blue skies and view of the Western Hills that impressed visitors in earlier centuries. Nor will he or she be awed by the massive walls and gates and the shining tiled roofs of the Forbidden City. The sky will undoubtedly be the murky brown gray of acrid pollution; only occasionally, after a day of strong winds, does it clear enough to reveal the Western Hills. Only two or three gates remain, together with fragments of the city walls. And while the Forbidden City still remains at the center of the city, it must be approached through heavy traffic on boulevards lined with skyscrapers. The physical and spatial character of the city has been so transformed in the last twenty-five years that it barely resembles what it used to be.

For older-generation Beijingren, and for those with appreciation of history and culture, the disappearance of the old Beijing as a perfectly designed city with precious monuments is a tragedy of major proportions. First-time visitors, however, follow the same recommended tour routes and visit the same important historical sites as those in the nineteenth and twentieth centuries did. The typical must-see sights recommended by guidebooks are virtually the same as those recommended by *Dumen jilue* or *Cook's Guide* or Juliet Bredon. They are the Forbidden City, the Temple of Heaven, the Great Wall, and the Ming Tombs. For shopping, a trip to Liulichang is essential. With more time, one can visit the

Summer Palace (Yiheyuan), the Lama Temple, the Northern and Back Lakes (Beihai and Houhai), and take in the shops at Wangfujing.

Most governments since the fall of the Qing have recognized the importance of Beijing's major historical sites not only in defining the city's identity but in attracting tourists. We have seen how Yuan Shikai, the first president of the republic, virtually commandeered the Forbidden City for his own use, but by the 1920s some parts of the palaces were open for public touring. During the Republican through Communist periods, however, most former princely mansions were appropriated for government departments, and many temples and native-place lodges were turned into schools or offices or else allowed to decay. During the Cultural Revolution, many historic sites were damaged by Red Guards, and their relics destroyed. With the economic boom of the 1990s, however, local authorities increasingly turned to reclaiming and restoring such complexes to their original state in order to increase tourism.

With the approach of the Olympics, national and local authorities together were engaged in an intensive effort to beautify the major sites. In 2006 the Temple of Heaven, the Hall of Supreme Harmony (Taihedian), pavilions at Prospect Hill (Jingshan) and Northern Lake (Beihai), and other monuments were all under scaffolding as they were repaired and repainted. Old museums were modernized, and new museums created to preserve the old. More homes of famous Beijing residents of the past were being restored so that they could be made accessible to the public. In addition to the mansions of Prince Gong and Song Qingling (widow of Sun Yat-sen and major Communist Party figure), those of celebrities such as author Lu Xun, eminent scholar and writer Guo Moruo, and opera star Mei Lanfang were already open. Ironically this accelerated program of historical preservation took place just as the scale of destruction of the old city had reached unprecedented proportions.

The Palace Museum

Any discussion of Beijing's historical sites and museums must begin with the Forbidden City, which is not only the city's most important focus but a vast museum as well. After Puyi was evicted from the Forbidden City in 1924, the warlord authorities decided to turn the entire complex, together with its storehouse of riches, into a national museum called the Palace Museum (Gugong bowuyuan). Their motive was to appropriate the palace as a symbol of national pride (and their own legitimacy), and also to bring under state control the pillaging of artifacts that had been going on continuously since the late Qing.[1] Historians, art historians, and other members of the intellectual elite were intensely involved in the cataloging and preservation of hundreds of thousands of pieces of art. The museum was opened to the public in 1925, but with only limited access to the halls and grounds. Over time the Palace Museum has come to symbolize not only the palace, halls, and grounds where the emperor and court lived and worked but also the immense collections of art and artifacts accumulated over centuries. Although these included countless precious gems, silk robes, and furs acquired for the court's use, their core was the imperial assemblage of paintings and calligraphy that the Qianlong emperor inherited, expanded, and had cataloged. An avid connoisseur as well as a devoted calligrapher and painter himself, the Qianlong emperor placed a vermilion imperial seal, often a very large one, on the paintings belonging to him, as collectors usually did. In addition to paintings and calligraphy, the palace also contained vast holdings of bronzes, porcelain, carved jade, and lacquerware as well as European clocks and curios.

With the threat of Japanese invasion after 1931, the main part of the art collection, along with documents and rare books, was transported out of Beijing for safekeeping. The journey, starting in 1933, of this selection of the finest paintings and objects from the Palace Museum was a major saga in itself. Assembled into twenty thousand crates, the collection was moved in various stages from Beijing to Nanjing and from there via different and difficult routes to the western city of Chongqing (Chungking), the wartime Nationalist capital. With Chongqing often suffering aerial bombardment, many objects were saved by dispersion among temples and shrines in Sichuan and Guizhou. After the war, the collection was reassembled in Chongqing and then in Nanjing, and in the end about twenty per cent of it was shipped to the island of Taiwan, where the Nationalist Party eventually retreated in 1949. For many years this part of the collection remained in storage with only a few pieces on display in Taichung (Taizhong) in the center of the island. In 1965 it was moved to a newly built National Palace Museum outside the capital city of Taipei (Taibei).

More than sixteen thousand crates, about eighty per cent of those that had left Beijing in the 1930s, did not go to Taiwan and were returned from Nanjing and Shanghai to Beijing, where they rejoined objects still in the Forbidden City. After the Cultural Revolution, the Palace Museum opened to the public again. Although the choicest paintings and art objects were in Taipei, this Palace Museum actually *was* the palace itself and had the advantage of location and authenticity. The museum started to emphasize the palace as the residence of the Qing emperors. As these emperors—particularly the three high Qing emperors Kangxi, Yongzheng, and Qianlong—were transformed in public discourse from feudal autocrats to great national heroes, the Forbidden City increasingly became a source of patriotic pride. In the 1980s, with the opening of China to contact with the West and increased international tourism, the Palace Museum played an even more visible role. As an important and attractive means for projecting China's image, the collections of both Beijing and Taipei began to travel overseas, mainly to European and American museums. Between 1974 and 2004 the Beijing Palace Museum mounted thirty-three exhibitions overseas, each on an increasingly large scale.[2] In 1996 the Taipei National Palace Museum sponsored a "blockbuster" comprehensive exhibition of its finest works in four cities in the United States, billed as "the third greatest exhibition of Chinese masterworks to travel to the West."[3] (The first was in London in 1935 and 1936, and the second in the United States in 1961 and 1962.) In 2005 the Beijing Palace Museum displayed its best works and objects at the Royal Academy of Art in London, an event described as a "landmark exhibition of works of art from the three most powerful rulers of China's last dynasty, the Qing."[4]

In the 1990s, and especially in the run-up to the Olympics, the Palace Museum underwent extensive repair and repainting. In addition to the sprucing up of the central halls, such as the Hall of Supreme Harmony, the restoration of the private quarters of the emperors and empresses in the inner or northern half of the Forbidden City was in progress. The upkeep of the Forbidden City poses enormous physical and financial challenges. Not only is the Gugong extensive in area, but the buildings are constructed of wood, as almost all traditional Chinese buildings were, and do not withstand the weather well. The few other palace-museums in the world—Versailles outside Paris, Topkapi in Istanbul, or the Hermitage in St. Petersburg—are made of sturdier materials and not so exposed to the elements. The Palace Museum renovations are very costly, and some foreign funding has been obtained. The Qianlong Garden, a complex of twenty-four buildings and extensive outdoor courtyards, will cost US$15 million to renovate. The World Monuments Fund, an American conservation group, is providing funding for the renovation of one section.[5] The complete rebuilding of the Palace of Established Happiness (Jianfugong), which had burned to the ground in 1923, has been undertaken by the Hong Kong–based China Heritage Fund, with contributions by U.S. foundations and corporations. (See Color Plate 13.)

Temples

In addition to the numerous large and small imperial palaces and gardens, Beijing's temples, both large and small, were its most characteristic public structures. Most were used as schools, factories, or offices after 1949. Many of their relics were destroyed during the Cultural Revolution, but most major structures remained. The Lama Temple, Yonghegong, was one of the most important temples in Beijing, and was somewhat exceptional in the early attention it received in the People's Republic. Once the palace of Qing princes, it was converted to a temple in the 1740s, was the central site for the "lama religion" or Tibetan Buddhism, and consistently received imperial attention. By 1949, however, it had fallen into considerable disrepair, but the new government soon decided to restore it. On the lunar new year in 1954, the temple reopened to the public for three days; Mao and other party leaders attended the ceremonies. Their motive, like that of the Qing emperors, was to win the favor of religious leaders in Tibet. In 1957 the Yonghegong was selected to be among the first thirty-nine cultural preservation sites (*wenwu baohu danwei*) by the Beijing city government, and in 1961 it was chosen as a national preservation site. In 1979 large-scale renovations took place, costing millions of yuan, and in 1981 the temple was formally opened to the public. (The ticket price was five *mao* (about twenty-five cents), which people thought extravagant compared to the new Summer Palace, Yiheyuan, which at that time charged only one *mao*.) Today the Yonghegong is one of the most visited tourist spots, but it also functions as a religious center and headquarters of the Chinese Lama Buddhist Association. Like all temples and other historical sites, the Yonghegong falls under multiple jurisdictions. Its religious activities are conducted by the Lama Buddhist Association, but its administration is under the city's Religious Affairs Bureau, which works closely with the Tourist Bureau.

A number of other temples in Beijing have received a new lease on life in recent years. Their buildings have been physically restored, but not necessarily their traditional functions. Most are classified as *wenwu* (cultural relics) that require *baohu* (preservation). Their restoration falls under the jurisdiction of the central government's Wenwu ju, Bureau of Cultural Relics, which is under the Ministry of Culture. Most temples, churches, and mosques are treated as cultural relics. Some are affiliated with, and sponsored by, religious associations. Others serve a more overt tourist function. As in the traditional governance of the city, overlapping functions and jurisdictions are the norm. (See Map 6 in Chapter 5 for the location of temples.)

One of the most important temples to be restored in the 1980s and 1990s was the Dongyuemiao (Temple of the God of the Eastern Peak), a Daoist temple with a rich history dating back to 1319 and even earlier.[6] Belonging to the Zhengyi branch of Daoist practice, the temple had a rather exclusive tradition of housing monks and novices, coupled with accessibility to everyday worshippers, who came to pray for their health, to settle their accounts at the end of the year, or to take care of other practical issues. From the Ming onward, it was one of the most popular temples in Beijing with many lay religious associations involved in helping to maintain it. In the Republican period its practices and beliefs were recorded by the famous historian Gu Jiegang, who pioneered the study of folklore and folk customs in China. From 1949 to 1995 the temple's buildings and premises were occupied by the Public Security Academy. Although the structures were not harmed, precious statues, stelae, and other relics were damaged or destroyed. The Chaoyang district authorities decided to restore the temple and in 1995 cancelled the contract with the police academy. The district government, with central government support, financed the physical restoration of the temple compound, which was fairly straightforward since the structures suffered from little damage. Rebuilding the statues and relics that had disappeared, however, depended on the memory of the last surviving monk from before 1949, who was invited to recall the details of the interiors of the worship halls and the former practices of the temple.

Today the Dongyue Temple is a good example of historical restoration and is an important cultural and tourist site in the Chaoyang district in the eastern section of the city—a district that has developed rapidly since the 1980s. A center for government offices, international businesses, foreign embassies, and the Western community, the Chaoyang district has a forest of gleaming skyscrapers and boulevards that seem sleeker and more prosperous than elsewhere in the city. Income from such enterprises has no doubt allowed the district to undertake cultural projects. The Dongyue Temple itself is an oasis of calm, but its original layout is marred by a busy four-lane street that separates its impressive signature green-glazed entrance arch, or *pailou*, from the rest of the temple. Figure 45, a photograph taken about 1913, shows a water-carrier, barebacked and with queue, approaching the famous *pailou* to cross through the cluttered southern entrance to the temple complex. At the same location today, the elegant *pailou* has been preserved on a grand plaza. The restoration of only the central structures of the temple was the subject of local controversy; the plan excluded the entire western section of the original temple complex, with additional shrines, and which more recently has housed shops and residences. (See Figure 46.)

The temple is not actually a religious center. No priests live or practice there, and no formal religious ceremonies are performed. The lively festivals and markets of the past have been reduced to a single event on the lunar new year, and the government tries to restrict organized religious activity. Yet ordinary people, young and old, do come to the temple to burn incense and pray for good results on exams, settlement of debts, good health, or even redress from wrongful accusations—a very practical "full-service" temple. Ancient stone tablets, dug out from under the pavement laid down by the Public Security Academy, stand as a grand testament to the history of the temple. And a Beijing Folklore Museum has been established in the rear halls with exhibitions about Beijing's past commerce, handicrafts, and other nonreligious practices. The museum also sponsors dance and acrobatic performances, and community activities, some involving children.

By contrast, other temples have had different experiences. Baiyunguan (White Cloud Temple), to the west of the old Inner City wall, is the most important Daoist temple that still functions as a religious center and is the seat of the Chinese Daoist Association and the Quanzhen school of Daoist practice. Monks live and work at the temple, and adherents are said to have more spiritual interests than the practical-minded worshippers at Dongyue Temple. At Baiyun Temple monks pray for longevity; at Dongyue Temple ordinary people pray for good grades or good fortune. Guanghua Temple, located in the Bell and Drum towers section of the city, is an example of a functioning Buddhist temple that still holds ceremonies on the first and fifteenth of each lunar month. On these occasions, the temple is open to the public all day. Lay members of the Buddhist association assist the monks in the ceremonies. Worshippers—predominantly, but not exclusively, women of middle age or older—chant the simple "A-mi-to-fo" central to popular Buddhist worship. All, even the younger worshippers, turn off their cell phones. At noon, a lunch of vegetables and a very large *mantou* (steamed bread) is served to hundreds. At the door, the Buddhist association gives out simple tracts explaining how Buddhism can bring calm and peace to believers. Other, smaller temples serve more earthly functions. At the Xianliang Temple (Xianliangsi), operated in part by a girls' school, there is a dispensary of Tongrentang, the famous Chinese medicine store. Medical personnel, patients, students, and tourists mingle in a rear courtyard. At Baoguosi, a Buddhist temple, a lively market takes place several days a week. More a flea market than a traditional market, it is a place where one can buy funky radios from the 1950s and Cultural Revolution memorabilia.

The Lidai Diwang miao, or Temple of Ancient Monarchs, restored and opened to the public in 2004, is a flashy example of imperial religion transmogrified into nationalist "kitsch." This large temple complex was established by the Ming emperors, and expanded by the Qing, for the purpose of venerating an orthodox line of Chinese emperors and eminent ministers and generals. By the Qianlong period there were 188 emperors and 80 eminent ministers and generals enshrined. With the departure of Puyi from the Forbidden City and the death of Sun Yat-sen, the temple was no longer used for imperial ceremonies. After 1931 it was used as a school, and in 1972 it became Beijing's Middle School No. 159. During the Cultural Revolution its cultural relics were seriously damaged. Finally in 2001 the Beijing city government and Xicheng district combined to relocate the school and restore the temple. An association for the preservation, utilization, and promotion of the temple was established in 2003, supported in part by the Xicheng district's overseas Chinese committee. Local contributions, as well as those from Taiwan and Hong Kong Chinese, supplemented government funding. Twice a year the temple enacts a major ceremony. In fall 2005 an ancestral ceremony was staged, with a procession headed by the "emperor" and his court, followed by representatives of several families from Hong Kong, clothed in ornately decorated and brightly colored satin jackets, paying tribute to their ancestors. (See Figure 47.) Historical museums occupy the buildings on the left and right side of the central courtyard. Dedicated to state religious ceremonies in the past, the Lidai Diwang miao seems now to be dedicated to fostering Chinese nationalism among overseas, Hong Kong, and Taiwan Chinese.

The Old City and Cultural Preservation

The preservation of historical monuments—or "cultural relics" in official terminology—takes place in isolation from their spatial and environmental context. The historic city that formed the context for these palaces and museums has largely disappeared. During the late 1990s and 2000s, controversy focused on the destruction of traditional neighborhoods, with their characteristic courtyard houses. The *hutong* and the courtyard houses (*siheyuan*) were the quintessential form of social organization in Beijing. Although after 1949 most Beijing residents eventually lived in the apartments set up by their work units, the *hutong* way of life represented the old Beijing and old local families (those who lived in the city before 1949). In "Old Beijing," through the Republican period, the *siheyuan* provided privacy for a large family and its servants in different chambers on four sides and a central courtyard that provided light, trees, perhaps a garden, and a common space. It signified a leisurely way of life hidden behind walls that yet permitted the small street life of peddlers and neighborly interactions. In the late twentieth century these houses and alleys deteriorated, and each dwelling was subdivided into smaller and smaller units that together housed perhaps ten or more families. Without modern plumbing and heating, such dwellings might in other contexts be described as slums, but because of their architectural charm and intimacy, living in a *hutong* was still a good way of life for many.

In the 1990s public distress about the destruction of *hutong* mounted. Although illegal demolition seldom reached the press, a network of protest developed. Fang Ke, a student of Wu Liangyong, respected Qinghua professor of architecture, undertook an investigation of *hutong* destruction. His book offered detailed documentation of the extent of demolition. Modestly published in 2000, it received wide circulation among intellectuals. In 2003 Wang Jun, a journalist, published *Chengji* (Record of a City), which was elaborately illustrated with photographs and sketches. It became an instant sensation and was reprinted several times. It not only focused attention on "what might have been" if Liang Sicheng's plan for Beijing had been heeded by party leaders in 1950, but it opened the eyes of a younger generation who had never seen the Old Beijing with its gates and walls, or lived in a courtyard house. When Wang lectured at Beijing University to an overflow audience, students—mostly from other parts of China—listened with rapt attention. Together with historical geographers, such as Beijing University's Yue Shengyang, Wang documented the disappearance of the Old Beijing and what he called the "War between the New and Old Cities."

In response to mounting criticism and its own misgivings, the Beijing municipal government in 2002 enacted regulations for the conservation of twenty-five historic districts in the Old City.[7] The concept of a spatially specific "Old City" (Jiucheng) replaced the earlier cultural notion of "Old Beijing." The Old City was in fact the Inner and Outer Cities of the Qing era. The new regulations for the Old City stipulated that the Second Ring Road, which followed the location of the old city wall, be a boundary around which a green belt would be maintained, and within which land use would be restricted, the height of structures regulated, their roofs slanted at the correct angle, and unobstructed views across the main axes of the ancient city preserved. In the old Imperial City, some modern structures that did not conform to the palace style would be demolished. The revival of traditional temples, stores (such as the Tongrentang), and folk customs and entertainment (such as Beijing opera and acrobatics) was encouraged, with a view toward tourism as well as entertaining the local population. A well known native-place lodge, the Huguang huiguan, where the Nationalist Party (Guomindang) had been founded in 1912, became a museum and site of Beijing opera performances.[8]

The twenty-five districts to be protected include fourteen within the old Imperial City (such as the Jingshan district and the Xihuamen district) and seven in the rest of the Inner City (outside the Imperial City but within the Inner City Wall, such as Fuchengmennei streeet or the Dongsi district). Four others (such as Dashalar and Liulichang) were in the Outer City. Within each of the twenty-five districts, the physical condition and architectural and historical value of buildings were to be assessed; some would be maintained and upgraded, and others would be torn down, including high-rise buildings. Regulations about construction and utilities were detailed for guidance in updating structures. Maintaining greenery within the districts was given a high priority. Roads should be widened as needed but with limits. The twenty-five districts contained 285,000 people; this overcrowding was to be alleviated by moving families to new parts of the city, with adequate compensation. Studies and plans for each district were made, and some were assigned to universities or architectural firms.

The conservation of twenty-five historic districts did not focus on the *hutong* per se but on maintaining and improving the overall historic appearance of these areas. The idea was to restore them to some semblance of an idealized past, not to maintain their current appearance at all costs. In fact, the plan specifically authorized the removal of 41 percent of the total population. The neighborhoods covered by the new rules constituted 17 percent of the entire old city, but coupled with the 200 buildings already registered as cultural heritage sites, the commission stated that the total controlled space was 38 percent of the Old City. In interviews, however, reporter Ian Johnson discovered that with all the exceptions and qualifications, the actual percentage of buildings that fell under protection was only 13 percent of the Old City.[9] Although the pace of demolition in Beijing did decline somewhat after the issuance of the regulations, there continued to be constant violations of the meticulous rules and very little enforcement.

Public anger about the ruthless destruction of the Old City mounted. The construction of Peace Boulevard (Ping'an dajie), a six-lane west to east roadway north of the Beihai, generated huge controversy because it cut a wide swath through historic buildings and many residences. Another even wider eight-lane boulevard paralleled this road in the southern part of the Old City (the former

Outer City) at the Zhushikou district (Guang'anmen dajie).[10] There were blatant violations of the rules about the height of buildings, the green zone, and clear sight lines. Classic views, such as the Bell Tower and Drum towers from the Back Lakes, were marred by skyscrapers. (See Figure 2.)

In the 1990s several activists formed a group to identify places that were being torn down illegally and raise public protest. Led by He Shuzhong, an energetic and idealistic preservationist, the Beijing Cultural Heritage Protection Center used several methods to expose such violations, focusing on those actions after 2002 that were in clear violation of the government's own regulations about conservation of the Old City. The center had a website that reported such news quickly, and a telephone hotline on which people could phone in violations that they spotted; and they staged polite public protests. The website was closed several times, and only in 2003 did the center receive official approval to become a nongovernmental organization (NGO). It is very difficult to achieve this status in China, and the few NGOs that exist are still subject to inspections and other forms of scrutiny. Despite its vulnerability and inadequate resources, the center has achieved modest success in bringing violations to the attention of the public. In 2004 when a Ming dynasty granary in the Dongsi shitiao area was about to be bulldozed for the construction of two high-rise apartment buildings, the center mobilized secondary school students in the neighborhood to stage a protest at the worksite. Under public pressure, the real estate developers decided to spare the granary buildings. Taking advantage of the situation, they named the structure the South New Granary International Towers and used the granary itself as the sales office for the apartments.

Such small victories, however, cannot stem the overwhelming tide. The Old City in its characteristic form has disappeared. What remains are pockets of preservation, with extremely high property values that have already driven out the previous residents and attract only wealthy Chinese and foreign clients. If the *hutong* represented not just an architectural design but also a way of life of ordinary Beijingren, the latter is disappearing almost without a trace. Lacking adequate plumbing, electricity, and heating, the *hutong* were not comfortable places for their crowded residents, and new high-rise housing on the outskirts of the city provides more space and convenience for those who have the means to move. In their place *hutong* are now becoming enclaves of commodified cultural heritage and "gentrification."

A couple of notable projects have attempted to preserve the character of courtyard housing, but with new construction. The Ju'er *hutong* project in the area of the Bell and Drum towers was designed by Qinghua University professor Wu Liangyong and his students. The plan involved two-storey apartment buildings built around courtyards. The local street life, including a small hotel, restaurants, bars, as well as traditional shops, was part of the project. Its objective was to design "a standard courtyard house unit that achieves an ideal balance of sunshine, ventilation, lighting and other environmental conditions on the one hand, and an intense use of land . . . on the other."[11] The Ju'er *hutong* project met these objectives admirably. Nevertheless, it received criticism for not being in the true one-storey Beijing style but rather a transplant of the Jiangnan, or southern, style of housing. Over the years, the older residents have been displaced by upwardly mobile professionals, including quite a few foreign tenants, who consider it a nice place to live.

The renovation of the historic Nanchizi district, just outside the southeast wall of the Forbidden City, generated huge controversy in 2002. Too many buildings that could have been restored were unnecessarily torn down, and families were evacuated without adequate compensation. (After Wang Jun made a confidential report to state authorities, the process of destruction was halted.) In their place new buildings in the old style were erected, some with two stories and underground swimming pools and Jacuzzis. An underground parking garage alleviated congestion. Such showcase homes were sold to wealthy customers from outside Beijing, reportedly at huge prices. Most of the controversy over the *hutong* has addressed either the disappearance of the Old City in physical terms or the plight of the displaced. Few or none have discussed the phenomenon of *hutong* gentrification, which is the inevitable and perhaps desirable consequence of maintaining one-storey housing in prime real estate districts. Only the very wealthy can afford this. The *Wall Street Journal* reported in 2005 that Rupert Murdoch and other Western tycoons were seeking to purchase courtyard houses, which they planned to renovate with swimming pools, game rooms, satellite dishes, and underground garages.[12]

In some districts the preservation of *hutong* has clearly been seen as good for tourism as well as real estate speculation. Courtyard homes around the Houhai (Back Lake) district were maintained by wealthy and sometimes high-ranking Chinese as well as a few foreigners. "Jimmy Jing," a banner descendant, and his family, have cleverly turned their courtyard home into a bed and breakfast. (See Figure 48.) The more impressive traditional homes, now with two-car garages, are sometimes used as settings for television commercials or movies. An idealized, prosperous Chinese family—grandparents, parents, and young child—poses in front of their beautiful home; but actually they are actors shooting a commercial for powdered milk. (See Figure 49.) Like the "gentrification" of Nanchizi, these showcase examples hardly address the overall problem of the disappearance of the distinctive characteristics of "Old Beijing." They are another example of the commodification of the past, which to many is not the same as historical or cultural preservation.

History for Sale

The preservation of historical and cultural relics, while necessary and welcome, has also raised many troubling issues. The Yuanmingyuan—the old Summer Palace—embodies most of the dilemmas in historical restoration. Repeatedly robbed of its artifacts by both foreigners and Chinese, the Yuanmingyuan grounds had been used as farmland and housed villages of farmers. After 1949 Zhou Enlai proposed that it be restored for public use, but instead, over the years, fifteen work units were located there and an estimated 270 families lived on the grounds.[13] After the Cultural Revolution, discussions resumed about the fate of Yuanmingyuan. Many, including Mayor Chen Xitong, wished to develop the extensive area into a tourist site, while others—scholars and preservationists—advocated preservation rather than restoration. In 1988 the European ruins and the Fuhai Lake area were opened to the public, but in the 1990s the other gardens were developed into a recreational park, with its large lakes available for boating, children's amusement, restaurants, and the like. The European ruins, so historically distinctive and so often photographed, became a subsection of Yuanmingyuan, with an additional entrance fee. (See Figure 50.) Many local people—especially from Beijing and Qinghua universities, which are adjacent to the grounds—felt that Yuanmingyuan had been downgraded from an overgrown, but magical, historical site into just an ordinary park; it was made too beautiful and lost its value as a historical artifact.

In 2005 a major scandal erupted over environmental violations by the Yuanmingyuan authorities. They needed to purchase water annually to replenish the large lakes because natural sources of water were retained upstream. Around 2004 they decided to line the lake bottoms with plastic so that water would not drain out naturally. When this project was exposed, both the public and the specialists in the Haidian district were scandalized. Such an extensive project threatened the district's natural drainage system and water table and denied adequate underground water to the trees, plants, and grass in the Yuanmingyuan itself. In April the Environmental Protection Bureau conducted a public hearing that included experts from many fields as well as various local groups. The vast majority concluded that the project should be terminated, but there was much resistance from other quarters. Both the national and city cultural relics bureaus denied ever having approved the project. The two major companies engaged in the lining of the lake bottom were both run by former officials of the Haidian district government, and there was a widespread perception of private interest and bureaucratic corruption. In August work began to remove the lake lining, and in September the Beijing Water Conservancy Bureau approved the diversion of two million tons of water from the Miyun Reservoir, north of Beijing city, to the Yuanmingyuan.

Many historians, archaeologists, and other specialists believe that the protection of cultural properties should be limited to preservation (*baohu*) and should not extend to restoration (*xiushan*). They argue that the beautification of the Forbidden City or the old temples destroys their essential *historical* character. There are those who feel that most of the restoration projects have been botched and serve the purpose of tourism and commerce, not culture and history. The Yongding Gate—the southernmost gate on the main axis leading to the Forbidden City, torn down in 1950—was rebuilt in 2004, but critics say that it is not a good copy. The term "fake antique" (*jia gudong*) is frequently used by experts. The question of authenticity is not easily answered. Is it wrong to re-create a structure that has already been demolished? Should buildings still standing be restored to their appearance at the time of their original construction, or should they be preserved only to the extent that they will not be irreparably damaged? For palaces and temples with centuries and layers of history, to which era should they be restored? Or should they look as they did in the early twentieth century—worn and faded, but distinctly recognizable? Should they look new or old or merely familiar? Which is more "authentic"? The China Heritage Fund had the resources and opportunity to rebuild the Palace of Established Happiness (Jianfugong) to be as close as possible to what it was at the time of its original construction in 1740, but others regard such exacting detail and lavish decoration as excessive. Many fear that the Olympics has only encouraged the ahistorical beautification of historical sites at the expense of authenticity. When the Chinese Olympic Planning Committee went to Athens, they said it was a shame that the Greek authorities had not fixed up the Acropolis to look nicer. Another rumor is that someone once suggested that the Hall of Supreme Harmony, the central palace in the Forbidden City, would make a splendid five-star hotel.

The commodification of history has become a major trend throughout China, but Beijing presents the greatest of opportunities. At the Yuanmingyuan, plans to reconstruct the European ruins have been resisted, but in Zhuhai, in Guangdong Province, a miniature Yuanmingyuan has in fact been a great tourist attraction and a huge financial success. Liulichang presents a conspicuous example of commodification. On the top ten list of tourist attractions in Beijing, Liulichang is the street where Chinese paintings, porcelains, and rare books are sold, and also a place where one can buy souvenirs, have a seal carved, or have a painting mounted or framed. But the Liulichang that one sees today is a 1980s re-creation of the Liulichang of the past, which evolved from a Yuan dynasty tile workshop and a supplier of materials for the construction of the Ming Imperial Palace. It was reconstructed in the early 1980s under the direction of the Beijing Cultural Relics Bureau for the purpose of attracting tourists. Although it has succeeded admirably in that regard, architects and scholars have denounced the project for its extravagant use of color, its mixture of architectural styles, its disregard of the surrounding neighborhoods, and its lack of "authenticity." To them Liulichang is an example of the destruction of any physical vestige of the past in order to construct an imagined ideal of "old Beijing."[14]

While projects such as Liulichang have been strongly motivated by profit opportunities, historical preservation serves an even larger purpose: the glorification of Chinese nationalism. The 2008 Olympics also serves this purpose. Beijing will be a showcase for the modern Chinese nation, and it will be a museum of China's magnificent past. The use of history for current purposes is not unusual in China or elsewhere, and Chinese rulers, both past and present, have developed the practice into a finely honed skill. The identification of history and nation with a single city over such a long and continuous period of time is, however, matched by only a few other world capitals.

Other historic world capitals have evolved different relationships with their pasts. In European cities, such as Vienna, Prague, or London, modern structures have blended more comfortably around older structures in part because the older structures, dating from the fifteenth to nineteenth centuries, are constructed of stone or brick and are less vulnerable to deterioration. More important, the pace of change was incremental; structures added in the nineteenth or twentieth centuries were modern at the time, but were of a scale that did not violate the proportions of the older structures. Taller buildings built since World War II generally have been relegated to the outskirts or confined to particular sections.

The scale of all European cities, in any case, is much smaller than that of modern Beijing.

In modern Istanbul, the appearance and atmosphere of the old Constantinople have been well preserved, while the city thrives as a bustling port and metropolis. Its incomparable location overlooking the Bosporus, and its iconic monuments—the Aya Sofya and the Blue Mosque—still serve to link the city with its many layers of Byzantine and Ottoman history. The modern city grows on the eastern side of the Bosporus, but it is no longer a capital. Unlike the Chinese capital, which moved to Nanjing in 1927 but returned to Beijing two decades later, the Turkish capital moved permanently to Ankara in central Turkey in 1923, when the Turkish Republic was founded.

In Japan, Tokyo was largely destroyed in the 1923 earthquake and leveled again by U.S. bombing at the end of World War II, and hence it is an almost entirely modern city. In any case, Tokyo (Edo) was established as the shogunal capital only in the seventeenth century, and Japan's truly ancient historical monuments—the great temples of the seventh century and later—are located in Kyoto and Nara, the sites of imperial capitals before 1868. Although they are, like Chinese temples, constructed of wood, Japan's Buddhist temples have been well preserved and maintained, and its most important Shinto shrines at Ise and Izumo have been periodically reconstructed and repaired.

Only Paris experienced a controversy over urban renovation comparable to the one that Beijing faces today. What tourists perceive as the quintessential Paris with its boulevards, parks, and monuments is in fact a mid-nineteenth-century creation designed by one visionary planner: Georges-Eugène Haussmann, who was commissioned by Napoléon III to design a new city that would reflect France's greatness and overcome the problems of squalor and overcrowding that characterized the old city. The broad boulevards were intended also to facilitate the transport of soldiers into the city to quell local insurrection. The project, which entailed the rapid destruction of most of the medieval city, met loud opposition. The Eiffel Tower, erected later for the Paris Exhibition of 1889, also was widely protested as a monstrous desecration of the city's architectural unity.

Today, few would deny that Paris is one of the world's most beautiful and charming cities, and the innovations so hated in Haussmann's time are now treasured. Could it be that in the coming century the new Beijing that now seems so unattractive will be seen as beautiful? Judging by today's attitudes, it would be difficult to predict such an outcome despite the glowing futuristic displays at the city planning museum. Beijing's city planning and design have not been the product of one vision, as in the past, but the dizzying outcome of contending political and economic forces. Twenty-first-century Beijing will never be a Paris.

But no other city could have Beijing's past and present. Throughout its history, Beijing has remade itself several times, but in the thousand-year progression from the Liao through the Jin, Yuan, Ming, and Qing dynasties (916–1912), the fundamental imperial capital design varied only in its size and particular location. When the Communist leaders chose Beijing as their capital in 1949, they set in motion an essential contradiction by using the city to legitimize not another dynasty, but a new and revolutionary regime. Soviet-style architecture served as the model for the ten great constructions and other public buildings of the 1950s, while Maoist grandiosity and the requirements of modernization dictated the dismantling of the city wall and most of its gates. Yet throughout the Mao years, the Forbidden City, Zhongnanhai, and Tiananmen—once symbols of imperial rule—maintained, and even increased, their importance as the focus of the party's power. In the 1980s Tiananmen Square, where the people had paraded in front of Mao, became a place where the people contested the power of the party leaders, and Tiananmen thus acquired yet another layer of meaning.

Since the 1980s, however, market economics and globalization have had an even greater impact on the city plan and its coherence. With the stimulus and opportunities created by the Olympics, Beijing is acquiring an international look full of skyscrapers and futuristic designs. The CCTV building has excited such attention that New York's Museum of Modern Art mounted an exhibition of its design in the fall of 2006, well before the scheduled completion of the building. It is this international look that Beijing wishes to project and that the younger generation embraces. The older generation, who remember the 1950s as a golden era, may regret that new commercial structures seem to overshadow the Great Hall of the People and other public monuments of the socialist past, just as the previous generation may have regretted the sacrifice of the city walls to socialist construction and modern transportation. Memories and tastes change. What was once regarded as ugly and stolid (Soviet-style architecture) may now be respected as symbolic of an earlier, more hopeful, era. What today seems monstrous or laughable (the three-egg complex at Xizhi Gate) may some day appear as an emblem of the early twenty-first century.

Through a millennium of change, Beijing has constantly drawn to itself outsiders and visitors, foreign and domestic, attracted by its political importance and centrality. Repression and control also have been constant forces; the city has been both open and closed. At the outset of the twenty-first century, however,

Beijing's attraction is stronger than ever. It is not tributary envoys or scholar-officials who come to the capital, but business people, intellectuals, and artists. The mutually dependent relationship between government and intellectuals, so troubled in the past, now shows its more positive side through increased support of higher education and research, and a more liberal policy toward artists and writers. The relationship between government and business, also so vexed in the past, is more synergistic than antagonistic at present, despite the collusion and corruption that are sometimes the underside of this synergy. An international city with an international look has produced, and will continue to demand, a degree of openness far beyond what has been experienced in the past.

Beijing has grown out of its historically familiar architectural space. Museums, monuments, and preserved areas serve as the physical embodiments of the past. But the city's present links to its history are not just architectural or spatial, and in the future, its identity will be framed less by a physical space and more by cultural, social, and economic developments.[15] Beijing will continue, nevertheless, to be a museum of the past and a showcase for the present as well as a highly visible national and international stage upon which many dramas will be enacted. The sleek, albeit crowded and polluted, twenty-first century Beijing *is* a different city from the imperial capital of the past, but its dynamism, as well as its contradictions, will continue beyond the Olympics and well into the future.

Notes

Chapter 1

1. *Cambridge History* 6:16–17; Farmer, 125.
2. Boyd, 62–3; Steinhardt, *Chinese Imperial City Planning,* 1–28.
3. *Cambridge History* 6:63–79.
4. *Beijing tongshi,* 3:90–92.
5. Jagchid, 79–80.
6. *Beijing tongshi,* 3:229–34; Naquin, *Peking,* 116–17.
7. *Beijing tongshi,* 3:66–69, 90, 229, 234, 245–54; Crump, 26; Wittfogel and Feng, 44–45, 79; *Cambridge History* 6: 43–153; Storey, 13.
8. Farmer, 125.
9. *Beijing tongshi,* 4:49–57, 223, 269–70; Steinhardt, *Chinese Imperial City Planning,* 130–36.
10. 225,000 households: *Cambridge History* 6:279; routes for transport: *Cambridge History* 6:297.
11. Kates, *HJAS* 7:3 (1942–43); *Cambridge History* 6:312–13; Naquin, *Peking,* 116.
12. 53 million: *Cambridge History,* 6:40, 278–80; culture: *Cambridge History* 6:313; Bush, 103; Naquin, *Peking,* 116.
13. Valued Chinese higher culture: Bush, 103–12; intermarriage, assimilation: *Cambridge History* 6:40, 281–83; Rawski, 7, 295; comparison to Liao: *Cambridge History* 6:40.
14. *Beijing tongshi,* 4:243, 371; *Cambridge History* 6:300–1.
15. Bush: 103–12; *Beijing tongshi,* 4:237, 294–95; *Cambridge History* 6:309–10; Crump, 24–30, 177–83; Dolby, 19–31.
16. A contemporary nomad-founded state located partly in northwest China, the Xi Xia (Tangut) empire (ca. 982–1227), also fell to the Mongols. (*Cambridge History* 6:154)
17. Rachewiltz, 189–216; *Cambridge History* 6:375–81; Naquin, *Peking,* 115.
18. *Cambridge History* 6:278, 620–21.
19. Camp near Zhongdu ruins: Farmer, 125; foundation of Dadu: Steinhardt, "Plan of Khubilai's Imperial City."
20. Steinhardt, "Plan of Khubilai's Imperial City," 137, 148.
21. Strength of the Chinese: Hok-lam Chan, *Toung Pao,* 123; native land: *Cambridge History* 6: 454–57; identify more closely: Rossabi, 131; appeal to audiences: *Cambridge History,* 6:472.
22. The simplified description of Dadu and its design presented here is based on the comprehensive work of Nancy Steinhardt.

23. *Cambridge History* 6:642; Steinhardt, *Chinese Imperial City Planning,* 154–55.

24. Because of the demands of water supply, the marker actually was not at the absolute center. The eastern wall was closer to the center than the western (Steinhardt, *Chinese Imperial City Planning,* 158–59). The marker was engraved with the words *zhongxin zhi tai,* "center marker."

25. Steinhardt, "Plan of Khubilai's Imperial City," 137–47.

26. Mongol camp: Elliott 102–5; close to herds: Wood, 83.

27. Steinhardt, *Chinese Imperial City Planning,* 130, 142–43.

28. Steinhardt, "Plan of Khubilai's Imperial City," 147–51; Steinhardt, *Chinese Imperial City Planning,* 130, 158.

29. Steinhardt, "Plan of Khubilai's Imperial City," 152–53; Rossabi, 28–30, 131–32.

30. Hok-lam Chan, *Toung Pao,* 134; Rossabi, 67; Steinhardt, *Chinese Imperial City Planning,* 153.

31. Learned Persians: *Cambridge History* 6:642; architect and artisans: Rossabi, 132, 135; Steinhardt, "Plan of Khubilai's Imperial City," 152, n33–34.

32. Rossabi, 133.

33. Observatory: Rossabi, 133; population: Hou, ed., 290 (varying between 418,000 in 1270 and 952,000 in 1327); *Cambridge History* 6:657 (not more than 500,000).

34. Naquin, *Peking,* 6–10; *Cambridge History,* 6:646.

35. Steinhardt, *Chinese Imperial City Planning,* 132–33.

36. By proxy: Rossabi, 134; half of each year: Rossabi, 133; *Cambridge History* 6:455–56; Steinhardt, "Plan of Khubilai's Imperial City," 154, n38; respite: Rossabi, 135.

37. *Beijing tongshi,* 4:271; Wood; Haeger.

38. Paper money: *Cambridge History* 6:299–301, 449; luxury: *Jiujing daguan,* 240; *Cambridge History* 6:561–62.

39. Presence: Mote, "Transformation of Nanking," 104, 138; security: Naquin, *Peking,* 10.

40. Population: Gernet, *Daily Life,* 28; Marco Polo: Polo (Moule-Pelliot); Wood, 84–88; 150.

41. Naquin, *Peking,* 53, 115.

42. Masterpieces: Crump, 24–30, 177–96; Dolby, 32–59; growth of publishing and literacy: *Cambridge History* 6:267–68; Brokaw and Chow, eds., 152–83.

43. Economic crisis: Tsai, 32; minor damage, some returned: Naquin, *Peking,* 119.

44. Farmer, 24, 136, 191.

45. Southern families: Naquin, *Peking,* 120–21; Farmer, 149; military population rose: *Cambridge History* 7:247.

46. Naquin, *Peking,* 120.

47. Gate names: Farmer, 126–27; large-scale by 1406: Tsai, 125; reached imperial, main city walls: *Jiujing daguan,* 14; some tried to escape: Tsai, 126–28; Geiss, 66–67; Annamese conscripts: Farmer, 130.

48. Farmer, 121.

49. Tsai, 127; *Cambridge History* 7:241.

50. Tsai, 127.

51. Farmer, 128.

52. Farmer, 127–28; Geiss, 69.

53. *Jiujing daguan,* 11–17.

54. Naquin, *Peking,* 113; Boyd, 64.

55. *Cambridge History* 7:240, 243; Naquin, *Peking,* 134; Farmer, 127–28.

56. *Cambridge History* 6:642; *Cambridge History* 7:244.

57. Population: Hou, ed., 290; became a magnet, *langfang* compounds: Geiss 50, 64, 70; state-sponsored hereditary craftsmen, Gernet, *Chinese Civilization*, 412–13.

58. *Beijing de hutong*, 69; Steinhardt, *Chinese Imperial City Planning*, 154–55.

59. Number of *hutong: Beijing de hutong*, 12, see also *Beijing tongshi*, 6:83, Dong, 74; Ming and Qing descriptions include Zhang Jue, *Jingshi Wucheng fangxiang hutong ji*, 1560; Yu Minzhong, *Rixia jiuwen kao*, 1785; Ju Yixin, *Jingshi fangxiang zhi* (?1900).

60. *Beijing shi*, 290–91; *Jiujing daguan*, 274.

61. *Beijing de hutong*, 15.

62. Laborers: Albert Chan, 135; Muslims: Albert Chan, 139; Geiss, 35.

63. Albert Chan, 123; *Beijing shi*, 166–69; Geiss, 35.

64. Geiss, 42.

65. *Beijing shi*, 168–69; *Beijing tongshi*, 6:82–84, 94–100.

66. Albert Chan, 133; Geiss, 83, 186.

67. *Beijing de hutong*, 25; *Jiujing daguan*, 65–70

68. Worse for walking, veils: Ricci (Trigault, trans.), 310.

69. Naquin, *Peking*, 270; Albert Chan, 132–35; *Jiujing daguan*, 240; Belsky, *JUH* 2000.

70. Albert Chan, 134–35; Geiss, 43.

71. Pauper's market and *neishi:* Geiss, 77–78; Forbidden City: Albert Chan, 134; state regulation: *Beijing tongshi*, 6:469–70.

72. The name of the painting is "Huangdu jisheng tu."

73. *Beijing tongshi*, 6:400ff; Brokaw and Chow, eds., 27–28.

74. Gernet, *Chinese Civilization*, 437.

75. *Bejing shi*, 310–16; Mote, *Imperial China*, 368, 756; Naquin, *Peking*, 274–76; Tun (Bodde, trans.) 1–24, 26–27, 42–43, 64–68.

76. Wares for sale: Geiss, 202; carriages could not turn around: Albert Chan, 131.

77. Albert Chan, 136.

78. *Beijing tongshi*, 6:482; *Beijing shi*, 310–16; Naquin, *Peking*, 274–76.

79. Geiss, 105.

80. *Beijing tongshi*, 6:477 ff; Spence, *Memory Palace*, 218; Naquin, *Peking*, 282–83; Geiss, 141–42, 172; Albert Chan, 141–45.

81. Mote, *Imperial China*, 819, 831.

82. Spence, *Search for Modern China*, 31.

83. Hummel, ed., 358–60; Mote, *Imperial China*, 820.

84. Rawski, 26, 118.

85. *Beijing tongshi*, 4:58.

86. *Beijing tongshi*, 7:219; Elliott, 103.

87. Naquin, *Peking*, 294.

88. Geiss, 23.

89. *Beijing shi*, 253–55.

90. L. S. Yang, 196.

91. Naquin, *Peking*, 300.

92. L. S. Yang, 196.

93. Dray-Novey, "Spatial Order and Police," 902–3.

94. Naquin, *Peking*, 300.

95. Mote, *Imperial China*, 832–33; Rhoads, 60; Rawski, 40–41; Naquin, *Peking*, 287–301.

Chapter 2

1. Crossley, *Translucent Mirror,* 233–35; Rawski, 247–49.
2. Spence, *Search,* 93–95.
3. Zhu, 97–148, 222–47; *Beijing shi,* 220; Steinhardt, *Chinese Imperial City Planning,* 172.
4. Rawski, 31.
5. Shih.
6. *China: The Three Emperors,* 410, no. 83.
7. Literary examples include the three hundred short poems in the ancient *Book of Songs,* the *Analects* of Confucius, and popular novels of many chapters. In visual art, the hand scroll of related paintings that the viewer unrolls sequentially, like the series of portraits of the Yongzheng emperor in different costumes discussed in this chapter, has a similar character. The scrolls recording the imperial birthday processions of 1713 and 1790 (at the end of this chapter) also exemplify episodic forms.
8. Boyd, 73.
9. *China: The Three Emperors,* 57–58.
10. Rawski, 33.
11. *China: The Three Emperors,* 57.
12. Naquin, *Peking,* 355.
13. *Beijing tongshi,* 7:161–62, 168–69.
14. Naquin, *Peking,* 337.
15. *Kangxi shengshi de gushi,* nos. 25–54.
16. *China: The Three Emperors,* 242–45; Hummel, ed., 915–20.
17. *China: The Three Emperors,* nos. 2, 15, 167, 173, 272.
18. Hummel, ed., 371; *China: The Three Emperors,* 272–75; Sullivan.
19. Sirén, 99; Naquin, *Peking,* 332–53.
20. Geiss, 86.
21. Malone, 66; Naquin, *Peking,* 318.
22. *Beijing tongshi.* 7:145.
23. Malone, 59–60; Hummel, ed., 917; Danby, 35–37; Naquin, *Peking,* 72–73.
24. *China: The Three Emperors,* nos. 30, 78.
25. *China: The Three Emperors,* 58–59.
26. Johnston 70, 335–37, 341. On Qianlong's filial devotion, see Kahn.
27. *Yuanmingyuan sishi jingshi* (Forty scenic spots, each with a poem composed by the emperor) (1745). In addition, twenty copper engravings preserve a memory of the European-style structures at Yuanmingyuan that otherwise would be lost. (Malone, 141ff).
28. Sirén, 126–27; Danby, 77–78.
29. Sirén; 125–37; Malone, 134ff; Danby, 68ff.
30. Danby, 76.
31. Sirén, 136.
32. Macartney, 271.
33. Malone, 141.
34. Sirén, 128.
35. Malone, 65, from introduction to *You zhi yuanmingyuan tu yong.*
36. The Garden of Long Spring, adjacent to Yuanmingyuan on the east, was distinct from the earlier Garden of Joyful Springtime. (*Chang* is written with a different character and pronounced in a different tone.) The Jingyiyuan garden was located

at Xiangshan, the Qiqunyuan adjacent to Yuanmingyuan on the southeast, the Chingyiyuan at Wanshoushan.

37. The Yiheyuan (Wanshoushan), built from 1886 to 1991. After 1860 Yuanmingyuan became as famous in successive phases of ruin as it had been as a summer palace in the eighteenth century.
38. Rawski, 146.
39. *Kangxi shengshi de gushi*, nos. 25–54; Kahn; Hummel, ed., 330–31, 372.
40. Ming palace eunuchs: Rawski, 163; Imperial Household Department supervised more than European royal courts: Rawski, 181.
41. Rawski, 166–67.
42. Spence, *Emperor of China*, 46–47.
43. Rawski, 165.
44. Zhu, 120.
45. Rawski, 163–64.
46. Spence, *Emperor of China*, 122; Elliott, 363.
47. Nicholas Wade.
48. Maidservants: Kovalevsky, II:42–43 (Dray, trans., 66); gossip: Kovalevsky, II:33–45 (Dray, trans., 64–66).
49. *Kangxi shengshi de gushi*, nos. 14–16.
50. Rawski, 171 ff.
51. Zhu, 121–33.
52. Spence, *Emperor of China*, 123.
53. *Guochao gong shi* KX 20/1/6 and 21/7/8; cited in Rawski, 193.
54. Rawski, 192–94.
55. *China: The Three Emperors*, 55.
56. Aisin Gioro Puyi, 49.
57. Cheng Qinhua, 47.
58. *Kangxi shengshi de gushi*, nos. 159–61.
59. Cheng Qinhua, 36–38; Rawski, 48.
60. Albert Chan, 134.
61. Rawski, 183.
62. Naquin, *Peking*, 306–8; *Kangxi shengshi de gushi*, nos. 164–85.
63. *Jinwu shili* 5.15–25, 7.11–12; Wade, Thomas F., 305.
64. Cheng Qinhua, 73.
65. *Jinwu shili*, 5.10; Thomas F. Wade, 206.
66. Dray-Novey, "Spatial Order and Police," 902.
67. Attiret letter: cited in Sirén, 125; Malone, 136; *China: The Three Emperors*, 242.
68. *China: The Three Emperors*, no. 120.
69. Jan Stuart in *China: The Three Emperors*, 68.
70. Later this development of art for dynastic purposes weakened because the government grew poorer. An echo of the high Qing affinity for realistic representation of the ruler occurred a century or more later, when the court embraced photography. (See Figure 6.)
71. *Wanshou shengdian* (1718) and later copies; Beurdeley and Beurdeley; Naquin, *Peking*, 349–51; *China: The Three Emperors*, nos. 24–25.
72. Ripa, 99–100.
73. Naquin, *Peking*, 349–51; *Kangxi shengshi de gushi*, nos.190–262; Dray–Novey, "Spatial Order and Police," 906.
74. Owen, preface to Waley; Keightley.

75. Qianlong left from Yuanmingyuan rather than Changchunyuan, and he entered the Forbidden City at the Xihua (western) rather than the Shenwu (northern) Gate.
76. *Qing neiwufu cang jingcheng quantu;* Dray-Novey, "Spatial Order and Police," 906.
77. This map, engraved on copper by Matteo Ripa, was reproduced in Europe in the 1730s. Earlier Ripa at Kangxi's request had made copper engravings of thirty-six views of the imperial retreat at Rehe. Later twenty copper engravings by Jesuits showed European structures at Yuanmingyuan. (Mungello, 61; Malone, 141.)
78. Du Jiang, Guo Chengkang, Liu Yuwen (all 1993): cited in Hevia, *Cherishing Men from Afar,* 242.

Chapter 3

1. Population: Han, 120; Naquin, *Peking,* 6.
2. Zhu (138) suggests that the Imperial City was a "wide buffer zone, an insulation gap."
3. Prohibitions: *Beijing tongshi,* 7:122–27; dominance of throne: Naquin, *Peking,* 410–28.
4. Elliott, 101.
5. Language, clothing, gestures: Rhoads, 60–63; language: Wadley; publishing: Brokaw and Chow, eds., 27–28.
6. Locations of banners: *Beijing tongshi,* 7: 217–22; most desirable: Naquin, *Peking,* 373; gates: *Jinwu shili,* 2.48–52; Brunnert and Hagelstrom, no. 801; Thomas F. Wade, 392, 394; Dray-Novey, "Spatial Order and Police," 910.
7. Elliott, 33–71; *Beijing tongshi,* 7: 139–45.
8. Kovalevsky, I:139, 147–49 (Dray, trans., 55, 59–60); Naquin, *Peking,* 572, 580–82; *Beijing shi,* 252.
9. Zhu, 61; Naquin, *Peking,* 397–98.
10. *Beijing tongshi,* 7:219, 222–23; Naquin, *Peking,* 375.
11. Land supports stipends: Naquin, *Peking,* 374; nonmilitary occupation: Crossley, *Orphan Warriors,* 54.
12. Naquin, *Peking,* 379–80; *Beijing tongshi,* 7:247–52.
13. *Beijing tongshi,* 7:244–59: Elliott, 305–44; Naquin, *Peking* 375–81.
14. Spence, *Emperor of China,* 124.
15. This section's sketch of the courtyard house is based on the detailed description by Boyd, 77–86, 111–16; Sirén 3–16. Number of *hutong* in Qing era: Dong, 73–74.
16. Boyd, 77–79.
17. *Beijing shi,* 318; Boyd, 82.
18. Mansions: Naquin, *Peking,* 392–94; inheritance of titles: Rawski, 77, 107
19. Boyd, 79.
20. Predominantly male: Barrow, 66; Macartney, 156; Kovalevsky, II:87 (Dray, trans.,72); hair ornaments: Tun (Bodde, trans.), 35.
21. Female dress: Rhoads, 62.
22. Rhoads, 60–62; Kovalevsky, II:5 (Dray, trans., 61–63).
23. Kates, *Years that Were Fat,* 95.
24. Tun (Bodde, trans.), 85.
25. Peddlers: Naquin, *Peking,* 625; ice: Tun (Bodde, trans.), 58; specialized: Swallow, 19–23.
26. Tun (Bodde, trans.), 87.
27. *Beijing tongshi,* 7:372–89; food security: Li and Dray-Novey.
28. Staunton, II:156–57.

29. *Jinwu shili*, 10.29.
30. Barrow, 282
31. Macartney, 158.
32. Zhu, 89.
33. Naquin, *Peking*, 366.
34. Wilson.
35. Cibot, *Mémoires* 8:217–19; on policing patterns, security-related street structures, and equipment, see Dray-Novey, "Spatial Order and Police."
36. Naquin, *Peking*, 19–21.
37. Naquin, *Peking*, 401–6.
38. Naquin, *Peking*, 504–8.
39. 213 temples in Outer City in 1800: Naquin, *Peking*, 423; 1851 census: *Jinwu shili*, 6.15–18; Stove God: Tun (Bodde, trans.), 17, 68, 98.
40. Naquin, *Peking*, 629.
41. *Beijing shi*, 290–291.
42. Zhu, 83–87; *Jinwu shili*, 7.71, 8.55–56, 9.8.
43. Albert Chan, 134; Belsky, *Localities*, 27.
44. *Dumen jilue*, 1875; *Beijing tongshi*, 7:266–68; Belsky, *Localities*, 41–54.
45. Belsky, *Localities*, 58–73, 193–216; Swallow, 80.
46. Kovalevsky, II:206–207 (Dray, trans., 77–78).
47. Brokaw and Chow, eds., 27–28, 175, 322.
48. Kovalevsky, II:7–8 (Dray, trans., 63–64).
49. Belsky, *Localities*, 85–94, 217–35, and "Urban Ecology."
50. Kovalevsky, II:148–49 (Dray, trans., 77).
51. Tun (Bodde, trans.), 116–20.
52. *Beijing tongshi*, 7:343–45; *Beijing shi*, 266–67, 344.
53. The following description of Qing theatrical entertainments is based in part on the work of Zhu (82–83) and Mackerras (92–144).
54. *Beijing shi*, 287–89; Zhu, 82; Kovalevsky, II:87 (Dray, trans., 72).
55. Kovalevsky, II:85 (Dray, trans., 71).
56. *Beijing tongshi*, 7:122.
57. Zhu, 83.
58. *Beijing shi*, 288.
59. Naquin, *Peking*, 282.

Chapter 4

1. Barrow, 61.
2. Barrow, 65
3. Kovalevsky, II:22–23.
4. Kovalevsky, I:145–46 (Dray, trans., 59)
5. Fortune, 350.
6. Fortune, 357.
7. Fortune, 361.
8. Fortune, 362.
9. Rennie, II: 52.
10. Kovalevsky, II: 23.
11. Dennys et al., 499–500.
12. Naquin, *Peking*, 363. Belsky, *Localities*, 64.

13. Naquin, *Peking,* 603–5. Belsky, *Localities,* 42–54, and Chap. 3 generally.
14. Belsky, *Localities,* 60–62, 238–42. Belsky argues that many fail to distinguish between scholar-official and merchant handicraft lodges, and that those who make the distinction underestimate the dominance of the scholar-official lodge in Beijing both before and after 1911.
15. Naquin, *Peking,* Chaps. 8 and 13.
16. *Dumen jilue, juan* 3.
17. *Dumen jilue, juan* 1.
18. Li and Dray-Novey, Table 2, 996, based on Han Guanghui.
19. Elliot, 287. See also Li and Dray-Novey, 1007.
20. Crossley, *Orphan Warriors,* 84–85.
21. Elliott, 288.
22. Rhoads, 50.
23. *Beijing tongshi,* 8:38.
24. Elliott, 313–22, on early poverty: Rhoads, 35; Crossley, *Orphan Warriors,* 147–48.
25. Li and Dray-Novey, on famine relief in Beijing.
26. Ibid. on changing forms of relief.
27. Naquin, *Peking,* 642–43, 667–70.
28. Rennie, II:120–21; Naquin, *Peking,* 660–62.
29. Naquin, *Peking,* 365. Also Naquin, *Millenerian Rebellion,* 176–185.
30. *Beijing tongshi,* 8:21–29.
31. *Beijing tongshi,* 8:21–26.
32. See Lillian M. Li, *Fighting Famine,* Chap. 4, on monetary crisis, and Gabbiani, Chap. 6, on 1850s as a major crisis period.
33. Point made by Gabbiani, 259.
34. Hevia, *Cherishing Men from Afar,* reinterprets the significance of the Macartney mission. The Amherst mission of 1816 reached the capital but was turned away in a misunderstanding over what can only be described as "scheduling."
35. Hevia, *English Lessons,* Chap. 2, gives a clear and detailed account.
36. Quoted in Hevia, *English Lessons,* 48.
37. Malone, 188.
38. Malone, 161.
39. Hevia, *English Lessons,* Chap. 4.
40. Malone, 187–88, quoting Boulger, *Life of Gordon,* 45–46.
41. Based on a discussion of loot in Hevia, *English Lessons.*
42. Rennie, I: 319, 329, 337.
43. Martin, *Cycle of Cathay,* Chaps. 6–7.
44. Thiriez, 19–26.
45. Freeman-Mitford p. xlix.
46. Trevor-Roper.
47. Martin, *Cycle,* 407.
48. *Beijing tongshi,* 8:286–88.
49. *Gudai Beijing,* 112; Smith, II:532.
50. *Beijing tongshi,* 8:332–33, 318–28; *Gudai Beijing,* 112–15.
51. Favier, 189–91, 308–20.
52. *Beijing tongshi,* 8:122–23; Naquin, *Peking,* 582–84.
53. Lutz, 132.
54. *Beijing tongshi,* 8:127–29; Stuart, 49. Lutz, 29–32.

55. *Beijing tongshi,* 8:129.
56. Naquin, *Peking,* 662–67; Lillian M. Li, *Fighting Famine,* Chap. 9.
57. Naquin, *Peking,* 663–64.
58. *Beijing tongshi,* 8:377–88.
59. Naquin, *Peking,* 620; Belsky, "Placing the Hundred Days."
60. Yue Shengyang, 522–28.
61. Belsky, "Placing the Hundred Days."
62. Spence, *Gate of Heavenly Peace,* 2.
63. Belsky, "Placing the Hundred Days," 148.
64. Favier, 306ff. See Bredon, Chap. 5, for a description of the "Sea Palaces" that be-
     came the preferred dwelling place of the empress dowager and site of Guangxu
     emperor's imprisonment. These were later part of the Zhongnanhai complex, the
     residence of warlord presidents and now top party leaders.
65. This account follows Cohen, Chap. 1.
66. Smith, I:239.
67. Harrington, 55–57.
68. Preston, 177–83.
69. Preston, 138; Smith, II:543–44.
70. Preston, 263, 266. Also Harrington, 59.
71. Preston, 271–74.
72. Preston, 162–63.
73. Smith, II:519–20.
74. Harrington, 84, which also has photograph of the destruction of the legations, as
     does Smith, facing II:722.
75. There were even group tours provided in September 1900. Hevia, *English Lessons,*
     260.
76. Hevia, 209.
77. Hevia, 222.
78. Hevia, 235.
79. Martin, *Siege,* 16.
80. This is the premise of Naquin, who ends *Peking* in 1900, not 1911.
81. Smith, II:528.
82. Smith, II:524.
83. *Beijing tongshi,* 8:368–70.
84. Gabbiani, 310–17.
85. Dray-Novey, "Twilight."
86. Quoted in Gabbiani, 375–76 and 364–80 generally.
87. Martin, *Awakening,* 204–5.
88. Gabbiani, 319–22, 384–86.
89. Gabbiani, 309–10, 318–19. Also *Gudai Beijing,* 105–10.
90. Gabbiani, 337–43.
91. *Beijing tongshi,* 8:380–83.
92. Jiujing *"Xingshi huabao,"* for example, on 18, 38, 72, 103, 126, 136.
93. Johnston, 75.
94. Rhoads, Chap. 3. Johnston on Prince Chun and other court intrigues: Chap. 4, es-
     pecially 60–61.
95. Rhoads, Chap. 1, has good background on Manchu-Han differences in this period.
     He argues that the Manchus were equivalent to the banner people, and although the

banners were originally multiethnic, the Manchus should be regarded "not so much an ethnic group as an occupational caste." Also, "the transformation of the Manchus . . . to an ethnic group began during the watershed decade of the late 1890s and early 1900s." (290–91). Crossley, *Orphan Warriors*, argues that this transformation had earlier origins, at the time of the Opium War and Taiping Rebellion (222).

96. Johnston, 335–40.
97. Li and Dray-Novey, Table 2. Data from 1882.
98. Gamble, *Peking: A Social Survey*, 97–99, states that there were about 300,000 Manchus in Beijing and the vicinity, and estimates that they constituted about 20 to 25 percent of the entire population around 1919.
99. Rhoads, 256–70. Also Crossley, *Orphan Warriors*, Conclusion.
100. Naquin, *Peking*, 697.

Chapter 5

1. Rhoads, 232–33.
2. Johnston, especially Chaps. 9 and 16.
3. Nathan, *Peking Politics*, 60.
4. Nathan, "Constitutional Republic." Strand, 8, states that Zhang Zuolin was "military dictator in Beijing 1926–28."
5. Musgrove, 139; and Strand, 10.
6. Gamble, *Peking: A Social Survey*, 29.
7. Shi, 32, 39; and Gamble, *Peking*, 71–73.
8. Shi, 34.
9. Strand, 68–72.
10. Gamble, *Peking*, 75–86.
11. Strand, 74, 77–78.
12. Dray-Novey, "Twilight of the Beijing Gendarmerie."
13. Wakeman, 18–22, 43–59. Xu, Chap. 8, p. 17.
14. The proportion of police to people was reduced from 59 to 1 in 1910, to 95 to 1 in 1917, and to 115 to 1 in 1933. Xu, Chap. 9, p. 10.
15. Wakeman, 18–22, 43–59. Xu, Chap. 9. p. 18.
16. Gamble, *Peking*, 461–62.
17. Strand, 105.
18. Burgess, 107–22. He estimated there were a total of 128 guilds functioning in Beijing.
19. Burgess, 211.
20. Burgess, especially Chap. 12. Also Gamble, *Peking*, Chap. 8.
21. Burgess, 77.
22. Strand, Chap. 5.
23. Strand, Chap. 8.
24. Luo Shuwei.
25. Zhou Qiuguang, 565.
26. [Cook's] *Peking*, 1–2.
27. Bredon, 21–22.
28. Bredon, 22, and Dong, 22.
29. Dong, 35–37, 42; Shi, 353–64. Shi points out that the circular railroad "rationalized" the railway connections but "constrained the population of the Inner City from spreading into the suburbs."

30. Dong, 40–42.

31. Dong, 67–69; Shi, 380–81.

32. Strand, Chaps. 2 and 3.

33. Zhang Fuhe, 26–34.

34. Dong,151. Zhang Fuhe, 162–63. On Henry K. Murphy, see Cody.

35. Stuart, 56. The Rockefeller Foundation employed similar guidelines in designing the Peking Union Medical College. State-of-the-art classrooms and laboratories were housed in buildings with Chinese exteriors. Bullock, 8, 78.

36. Dong, 82–86; Shi, 183–201.

37. Dong, Chap. 5, "Consumption," provides an excellent description of the spatial and hierarchical distribution of markets in the Republican period.

38. This description follows Dong, Chap. 5, especially 144–52 and 159–62.

39. This paragraph follows Dong, Chap. 6, "Recycling." The quotations are found on 172, 205.

40. Kates, *Years that were Fat,* 103.

41. Han, 129–34, 281–87.

42. Gamble, *Peking,* 30, 99–102.

43. Gamble, *Peking,* 38.

44. Tao Menghe, quoted in Dong, 215.

45. Xu, Chap. 9, p. 2.

46. Gamble, *Peking,* 268–73.

47. Gamble, "How Chinese Families Live."

48. Rhoads, 257–58. See above, Chap. 4, n98.

49. Gamble, *Peking,* 273; Rhoads, 261.

50. Wu Woyao, quoted and transl. in Crossley, *Orphan Warriors,* 177.

51. Dong, 157.

52. Strand, 30–31, 73.

53. Xu, Chap. 8, p. 8.

54. Gamble, *Peking,* 274–76.

55. Gamble, *Peking,* 276–78.

56. Li and Dray-Novey, 1018–19; Strand, 204–5.

57. Gamble, *Peking,* 283–303.

58. Dikötter, 140–61; Gamble, *Peking,* Chap. 12.

59. Gamble, *Peking,* 31; Bullock.

60. Campbell, 195.

61. Campbell, 201.

62. Shi, Chap. 5. Quote on 302.

63. Shi, Chap. 3.

64. Rogaski, Chap. 4.

65. Xu, Chap. 9, 43–50.

66. Lao She, *Camel Xiangzi,* 78–80.

67. Lao She, 564, 568.

68. *Biographical Dictionary,* III:133.

69. Weston, 118–21.

70. Chow, 49.

71. Schwarcz, 39–54.

72. Chow, Chap. 3. Quote on 73.

73. Chow, Chaps. 3 and 12.

74. Chow, 191–92.

75. Chow, 232–34.
76. Wilma Fairbank, 3–38; Spence, *Gate of Heavenly Peace,* Chaps. 6–8.
77. Wilma Fairbank, 23–83, 169–95.
78. Chow, 106–7.
79. This account follows Chow, 105–16.
80. Chow, 243–44.
81. Chow, 142–43.
82. Strand, 182–88.
83. Strand, 194–95.
84. Weston, 242–47.
85. Schwarcz, 158–60.
86. Israel, Chaps. 3–4.
87. Israel, 125.
88. Israel, 153–54. Edgar Snow was teaching journalism at Yanjing University at the time. P. 115.
89. This and the following account of the occupation depend heavily on unpublished works by Sophia Lee, "Education in Wartime Beijing" and "The Japanese in Wartime Beijing."
90. *Beijing tongshi,* vol. 9, 129–32.
91. Spence, *In Search of Modern China,* 482.
92. Bodde, xvii, 9, 12–13.
93. Lao She, *Teahouse,* 194–96. Trans. John Howard Gibbon. The "Eighth Route Army" refers to the most famous unit of the Red Army.
94. Naquin, *Peking,* Epilogue; Dong, Introduction.
95. Dong, 252, and Chap. 8 in general, surveys the many Chinese publications about old Beijing.
96. Trans. in Dong, 264.
97. Morrison, *Photographer in Old Peking.*
98. Arlington and Lewisohn, vi; Naquin, *Peking,* 686–702, reviews other Western and Chinese works about old Beijing.
99. Goldstein, especially 109, 149–50, 163–73.
100. Goldstein, 308–28.
101. Dong, Chap. 9, especially pp. 293, 298. Naquin, *Peking,* 697.

Chapter 6

1. Williams.
2. See Williams. Mao's words are found in Mao Zedong, "Opening Speech at the First Plenary Session of the CPPCC" (September 21, 1949) and "Proclamation of the Central People's Government of the PRC" (October 1, 1949) in Kau and Leung, *Writings of Mao,* Vol. I, p. 5, in Kao and Leung, eds., *Writings of Mao,* I:5, 10–11.
3. Zhou Yixing et al., 130; Wang Jun, 82.
4. Wang Jun, 86.
5. See Wang Jun, 37–112.
6. Zhang Yihe, 111.
7. Wilma Fairbank, 182
8. Wu Hung, 8.
9. Xie Yinming, ed., 151.

10. See Xie Yinming, ed., 150.
11. Wu Hung, 9.
12. Wu Hung, 22.
13. Chang-tai Hung, 459.
14. Chang-tai Hung, 463, 459.
15. Wu Hung, 8.
16. Zhou Yixing et al., 87.
17. See Saionji, 8.
18. *Beijing dang'an shiliao*, 60.
19. Basic grain supplies, such as rice and flour, were rationed in Beijing from 1953, cooking oil and cotton cloth from 1954. Legal residents received monthly coupons.
20. *Dangdai Zhongguo de Beijing*, II:401.
21. Ma Yinchu (1882–1982), earned his M.A. from Yale University (1910) and his Ph.D. from Columbia (1916), both in economics; he became president of Beijing University in 1951. Mao forced him to resign in 1960.
22. Spence, *Search*, 648–49.
23. The cadre ranking system had twenty-five grades. The highest, rank number one, was reserved for Mao and five other top leaders. College graduates automatically received rank twenty-one.
24. A few workers' residential areas were built near factories in Beijing after 1949. The five- or six-floor brick buildings looked like *dayuan*, but the size and facilities of each apartment were much smaller and more limited than those in *dayuan*.
25. Rae Yang, 50–51.
26. Rae Yang, 50–51.
27. Rae Yang, 51.
28. Zhang Yiwu, 12.
29. "Shuijian bao" were called "shengjian bao" in Shanghai. The changed name refers to a slightly different emphasis in cooking (*sheng* means raw and *shui* water). The process of making "shuijian bao" is to put raw dumplings on a hot wok, add water rather than oil, and keep the lid on until they are done.
30. Deng Youmei, "Xinxiang ji guren."
31. The Yan'an era refers to the period from the mid-1930s to the end of the war of resistance against Japan when the Communist party leadership was at Yan'an in northwest China.
32. Saionji, 31.
33. Li Zhisui, 345.
34. *Dangdai Zhongguo de Beijing*, II:455.
35. The interpretation of Mao's psychology suggested here is based on Schram, 62–82.
36. Spence, *Search*, 447–48, 492.
37. Rae Yang, 58–59.
38. Chang and Halliday, 506. It was almost a rule that provincial newspapers had to follow closely the lead of major Beijing newspapers in deciding what to reprint.
39. MacFarquhar and Schoenhals, 48–51, 82.
40. MacFarquhar and Schoenhals, 54–65.
41. A "revolutionary cadre" was defined then as one who had joined the revolution by the end of 1945 and had been ranked at grade 13 or above. Later students from families defined as the "Red Five Categories" (workers, poor and low-middle peasants, army officers, revolutionary cadres) were admissible to the Red Guards.
42. Yan and Gao, 58.

43. Yan and Gao, 59.
44. MacFarquhar and Schoenhals, 102.
45. Yan and Gao, 62–63.
46. Yan and Gao, 70.
47. Yu Sanle, 358.
48. Zhou Yixing et al., 215.
49. Young-tsu Wong, 187.
50. See Yan and Gao, 77.
51. Wen Jieruo, who had been educated in Japan and graduated from Qinghua University in Beijing, was accused as "veteran spy" because of her family background and fabricated evidence during the Cultural Revolution.
52. Wen Jieruo, 704–6.
53. This scene was partially represented on the screen in the film *Farewell My Concubine* (1993) by Chen Kaige.
54. Yan and Gao, 68.
55. Wilma Fairbank, 178–79.
56. Yan and Gao, 77.
57. *Dangdai Beijing Dashiji*, 222.
58. Yan and Gao, 76.
59. *Dangdai Zhongguo de Beijing*, II:403.
60. This film was adapted from a novel by Wang Shuo; see Chapter 7 for a discussion of him.
61. Spence, *Search*, 598.
62. Yan and Gao, 430–32.
63. Yan and Gao, 483–84.
64. Yan and Gao, 484.
65. Yan and Gao, 493.
66. Yan and Gao, 497.
67. Li Zhisui, 580–86, 592.

Chapter 7

1. See Shu Kewen.
2. Mann, 95.
3. *Dangdai Zhongguo de Beijing*, I:681.
4. Zhou Yixing et al., 299.
5. *Dangdai Zhongguo de Beijing*, I:407.
6. Zhou Yixing et al., 301–2.
7. Zhang Xinxin et al., 5.
8. The Second Ring Road, 23.3 kilometers (14.5 miles) long, with six overpasses, was completed in December 1980 at a cost of U.S. $120 million.
9. *Dangdai Zhongguo de Beijing*, I:692.
10. Berry, 113.
11. Zhou Yang's article actually was written collectively by a group of leading liberal intellectuals, including Wang Ruoshui (former chief editor of *People's Daily*) and Wang Yuanhua (former member of "the Hu Feng counterrevolutionary clique," so accused by the authorities in the 1950s). See Hong Zicheng et al., 242–43.
12. Quoted in Baranovitch, 11.

13. "Having Nothing" is the name of Cui Jian's rock band as well as the name of his best-known song.
14. Baranovitch, 19–20.
15. Baranovitch, 32.
16. Zha Jianying, 152.
17. Williams. The following quotations are also cited from this film, unless otherwise noted.
18. Zha Jianying, 153.
19. Baranovitch, 32
20. See Chen Sihe, 325.
21. Williams.
22. Spence, *Search*, 628.
23. Bailey, 220.
24. Zhou Yixing et al., 358.
25. Zhou Yixing et al., 360.
26. Zhou Yixing et al., 360.
27. See Bailey, 224–2.
28. Baum, 257–58.
29. Kristof, 71.
30. See Bailey, 226.
31. Bailey, 225.
32. Baum, 290.
33. Bailey, 226; *Dangdai Beijing da shiji*, 476.
34. Cheng Pei-kai et al., 502.
35. Cheng Pei-kai et al., 505.
36. Zha Jianying, 3.

Chapter 8

1. Beijing residents' average annual income just reached 1,182 *yuan* in 1987, compared to 365 *yuan* in 1978. But annual living expenses per person were 1,147 *yuan* in 1987 and only 359 *yuan* in 1978. (*Dangdai Zhongguo de Beijing,* II:460). Obviously, it would have been very hard for the majority of people to save to buy houses, except for those who became rich by operating private enterprises.
2. *Dangdai Beijing dashiji,* 664.
3. *Beijing shehui tongji baodao 2005,* 74.
4. *Beijing shehui tongji baodao 2005,* 264.
5. *Dangdai Zhongguo de Beijing* II:404
6. Xiang Biao, 294.
7. Xiang Biao, 340.
8. *Beijing wanbao* (Beijing evening paper), June 16, 2005.
9. Yan, 39.
10. See Broudehoux, 111–17.
11. Broudehoux, 118, 145.
12. Broudehoux, 118, 119.
13. Broudehoux, 120.
14. Broudehoux, 121.
15. Broudehoux, 123.

16. *Xinjing bao* (Beijing news), September 16, 2005.
17. Johnson, 111.
18. Jiang Weiwei.
19. Jiang Weiwei.
20. Johnson, 91, 93.
21. Johnson, 120.
22. Johnson, 115.
23. *Jinghua shibao* (Beijing Times), December 13, 2006.
24. Wang Jun, 15.
25. Johnson, 117.
26. See Yardley.
27. Belsky, 258.
28. Author interview with Shu Yi, 2002.
29. *Beijing shehui tongji baodao 2005,* 300.
30. This was the fourth reconstruction of Tiananmen. The previous three reconstructions were 1949–1954, 1958–1959, and 1976–1977.
31. Shu Kewen.
32. Wu Hung, 241.
33. Shu Kewen.
34. Author interview with Zhang Yiwu, 2005.
35. Wu Hung, 241.
36. See Shu Kewen.
37. Wilma Fairbank, 181.
38. See "CCTV by OMA. Rem Koolhaas and Ole Scheeren," *Architecture and Urbanism,* July 2005.
39. Andrew Yang.
40. Lubow.
41. The different opinions mainly focus on the cost and hiring of foreign architects, as shown in the conversation between Qinghua architecture professor Peng Pen'gen and Lubow in the latter's article.
42. Lubow.
43. Yardley.
44. Zheng Lianjie is a transnational performance artist. The photo taken in 2000 is titled "Time line" and is one of Zheng's performance works. The artist returned to Tiananmen with his nine-year-old son; the picture they are holding is of the artist's family in 1957, when he was not yet born.

Epilogue

1. The following account depends on Naquin, "Forbidden City," especially 341–44, and *Zijincheng* (Gugong bowuyuan 80 nian) 132.5 (2005).
2. Naquin, "Forbidden City," describes and analyzes these overseas exhibitions.
3. *Possessing the Past.*
4. *China: The Three Emperors.*
5. *New York Times,* August 2, 2006.
6. Goodrich's book is the major study of this temple in English. Naquin, *Peking,* and author interview with Chen Bali, November 10, 2005.
7. *Beijing jiucheng*

8. Belsky, 114, 233, 258.
9. Johnson, 168.
10. Johnson, 101, 160.
11. Wu Liangyong, 104.
12. *Wall Street Journal,* December 3, 2005.
13. Broudehoux, 64–66, and Wong, 188–94.
14. Zhang Liang, 183–88.
15. The leading historians of Beijing are mostly historical geographers, many of them students of the eminent Hou Renzhi. They include Li Xiaocong, Yue Shengyang, and Yin Junke.

Bibliography

Aisin Gioro Puyi. *Wode qianban sheng* [The first half of my life]. Beijing: Qunzhong chubanshe, 1964.

Architecture and Urbanism. Special issue. July 2005. (In Japanese and English.)

Arlington, L. C., and William Lewisohn. *In Search of Old Peking.* 1935. Beiping: Henri Vetch., 1935. Reprint Oxford: Oxford University Press, 1987.

Bailey, Paul. *China in the Twentieth Century.* Oxford: Blackwell Publishers Ltd., 2001.

Baranovitch, Nimrod. *China's New Voices: Popular Music, Ethnicity, Gender, and Politics, 1978–1998.* Berkeley: University of California Press, 2003.

Barrow, John. *Travels in China.* Philadelphia: W. F. M'Laughlin, 1805.

Baum, Richard. *Burying Mao: Chinese Politics in the Age of Deng Xiaoping.* Princeton, N.J.: Princeton University Press, 1994.

Baxun wanshou shengdian (Magnificent record of the emperor's eightieth birthday). Beijing, 1792.

Beijing dang'an shiliao 2002.4 [Beijing archives series 4.2002]. Beijing: Xinhua chubanshe, 2002.

Beijing de hutong [*Hutong* of Beijing] Ed. Weng Li. Beijing: Beijing Arts and Photography Publishing House, 1994.

Beijing jiucheng ershiwu pian lishi wenhua baohu qu baohu guihua [Conservation planning of 25 historic areas in Beijing Old City]. Beijing City Planning Commission. Beijing: Yanshan, 2002.

Beijing shehui tongji baodao 2005 [Beijing statistical report, 2005]. Ed. Cui Shuqiang. Beijing: Tongxin chubanshe, 2005.

Beijing shi [History of Beijing]. Beijing University Department of History. Beijing: Beijing chubanshe, 1999.

Beijing Social & Economic Statistical Report 2005. Comp. by Beijing Statistics Bureau. Beijing: Tongxin chubanshe, 2005.

Beijing tongshi [Comprehensive history of Beijing]. Ed. Cao Zixi et al. 10 vols. Beijing: Zhongguo shudian, 1994.

Beijing wanbao [Beijing evening paper] June 16, 2005.

Belsky, Richard. "The Urban Ecology of Late Imperial Beijing Reconsidered: The Transformation of Social Space in China's Late Imperial Capital City." *Journal of Urban History* 27:1 (November 2000): 54–74.

Belsky Richard. "Placing the Hundred Days: Native-Place Ties and Urban Space." In *Rethinking the 1898 Reform Period: Political and Cultural Change in Late Qing China.* Ed. Rebecca E. Karl and Peter Zarrow. Cambridge, Mass.: Harvard University Asia Center, 2002. pp. 124–57.

Belsky, Richard. *Localities at the Center: Native Place, Space, and Power in Late Imperial Beijing*. Cambridge, Mass.: Harvard University East Asia Center, 2005.

Berry, Michael. *Speaking in Images*. New York: Columbia University Press, 2005.

Beurdeley, Cécile, and Michel Beurdeley. *Giuseppe Castiglione: A Jesuit Painter at the Court of the Chinese Emperors*. Trans. Michael Bullock. London: Lund Humphries, 1972.

Biographical Dictionary of Republican China. Ed. Howard Boorman. 4 vols. New York: Columbia University Press, 1967–1971.

Bland, J. O. P., and Edmund Backhouse. *China under the Empress Dowager: Being the History of the Life and Times of Tzu Hsi*. London: William Heinemann, 1910.

Blofeld, John. *City of Lingering Splendour: A Frank Account of Old Peking's Exotic Pleasures*. London: Hutchinson, 1961; Boston: Shambhala, 1989 reprint ed.

Bodde, Derk. *Peking Diary: A Year of Revolution*. New York: Henry Schuman, Inc. 1950.

Boulger, Demetrius C. *The Life of Gordon*. 2 vols. London: T. Fisher Unwin, 1897.

Boyd, Andrew. *Chinese Architecture and Town Planning 1500 B.C.–A.D. 1911*. Chicago: University of Chicago Press, 1962.

Bredon, Juliet. *Peking: A Historical and Intimate Description of Its Chief Places of Interest*. 2nd ed. Shanghai: Kelly and Walsh, 1922.

Brokaw, Cynthia J., and Kai-wing Chow, eds. *Printing and Book Culture in Late Imperial China*. Berkeley: University of California Press, 2005.

Broudehoux, Anne-Marie. *The Making and Selling of Post-Mao Beijing*. New York: Routledge, 2004.

Brunnert, H. S., and V. V. Hagelstrom. *Present Day Political Organization of China*. Rev. N. Th. Kolessoff and trans. A. Beltchenko and E. E. Moran. Shanghai: Kelly and Walsh, 1912.

Bullock, Mary Brown. *An American Transplant: The Rockefeller Foundation and Peking Union Medical College*. Berkeley: University of California Press, 1980.

Burgess, John Stewart. *The Guilds of Peking*. New York: Columbia University Press, 1928.

Bush, Susan. "Literati Culture under the Chin (1122–1234)." *Oriental Art* 1969, 15 (1969):103–12.

Cambridge History of China, Vol. 6. Ed. Herbert Franke and Denis Twitchett. New York: Cambridge University Press, 1994.

Cambridge History of China, Vol. 7. Ed. Frederick W. Mote and Denis Twitchett. New York: Cambridge University Press, 1988.

Campbell, Cameron. "Public Health Efforts in China before 1949 and Their Effects on Mortality: The Case of Beijing." *Social Science History* 21:2 (Summer 1997): 179–218.

Chan, Albert, S. J. "Peking at the Time of the Wan-li Emperor (1572–1619)." In *Proceedings of the Second Biennial Conference*, International Association of Historians of Asia. Taibei, 1962. 2: 119–47.

Chan, Hok-lam. "Liu Ping-chung (1216–74): A Buddhist-Taoist Statesman at the Court of Khubilai Khan." *Toung Pao* 53 (1967): 98–146.

Chang, Jung, and Jon Halliday. *Mao: The Unknown Story*. New York: Alfred Knopf, 2005.

Chen, Nancy, Constance Clark, et al. *China Urban: Ethnography of Contemporary Culture*. Durham, N.C.: Duke University Press, 2001.

Chen Sihe ed. *Zhongguo dangdai wenxueshi jiaocheng* [Contemporary Chinese literary history] Shanghai: Fudan University Press, 1999.

Cheng, Pei-kai, and Michael Lestz with Jonathan D. Spence. *The Search for Modern China: A Documentary Collection*. New York: W. W. Norton & Company, 1999.

Cheng Qinhua. *Tales of the Forbidden City*. Beijing: Foreign Languages Press, 1997.

Cibot, Pierre-Martial. "De la ville de Pé-king." In Joseph-Marie Amiot, Pierre-Martial Cibot et al., *Mémoires concernant l'histoire, les sciences, les arts, les moeurs, les usage, & c. des Chinois, par les missionaries de Pe-kin*. Vol. 8. Paris: Nyon, 1782. pp. 217–19.

China: The Three Emperors, 1662–1795. Ed. Evelyn S. Rawski and Jessica Rawson. London: Royal Academy of Arts, 2005.

Chow, Tse-tsung. *The May Fourth Movement: Intellectual Revolution in Modern China.* Cambridge, Mass.: Harvard University Press, 1964; Stanford, Calif.: Stanford University Press, 1967.

Cody, Jeffrey W. *Building in China: Henry K. Murphy's "Adaptive Architecture," 1914–1935.* Hong Kong and Seattle: The Chinese University Press, 2001.

Cohen, Paul A. *History in Three Keys: The Boxers as Event, Experience, and Myth.* New York: Columbia University Press, 1997.

Cook's Guide. See *Peking.*

Crossley, Pamela Kyle. *Orphan Warriors: Three Manchu Generations and the End of the Qing World.* Princeton, N.J.: Princeton University Press, 1990.

Crossley, Pamela Kyle. *The Manchus.* Cambridge, Mass.: Blackwell, 1997.

Crossley, Pamela Kyle. *A Translucent Mirror: History and Identity in Qing Imperial Ideology.* Berkeley: University of California Press, 1999.

Crump, J. I. *Chinese Theater in the Days of Kublai Khan.* Tucson: University of Arizona Press, 1980.

Danby, Hope. *The Garden of Perfect Brightness: The History of the Yüan Ming Yüan and of the Emperors Who Lived There.* Chicago: Henry Regnery, 1950.

Dangdai Beijing dashiji (1949–2003) [Chronicles of contemporary Beijing, 1949–2003]. Beijing: Dangdai zhongguo chubanshe, 2003.

Dangdai Zhongguo de Beijing [Beijing in contemporary China]. 2 vols. Comp. Zhou Yixing et al. Beijing: Zhongguo shehui kexueyuan chubanshe, 1989.

Deng Youmei. "Xinxiang ji guren" [In memory of old friends]. *Beijing wenxue* [Beijing Literature], March 1997.

Dennys, Nicholas Belfield, ed. *The Treaty Ports of China and Japan.* London: Trubner and Co., 1867. Compiled and ed. N. B. Dennys. Written William F. Mayers, N. B. Dennys, and Charles King.

Dikötter, Frank. "Crime and Punishment in Early Republican China: Beijing's First Model Prison, 1912–1922." *Late Imperial China* 21:2 (December 2000): 140–61.

Dolby, William. "Early Chinese Plays and Theater" and "Yuan Drama." In Colin Mackerras, ed., *Chinese Theater: From Its Origins to the Present Day.* Honolulu: University of Hawaii Press, 1983. pp. 7–59.

Dong, Madeleine Yue. *Republican Beijing: The City and Its Histories.* Berkeley: University of California Press, 2003.

Dutton, Michael. *Streetlife: China.* Cambridge: Cambridge University Press, 1998.

Dray-Novey, Alison J. "Policing Imperial Peking: The Ch'ing Gendarmerie, 1650–1850." Ph.D. diss., Harvard University, 1981.

Dray-Novey, Alison. "Spatial Order and Police in Imperial Beijing." *Journal of Asian Studies* 52:4 (November 1993): 885–922.

Dray-Novey, Alison. "The Twilight of the Beijing Gendarmerie, 1900–1924." *Modern China: An International Quarterly of History and Social Science,* forthcoming July 2007.

Dumen jilue [Short account of the capital]. 1875 ed.

Elliott, Mark C. *The Manchu Way: The Eight Banners and Ethnic Identity in Late Imperial China.* Stanford. Calif.: Stanford University Press, 2001.

Fairbank, John King, and Merle Goldman. *China: A New History.* Cambridge, Mass.: Belknap Press of Harvard University Press, 1998.

Fairbank, Wilma. *Liang and Lin: Partners in Exploring China's Architectural Past.* Philadelphia: University of Pennsylvania Press, 1994.

Fang Ke. *Dangdai Beijing jiu cheng genxin: diaocha, yanjiu, tansuo* [Contemporary conservation in the inner city of Beijing: survey, analysis and investigation]. Beijing: Zhongguo jianzhu gongye chubanshe, 2000.

Farmer, Edward L. *Early Ming Government: The Evolution of Dual Capitals.* Cambridge, Mass.: Harvard University Press, 1976.

Favier, Alphonse. *Pékin: Histoire et description.* Peking: Imprimerie des Lazaristes, 1897.

Fortune, Robert. *Yedo and Peking.* London: J. Murray, 1863.

Freeman-Mitford, A. B. (Baron Redesdale). *The Attaché at Peking.* London: Macmillan, 1900.

Gabbiani, Luca. "Orpheline d'un empire: la ville de Pékin et sa gestion á la fin de la dynastie des Qing (1800–1911)" [Orphan of the empire: The city of Beijing and its administration at the end of the Qing dynasty (1800–1911)]. Ph.D. diss. Paris: Ecole des Hautes Etudes en Sciences Sociales, 2004.

Gamble, Sidney D., assisted by John Stewart Burgess. *Peking: A Social Survey.* New York: George H. Doran, 1921.

Gamble, Sidney D. *How Chinese Families Live in Peiping: A Study of Income and Expenditure of 283 Chinese Families Receiving from $8 to $550 Silver per Month.* New York: Funk and Wagnalls, 1933.

Geiss, James. *Peking under the Ming, 1368–1644.* Ann Arbor, Mich.: University Microfilms International, 1979.

Gernet, Jacques. *Daily Life in China on the Eve of the Mongol Invasion, 1250–1276.* Trans. H. M. Wright. New York: Macmillan, 1962. Stanford University Press, 1982.

Gernet, Jacques. *A History of Chinese Civilization.* Trans. J. R. Foster. New York: Cambridge University Press, 1982.

Goldstein, Joshua L. "Theatrical Imagi-Nations: Peking Opera and China's Cultural Crisis, 1890–1937." Ph.D. diss., University of California, San Diego, 2000.

Goodrich, Anne Swann. *The Peking Temple of the Eastern Peak: The Tung-yueh Miao in Peking and Its Lore.* Nagoya, Japan: Monumenta Serica, 1964.

Gudai Beijing chengshi guanli. [Urban administration in old Beijing]By Yin Junke et al. Beijing: Tongxin, 2002.

Haeger, John. "Marco Polo in China? Problems with Internal Evidence." *Bulletin of Song-Yuan Studies* 14 (1979).

Han Guanghui. *Beijing lishi renkou dili* [Beijing's historical demography and geography]. Beijing: Beijing daxue chubanshe, 1996.

Harrington, Peter. *Peking 1900: The Boxer Rebellion.* Oxford: Osprey, 2001.

Hevia, James L. *Cherishing Men from Afar: Qing Guest Ritual and the Macartney Embassy of 1793.* Durham, N.C: Duke University Press, 1995.

Hevia, James L. *English Lessons: The Pedagogy of Imperialism in Nineteenth-Century China.* Durham, N.C.: Duke University Press, 2003.

Hong Zicheng et al. *Zhongguo dangdai wenxueshi* [History of contemporary Chinese literature]. Beijing: Beijing daxue chubanshe, 1999.

Hou Renzhi, ed., *Beijing chengshi lishi dili* [Historical geography of Beijing]. Beijing: Beijing Yanshan chubanshe, 2000.

Hummel, Arthur W., ed. *Eminent Chinese of the Ch'ing Period, 1644–1912.* Washington, D.C.: U.S. Government Printing Office, 1943–44. Reprint ed., Taibei: Ch'eng-wen, 1967.

Hung, Chang-tai. "Revolutionary History in Stone." *China Quarterly* 166 (June 2001): 457–73.

Israel, John. *Student Nationalism in China, 1927–1937.* Stanford, Calif.: Stanford University Press, 1966.

Jagchid, Sejin. "The Kitans and Their Cities." *Central Asiatic Journal* 25 (1981): 70–88.

Jiang Weiwei. "Beijing Qianmen Dazhalan: you shenghuo biancheng huiyi" [Qianmen and Dazhalan in Beijing: Again life turns into memory]. *Chinese Youth Newspaper,* April 14, 2006.

Jiang, Wen. *In the Heat of the Sun.* (Film, 1995).

Jinwu shili [Gendarmerie regulations and cases]. Beijing: 1851.

Jiujing daguan [Old Beijing in panorama]. Ed. Fu Gongyue et al. Beijing: Renmin Zhongguo chubanshe, 1991.

Jiujing "Xingshi huabao": wan Qing shi jing baitai [The "Xingshi huabao" of old Beijing: The many views of late Qing urban life]. Ed. Yang Binyan. Beijing: Zhongguo wenlian chubanshe, 2003.

Johnson, Ian. *Wild Grass: Three Stories of Change in Modern China.* New York: Pantheon Books, 2004.

Johnston, Reginald F. *Twilight in the Forbidden City.* New York: D. Appleton-Century, 1934. Reprint ed. Hong Kong: Oxford University Press, 1985.

Ju Yixin. *Jingshi fangxiang zhi* [Capital Street Guide]. Beijing, 1900.

Kahn, Harold L. *Monarchy in the Emperor's Eyes: Image and Reality in the Ch'ien-lung Reign.* Cambridge, Mass.: Harvard University Press, 1971.

Kangxi shengshi de gushi [Stories of the prosperous age of Kangxi]. Beijing: Xueyuan chubanshe, 2004.

Kates, George L. "A New Date for the Origins of the Forbidden City." *Harvard Journal of Asiatic Studies* 7:3 (1943): 180–202.

Kates, George L. *The Years that Were Fat: The Last of Old China.* Cambridge, Mass.: MIT Press, 1967.

Kau, Michael Y.M., and John K. Leung, *The Writings of Mao Zedong, 1949–1976.* Vol. I, Armonk, N.Y.: M. E. Sharpe, 1986.

Keightley, David N. "Early Civilization in China: Reflections on How It Became Chinese." In Paul S. Ropp, ed., *Heritage of China: Contemporary Perspectives on Chinese Civilization.* Berkeley: University of California Press, 1990. pp. 15–54.

Kovalevsky, Egor Petrovich. *Puteshestvie v Kitai* [Journey to China]. St. Petersburg: Korolev, 1853. Translated in part by Alison J. Dray in "Excerpts from E. P. Kovalevsky's *Journey to China,"* *Papers on China* 22A (May 1969): 53–88.

Kristof, Nicholas D. "How the Hardliners Won," *New York Times Magazine,* November 12, 1989, 39–71.

Lao She (Shu Qingqun). *Camel Xiangzi* (1936). Trans. Shi Xiaojing. Hong Kong: Chinese University Press, 2005.

Lao She. (Shu Qingqun) *Teahouse* (1957). Trans. John Howard-Gibbon. Hong Kong: Chinese University Press, 2004.

Lee, Sophia. "Education in Wartime Beijing, 1937–1945." Ph.D. diss., University of Michigan, 1996.

Lee, Sophia. "The Japanese in Wartime Beijing, 1937–1945." Paper presented at the Conference on the Social, Economic and Cultural History of Modern East Asia," Ann Arbor, Michigan, November 5–6, 2004.

Li, Lillian M. *Fighting Famine in North China: State, Market, and Environmental Decline, 1690s–1990s.* Stanford, Calif.: Stanford University Press, 2007.

Li, Lillian M., and Alison Dray-Novey. "Guarding Beijing's Food Security in the Qing Dynasty: State, Market, and Police." *Journal of Asian Studies* 58:4 (November 1999): 992–1032.

Li Xiaobin. *Biange zai Zhongguo (1976–1986)* [Transformation in China: 1976–1986]. Hongzhou: Zhejiang sheying chubanshe, 2003.

Li, Zhisui. *The Private Life of Chairman Mao.* Trans. Tai Hung-chao. New York: Random House, 1994.

Liu, Sola. *Chaos and All That.* Trans. Richard King. Honolulu: University of Hawaii Press, 1994.

Lubow, Arthur. "The China Syndrome." *New York Times Magazine,* May 21, 2006.

Luo Shuwei. "Minguo chunian Tianjin de *yugong*." [*Yugong* of Tianjin in the early republic of China]. *Chengshi yanjiu* 21 (2002): 419–33.

Lutz, Jessie Gregory. *China and the Christian Colleges, 1850–1950.* Ithaca, N.Y.: Cornell University Press, 1971.

Macartney, George (Earl of Macartney). *An Embassy to China; being the Journal Kept by Lord Macartney during his embassy to the Emperor Ch'ien-lung, 1793–1794.* Ed. J. L. Cranmer-Byng. Hamden, Conn.: Archon Books, 1963.

MacFarquhar, Roderick, and Michael Schoenhals. *Mao's Last Revolution.* Cambridge, Mass.: Belknap Press of Harvard University Press, 2006.

Mackerras, Colin, ed. *Chinese Theater from Its Origins to the Present Day.* Honolulu: University of Hawaii Press, 1983.

Malone, Carroll Brown. *History of the Peking Summer Palaces under the Ch'ing Dynasty.* Urbana: University of Illinois, 1934. Illinois Studies in the Social Sciences, Vol. 19, No. 1–2.

Mann, Jim. *Beijing Jeep: The Short, Unhappy Romance of American Business in China.* New York: Simon and Schuster, 1989.

Martin, W. A. P. *A Cycle of Cathay, or China, South and North with Personal Reminiscences.* New York: Fleming H. Revell, 1896.

Martin, W. A. P. *The Siege in Peking: China against the World.* New York: Fleming H. Revell, 1900.

Martin W. A. P. *The Awakening of China.* New York: Doubleday, 1907.

Mennie, Donald. *The Pageant of Peking: Comprising Sixty-six Vandyck Photogravures of Peking and Environs from Photographs.* Shanghai: A. S. Watson, 1920.

Meisner, Maurice. *Mao's China and After: A History of the People's Republic,* 3rd ed. New York: Free Press, 1999.

Michael, Franz. *The Origin of Manchu Rule in China: Frontier and Bureaucracy as Intersecting Forces in the Chinese Empire.* Baltimore: Johns Hopkins Press, 1942.

Morrison, Hedda. *A Photographer in Old Peking.* 1985. Reissued Hong Kong: Oxford University Press, 1999.

Mote, F. W. *Imperial China 900–1800.* Cambridge, Mass.: Harvard University Press, 1999.

Mote, F. W. "The Transformation of Nanking, 1350–1400." In G. William Skinner, ed., *The City in Late Imperial China.* Stanford, Calif.: Stanford University Press, 1977. pp. 101–53.

Moule and Pelliot. See Polo.

Mungello, David E. *The Great Encounter of China and the West, 1500–1800.* Lanham, Maryland: Rowman and Littlefield, 2005.

Musgrove, Charles D. "Building a Dream: Constructing a National Capital in Nanjing, 1927–1937." In Joseph W. Esherick, ed., *Remaking the Chinese City: Modernity and National Identity, 1900–1950.* Honolulu: University of Hawaii Press, 1999.

Naquin, Susan. *Millenerian Rebellion in China: The Eight Trigrams Uprising of 1813.* New Haven, Conn.: Yale University Press, 1976.

Naquin, Susan. *Peking: Temples and City Life, 1400–1900.* Berkeley: University of California Press, 2000.

Naquin, Susan. "The Forbidden City Goes Abroad: Qing History and the Foreign Exhibitions of the Palace Museum, 1974–2004." *Toung Pao* 90:4–5 (2005): 341–97.

Nathan, Andrew J. *Peking Politics, 1918–1923: Factionalism and the Failure of Constitutionalism.* Berkeley: University of California Press, 1976.

Nathan, Andrew J. "A Constitutional Republic: The Peking Government, 1916–28." In *Cambridge History of China.* Vol. 12, Part I, pp. 259–83. Cambridge: Cambridge University Press, 1983.

Owen, Stephen. "Foreword to the 1987 Edition." In *The Book of Songs: The Ancient Chinese Classic of Poetry,* trans. Arthur Waley. New York: Grove Press, 1987.

Peking, North China, South Manchuria, and Korea. 5th ed. Peking: Thos. Cook & Son, 1924.

Polo, Marco. *The Description of the World.* Trans. A. C. Moule and Paul Pelliot. London: G. Routledge and Sons, 1938.

Possessing the Past: Treasures from the National Palace Museum. Ed. Wen C. Fong and James C. Y. Watt. New York: Metropolitan Museum of Art and National Palace Museum, Taibei, 1996.

Preston, Diana. *The Boxer Rebellion: The Dramatic Story of China's War on Foreigners that Shook the World in the Summer of 1900.* New York: Walker, 2000.

Qing neiwufu cang jingcheng quantu [Complete map of the capital kept in the Qing Imperial Household Department]. Beiping, 1940.

Rachewiltz, Igor de. "Yeh-lü Ch'u-ts'ai (1189–1243): Buddhist Idealist and Confucian Statesman." In Arthur F. Wright and Denis Twitchett, eds., *Confucian Personalities.* Stanford, Calif.: Stanford University Press, 1962. pp 189–216.

Rawski, Evelyn S. *The Last Emperors: A Social History of Qing Imperial Institutions.* Berkeley: University of California Press, 1998.

Rennie, David F. *Peking and the Pekingese during the First Year of the British Embassy at Peking.* 2 vols. London: J. Murray, 1865.

Rhoads, Edward J. M. *Manchus and Han: Ethnic Relations and Political Power in Late Qing and Early Republican China, 1861–1928.* Seattle: University of Washington Press, 2000.

Ricci. See Trigault.

Ripa, Matteo. *Memoirs of Father Ripa during Thirteen Years' Residence at the Court of Peking in the Service of the Emperor of China.* Trans. Fortunato Prandi. New York: Wiley and Putnam, 1846.

Rogaski, Ruth. *Hygienic Modernity: Meanings of Health and Disease in Treaty-Port China.* Berkeley: University of California Press, 2004.

Rossabi, Morris. *Kublai Khan: His Life and Times.* Berkeley: University of California Press, 1988.

Saionji Kôichi, *Beijing shi'er nian (1957–1969)* [Twelve years in Beijing]. Trans. Gong Niannian. Hong Kong: Wenjia chubanshe, 1971.

Schram, Stuart R. *Mao Zedong, a Preliminary Reassessment.* New York: St. Martin's Press, 1983.

Schwarcz, Vera. *The Chinese Enlightenment: Intellectuals and the Legacy of the May Fourth Movement of 1919.* Berkeley: University of California Press, 1986.

Shi, Mingzheng. "Beijing Transforms: Urban Infrastructure, Public Works, and Social Change in the Chinese Capital, 1900–1928." Ph.D. diss., Columbia University, 1993.

Shih, Chung-wen. "China's Cosmopolitan Age: The Tang, 618–907" (film). Burlington, Vt: Annenberg/CPB Collection, 1992.

Shu Kewen, et al. "Tiananmen guangchang duandaishi" [History of Tiananmen Square by period]. *Sanlian Weekly* 4 (May 2001).

Sirén, Osvald. *Gardens of China.* New York: Ronald Press, 1949.

Sjoberg, Gideon. *The Preindustrial City: Past and Present.* New York: Free Press, 1960.

Skinnner, G. William. "Introduction: Urban Development in Imperial China." In *The City in Late Imperial China.* Ed. G. William Skinner. Stanford, Calif.: Stanford University Press, 1977.

Smith, Arthur H. *China in Convulsion.* 2 vols. New York: Fleming H. Revell, 1901.

Spence, Jonathan D. *Emperor of China: Self-Portrait of K'ang-hsi.* New York: Vintage, 1975.

Spence, Jonathan D. *The Gate of Heavenly Peace: The Chinese and their Revolution, 1895–1980.* New York: Viking Press, 1981.

Spence, Jonathan D. *The Memory Palace of Matteo Ricci.* New York: Viking Penguin, 1984.

Spence, Jonathan D. *The Search for Modern China.* New York: W.W. Norton, 1999.

Staunton, George L. *An Authentic Account of an Embassy from the King of Great Britain to the Emperor of China.* 2 vols. London: Nicol, 1797.

Steinhardt, Nancy Shatzman. "The Plan of Khubilai Khan's Imperial City." *Artibus Asiae* 44 (1983): 137–58.

Steinhardt, Nancy Shatzman. *Chinese Imperial City Planning.* Honolulu: University of Hawaii Press, 1990.

Stevens, Mark. "Beijing's Walls Come Tumbling Down." *New York Times,* November 16, 2003.

Storey, Robert. *Beijing: A Lonely Planet City Guide,* 2nd ed. Melbourne, Australia: Lonely Planet Publications, 1996.

Strand, David. *Rickshaw Beijing: City People and Politics in the 1920s.* Berkeley: University of California Press, 1989.

Stuart, John Leighton. *Fifty Years in China.* New York: Random House, 1954.

Sullivan, Michael. *The Three Perfections: Chinese Painting, Poetry, and Calligraphy.* New York: George Braziller, 1999.

Swallow, Robert W. *Sidelights on Peking Life.* Beijing: French Bookstore, 1927.

Thiriez, Régine. *Barbarian Lens: Western Photographers of the Qianlong Emperor's European Palaces.* Amsterdam: Gordon and Breach, 1998.

Trevor-Roper, Hugh. *Hermit of Peking: The Hidden Life of Sir Edmund Backhouse.* New York: Alfred A. Knopf, 1977 (first Eng. ed. 1976).

Trigualt, Nicola, S. J. *China in the Sixteenth Century: The Journals of Matthew Ricci, 1583–1610.* Trans. Louis J. Gallagher, S.J. New York: 1953,

Tsai, Henry Shih-shan. *Perpetual Happiness: The Ming Emperor Yongle.* Seattle: University of Washington Press, 2001.

Tun, Li-chen. *Annual Customs and Festivals in Peking.* Trans. and annotated by Derk Bodde. Beiping: Henri Vetch, 1936; 2nd ed. rev., Hong Kong: Hong Kong University Press, 1965, 1987.

Wade, Nicholas. "Scientists Link a Prolific Gene Tree to the Manchu Conquerors of China." *New York Times,* November 1, 2005.

Wade, Thomas F. "The Army of the Chinese Empire: Its Two Great Divisions, the Bannermen or National Guard, and the Green Standard or Provincial Troops, Their Organization, Locations, Pay, & c." *Chinese Repository* 20: (1851): 250–80 (May), 300–340 (June), 363–422 (July). Canton: Printed for the Proprietors.

Wadley, Stephen A. "Altaic Influences on Beijing Dialect: The Manchu Case." *Journal of the American Oriental Society* 16 (1996): 99–104.

Wakeman, Frederic. *Policing Shanghai, 1927–1937*. Berkeley: University of California Press, 1995.

Wang Jun. *Chengji* [Record of a city]. Beijing: Sanlian, 2003.

Wanshou quge yuezhang [Songs for the imperial birthday] Beijing, 1790.

Wanshou shengdian [The imperial birthday celebration]. Beijing, 1718.

Wen Jieruo. "Living Hell" (from her memoirs). Ed. James L. Watson, trans. Jeffrey C. Kinkley. In *The Columbia Anthology of Modern Chinese Literature*, ed. Joseph Lau and Howard Goldblatt. New York: Columbia University Press, 1995. pp. 703–709.

Weston, Timothy B. *The Power of Position: Beijing University, Intellectuals, and Chinese Political Culture, 1898–1929*. Berkeley: University of California Press, 2004.

Williams, Sue. *China: A Century of Revolution* (documentary film). WGBH Boston, 1997.

Wilson, James Q. *Varieties of Police Behavior: The Management of Law and Order in Eight Communities*. Cambridge, Mass.: Harvard University Press, 1968.

Wittfogel, Karl A., and Feng Chia-sheng. *History of Chinese Society: Liao (907–1125)*. Philadelphia: American Philosophical Society, 1949.

Wong, Young-tsu. *A Paradise Lost: The Imperial Garden Yuanming Yuan*. Honolulu: University of Hawaii Press, 2001.

Wood, Frances. *Did Marco Polo Go to China?* Boulder, Colo.: Westview Press, 1996.

Wu, Hung. *Remaking Beijing: Tiananmen Square and the Creation of a Political Space*. Chicago: University of Chicago Press, 2005.

Wu, Liangyong. *Rehabilitating the Old City Beijing: A Project in the Ju'er Hutong Neighbourhood*. Vancouver: University of British Columbia Press, 1999.

Xiang Biao. *Kuayue bianjie de shequ—Beijing "Zhejiangcun" de shenghuoshi* [The community that crossed the borderline—a history of Zhejiang village in Beijing]. Beijing: Joint Publishing Co., 2000.

Xie Mian and Zhang Yiwu. *Dazhuanxing: hou xinshiqi wenhua yanjiu* [Great transformation: Culture studies at the post-new era]. Harbin: Heilongjiang jiaoyu chubanshe, 1995.

Xie Yinming, ed. *Jianzheng Beijing 1919–2004* [Witness to Beijing 1919–2004]. Beijing: Yanshan chubanshe, 2004.

Xinjing bao [New capital paper] September 16, 2005.

Xu, Yamin. In "Managing 'Wicked' Citizens in Republican Beijing: Social Changes, Civil Strife, and the Origins of China's Modern State." n.p., 2005. Chapters 8 and 9.

Yan, Jiaqi, and Gao Gao. *Turbulent Decade: A History of the Cultural Revolution*. Trans. and ed. by D. W. Y. Kwok. Honolulu: University of Hawaii Press, 1996.

Yan, Yunxiang. "McDonald's in Beijing: the Localization of Americana." In James L. Watson, ed., *Golden Arches East: McDonald's in East Asia*. Stanford, Calif.: Stanford University Press, 1997. pp. 39–76.

Yang, Andrew. "The Olympics Haven't Begun, but the Party Has." *New York Times*, June 26, 2005.

Yang, Lien-sheng. "Government Control of Urban Merchants in Traditional China." *Tsing Hua Journal of Chinese Studies* 8:1–2 (August 1970): 186–206.

Yang, Rae. *Spider Eaters*. Berkeley: University California Press, 1997.

Yardley, Jim. "Beijing's Quest for 2008: To Become Simply Livable." *New York Times*, September 28, 2005.

You zhi Yuanmingyuan sishi jingshi [Imperial Poems on the Forty Scenic Spots a Yuanmingyuan]/ Beijing, 1745.

You zhi Yuanmingyuan tu yong. (Lithographic facsimile of *You zhi Yuanmingyuan sishi jingshi*), Tianjin, 1887.

Yu Minzhong. *Rixia jiuwen kao* [Study of "Ancient Accounts Heard in the Precincts of the Throne"]. ca. 1785; reprint ed., Beijing: Beijing guji, 1983.

Yu Sanle. *Zaoqi xifang chuanjiaoshi yu Beijing* [Western missionaries and Beijing in early times]. Beijing: Beijing chubanshe, 2001.

Yue Shengyang. "Qingdai Xuannan chu de shiren wenhua" [The culture of Xuannan urbanites in the Qing era]. Ed. Hou Renzhi et al. Beijing: Yanshan, 2000. pp. 482–538.

Zha Jianying. *Bashi niandai renwu fangtan lu* [Interviews with figures of the 1980s]. Beijing: Sanlian, 2006.

Zhang Fuhe. *Beijing jindai jianzhu shi* [The modern architectural history of Beijing] (from the end of the nineteenth century to the 1930s). Beijing: Qinghua daxue chubanshe, 2004.

Zhang Jue. *Jingshi wucheng fangxiang hutongji* [Streets and alleys in the capital's Five districts]. 1560.

Zhang, Liang. *La naissance du concept de patrimoine en Chine XIXe-XXe siècles* [The birth of the concept of national heritage in nineteenth and twentieth century China]. Paris: Ipraus, 2003.

Zhang, Xinxin, and Sang, Ye. *Chinese Lives: An Oral History of Contemporary China*. Ed. William J. F. Jenner and Delia Davin. New York: Pantheon Books, 1987.

Zhang Yihe. *Wangshi bingbu ru yan* [The past is not going up like a wisp of smoke]. Beijing: Renmin wenxue chubanshe, 2004.

Zhang Yiwu. *Shijimo de chenzui* [Memoirs at the *fin-de-siècle*]. Tianjin: Baihua chubanshe, 1999.

Zhou Qiuguang. *Xiong Xiling juan* [Biography of Xiong Xiling]. Changsha: Hunan shifan daxue, 1996.

Zhou Xiaohong. *Zhongguo zhongchan jiaceng diaocha* [Survey of the Chinese middle classes]. Beijing: Shehui kexue wenxian chubanshe, 2005.

Zhou Yixing et al. *Dangdai Beijing jianshi* [A brief history of contemporary Beijing]. Beijing: Dangdai Zhongguo chubanshe, 1999.

Zhu, Jianfei. *Chinese Spatial Strategies: Imperial Beijing 1420–1911*. London: Routledge-Curzon, 2004.

Zijincheng (Forbidden City). *Gugong bowuyuan 80 nian* [Special anniversary issue of *Palace Museum*] 132:5 (2005).

Index